SUPERHEROES BEYOND

SUPERHEROES BEYOND

Edited by Cormac McGarry, Liam Burke,
Ian Gordon, and Angela Ndalianis

UNIVERSITY PRESS OF MISSISSIPPI / JACKSON

The University Press of Mississippi is the scholarly publishing agency of
the Mississippi Institutions of Higher Learning: Alcorn State University,
Delta State University, Jackson State University, Mississippi State University,
Mississippi University for Women, Mississippi Valley State University,
University of Mississippi, and University of Southern Mississippi.

www.upress.state.ms.us

Frontis illustration by James Brouwer

The University Press of Mississippi is a member
of the Association of University Presses.

An earlier version of chapter 11 was published as the article "We Need Another Hero: The
Incompatibility of Superheroes and Australia" in issue 89 (2018) of *Senses of Cinema*.

Copyright © 2024 by University Press of Mississippi
All rights reserved

∞

Library of Congress Cataloging-in-Publication Data

Names: McGarry, Cormac, editor. | Burke, Liam (Liam P.), editor. | Gordon,
Ian, 1954– editor. | Ndalianis, Angela, 1960– editor.
Title: Superheroes beyond / Cormac McGarry, Liam Burke, Ian Gordon, Angela
Ndalianis.
Description: Jackson : University Press of Mississippi, 2024. | Includes
bibliographical references and index.
Identifiers: LCCN 2023043898 (print) | LCCN 2023043899 (ebook) | ISBN
9781496850096 (hardback) | ISBN 9781496850102 (trade paperback) | ISBN
9781496850119 (epub) | ISBN 9781496850126 (epub) | ISBN 9781496850133
(pdf) | ISBN 9781496850140 (pdf)
Subjects: LCSH: Superheroes. | Superheroes—Social aspects. | Superhero
films—History and criticism. | Superhero television programs—History
and criticism. | Comic strip characters in motion pictures. | Comic
books, strips, etc.—History and criticism. | Comic books, strips,
etc.—Social aspects. | Comic book fans.
Classification: LCC PN6714 .S874 2024 (print) | LCC PN6714 (ebook) | DDC
741.5/352—dc23/eng/20231023
LC record available at https://lccn.loc.gov/2023043898
LC ebook record available at https://lccn.loc.gov/2023043899

British Library Cataloging-in-Publication Data available

CONTENTS

Foreword: Planetary Superheroes as Collective Daydream ix
    FREDERICK LUIS ALDAMA

Acknowledgments xiii
Introduction 3
    CORMAC McGARRY

SECTION 1: BEYOND MEN OF STEEL

Introduction: Beyond Men of Steel. 19
    ANGELA NDALIANIS

Chapter 1: All New, All Different, or No Normal?: Marvel Comics
and Superhero Diversity. 22
    NAJA LATER

Chapter 2: The Heart of a Hero: Disability and Humanity in the
Origin Stories of Marvel Studios' Superheroes 37
    ALEXANDRA OSTROWSKI SCHILLING

Chapter 3: Monstrosity, Mutation, and the World without Us 50
    OCTAVIA CADE

Chapter 4: *Midnight's Children* and *The Fortress of Solitude* as
Superhero Origin Stories 62
    JULIAN NOVITZ

Chapter 5: African American Viewers Watching *Black Panther*:
The Power of Representation 75
    SHEENA C. HOWARD

SECTION 2: BEYOND COMIC BOOKS

Introduction: Beyond Comic Books 95
　IAN GORDON

Chapter 6: Animating Sub-Mariner and Aquaman: Generational Taste
and the Moral Panic of the 1968 Television Season. 98
　DJOYMI BAKER

Chapter 7: The *Toy Biz* of Superheroes: Superhero Action Figures 111
　JASON BAINBRIDGE

Chapter 8: From Comic Books to Courtroom: Unmasking the
Intellectual Property behind the Superhero. 122
　MITCHELL ADAMS

Chapter 9: Capes, Tights, and Motherships: Superheroes and
New Transmedia Star Systems 135
　CORMAC McGARRY

Chapter 10: Super Fans or Toxic Madmen?: Fantasy, Reality, and
Marginalized Identities in Subversive "DIY Superhero" Indie Films 151
　JACK TEIWES

SECTION 3: BEYOND THE UNITED STATES

Introduction: Beyond the United States 173
　LIAM BURKE

Chapter 11: We Need Another Hero: The Incompatibility of
Superheroes and Australia 176
　LIAM BURKE

Chapter 12: Without Seeing the Dawn: Monstrous (Super)Heroes
and Philippine Myths in Mervin Malonzo's *Tabi Po* 192
　MARIA LORENA M. SANTOS

Chapter 13: Is There a Colombian National Superhero?:
How Colombian Superheroes Help Define Ethnicity and Race
in a Multicultural Society 208
　ENRIQUE URIBE-JONGBLOED and HERNAN DAVID ESPINOSA-MEDINA

Chapter 14: Where Does *Black Panther*'s Music Come From? Authorship, "the Other," and the Musical Representation of Africa in Hollywood 226
DAN GOLDING

Chapter 15: The Phantom in Aboriginal Australia: Educational Comics, National Identity, and Indigeneity 240
AARON HUMPHREY

About the Contributors 259
Index 264

Foreword

PLANETARY SUPERHEROES AS COLLECTIVE DAYDREAM

FREDERICK LUIS ALDAMA

Everywhere I turn these days I can satiate a seemingly bottomless pit of hunger for superheroes. From IMAX to my seventy-two-inch 4K living room wall mount TV. From printed 6x10s that line shelves at my local brick-and-mortar to Comixology digital downloads. From thirteen-inch laptop streams to hyperkinetic TikTok smartphone indulgences. And, unlike that time when I began my journey into LatinNerdom as a wet-behind-the-ears *chavalito* feasting on the adventures of only US-born and grown superheroes, today I can step easily into superheroic adventures from *all* our planet's nooks and crannies.

In superhero creation, distribution, and consumption, I'm riding a Tsunamic wave of transition and transformation—a superhero neo-Renaissance as we move from the regional (insular) to the global (expansive), from media to trans- and multimedia. But of course, superheroes—planetary superheroes—have been with us since time immemorial. Think Gilgamesh. Think Popul Vuh. Think Old Testament. Think Darangon. Think Ramayana. Think *Theogony*. Think *Saga of the Ynglings*. Inspired by the extraordinary league of scholars in this volume, I ask: Why the fascination today as much as deeptime yesterday with creating and consuming stories of superpowered humans and anthropomorphic creatures and sentient beings? Why *Superheroes Beyond*?

To begin to answer this, I can talk about superheroes as archetypes that express our shared evolution as a species of sensory, thought, and feeling systems. I can talk about them within the context of the epic heroic prototype narratives that we've spider-web spun out into the world. I can also, and arguably more straightforwardly, begin to answer this by framing our fascination with and creation of superheroes within our every-waking-hour quotidian activity of daydreaming. Just as we inhale and exhale automatically, so too do we daydream automatically. And, importantly, it is in our daydreams that we work through possible, plausible, and probable hypotheticals that often include a version of ourselves that tries out different ways to overcome challenges, obstacles—including bully revenge counterfactuals. It is in our daydreaming that we can turn fear and humiliation into joy, pride, and satisfaction. It is here that we can lead our past and present sense of self into new and differently possible future selves. We daydream and we future think, future act, future feel a limitless variety of these future selves.

No wonder, then, that we can't get enough superheroes. Superheroes and their stories are the materialization of this expansive process of imagining empowered future selves. Superhero comics in their many media formats invite us into the daydreams shaped and shared by others. Whether a single author/illustrator print comic or a multiple creator film, TV show, or streaming webisode, these superhero stories invite us into the cocreating of the daydreams of others. They offer options that might coincide, overlap, or take daydreaming in new directions. They can and do invite us to coexperience constructed and sculpted daydreams that lead to new thrilling ways of future thinking, acting, feeling, and self-constituting.

You might be wondering if all fiction does this. Yes—but with a crucial difference. By condition of experience and storytelling convention, stories that feature superheroes roll out the proverbial red carpet for our imagination, offering that especially fuzzy-warm and celebratory welcome that transitions from our individual daydream to the cocreating of daydreams of another. For me of late, this has led to the cocreative daydreaming with superheroes from across the planet: Filipino comic book and cartoon *Trese* (2021); Kenyan cartoon *Super Sema* (2021); India's Krrish film franchise; Chile's film *Mirageman* (2009); Koreas TV series *Strong Girl Bong-Soon* (2017); the French film *Comment je suis devenu super-héros* (2021); the British TV show *Misfits* (2009–2013); the Palestinian comic book *Gaza Man* (2014); the Malaysian comic book *Galaxioman* (2021); Australian Aboriginal TV show *Cleverman* (2016–2017); the legion of Islamic superheroes in the comic *The 99* (2007–2014) and the cartoon series of the same title (2011–2012); and the many other superhero stories discussed by the extraordinary league of scholars herein.

These and other superhero stories invite us to cocreate radically different daydreams, including in unbounded and powerful ways as older and younger possible selves. These days, too, I find myself especially drawn to those that invite me to cocreate daydreams of younger possible selves; those superhero stories that invite me to reach back to a phase of self-formation as a Latinx teen with limitless possibilities. Think of superheroes like Amadeus Cho (new Hulk), Kamala Kahn (new Ms. Marvel), Miles Morales (new Spidey), Reptil (Humberto Lopez), Riri Williams (Ironheart), Garfield Logan (Beastboy), Jake Hyde (Aqualad), Jessica Cruz (new Green Lantern), Nina Rodriguez (Blackbird), and of course Shuri and Nubia. Think of superhero films such as *Sleight* (2015), *Alita* (2019), *The Darkest Minds* (2018), *Logan* (2017), and *See You Yesterday* (2019), among others. Think of TV shows that feature, to different degrees of presence, BIPOC protagonists such as *Teen Titans* (HBO 2018–), *The Umbrella Academy* (Netflix 2019–), CW's *Naomi* (2022), *Maya and the Three* (Netflix 2021), and the more tween-than-teen *Raising Dion* (Netflix 2019–). Think of the vitality that the Latina medaled boxer, Yolanda Montez (Yvette Monreal) as the Wildcat II brings to an otherwise near-all white show like *Stargirl* (2020–). "For months I've been afraid to listen to myself. To be me. I'm not going to do it anymore," Montez announces, inviting those like me to revisit a time and place or ethnoracial and sociocultural surveillance and restriction to think differently about ourselves. They invite us to cocreate as *superheroic* those of us otherwise underrepresented, erased under the watchful eye of restrictive identity systems powered by xenophobia and queerphobia. And let's be honest, there's nothing like the endorphin washed brain when coexperiencing some superheroic warrior badassery.

Don't get me wrong. Not all superhero daydreams are made alike. Not all superhero stories invite us to cocreate daydreams that open us to new, limitless possibilities. For all of the extraordinary and original superhero stories like *Raising Dion* and *Sleight*, there are others like *The Boys* (2020), *Jupiter's Legacy* (2021), and *Man of Steel* (2013). Less daydream and more toxic nightmare, these latter narratives imagine limited and limiting, fearful and fear-creating superheroscapes that can't see beyond denigrative racist, sexist, and queerphobic stereotypes; that somehow see the world as all white—where are the brown people in Mark Millar, Garth Ennis, and Zack Snyder's superheroscapes?—and saved by white messianic figures: a gray-hair locked, translucent white Jesus-styled The Utopian in *Jupiter's Legacy*; the excessive screen-time presence of xenophobic and queerphobic Homelander in *The Boys*; the obsessive messianic reverence of Superman in Zack Snyder's *Man of Steel*—and the total absenting of people of color from his storyworld spaces.

Fortunately, in today's building of coinhabiting daydreams superheroscapes, the possible outweigh the simplistic; the complex outweigh the rotten, racist, queerphobic, and gender toxic. This doesn't mean that the good ones shy away from a past and present filled to the brim with violence, trauma, and systems of exploitation and oppression that target exploited and geopolitically bullied and persecuted peoples across the globe. They do show this. They also, however, invite us to cocreate daydreams that imagine different futures where we all have access to the resources and pathways to realize our full superheroic potentialities to act, heal, and transform our today into a better tomorrow and *beyond*.

ACKNOWLEDGMENTS

This collection, *Superheroes Beyond*, represents one of the final official outcomes of the Australian Research Council Linkage Project Superheroes & Me (LP150100394) with the Australian Centre for the Moving Image (ACMI). This project was initiated, developed, and led by Angela Ndalianis with outputs including a virtual reality experience *Superheroes: Realities Collide* (produced by the creative leaders at Visitor Vision, Craig Bowler and Charles Henden), the museum exhibition *Cleverman*, two international conferences, and numerous articles, book chapters, and edited collections. The editors are eternally grateful to Angela for her leadership of the project and her steadfast work in popular culture and superhero scholarship over her extensive career. It is hard to imagine a collection like this existing without Angela's support and guidance.

The editors would also like to acknowledge Cormac McGarry who carefully coordinated this transnational collection in the middle of a global pandemic while also finishing his PhD. Cormac's research on digital comics is due to make a major contribution to comics studies, and it is exciting to see his career develop.

Many of these chapters were first presented at the Superheroes Beyond conference held at ACMI. We would like to thank Helen Simondson, Amita Kirpalani, Russell Briggs, and the many other ACMI staff who made that event possible. We thank Frederick Luis Aldama for his generous introduction. Frederick's Eisner-Award-winning work on Latinx Superheroes has been crucial in widening the scope of superhero research. We hope that this book can add to that more expansive scholarship. We must also acknowledge the work of superstar artist James Brouwer, whose dynamic cover brings together the far-reaching streams of this ambitious collection. The team members at the University Press of Mississippi led by Katie Keene have been tremendously supportive and patient throughout this process, and the editors are very grateful for the care that they have taken with the collection.

Finally, and most importantly, we would like to thank the collection's fantastic contributors, who trusted us with their work and patiently waited for the publication to come together at a time of great change for the world and editorial team. Their research and contributions in this anthology will expand superhero studies into previously unchartered territory.

SUPERHEROES BEYOND

INTRODUCTION

CORMAC McGARRY

"Anyone can wear the mask. You can wear the mask. If you didn't know that before, I hope you do now." Miles Morales (Shameik Moore) tells this to the audience at the close of the Academy Award–winning film *Spider-Man: Into the Spider-Verse* (2018). It should not be an extraordinary or powerful thing to say. The literal function of a mask is to obscure and dissolve identity, after all. Surely anyone could always have worn the mask? But the requirements have been unspoken; tacit defaults of race, gender, orientation, and ableness have remained durable beneath its cover. Thus, when Miles Morales, a character of mixed race, assumes the mantle of Spider-Man, one of Marvel Comics's most famous heroes, and declares "anyone can wear the mask," it signals a moment. Not the first moment. And not the last. But a moment in which the transcendent capacity of the superhero as an archetype is visibly marked.

Superheroes, the fantastic avatars of wide cultural imagination, have often ironically labored under staid prescriptions of form and identity. This moment at the end of *Into the Spider-Verse* strikes against these prescriptions and instead encapsulates the increasingly transmedial and transcultural ways that superheroes are reaching beyond to speak to broader communities. No longer confined to the pages of comic books, no longer just white men in tights, in their unprecedented breadth and variety, superheroes can demonstrate an uncanny ability to reflect a squared circle. They are able to reach for globalization's utopian ideals of universality at the same time as readily embodying a broad spectrum of cultural specificities and lifting up the importance of the histories and identities which form them.

The representational power of the superhero archetype across countries, media platforms, and identities is at a never-before-seen peak. The incumbency of great power—you will not need reminding—is great responsibility and this responsibility falls on scholarship to critically engage with the new horizons of superheroism that dawn when anyone can wear the mask. This collection,

Superheroes Beyond, looks to meet that obligation by bringing together a wide range of scholars from across the globe and across a variety of disciplines. The novel approaches to the superhero brought forward by these scholars showcases the extensive cultural purchase of the cape and cowl, revealing new contexts and perspectives that eschew the expected boundaries of superhero analysis to instead go far beyond.

DIMENSIONS OF IMAGINATION

Superhero characters have traced the lines of a long-abiding frontier. It is a frontier that they continually transgress to find the measure of their scale, their scope, and their substance. Like the unstable molecules Reed Richards fabricates to clad his family in the distinctive uniforms of the Fantastic Four, the figure of the superhero is one that must constantly adapt and yet facilitate instant recognition. The superhero is both what literary theorist Mikhail Bakhtin would term a "chronotope" (84) that expressively transduces an ever-cascading series of historical moments, and also that which nonetheless exerts itself against this history in a serial process of reinvention. Semiotician and cultural critic Umberto Eco observed this as the tension between the superhero's mythological qualities and the "novelistic" imperatives imposed by its comic book readership (149). This is to say that, in order to function, the superhero must be an archetype that stands in constant "consumption" of itself (149). They must persistently cross the frontiers of their provenance and their moment of reception. More succinctly, this means that they are in constant negotiation between the accumulated histories that make them recognizable and the imperative to belong and be relevant to the "now" that media producers are selling into.

The need to be symbolically stable and yet produce innovation, adventure, and cultural introspection means that superheroes are at once timeless and uniquely the products of whatever time they happen to find themselves in. Ian Gordon draws on Angela Ndalianis to explain this as the superhero's survival requiring it to simultaneously "contain its own past, 'make way for the present and look towards its future'" (qtd. in Gordon 37). "Beyond" is thus built into the DNA of the superhero. This ability to consistently renegotiate its borders to present itself unchanged and still somehow spangled in the contemporary is the superpower that invests the archetype with such transhistorical, transcultural, and transmedial potency. One further aside from *Into the Spider-Verse* neatly articulates this quality. In a posthumous cameo, an ersatz Stan Lee sells Miles Morales a novelty Spider-Man costume. When Morales asks if he can return the costume should it not fit, the ersatz Lee grins and replies, "It always fits . . . eventually," coyly hinting at the process of perpetual becoming that the

Figure I.1. Miles Morales symbolically takes on a novelty costume reflecting a commercialized archetype whose scope he must challenge in order to "make the costume fit" (*Into the Spider-Verse*).

superhero is innately given to. The costume always fits because its dimensions are always raised from imagination.

The major caveat of the maxim above is, of course, the conclusion "eventually." In this, the line spoken by Lee synopsizes the contention of this collection *in nuce*: that the make-up of the superhero endows it with the transcendent potential to continually reach beyond itself, yet it has been prone to ossification and lag over time, becoming complacent with the dimensions of imagination that have proven successful. The phrase "dimensions of imagination" is one loosely adapted from film philosopher and theorist André Bazin. The phrase is offered here to underpin a conspectus of the superhero's relationship to form and culture. It also acts as a reflection on the parameters within which scholarship has sometimes helped to reify a particularly narrowly imagined archetype.

Bazin's treatise on the Western film genre offers a helpful starting point in charting the superhero's cultural role, providing a parallel that can be used to unpack the quandary of the iterative capacity of the superhero that Eco and others above have observed. Commenting on the fundamental nature of the genre, as Eco does for the superhero, Bazin remarks of the Western as being "born of an encounter between a mythology and a means of expression" (142). By this, Bazin linked the Western genre with cinema in an elemental way, suggesting that the distribution on screen of the American West's mythologized frontiers had raised the dimensions of those images to "become one with those of imagination" (142). In cinema, the Western genre had found a medium whose breadth and grain were connatural with its own dynamism and want of amplitude. The qualities of the Western "identifie[d] it with the essence of cinema" in the Hollywood mode (141), allowing Bazin to proclaim that the genre represented the "American film *par excellence*" (141).

One could argue, quite facilely, that the superhero was the alchemical product of a similar equation to the Western film genre: a folkloric collision captured and wrought in the four-color worlds of a new medium. Much like the Western's relationship to cinema, an intimate and abiding association was formed between the burgeoning superhero archetype and the comic book form. Superman, Jerry Siegel and Joe Shuster's promethean superhero, emerged to embody the beginning of this union, setting in motion a cavalcade of imitators and offshoots in what could be described as the only runaway train the Man of Steel has ever failed to stop. Over time, in an outcome that broadly mirrored Bazin's observation of the Western and cinema, the unique suitability of the comic book medium in expressing the imaginative potential of the superhero saw the genre become constructed and conventionalized as the American comic book genre *"par excellence"* (141). Ramzi Fawaz succinctly describes this, noting that

> the invention of the superhero [. . .] would cement comics as one of the most influential forms of twentieth century American popular culture, by linking the populist character of the comic book medium to a fantasy figure that embodied American ideals of democratic equality, justice, and the rule of law (6).

The representational capabilities of the comic book medium, in addition to the populist embrace of the form which Fawaz notes, together suggested that the imaginative dimensions of the superhero had found a seemingly ideal vehicle. William W. Savage Jr. sums this up well, observing, "Comic books could carry heroes beyond the limits of possibility imposed by radio [. . .] and film" (7). Echoing Bazin's view of cinema's singular suitability to fully capture the potential of the Western, Savage Jr. summates, "Comic book artists and writers could produce that which could be conceived" (7) or as Grant Morrison concisely put it, "No other popular form existed where spectacular scenes of men tossing planets at one another could be created with any degree of believability" (61). Thus, in a formative period, comic books offered the superhero its most commensurate environment. In Bazinian terms, the comic book elevated the dimensions of the superhero to its most realized form. In its pages, the costume seemed to fit without flaw.

This account of the superhero as the American comic book genre par excellence, however, involves its own degree of mythologizing. As Carleton Young famously expounds to James Stewart at the conclusion of *The Man Who Shot Liberty Valance* (1962), "When the legend becomes fact, print the legend." Scholarship of the superhero has previously been guilty of printing the legend. Indelibly yoked to the form of the comic book as its ideal home, the superhero has been equally subject to what Bart Beaty describes as the "Americanization of comics" (29).[1] In this way, Jerry Robinson's claim that "America and the comic strip were made for each other" (11) rehearses Bazin's formulation of the Western genre's elevation through cinema into an exemplar of American culture. The superhero as an embodiment of the comic book form described by Maurice Horn as "so American in its expression" (qtd. in Beaty 28) becomes similarly mythologized as an American archetype along these lines.

While the role of the United States in the development of comics and the superhero genre is not to be understated, scholarship has, at times, tended to draw the dimensions of the two so as to precisely exclude contributions that do not fit the legend. Beaty suggests this has been an attempt to avoid the positioning of comics (and by extension here, the superhero) "not as a narcotizing and alienating aspect of mass culture" but within the "sociological paradigm of societal reflection" (29). Beaty elegantly summarizes this line of argument: "[I]f comics cannot be art, it suffices that they are at least American" (29). By being firmly fastened to the comic book as its "defining content" (Morrison 4), the superhero has been similarly skewed. The privileging of the United States within this sociological paradigm, however, has ironically disbarred the superhero's broad capacity for societal reflection and critically ossified its location within comics so as to forestallingly exploit its status as a neglected cultural underdog. This, in particular, is something that the third section of this collection addresses. Mapping the superhero archetype beyond the United States serves as a corrective to the "Americanization" of the superhero.

As superheroes have escaped the bounds of the comic book to find great appeal and performative flexibility through animation, video games, television shows, and cinema, the critical guarding of the archetype against the critique of mass culture has come more into relief. Scott Bukatman notes this, observing that the "superhero film has displaced the superhero comic in the world of mass culture" (118). Mitch Murray suggests the result of the superhero's expropriation into the mass media of film and television has been to see it "discredited as the worst of mass culture" (45). Murray, however, also notes that this view is inescapably couched in longstanding arbitrations of mass culture as low culture, referring to such arbitrations as the "protector[s] of particular historical, and classed, perceptions of aesthetic achievement" (30). Murray's article is positioned as a riposte to the mass cultural critique which Beaty noted that comics scholarship had been doing its best to avoid. In meeting and dismantling many elements of this critique, however, Murray demonstrates that the protective Americanization of the superhero and the guarded focus of scholarship on its relationship with the comic book (at the expense of a wider view) were unwarranted. While the superhero is by no means innocent of naked commoditization, indeed the second section of the collection interrogates this, Murray

Figure I.2. *Black Panther: Wakanda Forever* (2022) explores Meso-American mythology in an enrichment of Namor (Tenoch Huerta), while elevating Black female characters in Shuri (Letitia Wright) and Riri Williams (Dominique Thorne) and setting up a streaming series for the latter.

notes that a number of "superhero works, most notably in the emergent web streaming medium, are upending the aesthetic and critical assumptions about what the superhero genre is and what it can do" (30). Rather than "typifying the evils of [mass] culture" (30) that some scholarly constructions of comics and the superhero have guarded against, the extension of the superhero into forms beyond the comic book has allowed the superhero to form a "shared cultural heritage" (Arnaudo 2) and a "figuration of our collective utopian fantasies" (Murray 31). The degree to which transmedia mechanisms have supported this extension of the superhero away from the critiques of mass culture and moral panics is analyzed in the second section of this collection.

The costume always eventually fits because its dimensions are always raised from imagination. This is, in its own way, a utopian figuration of the superhero. Yet, as the caveat implies, and as has been illustrated above, the dimensions of imagination sometimes need to be recalibrated and reconceptualized. If they did not, Miles Morales would have no reason to remind audiences that they too can wear the mask. If the unbalanced focus of scholarship on the superhero as the folk product of an American medium has been undertaken with a defensive strategy, the lack of research on how the costume is embodied outside a traditionally white masculine identity has little such excuse. A growing body of scholarship, however, has emerged to redress this lack. Carolyn Cocca's *Superwomen: Gender, Power, and Representation*, for instance, stands out as a particular exemplar of this redress. In her book, Cocca challenges why female representation among superhero characters has been relatively stagnant and observes that the proportion of female superheroes pales in comparison to the volume of their male counterparts (1). Even among the superhero's comparatively scant female representation, a series of other defaults endure. Cocca notes that most superhero types are "white and heterosexual and upper middle class and able-bodied" (1). As Cocca suggests, and the first section of this collection explores, these are defaults that media industries have slowly (and sometimes clumsily) begun to challenge.

Here the collection contributes to gaps in scholarship that Cocca and other researchers have identified as being in need of continued analysis. Sean Guynes and Martin Lund, for example, find the study of whiteness in superhero comics to be "nigh invisible" (24), while Scott T. Smith and José Alaniz observe similarly that disability "is largely absent in many recent studies of the superhero" (2). Ramzi Fawaz's *The New Mutants* makes a critical intervention in superhero studies using queer theory, once again recognizing the many fluid aspects of superhero representation that require further attention from scholars. Though the defaults of identity still largely persist for the superhero, they can be challenged by scholarship and by the continued transmedia proliferation of the archetype into the hands of more diverse creators who can give credence to the utopian ideal that the costume always eventually fits and its defaults can be overcome. The chapters which follow in this collection are part of this challenge and contribute to further broadening the definition of the superhero.

André Bazin's conception of the Western was drawn on above as a point of comparison for how the superhero has been mythologized as a cultural product. Both the superhero and the Western could conceivably be argued as having been born in fateful encounters between mythologies and means of expression, but they differ in a key regard, particularly as Bazin saw the Western. Where Bazin extols the timelessness and implacability of the western as a genre that inoculates itself against influence to retain its mythic permanence (140), the mythology of the superhero is one that continues to be porous to a persistent cultural pulse-taking. This has allowed the superhero to continuously redraw itself as new opportunities emerge for it to be creatively realized. The *Superheroes Beyond* collection offers its own take of the superhero's progress in creatively redrawing itself according to widening dimensions of imagination. In this, the collection contributes to an overdue debate about the expanding definition of the superhero. Following from the early interventions of Cocca, Fawaz, and Howard and Jackson (among others), this book organizes three sections of scholarship that provide a transhistorical appraisal on the degree to which industries have moved the archetype beyond men of steel and comic book synonymity and that challenges its conception as primarily being a cultural export of the United States.

SUPERHEROES BEYOND

Superheroes Beyond explores the complexity and cultural reach of the superhero under three sections—"Beyond Men of Steel," "Beyond Comic Books," and "Beyond the United States." These sections thematically relate the salient ways in which the superhero archetype has come to flexibly resist traditional placings within specific formal and sociocultural boundaries. The first section discusses the ways that the archetype has moved beyond simply recapitulating the "man of steel" figure that proliferated in the early boom of superheroes following the success of Superman. Increasingly, the superheroes on our shelves, and on our screens, are being pushed beyond assumed defaults of race, gender, sexuality, and ableness. Authors in this section reflect on the impact of audiences, creators, and industry in driving this move beyond men of steel, particularly casting light on what greater representation in the cape and cowl has meant for a wide range of people and communities. Naja Later opens this section and kickstarts this conversation with a chapter on Marvel Comics and its treatment of diversity. Marvel's All New, All Different epoch is discussed, which ushered in Jane Foster's Thor and Sam Wilson's Captain America among many other recastings of the publisher's premier heroes. Later illustrates how the industrial side of comics can cynically play a neoliberal game where diversity and representation rise and fall according to the stock value of its perceived cultural capital. The chapter navigates Marvel's All New, All Different era in this light, deconstructing its branding to demonstrate the problematic associations of representation with novelty and, in turn, suggesting better possibilities for superhero publishers pursuing a fuller breadth of the comics market.

Alexandra Ostrowski-Schilling continues the examination of Marvel's relationship with representation, this time focusing on depictions of disability in the Marvel Cinematic Universe (MCU). The chapter provides a detailed reading of how disability is linked to the actualization of the superheroic in three of the shared universe's tentpole characters: Robert Downey Jr.'s Iron Man, Chris Evans's Captain America, and Benedict Cumberbatch's Doctor Strange. Ostrowski-Schilling points out how the MCU's articulation of the hero's journey, particularly their origin stories, problematically engages with a number of real-world biases that distort experiences of disability. The chapter deftly draws on the contemporary social depiction of the "super crip" and Simi Linton's work on "overcoming narratives" to explore how disability has become expediently used to underline tragedy and set the superhero on their path to becoming symbols of moral virtue. Like Naja Later's chapter before it, however, Ostrowski-Schilling's analysis speaks to how representations of disability among superheroes can move beyond such unhelpful tropes.

Octavia Cade's chapter pivots the section into looking at the monstrous nonhuman as an extension of the superhero archetype. The thematic thread begun in Ostrowski-Schilling's chapter, examining what goes into the heart of a hero, is continued here as Cade's chapter also scrutinizes how moral probity constructs the superheroic. Focusing on ecological horror, Cade observes how the monstrous characters of the genre are disbarred from recognition within the superheroic mode in spite of performing many of its archetypal functions. Cade, however, following Ellen E. Moore, also makes the case that these characters throw into question the superhero's longstanding defense of the ordinary citizen as innocent by highlighting their culpability and passive complicity in perpetrating ecological deterioration. The chapter takes up this central contention to suggest how monstrous nonhumans—ranging from Swamp Thing to mutant bears and Godzilla—are challenging the boundaries of superhero definitions by creating their own status as ecological heroes.

The section's penultimate chapter continues to home in on how the links between identity formation and the superheroic can fuel the latter's expanding boundaries. Julian Novtiz's chapter examines the construction of literary superheroes using the format of the bildungsroman. In addition to progressing the section's insights into what it means to wear the mask, Novitz's chapter also offers a useful transition into the collection's second segment on the superhero archetype's proliferation outside of comic books. Analyzing Salman Rushdie's *Midnight's Children* and Jonathan Lethem's *The Fortress of Solitude*, Novitz reflects on how the bildungsroman structure of these novels places its burgeoning heroes within a complex social order, offering a nuanced appraisal of the superhero origin that is taken up particularly effectively by the literary medium of the novel. Novitz outlines how the narrative trajectory of these novels draws a parallel between the maturation of its protagonists and that of the superhero archetype itself. The chapter takes the notion of great power being tied to great responsibility and deftly identifies how this often contains a fallacy of agency that is readily uncovered by placing the superhero within the framework of the bildungsroman.

Sheena C. Howard closes this section, using a qualitative approach to articulate the profound resonances for African American viewers of the watershed superhero film *Black Panther* (2018). Howard uses focus-group research to examine the importance of how a Black-led superhero blockbuster has contributed to the development of robust self-concepts for young adult African American viewers. In her chapter, Howard employs uses and gratifications theory alongside a range of thematic analyses to organize the insights from her focus group research, presenting readers with a detailed picture of why *Black Panther* represents a portentous touchstone of the kinds of empowering representation superhero icons can offer. This focus and inquiry speaks to the heart of the collection.

While section one highlights representation as its primary concern, its chapters also showcase the wide gamut of different media that the superhero has come to malleably inhabit and take advantage of. The second section looks more specifically at this, demonstrating that where once the superhero seemed bound to the comic book, technologies have progressed, potential outlets have broadened, and superheroes have come to traverse this increasingly transmediated landscape of popular culture with great flexibility. Our first encounters with superheroes now take place in the dark of movie theaters or with thumbs on joysticks as readily as they do in the panels of comic books. Indeed, the superhero's modern-day configuration as intellectual property (IP) has taken it far from its origins to the tops of box offices and beyond. The franchise potential and sheer transmedia "spreadability" (Jenkins, Ford, and Green 3) of the superhero has transfigured it into some of the most bankable IP that conglomerates can get their hands on. The second section of the collection discusses how the superhero has become a spreadable phenomenon, moving from the "folk devils" of children's animation to toy lines, trademarks, and IP.

Djoymi Baker's chapter begins this section with an examination of how the superheroes synonymous with Saturday Morning Cartoons came to be viewed by some as the folk devils of children's television at the time. Animated superhero shows formed a core part of the Saturday morning programming block and their relative success within this block did much to calcify the perception of animation as a children's medium. Baker wades into the irony of this with a sharp analysis of how superhero animations such as *The Marvel Super Heroes* (1966) and *The Superman/Aquaman Hour of Adventure* (1967–68) were attended by a moral panic over their perceived violence and thus their suitability for children. Arising from this, Baker's chapter offers a nuanced account of how superhero shows became a staging ground in a battle of generational taste over how the medium of animation was to develop on television.

Baker's chapter demonstrates how Saturday Morning Cartoons were an entryway for many children into the world of superheroes. Jason Bainbridge explores a similar entryway as his chapter takes up the discussion of the superhero's transmedia potential by examining their history as the plastic paratext par excellence—the toy. In describing the "toyesis" of superheroes, Bainbridge details how toys have played a critical role in the saturation of the superhero throughout our media landscape. The chapter outlines the symbiotic relationship that has prevailed between superheroes and toys and how it has functioned to their mutual benefit. Dovetailing with Mitchell Adams's ensuing chapter, Bainbridge notes how toys have been at the center of legal wranglings around the very definition of the superhero and how toys, as a key commercial appendage, have long guided the evolution of the archetype both within and beyond its comic book roots.

The transfiguration of the superhero into IP is further elaborated in Mitchell Adams's chapter. He observes how superheroes, such as Batman and Superman, have become the golden geese that conglomerates have fought to maintain an iron grip on. As Adams explores, however, time may force that grip to loosen. In his chapter, Adams offers an insight into the courtroom battles and legal strategies undertaken in the pursuit of protecting the IP rights of many valuable superhero characters, observing how the efforts involved have helped fundamentally shape the law around IP and trademarking. Adams notes how the legal maneuverings of conglomerates are now being made to hold onto the value of key superhero IP as characters like Batman and Superman edge closer to becoming part of the public domain.

Leaving the courtroom to look up at the marquee, my own chapter examines how the protectionist attitudes of conglomerates towards the monopoly value of their superhero IP has created a Hollywood-like star system around them. As practices of consumption have shifted and become more transmediated, the chapter looks at how conglomerates may be retooling the superhero star system towards a new kind of value that is to be found in having multiple iterations of their stars available across different platforms simultaneously. The chapter explores how the value of the superhero star image can be shaped across a hierarchical network of transmedia systems, taking the youth-focused Marvel Rising franchise as a particular example. Where previously conglomerates had taken a view of audiences as unequipped to handle two or more versions of a character at one time, a new approach to the value of superhero stars could be seen to leave conglomerates asking just what is the maximum occupancy of a mask?

Jack Teiwes concludes the second section of this collection with an examination of a cluster of independent superhero films whose releases were perhaps obscured in the coinciding dominance of studio-backed superhero IP. Teiwes names a series of films among this cluster, including *Special* (2006), *Defendor* (2009), and *Kick-Ass* (2010), and makes the case for them as a significant subgenre of the superhero film with a number of distinct tropes. The "DIY superhero" film, as Teiwes dubs it, offers a subversive take on the superhero that conceptually grounds them in true-to-life diegeses. Through a series of common tropes, Teiwes argues that the DIY subgenre deconstructs the superhero such that, in a broad parallel to Julian Novitz's chapter, the superheroic power of its protagonists is revealed as a delusory agency whose ultimate pursuit may, as the chapter's title pointedly suggests, be a toxic fantasy.

The expansion of the superhero outside of comic books and into new media landscapes has been prolific, creating star systems and subgenres and driving the development of the media they have found themselves in. The expansion of the superhero, however, has not just been a transmedia venture. It has also been a transnational, transcultural, and globalized affair. The collection's final section details this global endorsement of the superhero archetype and highlights the vibrant history of superhero figures outside of the United States. Liam Burke opens this section by noting how the development of national superheroes has been stymied by the cultural hegemony that US superheroes have enjoyed. Analyzing the superhero landscape in Australia, Burke's chapter draws on a wide range of interviews with fans and creators to put forward a critical framework for uncovering the reasons behind Australia's dearth of national superheroes. The chapter uses this framework to then contextualize the development of a greater number of Australian superheroes, such as the eponymous hero of the Indigenous Australian television show *Cleverman* (2016–17), as local creators have emerged and local industries have strengthened.

Moving up to the Philippines, Maria Lorena Santos explores the commingling of local mythology, nation-building, and the superheroic. Santos's chapter adroitly navigates through the use of the superhero archetype by Filipino creators in a postcolonial reclamation of indigenous folklore. Looking particularly at Mervin Malonzo's graphic novel *Tabi Po*, Santos analyzes how its reimagining of figures from the history of Filipino nationalism as monstrous heroes denudes the myths of nation-building at the same time as engaging with the country's precolonial mythologies. In a corollary with Octavia Cade's chapter in the collection's first section, Santos explores how the archetype of the superhero is imbricated in the monstrous hero as a demonstration of moral complexities, especially those that attend to revolutionary histories.

The ability of the superhero to function as a transductive mechanism for the interpretation of national histories is also taken up in Enrique Uribe-Jongbloed's and Hernan David Espinosa-Medina's chapter on Colombian superheroes. Guiding the reader through an overview of the history of the comic book medium in Colombia, Uribe-Jongbloed and Espinosa-Medina set the scene for an examination of how the Colombian superhero can be used to parse the country's complicated circuit of race, ethnicity, and national identity. Drawing on ideological and close textual schemas from Leonard Rifas and Andrew J. Kunka, the chapter provides an appraisal of the development of superheroes that move beyond imported US tropes to more fully articulate the possibility of truly representative Colombian superheroes.

Dan Golding's chapter, like others in this section, grapples with the effects of the cultural hegemony that has long underpinned the superhero as a particularly North American archetype with strong roots in the United States. Examining the score to the MCU's *Black Panther*, Golding looks at how the film's musical accompaniments tell the story of its relationship with Africa and the African diaspora—a relationship where the critical darling of superhero representation may not have escaped the US cultural imperialism of the archetype or the prevailing whiteness of Hollywood scoring. Golding's chapter offers a nuanced analysis of how the music of *Black Panther* could be seen to amount to an approximation of African culture, perhaps mired in traditions that have often served to reify the Otherness of the nonwhite and non-Anglophone onscreen.

The section completes a circumnavigation of the globe, returning to Australia for Aaron Humphrey's concluding chapter on postcolonial iterations of Lee Falk's popular superhero The Phantom. Humphrey's chapter neatly aggregates a number of the prominent themes of the section. As Humphrey points out, The Phantom is somewhat uncanny as an incarnation of cultural imperialism. He is, after all, a literal white savior figure. This, the chapter contends, makes the character an interesting case study in transnational adaptation. Humphrey uses John Fiske's work on excorporation to analyze how localized iterations of The Phantom have seen the superhero rearticulated to serve in a range of community service campaigns and educational comics, particularly among Aboriginal Australians. Humphrey details how the excorporation of the superhero figure can ungird its relationship to cultural imperialism and allow it to be reimagined in different local and national contexts to promote a civic good.

Together, the contributors to this collection demonstrate a need for scholarship to take a more encompassing view of the superhero, expanding the understanding of the archetype by filtering it through the different lenses available across multiple fields of study. Their observations form important starting points needed to take stock of the superhero's far-reaching appeal, contributing the critical conversations required to bring scholarship into the present moment and beyond.

Note

1. Bart Beaty describes the "Americanization of comics" (29) as an appeal to locate comics within the purview of the folk culture of the United States rather than as vapid mass culture outside the realms of legitimate art. It is worth clarifying here that "Americanization" refers in principal to the United States. Comics and superhero traditions in Latin and South America are explored in the third section of the collection—"Beyond the United States."

Works Cited

Arnaudo, Marco. *The Myth of the Superhero*. Translated by Jamie Richards, The Johns Hopkins University Press, 2013.

Bakhtin, Mikhail. *The Dialogic Imagination*. Translated by Caryl Emerson and Michael Holquist, University of Texas Press, 1981.

Bazin, André. "The Western: Or the American Film Par Excellence." *What Is Cinema? Vol. II*, Translated by Hugh Gray, University of California Press, 2005, pp. 140–48.

Beaty, Bart. *Comics versus Art*. University of Toronto Press, 2012.

Bukatman, Scott. "Why I Hate Superhero Movies." *Cinema Journal*, vol. 50, no. 3, 2011, pp. 118–22.

Cocca, Carolyn. *Superwomen: Gender, Power, and Representation*. Bloomsbury Academic, 2016.

Eco, Umberto. "The Myth of Superman." *Arguing Comics: Literary Masters on a Popular Medium*, edited by Jeet Heer and Kent Worcester, University Press of Mississippi, 2004, pp. 146–64.

Fawaz, Ramzi. *The New Mutants: Superheroes and the Radical Imagination of American Comics*. New York University Press, 2016.

Gordon, Ian. *Superman: The Persistence of an American Icon*. Rutgers University Press, 2017.

Guynes, Sean, and Martin Lund, editors. *Unstable Masks: Whiteness and American Superhero Comics*. The Ohio State University Press, 2020.

Howard, Sheena C., and Ronald L. Jackson, editors. *Black Comics: Politics of Race and Representation*. Bloomsbury Academic, 2013.

Jenkins, Henry, Sam Ford and Joshua Green. *Spreadable Media: Creating Value and Meaning in a Networked Culture*. New York University Press, 2013.

The Man Who Shot Liberty Valance. Directed by John Ford, Paramount Pictures, 1962.

Morrison, Grant. *Supergods: What Masked Vigilantes, Miraculous Mutants, and a Sun God from Smallville Can Teach Us about Being Human*. Spiegel & Grau, 2012.

Murray, Mitch. "The Work of Art in the Age of the Superhero." *Science Fiction Film & Television*, vol. 10, no. 1, 2017, pp. 27–51.

Robinson, Jerry. *The Comics: An Illustrated History of Comic Strip Art*. G. P. Putnam's Sons, 1974.

Savage, William W., Jr. *Comic Books and America: 1945–1954*. University of Oklahoma Press, 1990.

Smith, Scott T., and Aláñiz José, editors. *Uncanny Bodies: Superhero Comics and Disability*. The Pennsylvania State University Press, 2019.

Spider-Man: Into the Spider-Verse. Directed by Bob Persichetti et al., Sony Pictures Releasing, 2018.

Section 1

BEYOND MEN OF STEEL

Introduction

BEYOND MEN OF STEEL

ANGELA NDALIANIS

In her 2016 book *Superwomen: Gender, Power, and Representation,* Carolyn Cocca reflects on how the "word 'superhero' pretty much assumes that the hero in question is male, and white, and heterosexual, and able-bodied" (6). Since that publication, successful superhero movies and TV shows such as *Wonder Woman, Black Panther, Watchmen, Captain Marvel,* and *She-Hulk: Attorney at Law,* as well as the growing popularity of characters like Miles Morales (aka Spider-Man), Ms. Marvel, and Harley Quinn on the comic book page have begun widening definitions of the "superhero" and challenging baked-in expectations of who can wear the mask. The contributions to this section probe representation in the superhero genre.

A leading figure in the underground Comix scene, Trina Robbins has written a number of books that highlight the role of women as characters and creators in comics. Describing Golden Age comic book superheroes, Robbins noted that "[a]side from their brightly colored longjohns, the one thing these heroes had in common was their gender" (54). In fact, when psychologist William Moulton Marston introduced Wonder Woman in 1941, he positioned the hero as a corrective to the "bloodcurdling masculinity" of comics (Lepore 187). However, for decades Wonder Woman was often the only woman character to headline a US superhero comic book. When women heroes did appear during the comic book industry's Golden and Silver Ages they were often super powered Smurfettes, rounding out all-male line-ups such as the Marvel Family (Mary Marvel), Fantastic Four (Sue Storm), and X-Men (Jean Grey). Representation for non-white heroes among mainstream comic book publishers was similarly limited. Marvel enjoyed success in 1966 with the introduction of Afrofuturist superhero Black Panther, but most Silver Age efforts to depict heroes of color tended to play upon wider popular culture trends with characters whose origins perpetuated stereotypes about Eastern mysticism (e.g., Shang-Chi) or inner-city crime (e.g., Luke Cage).

Moving into the 1980s team books with diverse rosters such as *X-Men* and *Teen Titans* began to widen representation in mainstream comics, but this diversity ironically coincided with a narrowing of comic book readership. In the late 1970s comic book publishers began moving from newsstand to direct distribution, which found dedicated comic book stores become for many the central hub of comic book fandom. These stores were often unwelcoming to newer readers and those that did not conform to an imagined comic book readership: straight, white men (Burke). This limited view of comic book culture continued through the 1990s, with women comic book characters often being hypersexualised or serving as narrative fodder to advance the male hero's arc. By the turn of the millennium marginalised fans were using digital distribution to circumvent comic book store gate-keeping and access comics. Fans and creators also used online platforms to critique the lack of diversity in the superhero genre though grassroots strategies like the Hawkeye Initiative, which used fan art to bring attention to the hypersexualised costumes and poses of women heroes.

Coinciding with the greater visibility of once marginalised fans, since the 2010s a greater number of women, members of the LGBTQ+ community, and creators of colour color have moved into the comic book industry where they have taken on key creative and editorial positions (Ndalianis). This era has also seen the introduction of new superheroes who are not straight white men (e.g., America Chavez, Ms. Marvel, and Ghost-Spider), while the mantle of long-standing heroes has passed to characters from backgrounds that mainstream comics traditionally ignored, such as Wolverine (Laura Kinney), Hulk (Amadeus Cho), and Blue Beetle (Jaime Reyes). This greater diversity has extended into adaptations of these characters including blockbuster films starring and directed by women and people of color like *Black Panther*, *Wonder Woman*, *Aquaman*, *Captain Marvel*, and *Shang-Chi and the Legend of the Ten Rings*.

A wealth of research has emerged that is interrogating how long-standing traditions of the superhero genre have been challenged by fans and creators to facilitate wider representation. This scholarship includes Eisner Award-winning books such as Frederick Luis Aldama's *Latinx Superheroes in Mainstream Comics*, Carolyn Cocca's *Superwomen: Gender, Power, and Representation*, and the edited collections *The Blacker the Ink* and *Black Comics*. The chapters in this section continue that interest by going beyond Men of Steel to unmask diversity of representation in the superhero genre.

Works Cited

Aldama, Frederick Luis. *Latinx Superheroes in Mainstream Comics*. University of Arizona Press, 2017.

Burke, Liam. "Harley Quinn and the Carnivalesque Transformation of Comic Book Fandom." *Transformative Works and Cultures*, no. 36, 2021.

Cocca, Carolyn. *Superwomen: Gender, Power, and Representation*. Bloomsbury Publishing USA, 2016.

Gateward, Frances, and John Jennings, editors. *The Blacker the Ink: Constructions of Black Identity in Comics and Sequential Art*. Rutgers University Press, 2015.

Howard, Sheena C., and Ronald L. Jackson II, editors. *Black Comics: Politics of Race and Representation*. Bloomsbury Publishing, 2013.

Lepore, Jill. *The Secret History of Wonder Woman*. Vintage, 2015.

Ndalianis, Angela. "Female Fans, Female Creators, and Female Superheroes: The Semiotics of Changing Gender Dynamics." *The Routledge Companion to Gender and Sexuality in Comic Book Studies*, edited by Frederick Luis Aldama, Routledge, 2020, pp. 310–28.

Robbins, Trina. "The Great Women Superheroes." *The Superhero Reader*, edited by Charles Hatfield, Jeet Heer, and Kent Worcester, University Press of Mississippi, 2013, pp. 53–60.

Chapter 1

ALL NEW, ALL DIFFERENT, OR NO NORMAL?

Marvel Comics and Superhero Diversity

NAJA LATER

INTRODUCTION

In 2015, Marvel announced that its new line of superhero comics would be branded as All-New, All-Different (ANAD) (Calia). In part a reference to the alternate universe the Marvel heroes now inhabited, this relaunch prominently featured a number of superheroes popularized by Marvel's blockbuster movies such as Iron Man, Thor, Hulk, Captain America, and Spider-Man.[1] Traditionally, these superheroes' secret identities were white male characters, but ANAD featured characters whose superhero aliases were passed along to women and people of color. This meant Iron Man was Riri Williams, a Black girl; Thor was an anonymous white woman later revealed to be Jane Foster; Hulk an Asian boy called Amadeus Cho; Captain America was Sam Wilson, a Black man whose usual role is the Falcon; Wolverine was a white woman called Laura Kinney; Hawkeye was a white woman called Kate Bishop; Spider-Man was a Black Puerto Rican boy, Miles Morales; Captain Marvel was a white woman called Carol Danvers, and her former alias Ms. Marvel was now a Pakistani American girl, Kamala Khan.[2] While the ANAD press releases did not explicitly announce these new protagonists' race and gender identities, the implication was clear: Marvel recognized the homogeneity of its superstar characters and was championing diverse representation. The *Wall Street Journal* titled the release "Diverse New Avengers," calling ANAD "a new wrinkle that marks the company's latest push for more diversity" and quoting *Avengers* writer Mark Waid's statement: "I like the fact that we ended up with an Avengers team with one white guy on it" (Calia). The press surrounding the ANAD brand emphasized diversity as the ultimate novelty: this inference only became clearer when the novelty wore off.

The ANAD approach was not to last. A notorious statement from Marvel executive David Gabriel to comic retailers in 2017 claimed:

> What we heard was that people didn't want any more diversity . . . They didn't want female characters out there. That's what we heard, whether we believe that or not . . . We saw the sales of any character that was diverse, any character that was new, our female characters, anything that was not a core Marvel character, people were turning their nose up against. (Bryant)

In clarifying the statement, Gabriel emphasized that Marvel would continue to introduce "unique characters that represent new voices and new experiences in the Marvel Universe and pair them with our iconic heroes" (Bryant). However, the "core" Marvel titles such as *Iron Man*, *Captain America*, *Thor*, *Hulk*, and *Wolverine* were returned to the original characters in the 2017–2018 Legacy relaunch and subsequent Fresh Start line shortly after some were rebranded as Marvel NOW! 2.0—one of Marvel's many cycles in the NOW! brand.[3] With "Legacy," many titles with marginalized protagonists were canceled (Lovett). Suzanne Scott argues that Gabriel's statement "has a subtextual goal: to attempt to quash further calls for diversity through the logics of market rationalization" (1–2). This demonstrated a number of issues with the ANAD initiative: the language of the branding; the difficulty Marvel experiences connecting to a wider readership; the difference between on-page diversity and empowering representation; and systematic problems in the genre and the industry. These problems can be related to the context and approach specific to ANAD.

This chapter proposes a number of strategies that could have averted the perceived failure of ANAD. Diversified creator hiring practices would allow for more nuanced and three-dimensional representation, addressing the systematic homogeneity of superhero publishing that extends beyond the pages of the comics. Other problems relate to distribution: more accessible retailing would allow for a more diverse and open-minded readership. Finally, a more complex and dynamic approach to superhero storytelling could improve representation of marginalized people in comics.

ALL NEW, ALL DIFFERENT: THE BRAND

To address the significance of ANAD as a branding strategy for these comics, I take a similar approach to Rob Lendrum in his essay "Queering Super-Manhood: Superhero Masculinity, Camp and Public Relations as a Textual Framework." Lendrum analyses Marvel's 2003 *Rawhide Kid* title and the 2002 press release that preceded it. *Rawhide Kid* was a revival of the 1950s gunslinger, now published under the adult-oriented MAX imprint (290). Lendrum's analysis demonstrates that while the Rawhide Kid is portrayed as camp in the text, the only clear identification of him as gay is in Marvel's marketing: "Marvel's press releases accompanying the release of the new *Rawhide Kid* comic book function to prepare a dominant public perception of the character property as homosexual when the actual text is ambiguous" (287). Even in the 2010 *Rawhide Kid* sequel issues, the character remains textually closeted. Lendrum argues: "By openly stating the Rawhide Kid is gay, Marvel boldly proclaimed itself as a progressive company, willing to take risks on sensitive issues such as homosexuality. Marvel's public relations officer, Brian Reinert said, Marvel is 'always interested in tapping into stories that are relevant today'" (290).

Reinert's use of "today" echoes the language of "All-New," implying that queer people, like the nonwhite characters and women of the ANAD titles, are a recently discovered novelty. Lendrum is highly critical of the marketing strategy for *Rawhide Kid*, claiming:

> Marvel has launched this series strictly to test the waters for new markets using sexuality as their lure. The clever textual framing of the series allows Marvel to step back if the water gets too hot. Following the contemporary trend in other forms of mainstream media, Marvel uses representations of homosexuality to generate income and expand its market, rather than progress the social inclusion of homosexuality. (298)

Rami Fawaz similarly defines superhero diversity as a neoliberal strategy, analyzing superheroes' physical malleability as an allegory for how "formerly vilified outcast social identities—for instance being gay or lesbian—have been revalued on the basis of their profitability" (10). Fawaz's and Lendrum's arguments apply just as well in 2015. This can be seen with Gabriel's statement that "diversity" was to blame for poor sales: the water got too hot, and diversity did not generate adequate income. The subsequent rollout of the Legacy branding exemplifies the stepping-back that Lendrum describes. This disappointing pattern in Marvel's branding strategies undermines the potential for powerful representation in the comics.

THE ALL NEW, ALL DIFFERENT APPROACH TO REPRESENTATION

ANAD demonstrated an attempt by Marvel to address the overwhelming whiteness and maleness of its biggest titles. As Sheena C. Howard and Ronald L. Jackson note, "oftentimes comics tell a story about White heroes and minority villains, White victors and minority losers, White protagonists and perhaps a minority sidekick. This sets up a dialectic that, although is quite public, leaves a concealed residue of minority inferiority" (13). In diversifying the representation of women and people of color in the center of these high-profile narratives, Marvel is seeking to change this metanarrative. This has the potential to create empowering and empathic representations of marginalized people by giving them the roles of powerful, well-recognized superheroes, rather than relegating them to sidekick, villain, or victim. This is a key difference between diversity, which refers to the quantity of marginalized characters, and empowering representation. The latter is a complex and subjective quality that does not intrinsically follow from the former. Albert S. Fu argues that "diversity initiatives often emphasize membership rather than equality and integration" (278). This may be contrasted with Winona Landis's analysis of Kamala Khan as Ms. Marvel, which she calls a "nuanced and multifaceted representation of Muslims and Islam, both through narrative content and its visual depictions" (190). The push for better representation of nonwhite, nonmale superheroes is deeply necessary work, with potential for far-reaching positive ramifications. There are also many risks of misplaced sentiments and well-intentioned mistakes. Branding this latest attempt as ANAD was one such mistake.

The ANAD superhero lineup was not entirely all-new, nor all-different. Many of the new character identities precede the ANAD flagship titles. The most prominent examples were in 2012, when Miles Morales became Spider-Man and Carol Danvers became Captain Marvel.[4] ANAD was a watershed for Marvel, where diversity was foregrounded as the 2015 branding strategy. The ANAD branding was not used comprehensively in the actual titles of the comics: it appeared more consistently in the publicity and press surrounding the comics themselves. This suggests Marvel was attempting to foreground their diversity initiatives for new readers, rather than established readers who may already be picking up titles in a comic book store.

This narrative device is not a twenty-first-century invention, either: James Rhodes was Iron Man, and Monica Rambeau was Captain Marvel in the 1980s (O'Neil et al.). ANAD, however, is groundbreaking in its scale and publicity, a conscious response to increasing pressure on major media companies like Disney to improve its representation of marginalized characters. If the strategic branding of "diversity" was not obvious in the initial promotion, "diversity" was openly labeled the culprit when ANAD did not meet Marvel's expectations.

This chapter does not seek to analyze individual comics in-depth, nor is its intent to rate the representation of marginalized characters in various ANAD titles between empowering and reductive. Kristen J. Warner analyzes this problem in her work on "plastic representation," wherein attempts to quantify representation of Black characters in film and television "resulted in a set of binary, nonscientific, underdeveloped metrics—positive and negative—that constitute a nebulous catch-all system" (33). As is often the case in a large-scale project with many creative teams, some of the ANAD titles are compelling, and others fall flat, and all will be subjective to marginalized readers' experiences.

The chapter discusses overarching patterns in the ANAD books, such as how the title characters deal with their new superhero roles, as these demonstrate how structural issues of the New/Different paradigm are played out on the pages. Analysis focuses on the context that framed these attempts at improving representation, to argue that the ANAD branding was an impediment to the often-genuine attempts at empowering storytelling within the individual titles.

Just as Marvel does in the ANAD line, the chapter focuses on race and gender representation. Other marginalized identities such as sexuality and disability are represented very differently in the superhero genre and were not foregrounded as examples of diversity in ANAD. There are many techniques for improving representation in storytelling, and the approach ANAD takes could be called "genderbending" and "racebending." While this technique can be empowering as a fan tactic, reclaiming homogenous ensemble casts and encouraging fans to read "against the grain," it becomes more problematic as a corporate strategy. Warner describes this in film and television, wherein casting actors of color for normatively white roles:

> [Y]ield a set of dueling consequences: first, that any representation that includes a person of color is automatically a sign of success and progress; second, that such paltry gains generate an easy workaround for the executive suites whereby hiring racially diverse actors becomes an easy substitute for developing new complex characters. (33)

The problems Warner raises are exacerbated by comics. The characters of comic books are literally two-dimensional, and very few racially diverse creatives are hired at all. While this technique does create new characters whose racial identities may shape their narratives, the problems of an "easy workaround" remain. Warner defines plastic representation as "a combination of synthetic elements put together and shaped to look like meaningful imagery, but which can only approximate depth and substance because ultimately it is hollow and cannot survive close scrutiny" (35). She argues, "Plastic representation uses the wonder that comes from seeing characters . . . who serve as visual identifiers for specific demographics in order to flatten the expectation to desire anything more" (35). This framework demonstrates the ingrained problems of ANAD's diversification strategies, where famous superhero mantles are passed on to marginalized sidekick characters.

Rather than reimagine Peter Parker, Steve Rogers, and Tony Stark as Black, the original white characters are sidelined so that new characters—Miles Morales,

Sam Wilson, and Riri Williams—can use the superhero personas of Spider-Man, Captain America, and Iron Man respectively. Williams must deal with the obvious gendering of "Iron Man," renaming herself "Ironheart" at Stark's suggestion. This leaves Williams in a similar position to many female predecessors with feminized aliases of exnominated heroes: Captain Marvel/Ms. Marvel, Hulk/She-Hulk, and Thor/Thor Girl. Ironically, these particular three have recently discarded their uncomfortably gendered names: Ms. Marvel, She-Hulk, and Thor Girl have been redubbed Captain Marvel, Hulk, and Thor (although initially ambiguous in the comic, the woman using "Thor" is not the same character as Tarene Olson, the original Thor Girl). The problem with these new titles being framed by Marvel as promotions is that it reinforces a hierarchical relationship between the original and "new" hero. Fu analyzes the example of Miles Morales becoming the new Spider-Man rather than Peter Parker being reimagined as a Black character: this is "not as radical as some critics claim," quoting Leonard Pitts's comment: "The 'real' Spider-Man remains Peter Parker" (279). A similar problem plays out in the ANAD title *Captain America* (Spencer and Acuña), where Sam Wilson is "promoted" from Falcon to Captain America. There is still a hierarchical relationship between two traditionally white and traditionally Black superhero roles. Wilson frequently grapples with the newfound celebrity and responsibility of being Captain America, confessing newfound admiration for Steve Rogers and his politically "neutral" Captaincy (Spencer and Acuña). Ultimately, this primes the reader for Rogers's triumphant return in "Legacy," putting Wilson back in his place as Falcon.

This approach suggests that the mantles of white men are aspirational; the highest honor for marginalized heroes is to ascend to the status of white manhood. Fu argues, "In both the workplace and superhero teams, social and cultural 'diversity' does not negate the glass ceiling that keeps white men in leadership positions" (278). The blessing of the original alias-bearers is paramount during the new characters' ascendance: the emotional conflict for characters like Wilson and Khan centers on the approval of the original Captain America and Ms. Marvel. The systems that uphold "Thor," "Iron Man," "Captain America," and "Hulk" as the greatest heroes in the Marvel universe are maintained, within the narrative universe and for readers. The potential for marginalized superheroes to rise to superstar status in their own right, with their own aliases, is precluded by this strategy. The superaliases are only made available to marginalized characters when the traditional heroes have vacated the roles—often temporarily. Even more troubling is how former sidekick aliases such as the Falcon and Ms. Marvel are passed down to new characters with different axes of marginalization: the new Falcon is a Mexican immigrant, and Ms. Marvel a first-generation Pakistani Muslim. For Captain Marvel and Ms. Marvel, a hero-sidekick imbalance is transferred from a white man and a white woman to a white woman and a woman of color (implying the alias "Ms. Marvel" can be used by a woman of color, now that a white woman does not need it anymore). While the comic itself deals with this in a frank but insightful way, the broader implications of this as a primary diversification strategy are problematic. It continues to centralize whiteness especially as the traditional and quintessential quality of a superhero.

DIVERSITY AS A MARVEL PROBLEM

It is important to contextualize the position of Marvel as a publisher in comics culture. While Marvel has become well-established as a household name due to the phenomenal success of their film adaptations, comics culture has shifted away from superhero supremacy. Webcomics, manga, and graphic novels represent a more culturally significant—and often more financially successful—portion of comics culture. In these areas, representation for creators, characters, and readers is already strongly improved for women, people of color, and queer people. Independent and "alternative" comics are already reaping the rewards of authentic representation, as this chapter will argue. Manga has a massive female readership; comics by women of color are incredibly successful with online fundraising; and graphic novels by women frequently make bestseller lists. Marvel and DC are relatively regressive and increasingly irrelevant as comics retailers: their key strength is in licensing and IP for screen adaptations. Marvel is struggling to catch up with—and capitalize on—the diverse landscape of broader comics culture since the 2010s. The hard work of empowering representation is already being done: just not within the traditional framework of the "Big Two" publishers.

The apparent failure of diversity in the comics market is a complex issue, which can be explained in a number of ways. Marvel's conservative core fanbase; the flawed metrics of measuring sales; the struggle to capitalize on the thriving paperback and digital markets; the lack of representation in creative teams; and the superhero genre itself are environmental factors that must be considered. These help to explain why ANAD may not have met projected numbers, and why the "failure" may be symptomatic of the ANAD brand itself rather than an endemic problem in comics culture.

FAN COMMUNITY ELITISM

There is an implicit assumption that readers are particularly interested in characters who share their racial and gender identities. That is, women fans prefer superheroines; Black fans prefer Black superheroes; and white male fans prefer white male superheroes. Of course, this is not necessarily true, although it is understandable why the white patriarchal paradigm of traditional superhero comics might be unattractive to marginalized fans. Scott notes of Gabriel's statement: "[T]he blame for Marvel Comics' sales slump lies with female comic book fans, particularly those who have vocally criticized comic books' lack of creative and representational diversity" (1). Efforts to create empowering representations of marginalized heroes have led to an increased visibility of marginalized fans and an expectation that marginalized fans will buy more superhero comics. This is bolstered by significant work on the part of writers like Kelly Sue DeConnick (*Captain Marvel*), G. Willow Wilson (*Ms. Marvel*), Eve L. Ewing (*Ironheart*), and Sina Grace (*Iceman*) to connect with marginalized fans on social media and promote their books. The excitement from fan sites like *Geeks of Color* and *Women Write about Comics* suggests that ANAD was eagerly—if cautiously—anticipated (Overland).

While attracting marginalized fans to the mainstream titles, the ANAD strategy also sought to broaden the horizons of Marvel's core readership. This traditional readership is a cornerstone in superhero publishing, as major publishers have courted their loyalty since the 1990s (Pustz 17–18). This demographic is predominantly white and predominantly male, due to the symbiotic problems of over-representation on the page and the narrowness of comic book store culture (Pustz 5). Marvel has endured by supplying reliable, predictable white male superheroes to reliable, predictable white male readers. Marketing comics as a cultural underdog, Marvel forged a strong relationship with readers who buy single-issue superhero titles in specialist comic stores (often to the exclusion of other readers). Scott quotes Gabriel in calling these fans the "'meat and potatoes' fanboy base, a code phrase used within the comic book industry to justify abandoning diversity titles and initiatives" (2). These readers are fiercely loyal to the brand, to the point where some vocal fans are defensive or even hostile to change.

ANAD represents a compromise between new readers, attracted by the less-tokenistic representations of themselves, and old readers who will (hopefully) buy *Spider-Man* and *Captain America* comics regardless of who wears the mask. I was told by a retailer: "These guys *will not* buy anything else. It's the only way to get them to read books about women or not-white-guys." To the traditional reader base, diversity *was* all new, and all different. This is where the branding of ANAD works to the detriment of both marginalized or hegemonic fans: to the former, being a woman or nonwhite is *not* new or different. To the latter, the improving representation is framed as disruptive and out-of-character.

MEASURING SALES: TRADE PAPERBACKS AND DIGITAL COMICS

A key problem in the claim that diversity does not sell is the different ways that marginalized readers buy comics. Marvel renews or cancels its titles based on the number of periodicals preordered through specialist comic stores. This metric for success heavily favors buyers who are familiar with the arcane machinations of the comic book pull list. To establish a pull list and have one's purchasing habits recognized by this metric, one must have a local comic book shop; one must have an account at that shop; one must know which titles to preorder; and one must know the date to preorder them. This specialized process is not intuitive and can be part of the generally intimidating experience of a new reader in a comic book shop. Comic book stores have a reputation for the bullying of new and unfamiliar readers by other customers and even employees (Pustz 8). I run a comic club for women, and most club members have stories of being treated poorly in other comic stores. While many stores are seeking to address this with open support for marginalized readers and firm antiharassment policies, this culture is slow to change. For a marginalized fan interested in reading *Thor* for the first time, this process of supporting the book becomes incredibly fraught. Marvel is quick to cancel titles with inadequate preorder numbers, which leaves very little opportunity for new readers to discover and buy the title.

The problematic culture of comic book stores and the inconvenience of buying single-issue books has led many new readers to other markets (Alverson). Mainstream bookstores have seen growing sales in graphic novels and trade paperbacks (collected editions of single issues), attributed to a broadening readership including marginalized fans.[5] Generally speaking, the graphic novel market has stronger representation of marginalized creators and characters: the *New York Times*' paperback graphic novel bestseller list in 2017 features Raina Telgemeier in the top three spots, followed by John Lewis's autobiography; *Love Is Love* (an edited collection in aid of survivors of the Pulse massacre); Alison Bechdel; Marjane Satrapi; and Victoria Jamieson ("Paperback Graphic Books"). This is to say nothing of manga, a genre which has introduced a generation of young women across the globe to comics. Similarly in trade paperbacks, superheroes like *Ms. Marvel* and *Thor* sell better than they do in periodical sales. Rose Moore describes how "compared to single issue sales, trade paperbacks are killing it when it comes to diversity." The statement "diversity doesn't sell" may have reflected Marvel's overall sales, rather than just single issues, but many of ANAD's titles had only released a handful of trade paperbacks—the market where they stood to profit the most—before their cancelation.

Digital comics have seen a similar boom to paperbacks: the approachable interface, anonymity, and convenience of sites like comiXology make buying comics easy. The inaccessibility of brick-and-mortar stores, as well as the higher price point, can be avoided by new and marginalized fans. ComiXology's 2015 sales reflect the fact that diversity *does* sell on a digital platform: *Silk, Ms. Marvel*, and *Thor* were the top superhero titles. This would be supported by the continuation of *Moon Girl, The Unbeatable Squirrel Girl,* and *Gwenpool*; Marvel titles whose print runs have been supported by digital sales. Susana Polo argues that anecdotal and commonsense evidence points to more diverse reader demographics in digital sales, while Howard and Jackson describe how online communities have mobilized Black fans and creators, "enabling new economic structures to develop" (73–74).

Beyond Marvel, the paperback and digital markets demonstrate popularity for books with marginalized characters. By 2018, independent comics like *Saga, Monstress,* and *Paper Girls*—all with women in the lead roles—were bestsellers in the paperback market. Howard and Jackson describe how Black fan communities have been able to network online and circumvent "the ossified direct sales model . . . that shut out many alternative voices" (74). They cite comiXology's attraction for readers who have never read traditional comics, and the potential for Black webcomic creators to find success. Indeed, comics crowdfunding initiatives by women of color have had spectacular success: Spike Trotman's Iron Circus Comics, Ngozi Ukazu's *Check, Please!*, and Mildred Louis's *Agents of the Realm* are outstanding examples. All of this suggests that diversity *does* sell—in the right market.

CREATIVE TEAMS STILL LACK DIVERSITY

Another issue that may have hindered the ANAD line was the homogeneity in the creative and editorial teams of Marvel. This has been an ongoing problem in superhero publishing, where women and creators of color are especially underrepresented in writing and editing roles. This suggests that while Marvel was aiming to champion diversity at the superficial level of characters, there have not been systematic changes to support real marginalized creators. Warner calls attention to this issue in the film and television industries:

> The problem with such a line of thinking is that quantifiable difference alone often overdetermines the benchmarks of progress and obscures the multifaceted challenges inherent in booking roles as well as securing work on writing staffs, directing gigs, or even reaching executive gatekeeper status—thus privileging the visible (actors) over all other cinematic and televisual functions. (35)

In the comics industry, this problem of "diversity as an artificial additive and not a substantive contribution," as Warner calls it, is exacerbated by the characters being two-dimensional illustrations; no actors even need to be hired (36). This has led to some significant critiques of ANAD titles. Paige Allen notes that *Invincible Iron Man*, written by Brian Michael Bendis, shows a "shallow understanding of Black experiences." Landis applauds a counterexample in *Ms. Marvel*, where editor Sana Amanat and white writer G. Willow Wilson are both Muslim women, and Wilson's "religious practice allows her to be sensitive, thoughtful, and reflective about her representation of a Muslim superhero" (198). While it's certainly possible for white male creators to tell nuanced and empowering stories about women of color, the overall makeup of the creative teams during ANAD shows a prioritization of fictional marginalized people over real ones. Marvel has endeavored to address this by hiring celebrated writers such as Ta-Nehisi Coates, Roxane Gay, and Sina Grace. However, all three writers dealt with cancelations due to lack of single-issue preorders (a particularly conservative market compared to trade paperbacks). Grace, a queer writer penning *Iceman* (the first Marvel superhero comic with a gay title character), criticized editorial staff for stating the book was "too gay" and the lack of support for the cyberbullying that disproportionately affects marginalized creators. This suggests Marvel is more comfortable with diversity on the page, where it remains two-dimensional.

GENRE AND SERIALITY: SUPERHEROES REINFORCE THE STATUS QUO

The difficulty of creating meaningful, systematic changes in representation is caught up in issues around genre and seriality. Serial narratives function through a careful balance of deviation and conformity to remain interesting and cohesive. Long-running superhero serials like *Iron Man*, *Captain America*, *Hulk*, and *Thor* require a remarkable degree of malleability to survive. These comics experiment with art styles, themes, emotional tones, ideologies, target audiences, creators, and characters. The central characters of Tony Stark, Steve Rogers, Bruce Banner, and Thor Odinson have quit, died, and renamed themselves; they have been replaced, reassigned, cloned, and rendered obsolete, before ultimately returning to their roles. A conservative reading of the superhero genre argues that this ultimate return is inevitable: the superhero narrative depends on a serial deviation from, and restoration of, the status quo. The archetypal goal of the superhero, to "save the world," requires an agreement between the reader and the character that the world as we know it deserves to be saved. This perpetual reinforcement of hegemony, along with the übermensch-like qualities of the long-running superhero characters, leaves little opportunity for empowerment of marginalized people. The long history of a character like Thor allows him to accrue a "legacy": his return, upon the inevitable death of Jane Foster, was branded under the Legacy relaunch. This language legitimizes characters like Thor as the prodigal sons, serially compelled to restore hegemonic order.

DIFFERENCE AND OTHERING

The language of the ANAD brand itself was a significant factor in undermining the comics' potential for empowerment. The language is at best disingenuous and at worst, self-sabotaging. While diversity *is* different for Marvel's core superhero lineup—and "different" ostensibly refers to the rebooted universe the characters now exist in—the branding clearly alludes to diversity as difference. This language contributes to the process of Othering, reinforcing whiteness and maleness as the norm. The phrasing of "new" equally contributes to the framing of empowering representation as a gimmick, easily discarded when diversity is no longer "new." It suggests that the past scarcity of superheroes of color was incidental, rather than an effect of white supremacy in American popular culture. If these allusions were not clear enough in the launch of ANAD, "diversity" was centered as the problem during its cancelation.

No matter how well intentioned the comics themselves, their branding under ANAD set them up as temporary novelties, and the diversity highlighted by the launch became the scapegoat after the novelty wore off. Scott argues: "Just as 'meat and potatoes' evokes a sense of stasis and stability, comfort and conformity, the anxieties underpinning [Gabriel's statement] (and indeed, undergirding misogynist pushback to the mainstreaming of fan culture) are rooted in fear of change" (3). This is affirmed by the Legacy line, as white male heroes are branded as the true inheritors of their own mantles and long-time readers are rewarded for their sufferance of temporary diversity. Legacy grounds the white male heroes in the past and secures their futures, reaffirming Marvel's hegemonic narrative.

NO NORMAL/NEW NORMAL

While many of the comics released under the ANAD brand show genuine effort at empowering underrepresented groups, the language of Marvel's branding shows a bad-faith effort that appears to be built to fail. This demonstrates some of the complex struggles in changing the genre and the industry, and the common setbacks in trying to improve diversity without challenging the systems that precluded it in the first place. A better example of empowering language can be seen in the critically acclaimed *Ms. Marvel* comics featuring Kamala Khan in the role of Ms. Marvel. The first *Ms. Marvel* trade paperback was released in 2014 with the subtitle *No Normal* (Wilson and Alphona). This choice of subtitle suggests a dramatically different approach from framing a non-white female superhero as "new" and "different." Instead, the preconception of "normality" itself—whiteness and maleness, in this context—is rejected.

This ideology is emphasized in the eleventh issue of the comic, when Khan says: "My new normal is no normal" (Wilson and Alphona). Ostensibly, she is articulating her new life as a superhero. As a reflection on the superhero publishing industry, however, Khan is speaking to the potential for a shifting paradigm that discards the expectations of an outdated status quo. These values are reflected holistically in many aspects of the comic: writer G. Willow Wilson imbues the superhero archetype with Muslim values, and Adrian Alphona's art evokes an indie style that avoids exploitative portrayals of young women. The title is a bestseller in trade paperback format, generally agreed to be a more diverse readership: certainly, it is much more accessible to newcomers and welcomes readers who may have previously been deterred by superhero comics. *Ms. Marvel* exemplifies how Marvel can keep in step with the thriving market outside superhero comics, by rejecting the preconceived limitations on superhero storytelling.

CONCLUSION

The success of a title like *Ms. Marvel* proves that "diversity" is not an insurmountable obstacle in comics publishing, even and especially for a long-established company like Marvel. The perceived failure of "diversity" spoke much more of problematic branding choices by Marvel than any problem endemic to superheroes, fandom, or comics publishing. This chapter isolated the phrase "All-New, All-Different" as a disingenuous and limiting label, in an effort to demonstrate how the negative ramifications of the brand could be avoided. Outside single-issue superhero comics, comics with strong representations of marginalized people have proven to be commercially successful and critically celebrated. This demonstrates an excellent opportunity for Marvel to adapt to the changing paradigm to support marginalized characters, creators, and readers.

Notes

1. Many ANAD comics included team titles and a number of smaller titles led by characters of color and women such as *Black Panther, Blade, Mockingbird, Patsy Walker AKA Hellcat*, and *Silk*. The central novelty of the brand, however, was the re-assigning of the "core" superhero

solo titles to new characters. These titles, and the way they were framed by ANAD, are the focus of the chapter.

2. A number of these characters, notably Morales, Bishop, Danvers, and Khan, had been using the aliases of Spider-Man, Hawkeye, Captain Marvel, and Ms. Marvel for years before ANAD. However, ANAD represents a watershed, with the marketing positioning marginalized characters centrally and in greater numbers than before.

3. The problematic branding of diversity with the buzzword "now" carries similar connotations to the "all-new" moniker. This is analyzed later in the chapter.

4. The circumstances under which Morales inherited Spider-Man and Danvers inherited Captain Marvel were complex. Miles Morales became Spider-Man only in Marvel's "Ultimate" universe, an alternate timeline to the mainstream "616" universe. Peter Parker continued as Spider-Man in the mainstream comics until ANAD brought Morales to 616. After years of legal issues between Marvel and DC over the use of "Captain Marvel" as a comic book title or a character, the defunct Marvel-owned character known as Captain Marvel, an alien called Mar-Vell, was killed off. When Marvel (the company) regained the rights to publish *Captain Marvel* (the comic title), the lead character role was appointed to fan favorite Carol Danvers, Mar-Vell's former sidekick. These were relatively low-risk experiments for Marvel as a company, and their success paved ground for ANAD.

5. Trade paperbacks are usually released within a few months of the final single issue of the collection, which can mean six months waiting between issue 1 and the paperback. While the wait can be daunting for fans excited to read and discuss the title, trade paperbacks are usually better value and significantly more durable than single issues.

Works Cited

Allen, Paige. "Riri Williams and the Limits of Representation." *Geeks of Color*, 23rd June 2017, https://geeksofcolor.co/2017/06/23/comics-riri-williams-and-the-limits-of-representation/.

Alverson, Brigid. "NYCC Insider Sessions Powered by ICV2: A Demographic Snapshot of Comics Buyers." *ICV2*, 18 October 2017, https://icv2.com/articles/news/view/38709/nycc-insider-sessions-powered-icv2-a-demographic-snapshot-comics-buyers.

Bryant, Jacob. "Marvel Exec Backpedals after Suggesting Diversity to Blame for Comic Book Sales Slump." *Variety*, 3 Apr. 2017, https://variety.com/2017/biz/news/marvel-exec-blames-diversity-women-comic-sales-slump-1202021440/.

Calia, Michael. "Marvel Reveals Inside Look at Diverse New Avengers Lineup." *The Wall Street Journal*, 24 June 2015, https://blogs.wsj.com/speakeasy/2015/06/24/diversity-reigns-in-marvels-new-avengers-lineup-exclusive/.

Fawaz, Rami. *The New Mutants: Superheroes and the Radical Imagination of American Comics*. New York University Press, 2016.

Fu, Albert S. "Fear of a Black Spider-Man: Racebending and the Colour-line in Superhero (Re)casting." *Journal of Graphic Novels and Comics*, vol. 6, no. 3, 2015, pp. 269–83.

Grace, Sina. "As Pride Month Comes to a Close, It's Time I Spoke Candidly about My Experience at Marvel Comics." *Tumblr*, 29 June 2017, https://sinagrace.tumblr.com/post/185915075613/as-pride-month-comes-to-a-close-its-time-i-spoke.

Howard, Sheena C. and Ronald L. Jackson II. *Black Comics: Politics of Race and Representation*. Bloomsbury, 2013.

Landis, Winona. "Ms. Marvel, Qahera, and Superheroism in the Muslim Diaspora." *Continuum: Journal of Media & Cultural Studies*, vol. 33, no. 2, 2019, pp. 185–200.

Lendrum, Rob. "Queering Super-Manhood: Superhero Masculinity, Camp and Public Relations as a Textual Framework." *International Journal of Comic Art*, vol. 7, no. 1, 2005, pp. 287–303.

Lovett, Jamie. "Marvel Legacy: Who Is the Returning Character?" *comicbook*. 5 Sept. 2017, https://comicbook.com/marvel/2017/04/26/marvel-legacy-returning-character/.

Moore, Rose. "Comics Sales Figures Prove to Marvel: Diversity Isn't The Problem." *Screenrant*, 27 Jan. 2018, https://screenrant.com/marvel-diversity-comic-sales-single-issue/.

O'Neil, Denny, et al., *The Invincible Iron Man*, no. 169, Marvel, Apr. 1983.

Overland, Kat. "Surface Tensions: Character vs. Creator Diversity." *Women Write about Comics*, 28 July 2015, https://womenwriteaboutcomics.com/2015/07/surface-tensions-character-vs-creator-diversity/.

"Paperback Graphic Books." *New York Times*, 29 Jan. 2017, https://www.nytimes.com/books/best-sellers/paperback-graphic-books/2017/01/29.

Polo, Susana. "ComiXology's Numbers Indicate Female Characters Dominate Digital Comics Sales." *Polygon*, 14 Apr. 2015, https://www.polygon.com/2015/4/14/8410771/digital-comics-female-characters.

Pustz, Matthew. *Comic Book Culture: Fanboys and True Believers*. University of Mississippi Press, 1999.

Scott, Suzanne. *Fake Geek Girls: Fandom, Gender, and the Convergence Culture Industry*. New York University Press, 2019.

Spencer, Nick, and Daniel Acuña. *Captain America*, no. 1, Marvel, Oct. 2015.

Warner, Kristen J. "In the Time of Plastic Representation." *Film Quarterly*, vol. 7, no. 2, 2017, pp. 32–37.

Wilson, G. Willow, and Adrian Alphona. *Ms. Marvel: No Normal*, Marvel, 2014.

Wilson, G. Willow, and Adrian Alphona. *Ms. Marvel*, no. 11, Marvel, Feb. 2015.

Chapter 2

THE HEART OF A HERO

Disability and Humanity in the Origin Stories of Marvel Studios' Superheroes

ALEXANDRA OSTROWSKI SCHILLING

Heroes need origin stories. From the death of Batman's parents to the oppression and persecution of Marvel's mutants, these stories serve both as motivators for heroes to become heroic and as audience entry points into the world of the story itself. They also subtly demonstrate why certain characters are able to become heroes. Heroism is often linked to the physical feats a character can achieve, implying that heroes should, generally, have superbodies (or at least "normatively" abled ones) as well as superpowers. Heroes are also expected to be exceptionally moral; they are asked to act as beacons of goodness for the average person to take inspiration from and strive to be like. Within the origin stories of the Marvel Cinematic Universe (MCU), however, these narratives have become tied to disability in a troubling way.

This chapter explores how the MCU uses disability as a narrative device in its origin stories to guide heroes into what it deems to be proper heroic morality, before "curing" or making negligible said disability. After clarifying the meaning of morality in this context, the chapter demonstrates how Western popular culture continuously links disability and morality, while explaining the key concepts of the "supercrip" and the overcoming narrative. From there, the idea of disability necessitating a "tragic" origin story ties the notions of the supercrip and the overcoming narrative to the MCU's portrayal of disability in its superheroes. This chapter uses three MCU heroes—Captain America (Steve Rogers), Iron Man (Tony Stark), and Doctor Stephen Strange—to show how disability is used as a narrative device to promote morality in heroes' origin stories and to consider why the ends of these arcs signal a neglect of true positive disability representation. This chapter concludes with a brief discussion of the multifaceted nature of this topic and offers suggestions on how the MCU might move forward with its representations of disability.

FROM ETERNAL CHILD TO SUPERCRIP

What does it mean for superheroes to be expected to be "moral"? Marvel's origin stories—whether in comics or in cinema—often serve not only to begin a character's story, but to highlight their shortcomings, showing that "most Marvel heroes have flaws that make them recognizably human" (Levine). "Recognizably human," in this case, is more abstract than the literal quality of existing as a human being, instead referring to the tendency for Marvel heroes to experience relatable challenges and imperfections of character (for instance, Spider-Man's financial struggles or Iron Man's alcoholism). This chapter uses two definitions of morality concurrently. The first defines morality as "certain codes of conduct put forward by a society or a group," with the "group" here being hegemonic Western popular culture (Gert and Gert). The second expands on these "codes," defining morality as "principles relating to right and wrong or good and bad behaviour" ("Definition of morality"). Societies may differ in the exact intricacies of their moralities, but certain activities are consistently looked upon as morally wrong—such as "murder, theft, lying, and breaking promises" ("Ethical Theory"). Many everyday acts are seen as simply morally neutral, such as watching television, or choosing a certain food to eat. Others are morally obligatory: "morally right acts one ought to do . . . they are moral duties" such as "keeping one's promises and providing guidance and support for one's children" ("Ethical Theory"). There are also morally supererogatory acts: "morally right activities that are especially praiseworthy and even heroic . . . They aren't required, morally, but if they are done it is an especially good thing" ("Ethical Theory"). These may range from donating to charities to saving someone's life.

The "notion of the superhero as human [is] linked to the notion of morality" (Jeffery 176). Therefore, if, when stripped of wondrous powers or abilities, a superhero is as "human" as anyone else, the hero falls under the same obligations to abide by those "codes of conduct" that make up morality. The Oxford Dictionary defines a hero as "a person . . . who is admired by many people for doing something brave or good." In the case of superheroes, this "brave or good" act is likely to be a morally supererogatory act—it may be fantastical, but it will, importantly, be morally *right*. As one condition of being a superhero, then, the hero must follow a set of morals that is seen by hegemonic society to be right and proper. Throughout this chapter, the terms "proper heroic morality" and "proper morality" are applied to refer to this concept of superheroes being obligated by society to perform morally right and morally supererogatory acts.

Morality and disability have been linked in Western literary and social history for some time. Before the 1950s, two opposing, but equally degrading, tropes were often used to try to explain disability. The first described disabled individuals as "savage and devilish beings... with no morals or laws," reasoning that disability was a punishment enacted for moral or personal failings (Desjardins 73). The other trope depicted disabled people as "eternal children, angelic and pure beings... with no malice or vices" (73). This evoked ideas of poor, innocent creatures tragically struck by the horrors of disability. Disability—and by extension disabled people—were defined as inherently undesirable, which was either well deserved or terribly unfortunate, but never positive or simply neutral.

Hegemonic culture continues to link disability and morality today in altered forms that are often mistakenly viewed as progress. Instead of thinking of disabled individuals as "angelic children," they are inspiring figures, made one-dimensional in their goodness and purity. One of the most widespread iterations of this linkage is the "supercrip," a disabled figure presented for the pleasurable consumption of nondisabled people. The supercrip is an "inspirational disabled person" or "role [model], lavishly lauded in the press and on television... deeply moving to most nondisabled [people] and widely regarded as oppressive by most disabled ones" (Shapiro 16). These figures are celebrated as heroic, inspiring, or talented just for getting out of bed and existing (Young). None of this would be seen as incredible or inspirational without these individuals being disabled, and to label them as such ascribes to a model which believes that "to live with a disability makes you exceptional... [because it] is a Bad Thing" (Young). Just as the "eternal child" was pure and innocent simply for being disabled, so here the supercrip is imbued with inspirational power, carrying the same "feel-good" connotations of positivity, stereotypical "goodness," and morality. "The purpose of [the supercrip]," Stella Young says, "is to inspire you [as the nondisabled viewer], to motivate you, so that we can look at them and think, 'Well, however bad my life is, it could be worse. I could be that person.'"

Not only is the supercrip ideal patronizing and harmful, but it also segregates disabled people from the rest of the population, ascribing to them incredible power simply for existing while disabled. The supercrip supports the idea that "'only some kind of superhero could possibly live a meaningful life with... any serious disabling condition'" (Alaniz 32). As José Alaniz writes, the disabled individual is pushed to

> escape the confining strictures of the "tragic, pathetic crip" role and don a new super-identity—passing not as normal, but as *supranormal*... In going from one extreme of marginality to the other, what the supercrip leaps over... is not tall buildings but "normality," which lies presumably somewhere in the broad middle, as inaccessible as ever. (32–33)

The nondisabled world refuses to accept disabled individuals as merely *normal people*. It instead insists that they be defined by dominant ideas about disability as a concept—whether lauded or pitied, ridiculed or put on a pedestal, disability consistently acts as a signifier to hegemonic culture that a person is "other than."

This is further complicated by the idea of an overcoming narrative, which views disability as a personal affliction to be overcome.[1] The overcoming narrative asks those with disabilities to do the work of navigating an inaccessible world; rather than expecting curb cuts, wheelchair users "should learn to do wheelies and jump the curbs" (Linton 18). This locates disability firmly within the person, rather than within society's refusal to create accessibility (Young). The supercrip is perhaps the pinnacle of overcoming narratives, lauded for their ability to achieve supranormality and "surpass" disability. Supercrips in popular culture often become disabled through "origin stories," assumedly a traumatic event—a birth defect, a war injury, a car accident. This "disabling" moment is assumed to have pushed them to "overcome" their "undesirable" disability and ascend to supranormality.

This is where popular culture's supercrips and the MCU's superheroes intersect: at the lines of supranormality, morality, and traumatic origin stories. Both supercrips and MCU's superheroes are placed on pedestals outside of normality and humanity; both are treated as beacons of "goodness" and as inspirational for the average person; and both have overcoming-based origin stories. The MCU adopts a troubling trend of using disability as a narrative device in its origin stories, playing on tropes of overcoming and the supercrip (supercripdom) familiar to modern audiences to imbue its heroes with proper morality and "goodness." When heroes have completed their moral arc, disability is truly overcome. Heroes are rewarded with a "cure," or through being made "abledisabled," wherein those who are in some way disabled display no observable ill effects, impairments, social stigma, or struggles with inaccessibility. Once again, disability becomes nonnormative, tragic, and a way to inspire others; it is a plot device instead of an opportunity for representation.

"MAYBE WHAT WE NEED NOW IS A LITTLE GUY": CAPTAIN AMERICA

Steve Rogers (Captain America) is perhaps the easiest of the MCU's heroes to see reflected in narratives of overcoming and supercrip-dom. He, like all heroes, is meant to be an inspirational figure, although set apart from the others, his journey to heroic morality is already complete by the time we meet him. *Captain America: The First Avenger* (2011) makes quick work of setting this up. Audiences of the film are introduced to Rogers (Chris Evans) in a military recruitment center, waiting to be examined by a doctor for fitness for service in World War II. Bare-chested, standing at the front of a line of other shirtless men, Rogers's physical "lack" is emphasized; he is much shorter and smaller. However, when asked if the prospect of dying in war makes him reconsider joining the military, Rogers answers with a confident, "Nope." Moments later, he is denied from service by the doctor, told he would be "ineligible on [his] asthma alone." The camera tilts down to show a "Summary of Patient Health Issues," including high blood pressure, heart palpitations, and chronic colds. The next scene shows Rogers standing up to a moviegoer disrespecting the prefilm military advertisements, and is consequently beaten up in an alley for it. When knocked down, though, Rogers scrambles to his feet, uttering his oft-repeated line: "I can do this all day."

Why is it so important that Rogers be disabled, rather than an "average" man who turns into a superhero? Without his disabilities and weakness, Rogers would not be as "inspiring" to audiences and would not be able to serve as that aforementioned disabled figure whom nondisabled audiences can look at to think "[I]t could be worse," and "[I]f they can do it, so can I" (Young). It would not be so shocking or unusual to see an "average" man stand up after getting knocked down; we are impressed and inspired because of Rogers's disabilities, regardless of catchy lines. He is a walking advertisement for the overcoming narrative, his origin story clearly showing someone who does not let his disabilities stop him. Rogers tells his close friend Bucky Barnes (Sebastian Stan) that "there are men laying down their lives [in the war]," and that he has "no right to do any less than them." At first glance, this may seem like an innocuous enough statement. Yet as Young points out, Rogers comes to belong within a context of what is colloquially dubbed "inspiration porn"; a concept expressed through such imagery as a poster of a man with one leg swimming, captioned "The only disability in life is a bad attitude," or a boy in a wheelchair holding a basketball, captioned "Your excuse is invalid."

When Rogers finally *is* accepted into the US Army, it is because of his morality and heroic "goodness." "I don't want to kill anyone; I don't like bullies," he tells Dr. Abraham Erskine (Stanley Tucci), an escaped German Jewish scientist working with the military and who is looking for someone to test a supersoldier serum on. The serum enhances everything a person is, both physically and morally. Erskine wants to use it on Rogers because of his strong morals, which the film posits he has *because he is disabled*. "There are already so many big men fighting this war," Erskine says, "maybe what we need now is a little guy." But that is not quite true. The serum is intended to enhance Rogers's body to the height of physical perfection, which Erskine knows. Perhaps what he really means is that they need someone who is morally sound, harkening back to the early ideas positing an innocent "goodness" associated with disability. Of course, there is some truth to his statement: those who have experienced oppression are less likely to visit the same unkindness upon others. Rogers knows what it is to be treated badly, and to rephrase his earlier statement, he doesn't want to *kill* bad people, but wants to *help* others being "bullied." Still, the underlying message is that Rogers has achieved moral purity because he is disabled. Notably, the villain of the movie, the Red Skull (Hugo Weaving), has also used the serum, but due to his inherent moral failings, he becomes monstrously disfigured. If you are not ready to be a hero, the film seems to say, you will become disabled as punishment. Rogers, however, imbued with heroic morality because of his disabilities, is ready to "overcome" them.

Ultimately, Rogers is selected to receive the serum because of one very telling act. In a test where a dummy grenade is thrown in the middle of the recruits' exercises, the other men run away and brace themselves for the explosion. Only Rogers runs toward the grenade, curling on top of it and commanding others to get away. He is willing to sacrifice his impaired, disabled body for the "perfect" bodies of others. This is the final action the MCU deems necessary in his moral arc. From here, Rogers "overcomes" one last time, pushing through the pain of the serum's transformation to become the hypermasculine ideal. Bathed in a blinding white light, unsubtly alluding to purity, Rogers emerges from the chamber in which he received the serum with a glistening, sculpted, hyper-able body. He becomes supranormal at the same time he becomes a superhero, never touching the middle ground of "normality." Disability is no more than a narrative device, used to make Rogers "good" and then triumphantly banished to the realm of the unwanted and undesirable. The film dangerously assumes, and perhaps even implies, that this is a moment of joy for Rogers—who would not want to be a superhero? Who would not want to be "cured," to have a "perfect" body, to eliminate disability, assumed to be a burden?

Rogers's origin story is not just about him gaining the body and powers of what the MCU claims a superhero should be, it is also about him doing away with his "lesser," disabled body. The film shows it would be impossible for Rogers, as he once was, to be Captain America; audiences watch him struggle in basic training to do even light physical activity. The MCU desires the morality assumed to come from disability, but does not want one of its core heroes to be so unmistakably disabled. Even after his transformation, we are assured that Rogers's heart is still what makes him Captain America: when Erskine is killed, he looks to Rogers and gently touches his chest where his heart is, silently evoking his earlier words that Rogers should be "not a perfect soldier, but a good man." This origin story implies that without having "suffered" through life as a disabled man, Rogers would never have achieved the pure, innocent goodness that lies at the center of his heroism, inherently tying his ascension to the superhuman to his erased disability.

PROVING MORALITY: IRON MAN

What about a hero who doesn't start out disabled? How are they to have a heart? The poster child for moving from "selfishness to selflessness" in the MCU is Tony Stark (Iron Man) (Markus and McFeely). A billionaire weapons developer, Stark (Robert Downey Jr.) starts out in the film *Iron Man* (2008) as a self-obsessed, carefree playboy, far more concerned with his own self-interest than helping others. He lacks the traditional "goodness" and morality the MCU desires for its heroes. He is unbothered by his position as an arms dealer and being nicknamed the "Merchant of Death," irreverently quipping, "I love peace. I'd be out of a job with peace." During a weapons presentation for the US military in Afghanistan, Stark is injured in a terrorist attack on his convoy, carried out by his own weapons. Here, then, is the tragic origin event of disabling, and soon we will watch the rise of a hero to overcome it.

As Rogers's origin story harkened back to the "pure" disabled person, Stark's calls back to disability as punishment—specifically, punishment for his lack of morality. He is injured by his own weaponry, with shrapnel in his chest and inching toward his heart. The weapons he profited from now threaten his literal heart, and he must have a metaphorical change of heart to survive and become a hero. Stark is saved by his fellow captive, Yinsen (Shaun Toub), and the two men work to make an arc reactor. The arc reactor—a fictional clean energy source—is to function as an assistive device to keep the shrapnel from Stark's heart indefinitely and to power the Iron Man suit he will use to escape from captivity. His assistive device powers both his human body and the suprahuman exoskeleton he wears as armor, protecting his disabled body both inside and out.

As Stark escapes captivity, a dying Yinsen pushes his journey toward heroic morality forward, urging Stark not to waste his life by remaining isolated in his wealth and selfish in his motives. Back in America, Stark shuts down the weapons manufacturing branch of his company, saying he "had his eyes opened" by experiencing firsthand the devastating potential of his weapons and asserting that he "doesn't want a body count to be [his] only legacy." Simultaneously, Stark is able to become both supercrip and superhero, overcoming the immediate threat of his disability, building the Iron Man armor, and vowing to do good for others. He is not, perhaps, the most obvious beacon of inspiration, but he is working toward reversing the harm he has done, bolstering his own heroic morality in the process.

Once again, the MCU uses disability as a narrative device rather than an opportunity for representation. There is no discussion of the actual physical effects a major surgery and a prosthetic implant like the arc reactor would have on someone, only of the way the event impacted Stark's morals. "I shouldn't be alive," he says, "unless it was for a reason"—and that reason is for him to be a hero. The arc reactor is proof of Stark's disability, and it becomes "Proof That Tony Stark Has a Heart," which are words engraved on an older model of the reactor, gifted by his love interest. Stark's disability becomes proof that he is a morally good person; he has both overcome the literal physical threat to his heart and fulfilled the moral imperative to become a better person, stepping into the realm of the superhuman in the process. Just as disabled individuals are encouraged to "rise above" their disabling origin events, so we see Stark working to "rise above" his. In place of more overt physical overcoming, however, the film overlays moral growth and a sense of heroic good.

Stark's path through morality is nonlinear: he is not immediately "cured" or made able-disabled in *Iron Man*, because he still needs to work on becoming more morally worthy of the title of hero. In *Iron Man 2* (2010), Stark makes reckless decisions in response to being poisoned by the arc reactor. The MCU seems to say that if his response to looming death is to use the Iron Man armor as a party trick while intoxicated, then his moral growth requires further development. *Iron Man 2* concludes with Stark finding a solution to the poisoning but still needing the arc reactor.

In *Iron Man 3* (2013), it is no longer a physical ailment that threatens Stark's body, but a mental one: he has developed panic attacks and what is coded (but not named) as posttraumatic stress disorder (PTSD) from his heroic but traumatic experiences with the Avengers. While to see a hero with panic attacks on screen is a unique and welcome change, it still somewhat represents an overcoming narrative. After pulling over because of a panic attack while driving, Stark is prompted by a friend that, as a mechanic, he can "just build something," which immediately snaps him out of it. After that point, his panic attacks dissipate, hinting that if Stark is heroically competent, he is also mentally (and physically) competent in overcoming his disabilities. Prior to this, the film did well in showing the actual *effects* of anxiety on Stark's life, and overall, it is not the most egregious case of disability erasure in the MCU. Nonetheless, this is the last time Stark is mentioned as or seen having a panic attack, or is quite so clearly seen dealing with the effects of anxiety. At the end of *Iron Man 3*, Stark seems to have finally completed his journey to heroic morality, claiming the role of Iron Man for himself, rather than as a man in a suit of armor. *He* is now a hero—and what is a hero to do about their disability? Stark undergoes what seems to be a relatively simple surgery to remove the shrapnel and arc reactor, even tossing the once-precious device into the ocean. Disability here is literally a disposable device, and Stark no longer needs proof of his disability to prove he has a heart. It has functioned as a guiding force for his moral journey throughout his extended origin story, serving as a reminder that he still has work to do before he can claim *himself* as a hero and his body as able.

CONSOLATION PRIZE: DOCTOR STRANGE

Doctor Stephen Strange (Benedict Cumberbatch) does *not* have his disability cured at the end of his heroic journey in the film *Doctor Strange* (2016)—but unfortunately, the MCU still follows the same trend, using disability as a plot point instead of a meaningful opportunity for representation. A brilliant, rich, and arrogant surgeon, Strange is in a car accident and consequently develops nerve damage and tremors in his hands, effectively ending his surgical career. Like Stark, Strange's disability can be read as a punishment for his moral failings—he talks down to others, is obsessed with his own fame, and contemplates a patients' usefulness to his career before considering how to help them. Instead of instantly beginning to learn morality when disabled, Strange is desperate to "cure" himself. This leads him on a journey to magic and mysticism, and eventual superheroism. At the same time, he is transformed into a more heroically moral person, having been humbled by the "uselessness" he feels following the nerve damage. Positively, the film demonstrates that able bodies are not a prerequisite for magic powers. However, the use of disability as a narrative device still creates major problems with representation.

More so than the other origin stories discussed, the entire narrative of *Doctor Strange* is tied to the "tragic" origin event of Strange's nerve damage. Strange is not simply a hero who *happens* to be disabled, he is a hero *because* he was disabled and sought to "cure" himself, *and* because his disability sent him on a moral journey. Unlike Rogers, whose "cure" came from outside himself, and Stark, who did not initially seek to completely "cure" himself, Strange's story would not have happened without his disability and his desire to erase it. Interestingly, there are two disabled minor characters in the film; Hamir (Topo Wresniwiro), a character with one hand; and Jonathan Pangborn (Benjamin Bratt), who was formerly quadriplegic. Despite having access to near-identical magical abilities, and more experience than Strange in the mystical arts, neither of these disabled men is the hero. This is because neither of their disabilities led them through an on-screen moral arc, and because we do not see either character experience an origin event. This reinforces the MCU's tendency to use disability merely as a narrative device bolstering their heroes' journeys rather than simply a trait some heroes possess. If Strange's nerve damage was not the gateway to magical powers, and was instead something he had always had, this narrative trend suggests that there would have been no means for his moral development—unless his disability had already imbued him with "goodness" like Rogers.

While it is a step forward that Strange's disability remains, the actual representation of said disability is troubling. The biggest effect of Strange's nerve damage is his inability to perform surgery, and this is seen mostly through his arrogant anger at no longer being the best in the business. Rather than a more thoughtful exploration of how such an impairment might affect the average person, a rich, haughty man's obsession with "fixing" himself is instead presented, which the audience may struggle to emotionally connect with or understand. The film does not dedicate time to bring about this understanding, and instead conveniently presents Strange with a "consolation prize" for his disability if he can change his morals: magical powers.

Strange's innate skill with magic "overcompensates for a perceived physical defect, difference, or outright disability," occasionally even "banishing [the perceived disability] to the realm of the unseen, replacing it with raw power and heroic acts" (Alaniz 36). Here, Strange enters the role of the supercrip, transforming into an "inspirational" figure. His mentor, the Ancient One (Tilda Swinton), practically recites the "Your excuse is invalid" poster referenced earlier to Strange when he complains during training that his initial difficulty in using magical abilities stems from his nerve damage, showing him that Hamir is still a capable magic-user. Soon after this, Strange is able to begin mastering magic, "overcoming" his disability through magical overcompensation. Instead of representing the reality of living with an impairment, Strange's nerve damage is generally shown as either horribly tragic or effectively negligible, with the tremors sometimes even disappearing as he overcompensates through his use of magic (or the nondisabled actor forgets to perform them). Because of this, Strange could be read as able-disabled. In real life, there is of course nothing remarkable about the shifts in intensity of disability, but in film, where audiences rely on visuals and dialogue for representation, it should not go unnoticed when disability quietly becomes completely invisible. In the end, it becomes clear that Strange's disability was not truly about representation, but is instead a device to enable heroic morality. Once again, a hero cannot just happen to have a disability—it must be utilized, then made nearly invisible or erased entirely.

And what of the character Jonathan Pangborn mentioned earlier? Pangborn, Strange learns, "cured" his paraplegia through magic, but at the cost of concentration and energy use; he must choose between doing magic in the traditional sense or channeling it into a "cure." Strange, too, has this choice, and it is both notable and unsurprising that he chooses to keep his powers. On one hand, a hero actively chooses to remain disabled. On the other hand, the film asks, who would not choose to abandon a life of surgery to be a magical superhero? And, as a "consolation," the "rules" of magic certainly would seem to allow Strange to reverse his decision at any time. So, while Strange *is* able-disabled *by choice*, he is also vastly overcompensating through magical superpowers, and he is also aware that he can "cure" himself at any time. In the end, Pangborn's power is taken from him entirely by the rising villain, leaving him crumpled on the floor, once more quadriplegic in what is played as a tragic, horrifying event—because, once more, disability *must* be inherently undesirable.

TROPES AND TRAITS

It should be noted that the MCU's disabled heroes are not universally received in a negative light, both by those within the disabled community and by its allies. In an opinion piece on *Doctor Strange*, Alyssa Rosenberg points out that "in a culture that often suggests the most logical response to disability is to choose death," Strange's choice to keep his disability is an important one. Rosenberg still takes care to note that "Even after his accident, Strange occupies the tall, dashing form of Benedict Cumberbatch; even if his hands shake, his body is still capable of a great deal, including eliciting excessive swooning." This is often where disability representation in movies such as this ends up: not going far enough. It is a multifaceted consideration, and these considerations must be taken all at once: it is positive to see representation at all, but still harmful to see poor representation; it is good that the MCU acknowledges disability, but disappointing that it seems only to be interested in using it to invoke morality.

Possibly the MCU's best and most consistent representation of disability, as of 2019's *Avengers: Endgame*, is Stark's best friend, James "Rhodey" Rhodes (Don Cheadle). After sustaining a spinal cord injury, we see Rhodes learning to walk with custom braces designed by Stark. Aside from a few lines here and there, this is the last time his disability is discussed. Unlike Strange, however, it does not visually disappear. Outside of the Iron Man–based armor that Rhodes wears as an Avenger, code named War Machine, he continues to wear the braces, complete with unobtrusive blue lights on the sides. As a side character, this amount of attention makes sense; Rhodes acknowledged the adjustment that he had to make at the end of *Captain America: Civil War* (2016), and by *Avengers: Infinity War* (2018) and *Avengers: Endgame* (2019), his small amount of screen time is dedicated to his work as an Avenger. As Valerie Kalfrin, whose son has spina bifida and was excited to see Rhodes with his leg braces, points out, "it's rare in a mainstream film to see a character whose disability is just a trait, such as skin or hair color, that doesn't completely define the person." Stark had a chance to be represented in this way, but the constant connection of his arc reactor and disability to his heroic morality hindered this. Rhodes represents a small but significant step forward in the MCU's representation of disability, where his origin story is not rooted in disability (he was an Avenger before his injury). Here is a way for disability not to become "something 'other,' something not understood or to be pitied" (Kalfrin). Of course, it is a more complex issue than a single minor character can absolve, especially considering that Rhodes's immediate use of braces might imply that he *needed* to walk again to continue on as an Avenger.

The idea of "cures" and "fixing" is complicated, and rightly so. The concerns raised do not come from those in the disabled community who see themselves in the MCU's variously disabled heroes, but from the messages these films may carry to nondisabled viewers or to disabled viewers who then see themselves as needing to change, be "cured," or become supercrips, possibly exiting the theater believing that "disability and superheroics do not mix" (Alaniz 25). The MCU still has work to do in disability representation, especially concerning their usage of disability as a moral bolster and narrative device. Those crafting the MCU's superheroes must be conscious of the way disability does and does not enter their heroes' stories, for they run of the risk of reinforcing the idea that heroes can come *from* disability but cannot *be* disabled, halting representation at the point of origin.

Note

1. For an analysis of the textual and cultural use of the idea of overcoming disability, see Titchkosky, *Reading & Writing Disability Differently: The Textured Life of Embodiment*, especially chapter 6.

Works Cited

Alaniz, José. *Death, Disability, and the Superhero: The Silver Age and Beyond*. University Press of Mississippi, 2015.

Avengers: Endgame. Directed by Anthony Russo and Joseph Russo, Walt Disney Studios Motion Pictures, 2019.

Avengers: Infinity War. Directed by Anthony Russo and Joseph Russo, Walt Disney Studios Motion Pictures, 2018.

Captain America: Civil War. Directed by Anthony Russo and Joseph Russo, Walt Disney Studios Motion Pictures, 2016.

Captain America: The First Avenger. Directed by Joe Johnston, Paramount Pictures, 2011.

"Definition of morality." *Morality Noun—Definition, Pictures, Pronunciation and Usage Notes/ Oxford Advanced Learner's Dictionary at OxfordLearnersDictionaries.com*, https://www.oxfordlearnersdictionaries.com/us/definition/english/morality.

Desjardins, Michel. "Ideology, Archetypes and Eroticism: The Extraordinary New Sexuality of People Labeled Intellectually Disabled." *Rethinking Disability: World Perspectives in Culture and Society. 2nd, Rev. Ed*, edited by Patrick Devlieger, 2nd ed., Garant Publishers, 2016, pp. 73–82.

Doctor Strange. Directed by Scott Derrickson, Walt Disney Studios Motion Pictures, 2016.

"Ethical Theory." *Ethical Theory—MU School of Medicine*, University of Missouri, 2020, https://medicine.missouri.edu/centers-institutes-labs/health-ethics/faq/theory.

Gert, Bernard, and Joshua Gert. "The Definition of Morality." *Stanford Encyclopedia of Philosophy*, Stanford University, 8 Sept. 2020, https://plato.stanford.edu/entries/morality-definition/.

Iron Man. Directed by Jon Favreau, Paramount Pictures, 2008.

Iron Man 2. Directed by Jon Favreau, Paramount Pictures, 2010.

Iron Man 3. Directed by Shane Black, Walt Disney Studios Motion Pictures, 2013.

Jeffery, Scott. *The Posthuman Body in Superhero Comics: Human, Superhuman, Transhuman, Post/Human*. Palgrave Macmillan, 2016.

Kalfrin, Valerie. "My Son Finally Has . . ." *The Hollywood Reporter*, 1 May 2018, www.hollywoodreporter.com/heat-vision/avengers-infinity-war-showed-my-son-a-hero-like-him-war-machine-1107350.

Levine, Robert. "FILM; Does Whatever a Spider (and a C.E.O.) Can." *The New York Times*, 27 June 2004, https://www.nytimes.com/2004/06/27/movies/film-does-whatever-a-spider-and-a-ceo-can.html.

Linton, Simi. *Claiming Disability: Knowledge and Identity*. New York University Press, 1998.

Markus, Christopher, and Stephen McFeely. "An Evening with Avengers: Endgame Screenwriters Christopher Markus and Stephen McFeely." 16 May 2019. Emerson Colonial Theatre, Boston, MA.

Rosenberg, Alyssa. "'Doctor Strange's' surprisingly thoughtful . . ." *The Washington Post*, 3 Nov. 2016, https://www.washingtonpost.com/news/act-four/wp/2016/11/03/doctor-stranges-surprisingly-thoughtful-exploration-of-disability/.

Shapiro, Joseph P. *No Pity: People with Disabilities Forging a New Civil Rights Movement*. Times Books, 1994.

Titchkosky, Tanya. *Reading & Writing Disability Differently: The Textured Life of Embodiment*. University of Toronto Press, 2007.

Young, Stella. "I'm Not Your Inspiration, Thank You Very Much." TED. TEDxSydney, Sydney, Australia, www.ted.com/talks/stella_young_i_m_not_your_inspiration_thank_youz_very_much/up-next?language=en.

Chapter 3

MONSTROSITY, MUTATION, AND THE WORLD WITHOUT US

OCTAVIA CADE

The week of December 6, 2018, the week that the *Superheroes Beyond* conference took place in Melbourne, Australia, thousands of the city's schoolchildren took part in a march to protest their government's lack of action towards climate change. They are not the only ones to be so concerned. Over the past few decades, there has been a growing awareness of the threat that human impact has had on the environment. Superhero stories are not immune from this awareness. That said, superhero stories do not always productively engage with ideas of responsibility and blame; to do so may lead to a more creative interpretation of ecological superheroes by an increasingly aware and engaged audience.

In her discussion of sustainable superheroes, Ellen E. Moore focuses on the concept of technological solutions, often bankrolled and developed by superheroes such as Tony Stark (Iron Man). This helps to "reassure audience members that a viable 'fix' for environmental problems will come eventually when 'the world is ready,'" and that "the solution to serious environmental problems need not come from individual or societal efforts" to reimagine patterns of consumption and ecological exploitation (Moore 204). Under such scenarios, responsibility for solution making is removed from consumers, and this removal absolves them from the guilt of contributing to the problems in the first place. As Moore points out, the traditional superhero narrative—in which the superhero protects ordinary people from evil governments or supervillains—falls apart when those ordinary people are themselves the culprits. It is ordinary people filling the oceans with plastic, she argues, ordinary people who are causing deforestation, and miraculous technological solutions ignore their culpability. Moore argues that "the reason why these [superhero] films are so focused on environmental fixes rather than the problems themselves seems to be because this would shift the identity of the villain to the human population that the superhero is sworn to protect" (207).

One way to reinterpret the ecological superhero, and to bring this general culpability to the forefront of the narrative, is to present the nonhuman, even the monstrous nonhuman, as ecological superhero, thereby privileging, within the narrative, the experiences of nonhuman organisms. This brings human culpability into focus, as the threats addressed by the nonhuman superhero originate from human behavior and human environmental choices. Notable, however, in the construction of an ecological superhero, are the connections between the monstrous, the mutated monstrous, and both natural and (human) constructed environments.

The superhero as ecological monstrous is fully explored in Alan Moore's series *Saga of the Swamp Thing* (1984–1987). This series raised "issues of air and water pollution, the greenhouse effect, nuclear weapons testing, pesticide use, littering, desertification, toxic waste, acid rain, deforestation, soil erosion, animal testing, and vivisection" (Gray 47). Swamp Thing could thus be seen acting as a defender not only of the swamp but of other exploited and degraded ecologies. This is a defense motivated primarily by Swamp Thing's increasing identification with his wetland home. He is what Rikke Platz Cortsen refers to as a "conscious swamp" (398). As the Floronic Man observes in *Saga of the Swamp Thing: Book One,* "He is perfectly at one with the swamp. He feels what it feels, knows what it knows . . . what must it be *like*? To spread out with the water hyacinths in an implacable, choking net, to know the gray dreams of the Spanish moss" (72). This identification is more than mental: the Swamp Thing puts down taproots. He grows tubers and fruit; his entire body is a pulpy mass of vegetation.

Despite this nonhuman biology, however, he is also a creature of borderlines—having the human memories of the scientist Dr. Alec Holland, the Swamp Thing is neither entirely vegetable nor entirely human. He is a liminal creature, one who exists on the boundaries of species as well as environments. Discussing liminality in the context of ritual practices, Victor Turner describes liminal individuals as "necessarily ambiguous . . . these persons elude or slip through the network of classifications that normally locate states and positions in cultural space" (95). That ambiguity allows him to represent the nonhuman world and articulate—in a very human way—the general public's failure of environmental responsibility in a way that Ellen E. Moore's "technological" superheroes frequently do not.

COME OUT OF THE SWAMP: THE INFLUENCE OF THE ECOSYSTEM

As a liminal creature, the Swamp Thing is an entity that inspires suspicion. Justin M. Nolan and colleagues, for instance, observed in their study of human reactions to the zoological that there was "considerable ambivalence surrounding liminal creatures that transcend the nature/culture divide" (132). That ambivalence is present in reactions to Swamp Thing. While he can be applauded for his ecological activism and human qualities, he is also frequently perceived as monstrous, threatening, and uncontrollable—characteristics more closely associated with the natural and the nonhuman. That perception is unsurprising, and it is underlined by the wetland environment that he identifies with and in which he makes his home. Swamps and marshes, in particular, are fertile ground for monstrosity being ambiguous places themselves; sites of quicksand and untrustworthy ground. They are neither water nor land, but a shifting amalgam of both: places of boundaries and border crossings, where the littoral becomes liminal. This innate instability leads to perceptions of such environments as being both threatening and inherently suspicious. William Howarth states that "For thousands of years, the human attitude towards wetlands was consistently negative: they were read as dangerous, useless, fearful, filthy, diseased, noxious" places (58). For individuals unsympathetic to Swamp Thing, these are accurate descriptors for character as well as setting. Any creature that chooses to make a home in the swamp, who values the very instability of place that renders that environment threatening, must be threatening themselves— as Piret Pungas and Ester Võsu note, the ambiguous and difficult to navigate grounds of mires may "become refuges for social outcasts" (93) who cannot be trusted in normal society.

This negative perception of littoral ecosystems, such as that described above by Howarth, can be puzzling considering their biological value. Despite their popular perception as dangerous and untrustworthy environments, wetland ecosystems such as swamps are, nonetheless, places of high biodiversity. Furthermore, resilience—which in this context describes the ability of an ecosystem to resist or recover following disturbance or environmental change—is frequently and positively associated with biodiversity. By defending his wetland ecosystem from toxic waste dumping, for example, Swamp Thing is protecting the biodiversity and consequently the resilience of the swamp ecosystem as a whole.

This is an unalloyed environmental benefit. The current and critical decrease in global biodiversity is a threat to the continued function of these ecosystems. Garry Peterson and colleagues comment, for instance, "The consequences of species loss may not be immediately visible, but species loss decreases ecological resilience to disturbance or disruption. It produces ecosystems that are more vulnerable to ecological collapse" (16). The consequences of such reduced environments can be severe. The compromised wetlands of Louisiana, for example—home to the Swamp Thing—had a "lost storm protection value ... of USD 1.1 billion" following Hurricane Katrina, and the increasing impact of climate change upon ecology is unlikely to mitigate future losses of this kind (Costanza et al., 247).

The diversity and species richness that characterizes *natural* liminal spaces, however, is less frequently found in the *created* environmental liminal. An example of this can be seen in the Verdun region of France, where a 1200 km² km area, Zone Rouge, was badly affected by the fighting of World War I. Following the war, Zone Rouge was fenced off by the French government and remains so to this day, largely due to contamination and unexploded ordinance. In some areas, the after-effects of heavy shelling have prevented recolonization by vegetation due to hydric soils (Hupy 180). In other areas, the soils have been so contaminated with heavy metals and arsenic from chemical weaponry that "vegetation will still not grow due to the polluted soils" (Hubé 206). Naturally, the villages and farmland that once existed within this region had to be abandoned. Verdun's Zone Rouge is therefore a liminal place itself: it is human-created, and full of human artefacts, but humans are unable to live there.

In some areas of Zone Rouge, however, ecosystem recovery is occurring, due to the fact that, as Peter Coates argues, "No Man's Land can also be Many Creatures' Land" (501). A hundred years without significant human presence has, despite the challenges of the region, allowed the recolonization of a number of plant and animal species. In at least one instance, that of the yellow-bellied toad (*Bombina variegate*), colonization was from an animal that did not previously live in the region but was able to migrate there due to the new environmental conditions, specifically ponds created by exploded artillery shells (Kornei 71). However, the ability to survive in created liminal areas like Zone Rouge can result from more than simple opportunity, and it is an ability that the fans of superheroes are more than familiar with.

Nonhuman ability to survive environmental risk factors that would severely damage normal humans is reflected in a number of superhero narratives where the protagonist has such survival skills. This not only links the nonhuman and the superhuman in terms of tolerance and habitat, it also offers insight on real world spaces. If such spaces are, through the actions of humans, made inhospitable for human life, then the empty ecological niche may be filled by the natural—as in the case of the yellow-bellied toads—but it may also be filled by the mutated and the monstrous. In superhero contexts, exposure to high levels of radiation, for instance, can result in characters such as Dr. Bruce Banner, who mutated into the Hulk as a result of accidental exposure to gamma radiation on a bomb testing field. Dr. Chen Lu, on the other hand, deliberately exposed himself to radiation in the hopes of acquiring mutant superhuman powers and succeeded in doing so, becoming known as Radioactive Man (O'Doherty et al. 2). Exposure to sufficient radiation may indeed cause mutation, but beyond the mutated individual is the mutated community or ecosystem. The superhero that represents ecosystem—as Swamp Thing does—rather than a single species inside that ecosystem, is uniquely placed to query assumptions of blame and responsibility within the narrative.

THE MUTATED MONSTROUS: JUSTICE, CULPABILITY, AND THE NONHUMAN SUPERHERO

Perception of mutation can differ depending on the type and severity of the mutation, and of the mutant's capacity for understanding and communication. A mutant superhero able to vocalize their thoughts, and able to be understood by the humans around them, can more effectively advocate for themselves and their environments. Such advocacy is deemed to be a human rather than a nonhuman—or even a mutant—characteristic and is capable of demanding human allegiance despite any perceptions of monstrosity that come with mutant status. Audiences expect some level of reasoned communication, of reasoned *discrimination*, with mutant superheroes. They do not expect the same with, for example, a mutant alligator lurking in urban sewer systems. For this reason, it is arguably far easier for that audience to identify with the mutant human than with the mutant nonhuman.

If the mutated human may retain audience identification and sympathy, the mutated *nonhuman*, especially the mutated animal, is more often perceived as simply monstrous. These creatures are seen as destructive and dangerous, taking on, by association, the perception frequently given to the created liminal environments that spawned them. Yet some of these mutated monsters are developed enough, or charismatic enough, to engender the same sympathy that is regularly given to the mutant superhero. This sympathy can then extend to what the monster *does* as well as what it *is*—even when the victims of those actions are human. Sympathy for the mutated monstrous, then, can override audience identification with victimized human characters, leading that audience to side with the monstrous and the mutant over their own species in-group. Notably, this is something that extends to liminal environments. Sympathy for the Swamp Thing, for instance, can lead to readers valuing the swamp he inhabits, even when they may not care to experience the reality of swamps for themselves.

Examples of such sympathetic monsters may include Godzilla, mutated by nuclear radiation in the 1954 film of the same name, or the giant bears of the 1979 eco-horror film *Prophecy*, hideously altered by toxic chemicals when a paper mill illegally contaminates the environment by dumping methyl mercury into a forest water source. *Prophecy* provides an excellent example of an apparent single villain causing ecological devastation. The owner of the paper mill is not only responsible for the poison and subsequent mutation of the ecosystem (methyl mercury being a recognized mutagen) but is actively involved in covering it up. As the film progresses, however, and the investigative team and the mill owner are hunted by mutant bears, it becomes clear that the local government has been looking the other way as well. The local government does not visibly appear in the film but exists in the background as silent and faceless supporter. Guilt, in *Prophecy*, initially appears to be individual, but comes to be understood as systemic.

Furthermore, although the monstrous bears of this mutant ecosystem are blindly destructive and blindly bloodthirsty, they are clearly not presented as the villains of the film. The bears' appearance is both horrifying and pathetic. Their mutations appear *painful*, and the prospect of animals suffering, perhaps even tormented to insanity, is not usually conducive to audience indifference. That the most dangerous of the bears is a mother protecting her cubs is a further plea for sympathy. The monstrous bear becomes, through her actions, something to identify with, even when her inability to discriminate between the relative guilt of human characters further underlines both her monstrosity and her nonhuman status. The paper mill owner dying at the paws of his own (unintended) creation is moreover presented as being something like justice. The mill owner, having mutated an entire ecosystem through his polluting activities, has created an unnatural and hostile environment; but that environment, however disturbing, is not at fault for its own exploitation. The bears may be monstrous, they may even be murderous, but their hideous mutations have been inflicted upon them. In fighting back against the direct causes of their own distress, they become de facto protectors of their ecosystem, in the same way as Swamp Thing protects his own habitat from the corrupting effects of pollution. If Swamp Thing is perceived as heroic for these acts, why not the bears?

Monstrous or mutant status does not, after all, preclude a superhero label: the Hulk, for instance, is an immensely destructive force, both mutant and monstrous, and yet he is certainly presented as a superhero, capable of saving others. (Indeed, that monstrous mutant status is what grants the superhero identity in the first place. Would Dr. Banner be perceived as a superhero if the Hulk did not exist?) The mutated and monstrous nonhuman who acts as an agent of justice against those who exploit and contaminate the environment can also be seen in the Godzilla franchise, which illustrates a particularly interesting commentary on mutation and the responsibility behind it. The franchise spans over thirty films, but two in particular are useful for the purposes of this chapter. In the original film, *Godzilla* (1954), Godzilla is exposed to hydrogen bomb testing, and the resultant mutation makes him even more lethal. The film ends on a warning note: radiation has created one monster. What will future nuclear testing create? In *Godzilla* (2014), a different radioactive species arises, and Godzilla successfully battles the new mutants and returns to the sea, thereby aiding the humans who caused the radiation problem in the first place. Admittedly, this 2014 version of Godzilla is not helping humans deliberately; he has no real interest in them at all. From Godzilla's perspective, the only relevance that humans have for his life is that their activities were responsible for his mutation. They are, essentially, culpable—but culpable on what level? This question leaves the 2014 film with an odd sort of tension that was entirely absent from the first rendition: Godzilla may be a monster, but—like the monstrous or mutant superhero—is he a savior as well?

Certainly, he has become so within Japan. The cultural perception of Godzilla as superhero in Japan has partially stemmed, so William M. Tsutsui argues, from his being an underlying "metaphor for the expression of Japanese identity in the nation's long, unresolved postwar" history (4). That metaphor is unreservedly associated with the development and use of atomic bombs. Godzilla itself has long been recognized as a metaphor for nuclear warfare, laying waste to Tokyo as the 1945 nuclear bombing of Japan similarly did to Hiroshima and Nagasaki. Tsutsui goes on to observe the impact of culture on reception, noting that the "disjunction is especially stark between Godzilla as frequently seen abroad . . . and the monster accessible to Japanese viewers" (5) due to differing experiences of atomic warfare. Susan J. Napier, however, comments that the 1954 film had such universal appeal because it not only addressed the Japanese experience of nuclear war, but it also allowed American audiences to "work through their own nuclear-age anxiety" (332). This "working through" on the American side, however, may arguably be cut short with the monster's death, with Chon Noriega stating that "Godzilla's death represses American guilt and anxieties about nuclear weapons" (70). Nancy Anisfield agrees, stating that the film's "catharsis serves to vent emotion which, in turn, represses nuclear guilt" (55). The dramatic death of the monster does end the problem, of course (apart from those pesky future occurrences), but it also ends, in some way, the responsibility. The problem is over, and it is time to move on.

This kind of absolution is reminiscent of the superhero-spawned technological solution to environmental problems, described by Ellen E. Moore above. It packages responsibility and hands it off, isolating the central conflict from society as a whole, in much the same way as Zone Rouge isolates the dangerous liminal spaces humanity has created from everyday human life. Swamp Thing, leaving his disdained home to actively confront the ecological villains outside it, refuses, in part, this tactic of isolation. Hindi Krinsky argues that Alan Moore's

Swamp Thing "challenges how readers interact with the environment, forcing them to directly engage with nature," which allows the natural world to become the "lead character, main subject, and narrative axis" of the *Swamp Thing* narrative (231). Such direct engagement encourages interaction and, ultimately, responsibility. Similarly, if the Godzilla franchise can be understood by two cultures as a way to address questions of responsibility and guilt when it comes to atomic war, then it can also be extended to address questions of responsibility and guilt when it comes to the environmental damage that war can cause, and its protagonist (or conversely, antagonist), in addressing those questions, can approach superhero status from an ecological rather than a wartime perspective.

The responsibility the average, ordinary, protected-by-superhero citizen has for the state of the world is often entirely absent, with blame instead given to an individual character or organization that can more easily be represented within a narrative. It is the military and the paper mill owner who are responsible. It is mad scientists and big business. That citizens fund the military and the scientists, and that voters tolerate bad business and environmental practices, participating in and implicitly supporting those practices with their consumer choices, is conveniently glossed over. Their responsibility is perceived as either lesser, separate, or absent entirely. Godzilla and the mutant bears of *Prophecy* make no such distinction. Their reactive destruction does not discriminate between the soldiers and scientists and mill owners who actively polluted the environment and the taxpayers and voters and consumers who passively allowed them to do it.

There is no traditional superhero, not even the most ecologically inclined, who can defend against such universal indifference and such universal irresponsibility. Such has been left, on rare occasion, to villains (albeit sometimes sympathetic villains). The Floronic Man, who Maggie Gray argues represents "some of the misanthropic attitudes of deep ecology" (48), is a far more radical character than Swamp Thing, and far more biased against humanity, ultimately advocating genocide in order to allow the other species of the world—particularly the plant species—to recover from the damage that humanity has caused them. It is clear from the example of Zone Rouge that even deeply devastated environments can, in the absence of further anthropogenic stressors, show both resilience and recovery, so the Floronic Man's argument has a legitimate basis. "You have waged bitter and undeclared war upon The Green, gutting the rainforests, mile after mile, day after day," he says, "If allowed to live, you will kill your planet. You must be removed" (112). The Floronic Man has arguably a much more clear-cut understanding of both responsibility and blame; like Godzilla and the *Prophecy* bears he does not discriminate between levels of responsibility. However, he cannot be said to be unbiased; his desire to remove all animal life from the Earth in favor of plants is both chosen, excessive, and counterproductive (he does not address, for instance, that this cause of action would see the extinction of all insect and bird-pollinated plants).

Michael Bradshaw notes that care is taken, in *Swamp Thing*, to make the villains "as revolting as possible," and this is an understandable tactic which gives an unpleasant face to the (apparent) producers of environmental problems (129). The pleasure that the audience of *Prophecy* is clearly meant to feel at the death of the poisoning paper mill owner, for instance, is a result of his deeply off-putting character. What this tactic can fail to take account of, however, is that villains have their own (cultural, social) ecosystems. They do not exist in a vacuum any more than liminal superheroes from liminal environments do. Taking account of that villainous ecosystem, however—acknowledging that the villains have the active support of much of the general population—renders the producers of environmental problems a faceless, amorphous mass. Perhaps, then, the most effective superhero to counter this mass is the one who does not—who literally cannot—discriminate. The nonhuman mutated monstrous, living in created liminal environments and without the capacity for reasoned communication, may therefore be the least biased, most objective distributor of justice; a quality of character every aspiring superhero is expected to possess.

THE MIRROR OF THE MONSTROUS: THE FUTURE OF ECOLOGICAL SUPERHEROES

Superheroes such as the Swamp Thing may have a strong ecological focus of their own, and they might protect their own natural liminal zones from human encroachment, but they retain within themselves some level of identification with human actors and some capacity for moral judgement. Individuals who do not harm the swamp are safe, while those who would pollute it are viable targets. Mutant animals, on the other hand, are indiscriminately vicious to any human being in their vicinity. They are perceived as lacking the moral capacity for judgment. The mutant mother bear of *Prophecy*, for instance, attacks both the owner of the paper mill, who has been polluting the environment with mutagenic chemicals, and the people protesting that pollution. This perception of indiscriminate monstrosity remains even when the mutant creature's role within the narrative is effectively similar to that of the superhero.

Scott Bukatman comments that horror, as a genre, "has long sought to awaken compassion for the monster and its plight" (185–86). This sympathetic concept of the monstrous is certainly not new and dates, perhaps, from Mary Shelley's 1818 novel *Frankenstein*. Bukatman argues that this compassion results from a shift in perspective, as a previously objective and observant audience is brought "into the mind of a monster" (186). Notable here is the word "mind." It implies a thinking creature, one able to reason and communicate. The humanization of a monstrous creature is an exercise in empathy that rests on the ability to identify with the thought processes of that creature. Frankenstein's monster and the Swamp Thing—even the Floronic Man—may not present as human, but their thinking is understandable to humans and evokes sympathy for their monstrous selves and, perhaps, recognition of their liminal status (part human and part nonhuman). Harder, perhaps, is the humanization of monstrous creatures that are not popularly perceived to think in humanly comprehensible ways. Nonhuman animals, for instance, or even plants, are frequently acknowledged as having *feelings*, instincts as opposed to reason, but even these are sometimes dismissed. Bukatman, after all, uses the phrase "into the mind of a monster" instead of, "into the heart of a monster," which might be more likely to privilege instinct rather than thought.

From our human, rationalist perspective, monstrous nonhuman mutants often attack innocent humans who are not immediately threatening. But how do we define *innocence* and *immediacy*? Superhero narratives tend to privilege the importance of choice, of individual ethical action, and of personal responsibility. Yet who is responsible for climate change? Who is responsible for microplastics entering the marine ecosystem or the production of toxic or nuclear waste? Such responsibility is global and communal. Humans are deliberately creating liminal spaces in nature; ambiguous spaces where established ecologies break down and can no longer function, and spaces where degraded ecologies can slowly recover only when not burdened further by human presence. For other species, the world would be materially better without humans in it, and the instinctive awareness of this, come out of both the monstrous, mutated nonhuman and their human-created liminal environment. If their capacity for self-defense is *increased* through mutation, then these creatures approach superhero status of their own. After all, if the Swamp Thing has tacit audience approval to destroy threats to the functioning ecology of the swamp, can we really give less approval to the actions of mutant bears defending their own habitat from perceived threat?

The existence, therefore, of mutant, ecologically focused superheroes, especially those who identify with liminal environments such as swamps, may be an early argument for different superhero identifications entirely, and for the reinterpretation of mutant nonhuman monsters, such as Godzilla, as superheroes in their own right. Engagement with the idea of the sympathetic mutant, springing as it does from superhero narratives, may, through ecological horror, provide a metaphor for understanding the causes and consequences of mutation in species other than our own.

It may be that, in the context of ecological sustainability, a mass destruction of liminal- and mutant-producing humanity by the mutated monstrous is, for the planet, the most superhero-like act that monstrous can achieve.

Works Cited

Anisfield, Nancy. "Godzilla/Gojiro: Evolution of the Nuclear Metaphor." *Journal of Popular Culture*, vol. 29, no. 3, 1995, pp. 53–62.

Bradshaw, Michael. "The Sleep of Reason: Swamp Thing and the Intertextual Reader." *Alan Moore and the Gothic Tradition*, edited by Matthew J. A. Green, Manchester University Press, 2015, pp. 121–39.

Bukatman, Scott. "Frankenstein and the Peculiar Power of the Comics." *Global Frankenstein*, edited by C. M. Davison and M. Mulvey-Roberts, Palgrave Macmillan, 2018, pp. 185–207.

Coates, Peter. "Borderland, No-man's Land, Nature's Wonderland: Troubled Humanity and Untroubled Earth." *Environment and History*, vol. 20, no. 4, 2014, pp. 499–516.

Cortsen, Rikke Platz. "Full Page Insight: The Apocalyptic Moment in Comics Written by Alan Moore." *Journal of Graphic Novels and Comics*, vol. 5, no. 4, 2014, pp. 397–410.

Costanza, Robert, et al., "The Value of Coastal Wetlands for Hurricane Protection." *AMBIO: A Journal of the Human Environment*, vol. 37, no. 4, 2008, pp. 241–49.

Godzilla. Directed by Ishirō Honda, Toho, 1954.

Godzilla. Directed by Gareth Edwards, Warner Bros. Pictures, 2014.

Gray, Maggie. "A Gothic Politics: Alan Moore's *Swamp Thing* and Radical Ecology." *Alan Moore and the Gothic Tradition*, edited by Matthew J. A. Green, Manchester University Press, 2015, pp. 42–62.

Howarth, William. "Reading the Wetlands." *Place in Context: Rethinking Humanist Geographies*, edited by Paul C. Adams et al., University of Minnesota Press, 2001, pp. 55–83.

Hubé, Daniel. "Industrial-scale Destruction of Old Chemical Ammunition near Verdun: A Forgotten Chapter of the Great War." *First World War Studies*, vol. 8, no. 2–3, 2017, pp. 205–34.

Hupy, Joseph P. "The Long-term Effects of Explosive Munitions on the WWI Battlefield Surface of Verdun, France." *Scottish Geographical Journal*, vol. 122, no. 3, 2006, pp. 167–84.

Kornei, Katherine. "Life after War." *Discover*, vol. 39, no. 4, 2018, pp. 70–72.

Krinsky, Hindi. "Mean Green Machine: How the Ecological Politics of Alan Moore's Reimagination of Swamp Thing Brought Eco-consciousness to Comics." *Plants and Literature*, edited by Randy Laist, Brill Rodopi, 2013, pp. 221–41.

Moore, Alan. *Saga of the Swamp Thing: Book One*. DC Comics, 2009.

Moore, Ellen E. *Landscape and the Environment in Hollywood Film*. Palgrave Macmillan, 2017.

Napier, Susan J. "Panic Sites: The Japanese Imagination of Disaster from Godzilla to Akira." *Journal of Japanese Studies*, vol. 19, no. 2, 1993, pp. 327–51.

Nolan, Justin M., et al., "The Lovable, the Loathsome, and the Liminal: Emotionality in Ethnozoological Cognition." *Journal of Ethnobiology*, vol. 26, no. 1, 2006, pp. 126–39.

Noriega, Chon. "Godzilla and the Japanese Nightmare: When 'Them!' Is U.S." *Cinema Journal*, vol. 27, no. 1, 1987, pp. 63–77.

O'Doherty, Jim, et al., "Real-Life Radioactive Men." *Superhero Science and Technology*, vol. 1, no. 1, 2018.

Peterson, Garry, et al., "Ecological Resilience, Biodiversity, and Scale." *Ecosystems*, vol. 1, no. 1, 1998, pp. 6–18.

Prophecy. Directed by John Frankenheimer, Paramount Pictures, 1979.

Pungas, Piret and Ester Võsu. "The Dynamics of Liminality in Estonian Mires." *Liminal Landscapes: Travel, Experiences, and Places In-between*, edited by Hazel Andrews and Les Roberts, Routledge, 2012, pp. 87–102.

Tsutsui, William M. "Introduction." *In Godzilla's Footsteps: Japanese Pop Culture Icons on the Global Stage*, edited by William M. Tsutsui and Michiko Ito, Palgrave Macmillan, 2006, pp. 1–9.

Turner, Victor. *The Ritual Process: Structure and Anti-Structure*. Cornell University Press, 1989.

Chapter 4

MIDNIGHT'S CHILDREN AND *THE FORTRESS OF SOLITUDE* AS SUPERHERO ORIGIN STORIES

JULIAN NOVITZ

INTRODUCTION: LITERARY SUPERHEROES

Chris Gavaler notes that the small but growing canon of literary superhero novels often tend to focus on pessimistic or antiheroic deconstructions of superheroic identity ("The Anti-Superhero" 33–35). Works like Thomas Pynchon's *Gravity's Rainbow* (1973) and Robert Mayer's *Superfolks* (1977) both focus on embittered or failed superheroes in ways that predate and anticipate Alan Moore's influential graphic novel *Watchmen* (1986–87), where the simplistic optimism often associated with superheroic identities is revealed to be insufficient and ineffectual in challenging the complex power structures and prejudices of the modern world. Later literary superhero novels have followed this trend. David J. Schwartz's *Superpowers* (2008) and Perry Moore's *Hero* (2007) both explore the disillusionment of emergent superheroes as they confront the limitations of their identities, while Austin Grossman's *Soon I Will Be Invincible* (2007) and Matt Carter's *Almost Infamous* (2016) explore and critique the hypermasculine and conservative attitudes that often underpin superheroic narratives. While nuanced and thoughtful critiques of superheroic tropes are certainly found in other media, Gavaler argues that this is an almost "formulaic" element of prose superhero novels, writing, "In literary fiction, the symbol of absolute victory is demythologized through the reversal of its most defining genre expectations: superheroes become ineffectual heroes in a world of complex morality" (34).

This chapter examines Salman Rushdie's *Midnight's Children* (1981) and Jonathan Lethem's *The Fortress of Solitude* (2003) as both literary superhero novels and bildungsroman narratives. A bildungsroman can be understood as a work that focuses on the formation of its protagonist's character, following them through a learning process or apprenticeship that ends in hard-won maturity (Boes 230–32). Where works like *Gravity's Rainbow* and *Superfolks* deal with the termination of superhero careers, featuring heroes who have become too passive and disillusioned to take meaningful action, Rushdie's and Lethem's novels operate as origin stories, exploring the desire to effect change and the belief in individual power and agency. However, in both *Midnight's Children* and *The Fortress of Solitude*, the journey of the protagonists towards maturity means accepting the futility of such attempts and acknowledging that the identity or ideal of the superhero has not only lost its meaning in a contemporary world, but was always illusionary. In this sense, their bildungsroman structures work to subvert and reverse the expected optimism and idealism represented by the origin story in superheroic narratives.

SUPERHERO ORIGIN STORIES

In his examination of Golden Age Superman comics, Umberto Eco observes that superhero stories often operate as loops that offer the pretense of meaningful incident while inevitably returning the hero to a status quo situation at their conclusion, thus preserving the mythic permanence of the superhero figure (15–16). While superhero narratives have become more sophisticated than the self-contained episodic adventures that Eco considers, frequent reboots and retroactive continuity adjustments to screen and comic book superhero properties can result in years or decades of complex storytelling being discarded, so as to return familiar heroes to a more recognizable and accessible state. But while superheroes are repeatedly reimagined and updated, the substance of their origin stories remains largely consistent (barring the occasional "what if?" experiment). This is true to the extent that origin stories could be considered the only permanent and generally unalterable storylines in the superhero canon (barring essentially cosmetic adjustments like the time period, or whether the spider is radioactive or genetically modified, etc.). While relationships, deaths, rivalries, and conflicts can be constantly rewritten, the story of how superheroes acquire their powers and purpose is fundamental to their identity. Though they often have their roots in tragedy and suffering, origin stories are usually optimistic in nature, with the hero either discovering, acquiring, or cultivating an ability that makes them special, and also resolving to use it altruistically (Rosenberg 5). In this sense, it could be argued that the typical superhero origin story has a clear parallel with the optimism of the bildungsroman in its classic form, where their hero's trials typically result in the discovery of their place or position within a welcoming social order (Boes 232).

The darker comic book deconstructions of superheroic identities that became popular from the 1980s typically focus on possible developments and endpoints for the careers of their superhero characters, rather than reimagining or revising their origins. Frank Miller's *The Dark Knight Returns* (1986) and Alan Moore's *Watchmen* both feature embittered, violent, older superheroes whose compromised and conflicted later careers are contrasted with their idealistic origins. Later comics such as *Kingdom Come* (1996) and *Old Man Logan* (2008–09) question the sustainability of superheroic idealism by placing their aging protagonists in dystopian environments that are arguably indicative of their failure to make a lasting difference in the world. The tendency towards antiheroic deconstruction that Gavaler identifies in literary superhero novels also typically associates aging and maturation with the breakdown of the superheroic identities. Both *Hero* and *Almost Infamous* feature older superhero characters corrupted by power. *Soon I Will Be Invincible* depicts aging superheroes and villains who are sinking into a state of ennui as a result of their repetitive conflicts. After (relatively) optimistic beginnings, the superhero characters in *Gravity's Rainbow* and *Superfolks* succumb to passivity. Works that attempt to subvert the optimism of superhero origin stories are therefore relatively rare—without the acquisition of powers and the resolve to use them for good there is no superheroic identity to deconstruct. Even comics that purport to present a cynical or subversive take on superhero origins, like *Kick-Ass* (2008–10) and *The Umbrella Academy* (2007–13), involve their protagonists essentially reaffirming the value of their superheroic identities and missions. While there is arguably an emerging subgenre that reimagines conventional superhero origins as horror stories or disasters—for example, *Chronicle* (2012) and *Brightburn* (2019)—these works do not critique the customary optimism and idealism of superhero origin stories, but suggest that the absence of these qualities will result in monsters and villains.

It is possible to argue then, that there is often a nostalgic sentiment at work in antiheroic deconstructions of superheroic identity. These deconstructions (whether in comics, on screen, or in the small canon of literary superhero novels identified by Gavaler) work to erode the mythic permanence of the figure of the superhero, featuring superhero characters who are forced to abandon or discard their initial optimism and idealism, either due to personal flaws or the increasing complexities of the contemporary world. For these deconstructions to work, however, the superhero origin story must remain "real" and inerasable in its significance. The remembered or implied optimism of the superheroic origin is needed to provide a point of contrast with superhero characters' contemporary compromises, often creating a longing on the part of both characters and readers for the simpler mode of heroism that it represents. *Midnight's Children* and *The Fortress of Solitude* are therefore unusual works in that they not only offer a deconstruction of the figure of the superhero, but also critique and contest the permanent "reality" of the optimistic superhero origin story. In both novels, this critique emerges from the protagonists' journey towards maturity and their discovery of the true nature of the social world that they are situated within.

Franco Morretti observes that in a bildungsroman novel, the protagonist's internal and external conflicts are typically resolved through the realization that they are not a heroically exceptional figure and that they are ready to accept their rightful place in society and submit to its mores and strictures (45–47). This discovery was typically presented as a happy outcome in the classic bildungsroman novels of the late eighteen and early nineteenth centuries. Yet Stella Bolaki argues that later engagements with the form offer more subversive and critical perspectives on the social order that surround and shape their protagonists, with maturity emerging through their apprehension of its inequities and injustices (10–13). In both *Midnight's Children* and *The Fortress of Solitude* the fulfilment of the protagonist's bildungsroman comes with the realization that the egalitarian ideal of a superheroic identity cannot surmount or remove them from the entrenched and coercive systems of power and privilege that shape their existence.

MIDNIGHT'S CHILDREN

Rushdie's novel is a multigenerational family narrative that explores the history surrounding India's independence from the United Kingdom and its partition from Pakistan. Due to the supernatural abilities of its title characters—the "Midnight's Children," who were all born in the hour following India's independence—the novel has often been classed as a magic realist work, where the conventions of fantasy and realist fiction are fused in a way that normalizes magical events (Degirmenci 58). Fredric Jameson argues that magic realism has become a staple of postcolonial literature because it is uniquely suited to exploring communities that are undergoing radical transitions. The genre therefore offers a means of expressing the conflicting and competing traditions and perceptions of reality that operate in these contexts (15). However, as Neil Kortenaar notes, the magical powers acquired by Rushdies's Midnight's Children have no specific association with any elements of Indian folklore or religious and spiritual traditions. It is, thus, difficult to read this element of the novel as operating in a conventional magic realist mode—where Indigenous spirituality exists alongside (and occasionally contests) materialist outlooks and preoccupations (766–68). Rather, the diverse powers possessed by the Midnight's Children recall the differing, inconsistent abilities of comic book superheroes:

> From Kerela, a boy who had the ability of stepping into mirrors and re-emerging through any reflective surface in the land . . . and children with powers of transformation . . . I found a water divining youth . . . a sharp-tongued girl whose words already had the power of inflicting physical wounds . . . There was a boy who could eat metal and a girl whose fingers were so green they could grow prize aubergines in the middle of the Thar desert. (Rushdie 276–77)

Gavaler (36) and Degirmenci (60–61) have noted the similarity of the Midnight's Children to Western superhero teams, and the catalyst for their powers—India's independence—could be likened to the emergence of the mutant gene in the *X-Men* series, or the cosmic rays that transform the Fantastic Four. Indeed, this sudden explosion of diverse superpowers is intimately connected to the initial potential of India to operate as a secular, egalitarian, and broadly inclusive state. The powers of the Midnight's Children do not arise out of any particular religious or spiritual tradition, and are bestowed regardless of wealth, class, or region. Degirmenci argues that the random, erratic nature of the powers described in *Midnight's Children* allows Rushdie a means to "secularize" the magical component of his realist novel. Its presence does not imply the re-emergence of a singular, more authentic mode of spiritual awareness in a postcolonial world, but the overwhelming directions and possibilities presented by the idea of a diverse, yet united independent India (Degirmenci 64–65).

Midnight's Children, however, implies that even from the moment of India's independence, this potential is already starting to wane. The children born in the first minute of the hour have the greatest powers—alchemy, flight, time travel, sorcery, and conjuration—but those born later have less impressive abilities. The novel's narrator, Saleem, observes: "Those children born in the last seconds of the hour were (to be frank) little more than circus freaks" (Rushdie 275). The further one travels from the moment of India's independence, the more its (secular) magic starts to fade. Born at the very stroke of midnight, however, is Saleem himself, who has the gift of telepathy; and Shiva, with the power of strength and destruction. Together they sit at the center of the plot, in which a superhero and a supervillain are born in the same second and each embody, through their power, a different potential for the newly independent India. The ability to communicate and unify is posed against the ability to coerce and repress.

It comes as no surprise that Shiva proves to be the ultimate victor in the anticlimactic non-confrontation between the two. Upon discovering his own powers and those of his peers, Saleem sets out to telepathically link the Midnight's Children, creating the "Midnight's Children Conference" in his head. Saleem is convinced that these powers must have some kind of meaning and can be used to affect positive change: "The thing is, we must be here for a *purpose*, don't you think? I mean there must be a *reason*, you must agree?" (Rushdie 305–6).

Upon being contacted, however, Shiva brutally undercuts the optimism of Saleem's attempted superhero origin, saying: "What *purpose*, man? . . . For what reason you're rich and I'm poor? . . . Man, I'll tell you—you got to get what you can, do what you can with it, and then you got to die. That's reason, rich-boy" (Rushdie 306).

Saleem is determined that all members of the conference should be considered as equals. Shiva, however, argues that he and Saleem, as the two most powerful members, should impose their will on the others, becoming "joint-bosses" of the other children so as to use them for their own benefit (305). Saleem is dismayed by Shiva's intentions, but is unable to exclude or effectively counter him due to his feelings of guilt. Saleem and Shiva had been switched at birth, allowing Saleem to grow up within the comfort of a wealthy family, while Shiva was confined to poverty. Where Saleem was lauded as the first child born in the newly independent India, Shiva's birth passed unmentioned. This initial injustice works to immediately undermine both the egalitarian potential of an independent India and Saleem's collectivist intentions for the Midnight's Children Conference itself. Saleem's privileged position allows him to optimistically believe that individual power must have some greater meaning and purpose, whereas Shiva's experiences of oppression and deprivation have convinced him that those with power will inevitably use it for their own betterment, despite their professed intentions (Manzo 74–76).

Shiva is ultimately proven right by the disintegration of the Midnight's Children Conference, who, despite Saleem's best efforts, are unable to decide on a collective identity or purpose. As they grow older, the unifying potential of their diverse powers is insufficient to overcome regional and class-differences:

> I found children from Maharashtra loathing Gurjaratis; and fair-skinned Northerners reviling Dravidian "blackies"; there were religious rivalries and class entered our councils. The rich children turned up their noses at being in such lowly company; Brahmins began to feel uneasy permitting even their thoughts to touch the thoughts of untouchables; while among the low-born the pressures of poverty and Communism were becoming evident. (Rushdie 353)

The fracturing of the Midnight's Children Conference in the novel mirrors growing disharmony in post-Independence India (Heffernan 474–75). While the secular magic possessed by the children expresses the remarkable, world-changing spirit of the independent state, their inability to transcend old hierarchies of privilege and prejudice leaves them, like the state itself, vulnerable to repressive forces. In the end, Saleem and his fellow Midnight's Children are betrayed by Shiva, who aligns himself with the government and identifies the Midnight's Children as a threat to its authority. During the twenty-one-month period of "Emergency" declared by Indira Ghandi, the Midnight's Children are rounded up with the coerced assistance of Saleem, and those who are not murdered are forcibly sterilized, stripping them of their powers.

As befits the protagonist of a bildungsroman novel, Saleem offers a double-voiced narration on these events. This captures both the optimism and idealism of his youthful attempts to organize the Midnight's Children Conference into a force for good, and charts his journey through disillusionment, horror, guilt, and eventual resignation (Kortenaar 768). Alongside this, Saleem's adult voice admits that the Midnight's Children did not just fail in their purpose, but never really had a purpose to begin with. With the pretence of superheroism stripped away, he concludes that the Midnight's Children were "just a bunch of kids," bereft of a higher calling (Rushdie 228). He concludes that if the Midnight's Children had any purpose then it was to be consumed by more powerful and predatory forces—conceding "that the purpose of the Midnight's Children might be annihilation; that we would have no meaning until we were destroyed" (262). As an adult, Saleem can recognize that the destruction of the Midnight's Children allows the state to assert its tyrannical centrality, brutally supplanting them as the metaphorical spirit of India (Degirmenci 62). The Midnight's Children Conference initially includes hundreds of individuals with unique superpowers, but by the end of the novel, only Shiva's singular powers of might and aggression remain. Where the youthful Saleem sees himself as uniquely connected to the nation and perceives Shiva as an anti-social outsider, in the end Shiva's authoritarian sensibilities are endorsed by the state apparatus and it is Saleem who is cast aside (Kortenaar 778–79).

In the fashion of a bildungsroman protagonist, Saleem's journey towards maturity involves him coming to understand the reality of his social world and his place within it. As a child, Saleem could see himself and his fellow Midnight's Children as superheroic embodiments of the potential of India, with the power to shape its development and direction, but as an adult he is left with the hard lesson that he was never central to any understanding of India. Rather, Saleem recognizes that the evolution of the state has been central in shaping him, finally understanding himself not as an active and heroic force, but as "the sum total of everything that went before me, of all I have seen done, of everything done-to-me" (Rushdie 457). His individual power and good intentions are revealed to be meaningless in the face of this history, and his expectations have been problematically shaped by his own, undeniable privilege (Manzo 174–76). The novel ends on an ambiguous note—it is unclear whether

Saleem can continue to live with this knowledge or whether he will literally disintegrate, as he anticipates, on his thirty-first birthday, representing the final expiration of the idea of India as a united, egalitarian state.

THE FORTRESS OF SOLITUDE

Jonathan Lethem's *The Fortress of Solitude* presents a no-less pessimistic derailment of the superhero origin story via the difficult lessons of its protagonist's bildungsroman-like journey from naivety to maturity. Set in New York in the 1970s, *Fortress of Solitude* follows the lives of Dylan and his African American friend Mingus as they grow up in Brooklyn. Their otherwise ordinary trajectories are interrupted by an elderly, drunken superhero who passes a ring that can bestow the gift of flight to Dylan, with the exhortation to "fight evil" (Lethem 150). Dylan is unable to use the ring on his own, so he recruits Mingus to take on the role of a costumed superhero "Aeroman" whom they jointly create.

The first section of the novel, related in the third person, appears to give equal weight to Dylan and Mingus as dual protagonists, emphasizing the parallels between them as it builds to their creation of the Aeroman persona. They are both growing up without mothers and with distant, artistic fathers, and are united by a shared love of comic books. As a component of their first meeting as neighbors, Mingus introduces Dylan to Marvel Comics, and they both keenly identify with its stable of conflicted, alienated, and self-doubting superheroes, observing the desirability and the challenges of maintaining a secret identity (Coughlan 198–99). Dylan in particular is arguably cast as a parallel of Peter Parker: studious, quiet, socially awkward, frequently bullied, and ready to be transformed via his acquisition of a superpower.

The superheroic origin story in this opening section is complicated by a number of factors. First, while the powers of the ring are shared between the two of them, it is initially bestowed upon Dylan, and he therefore considers it to be his property and his responsibility. The dying Black superhero Arthur Doily gives the ring to Dylan in the same way that the wizard Shazam imbues Billy Batson with his power, or how Alan Scott and Hal Jordan are given the ability to become the Green Lantern by a mystical talking lantern and a dying alien, respectively. However, as Gavaler notes, this trope from Golden and Silver Age comic books—where a figure that is coded as alien or "oriental" passes their unique power to a "chosen" white protagonist—has uncomfortable imperialist undertones ("The Imperial Superhero" 110). Gavaler identifies this as the continuation of the late-nineteenth and early-twentieth-century fantasy where Western proto-superhero characters like Spring-heeled Jack,

Tarzan of the Apes, or Mandrake the Magician would acquire the "culture of the other" and excel within it (109–10). In this sense, it is awkward for Dylan, a white child living in a predominately Black neighborhood—arguably as a part of the first wave of gentrification that will destroy its unique character (Godbey 132–33)—to be marked as the chosen one within this superhero origin narrative. Bildungsroman protagonists typically begin their journeys with the belief that they are heroically exceptional in some way (Moretti 46), so Dylan is naturally receptive to the idea that he is marked for a special destiny. This is reflected in the way he holds himself apart from his peers at school and in the neighborhood, repeating his mantra "Not in Jail, Just Visiting" as he works his way towards a scholarship to a (largely white) high school in Manhattan and later to the elite Camden liberal arts college (Lethem 239).

The way in which Dylan assumes his specialness and primacy (at least subconsciously) is challenged by the fact that Mingus is much more naturally suited to the assumption of a superheroic identity. He is presented from a young age as being charismatic and magnetic. Furthermore, his father is a significant R&B musician, and in a novel where musicians are arguably characterized and discussed as if they were contemporary superheroes, this would seem like a lineage that destines him for great things (Dore). In the first section, Mingus could be seen as pursuing another common path towards superheroism, where a special heritage or descent is the source of superheroic power (Nama 137–38). This is reinforced when Dylan discovers that Mingus is able to use the power of the ring easily and in the open (where Dylan is only able to fly when no one else is watching). Thus, while they profess to be equal partners in the creation of the Aeroman identity, Mingus is the only one to don the makeshift costume, fly, and fight crime directly.

Dylan is essentially regulated to the role of sidekick as they spend a summer foiling muggings and robberies around Brooklyn, an interesting inversion of the trope noted by Kolton Harris and Anna Scott, where Black superheroes typically first emerge as supporting characters in the narratives of white superheroes (9; 296). Despite this, Dylan still sees the ring as belonging to him and attempts to regulate its use, eventually withdrawing from the Aeroman dynamic when he feels Mingus is using it irresponsibly. Dylan's later decision to recover the ring from Mingus inadvertently precipitates a tragedy, where Mingus is forced to shoot his grandfather in order to protect his father and, it is implied, Dylan. In this sense, Dylan's assumption that he has the principle right to their shared superpower—befitting his role as both a bildungsroman protagonist and the "chosen" recipient of power in a superhero origin story—works to unravel the life of his friend.

The superhero origin story in the novel's opening section is further complicated by the events of its concluding section, which takes place twenty years later. Mingus has been repeatedly in and out of prison, while Dylan has moved to the West Coast, where he works as a music journalist and writer. Dylan's trajectory in the opening section is recast in a troubling light by the revelations about his adult life—particularly with regard to his veneration and jealousy of Mingus. The section opens with Dylan's Black girlfriend calling him out for his fetishization of Black people, music, and culture, suggesting that she feels she has been "collected" in the same way he collects R&B and Blues records by Black artists. As Godbey argues, Dylan views Black culture as a source of authenticity in his life, one that he feels entitled to share in as a result of his upbringing living among Black neighbors and friends (135–36). Dylan's entitlement is demonstrated through the ways that he lives vicariously through Mingus depending on his social networks and connections, "sharing" the Aeroman persona, and appropriating Mingus's graffiti tag (Coughlan 214). Later in life, he also uses his knowledge and experience of Black culture to create a "streetwise" persona for himself at Camden College, so as to impress his exclusively white peers. Dylan's bildungsroman trajectory in the final section of the novel involves him coming to appreciate how this is exploitative and that, despite his repeated construction of himself as a victim, his actions have caused harm to a number of Black characters in the novel and to Mingus in particular.

In the wake of the confrontation with his girlfriend, and his mixed feelings over the notes that he has written for a compilation of Mingus's father's music (which he felt was a genuine tribute, but which his editor dismisses as self-inflating grandiosity), Dylan resolves to return the ring to Mingus and encourage him to use it to escape his current imprisonment. Mingus refuses this attempt by Dylan to assuage his guilt, directing him to instead give the ring to Dylan's old childhood bully and tormentor, Robert Woolfrock, who is suffering behind bars. Dylan does so, but either forgets or deliberately fails to tell Robert that the power of the ring has changed and that it now grants invisibility but not flight. Robert dies when he leaps from the prison watchtower, causing Dylan to recognize his action, and himself, as decidedly untrue to the superheroic ideal: "I had resurrected Aeroman to kill Robert Woolfrock . . . Aeroman was nothing if not a [B]lack body on the ground" (Lethem 501).

In the final section, Dylan is forced to take stock of what has resulted from his superheroic origins and from the naïve belief that he (and possibly Mingus) could fight evil. His unwillingness to relinquish the superpower, and the sense of himself as uniquely chosen, inadvertently resulted in Mingus's initial imprisonment. His later attempt to make amends only caused the death of Robert Woolfrock. On the other hand, Mingus, who was naturally more heroic in spirit and ability was unable to use the power of the ring to affect any significant change at all. Aside from thwarting minor street crimes, his only major accomplishment was spraying his tag "Dose" on the Brooklyn correctional institute where he would later be imprisoned, "ironically signing himself up for incarceration" (Coughlan 211).

As a bildungsroman protagonist, Dylan's journey concludes with him coming to understand the truth of the world and his place within it, much like Saleem does in *Midnight's Children*. Where he had previously perceived himself as a bullied victim elevated to a special, heroic status through the receipt of a superpower, the conclusion of *The Fortress of Solitude* reveals that he was always powerful and protected within the American social order. In observing Mingus's trajectory in the final stages of the novel, Dylan is forced to confront his own privilege and therefore also the inauthenticity of the ways he has periodically laid claim to aspects of Black life and culture as an alternative or secret identity. While as children they both constructed their neighborhood as a prison, Dylan was the only one afforded the agency and opportunity to escape it, superpowers or no (Sharma 671). Furthermore, despite the repeated emphasis on the ways that Dylan is bullied while growing up by his Black neighbors and classmates, his whiteness nonetheless affords him privilege and protection. Dylan is spared the serious violence meted out to Black youths in the neighborhood, is repeatedly protected by Mingus, and even, subtly, by Robert Woolfrock on at least one occasion. Later in his adult life, he is able to easily escape the grotesque and violent outcome of his one, darkly farcical attempt to adopt the guise of Aeroman without Mingus. Finally, after passing the ring to Robert and becoming trapped inside a restricted prison wing, he is able to talk his way out of an encounter with the guards without consequence. It could be argued that by the end of the novel, Dylan's trajectory reveals that whiteness, and not the paltry and ultimately ineffectual gift of flight, is the true superpower.

In the end, *The Fortress of Solitude* cements its protagonist's movement towards maturity and self-knowledge through the realization of the futility of superheroic optimism and idealism. A superpower is insufficient to bridge the gap in power and privilege that divides Dylan and Mingus as adults, just as it is unable to arrest the chaos and turbulence of India's first decades of independence in *Midnight's Children*.

CONCLUSION

Midnight's Children and *The Fortress of Solitude* are both overtly presented as bildungsroman novels, where the protagonists attempt to form their identity within particular social and cultural contexts. They are also both superhero origin stories, where the protagonists discover special powers and resolve to use them for good. While these elements may seem naturally connected—in that both bildungsroman narratives and superhero origins are stories of formation—the bildungsroman element to these novels works to complicate, subvert, and ultimately nullify the optimism that is essential to superhero origins. As Moretti observes, a bildungsroman narrative is customarily one where the protagonist comes to discover that their life is not a model but rather a lesson. In the classic bildungsroman, protagonists act as if they are in a romance novel—as heroes with a fixed destiny—but, through misadventure, come to realize that they have misunderstood their own nature (Moretti 71–72). The realization of the truth leads them to a hard-won maturity but inevitably shatters the dream of heroism. Their heroic identity is not lost or rendered unsustainable; rather it is revealed to be misguided or illusionary. Through their bildungsroman structures, *Midnight's Children* and *The Fortress of Solitude* deny the nostalgia that is often a component of superhero narrative deconstructions, not only deconstructing the mythic, timeless figure of the superhero, but also critiquing the inherent optimism of superhero origin stories. While exploring very different contexts, these novels both suggest that optimism about individual power and agency works to obscure the entrenched systems of privilege and power that unavoidably compromise both their protagonists.

Works Cited

Boes, Tobias. "Modernist Studies and the *Bildungsroman*: A Historical Survey of Critical Trends." *Literature Compass*, vol. 3, no. 2, 2006, pp. 230–43.

Bolaki, Stella. *Unsettling the Bildungsroman: Reading Contemporary Ethnic American Women's Fiction*. Brill, 2011.

Brightburn. Directed by David Yarovesky. Sony Pictures, 2019.

Carter, Matt. *Almost Infamous: A Supervillain Novel*. Talos Press, 2016.

Chronicle. Directed by Josh Trank. 20th Century Fox, 2012.

Coughlan, David. "Jonathan Lethem's *The Fortress of Solitude* and *Omega the Unknown*, a Comic Book Series." *College Literature*, vol. 38, no. 3, 2011, pp 194–218.

Degirmenci, Ash. "The Nation and the Supernatural in Salman Rushdie's *Midnight's Children*." *Interactions*, vol. 24, no. 1–2, 2015, pp. 57–67.

Dore, Florence. "The Rock Novel and Jonathan Lethem's *The Fortress of Solitude*." *Nonsite.org*, no. 8, 2013.

Eco, Umberto. "The Myth of Superman." *Diacritics*, vol. 2, no. 1, 1972, pp. 14–22.

Gavaler, C. "The Anti-Superhero in Literary Fiction." *Image & Narrative*, vol. 17, no. 3, 2016, pp. 32–45.

Gavaler, C. "The Imperial Superhero." *Political Science and Politics*, vol. 47, no. 1, 2014, pp. 108–11.

Godbey, Matt. "Gentrification, Authenticity and White Middle-Class Identity in Jonathan Lethem's *The Fortress of Solitude*." *Arizona Quarterly*, vol. 64, no. 1, 2008, pp. 131–51.

Grossman, Austin. *Soon I Will Be Invincible*. Vintage, 2007.

Harris, Kolton. *Flying in Place: Black Superheroes and Their Origin Stories*. Connecticut College, Honour's Dissertation, 2014.

Heffernan, Teresa. "Apocalyptic Narratives: The Nation in Salman Rushdie's *Midnight's Children*." *Twentieth Century Literature*, vol. 46, no. 4, 2000, pp. 470–91.

Jameson, Fredric. "On Magic Realism in Film." *Critical Enquiry*, vol. 12, no. 2, 1986, pp. 301–25.

Kortenaar, Neil. "Salman Rushdie's Magic Realism and the Return of Inescapable Romance." *University of Toronto Quarterly*, vol. 71, no. 3, 2002, pp. 765–85.

Lethem, Jonathan. *The Fortress of Solitude*. Doubleday, 2003.

Manzo, Kerry. "Making the Invisible Visible: Privilege, Shame and Guilt in *Midnight's Children*." *South Asian Review*, vol. 35, no. 1, 2014, pp. 169–85.

Mayer, Robert. *Superfolks*. Dial Press, 1977.

Millar, Mark. *Kick-Ass*. Icon Comics. 2008–10.

Millar, Mark, and Steven McNiven. *Old Man Logan*. Marvel Comics, 2008–09.

Miller, Frank. *The Dark Knight Returns*. DC Comics, 1986.

Moore, Alan. *Watchmen*. DC Comics, 1986–87.

Moore, Perry. *Hero*. Hyperion Books, 2007.

Moretti, Franco. *The Way of the World: The Bildungsroman in European Culture*. Verso, 1987.

Nama, Adilfu. "Color Them Black." *The Superhero Reader*, edited by Chris Hatifield et al., University Press of Mississippi, 2013, pp. 252–68.

Pynchon, Thomas. *Gravity's Rainbow*. Viking, 1973.

Rosenberg, Robin S. "Our Fascination with Superheroes." *Our Superheros, Ourselves*, edited by Robin S. Rosenberg, Oxford University Press, 2013, pp. 3–18.

Rushdie, Salman. *Midnight's Children*. Jonathan Cape, 1981.

Sharma, Devika. "The Color of Prison: Shared Legacies in Walter Mosley's *The Man in My Basement* and Jonathan Lethem's *The Fortress of Solitude*." *Callaloo*, vol. 37, no. 3, 2014, pp. 662–75.

Schwartz, David J. *Superpowers*. Broadway Books, 2008.

Scott, Anna. "Superpower vs. Supernatural: Black Superheroes and the Quest for a Mutant Reality." *Journal of Visual Culture*, vol. 5, no. 3, 2006, pp. 295–314.

Waid, Mark, and Alex Ross. *Kingdom Come*. DC Comics, 1996.

Way, Gerald. *The Umbrella Academy*. Dark Horse Comics, 2007–13.

Chapter 5

AFRICAN AMERICAN VIEWERS WATCHING *BLACK PANTHER*

The Power of Representation

SHEENA C. HOWARD

INTRODUCTION

There was a lot of excitement for the film *Black Panther* when plans for its production were announced in 2014. The film was released in the United States during Black History Month in 2018. However, early excitement versus the actual execution of the plot, storyline, and performance of the film as it relates to audiences can be drastically different. After its release, the film received largely positive reviews, particularly from African American reviewers and movie-goers, inspiring people to have critical conversations around race and social justice (see Tompkins). This chapter takes these critical conversations as its central inquiry and draws on focus-group research conducted shortly after the film's release to engage with the impact of the film's reception on the young adult African American audience in particular.[1] By employing uses and gratifications theory in conjunction with this research, this chapter offers a unique insight into how the runaway success of a Black-led superhero blockbuster has influenced the shaping of Black self-concepts among adolescent viewers. The first section of this chapter will contextualize the comic book history of Black Panther and discuss, historically, how the character directly ties into political and social issues in the comics industry as well as society. This structure will give the reader a better sense of why there was much early excitement for the film, while detailing some of the aspects that propelled the stratospheric success of the film, particularly as it relates to the Black community. Thus, the reader will be able to contextualize the importance of research around the various aspects of the film's story, characters, and plotline as well as the film's special impact on Black audiences.

BLACK PANTHER: THE CHARACTER

The silver screen debut of Black Panther was accompanied by great fanfare. Joseph Tompkins compendiously notes how the "film stands, quite ceremoniously, as a film of many firsts—the first 'black blockbuster,' the first Marvel film to feature a Black superhero [in a title role], Black director and mostly Black cast, [and] the first film to get a studio-funded Oscars 2019 campaign," ("Woke Hollywood"). Tompkins goes further, observing that *Black Panther* has been deemed a watershed moment in the cultural history of African American people, describing it as "a radical and revolutionary cinematic breakthrough whose commercial success bodes well not only for the Walt Disney Company, its corporate proprietor, but the Black community as a whole" ("Woke Hollywood"). But how is the modern-day film *Black Panther* situated within the history of Black Panther the comic book character?

Black Panther is considered the first Black superhero in mainstream comics; however, Black Panther's publication history is spotty, at best. The character was featured in *Jungle Action*, issues 5 through 24, in two self-contained, multichapter stories, "Panther's Rage" and "Panther vs. the Klan," between November 1973 and November 1976. After this appearance, the character received his first solo series; *Black Panther* volume 1, by Jack Kirby, that ran a mere fifteen issues from 1977 to 1979. The Black Panther then appeared in two miniseries, *Black Panther: Cry the Accursed Country!* (1988), written by Peter Gillis with art by Denys Cowan, and *Panther's Prey* (1990), written by Gene Colan with art by Dwayne Turner. The series that defined the character for modern readers was *Black Panther* volume 3, written in 1998 by comics pioneer, Christopher Priest, and with art by Mark Texeira.

Priest's writing of Black Panther served as the inspiration for Marvel Studios' *Black Panther* film (Riesman 71). He is the first Black writer to work full-time at either Marvel or DC, starting with his first regular writing job back in 1983 (71). Ta-Nehisi Coates, who wrote *Black Panther* for Marvel Comics from 2016 until 2021, has opined that Priest "had the classic run on Black Panther, period" (quoted. in Riesman 72). Coates reflects that "People had not put as much thought into who and what Black Panther was before Christopher started writing the book. . . . While previously, the panther had been written as a superhero, [Priest] thought that Black Panther was a *king*" (72). Abraham Riesman suggests that it is "doubtful there'd even be a movie about him today if not for Priest's refurbishing" (72).

Priest transformed T'Challa, the king of the African nation Wakanda, into one of the most powerful and dangerous characters in the Marvel Universe (Howard 50). Because Marvel struggled with racialized market fears, Priest's run of the comic included a white American government agent, Everett K. Ross, as a sidekick to interpolate T'Challa. The opening narrative arc of Priest's 1998 *Black Panther* series was called "The Client." "The Client" laid out a mystery about a murder in Brooklyn, while a refugee crisis threatened Wakanda's borders. Black Panther had to solve the murder, prevent a civil war, and ultimately steal the Devil's soul in order to prevail (Howard 101). Priest blended humor, politics, and economics into his run of *Black Panther*, laying the foundation for Marvel's cinematic adaptation.

In 2005, Reginald Hudlin opened up his run of the series with "Who Is the Black Panther?" Hudlin's version of Black Panther refused to capitulate to racialized notions of the comics market. As such, Wakanda is depicted as an extraordinary nation with the ability to defend itself. Embedded in Hudlin's narrative is a utopian Black nationalism and a proto-Afrofuturism (Howard 101). Hudlin introduces the reader to the technological advancements of Wakanda, while digging into colonization through a Black reimaging of oppression. The series allows the reader to grapple with what the continent of Africa would have been like without five hundred years of colonialism, slavery, and foreign interference. As expected, Hudlin's run of Black Panther faced blowback from white male readers; however, the series was popular (see Burroughs 55).

BLACK PANTHER: THE MOVIE

Understanding the publication history of Black Panther allows us to contextualize why a film production headlined by the character may have been fraught. The importance of the film and its fan anticipation is redoubled in this light. It fell on director Ryan Coogler to deliver a storyline and plot that would live up to the expectations and hype. Coogler remarked of this that "I think the pressure is kind of always going to be there. I've had a chance to make three feature films, each one of them had its own very specific type of pressure. In the process of it, it feels insurmountable each time" (quoted. in Williams).

The early prescreenings of the film received rave reviews and a grassroots fundraising endeavor to subsidize private screenings of *Black Panther* for kids across the country began ("Woke Hollywood"): "Dubbed the #BlackPanther-Challenge, this campaign emerged as the brainchild of Fredrick Joseph, a New York City marketing consultant who was inspired by *Black Panther's* 'positive Black representations' to start a GoFundMe drive in order to buy tickets for the Boys and Girls Club of Harlem" ("Woke Hollywood"). The fund received many donations, including donations from high-profile celebrities and politicians such as Chelsea Clinton, Ellen DeGeneres, and J. J. Abrams. Tompkins notes that "'the trend went viral' [and] [s]oon donations were flowing into more than five hundred similar GoFundMe campaigns across the country, raising a total of $775,000" ("Woke Hollywood"). In addition, student groups, sports teams, teachers, businesses, and Hollywood stars were all organizing their own sponsored screenings of the film. The point, as Octavia Spencer pointed out on Instagram right before buying out a theater in Mississippi, was "to ensure that all our brown children can see themselves as a superhero" ("Woke Hollywood"). The verdict was out; Black audiences were viewing the film as positive. The film thus engaged with image activism, presenting fresh, new, and uplifting imagery of the Black community. These acts of charity and activism in real life largely mirrored the call to action that the film itself advocated for. Tompkins sums this up well, noting that "the film ends with a call for action when the hero T'Challa (played by Chadwick Boseman) makes his way to Oakland with his sister to perform 'outreach' for poor Black kids" ("Woke Hollywood"). Likewise, the postcredits scene also serves as an onscreen mirror to the film's inspired advocacy when T'Challa announces to the United Nations that Wakanda will share its wealth. Not only did the film feel good, but it motivated people to act. That is, "the feel-good theme of Black benefaction parallels the philanthropic discourse of the #BlackPantherChallenge" ("Woke Hollywood").

Ultimately, this study provides insight into the specific impact of the film on African American young adult viewers around concepts related to social stereotypes, self-concept, and Black audience perceptions of representation.

MEDIA USE AND YOUNG ADULT AUDIENCES

Emerging scholarship suggests the media plays a prominent role in shaping self-conceptions, both by supplying ideals to internalize (for instance, the thin ideal) and by providing feedback about the importance of one's social group, values, or status (Ward 284). Indeed, media use is quite high during adolescence, comprising 7.5 hours of each day and so offering an abundance of materials for identity construction (Davies and Gentile). L. Monique Ward has observed that for marginalized groups, in particular, mainstream media can be seen to offer critical insight into how the world at large views their group, its members, and their contributions (284).

YOUNG ADULT AUDIENCES, SELF-CONCEPT, AND STEREOTYPES

This research seeks to explore (1) what motivated African American young adults to view the film; (2) what impacts, if any, the film had on self-concept; and (3) other uses/gratifications the film fulfilled as it relates to the African American young adult population. The researcher expected topics around

Black self-concept and in-group dynamics to be readily apparent throughout the focus-group research due to the content and nature of the film. As such, this brief section touches on current research findings around self-concept stereotypes and minority audiences.

Research has found correlations between exposure to racial stereotypes in media and the development of negative attitudes towards the out-group (see Piotrowski 47; Fujioka 52). In addition, in *Stereotypes in the Media: So What?*, Bradley Gorham suggests that racial stereotypes in the media contribute to racial myths, which are sustained via repeated exposure. As a result, these myths inform how individuals process subsequent information about the group or individual that is stereotyped (229). Research also shows that Black children exhibit a preference for Black characters and television series (see Gorham 230; Adams-Bass et al., 367). These findings are significant, as this chapter examines young adult African American responses to a film that consists of predominantly Black characters and cast members.

Television has been considered an influential source of information that plays a role in constructing viewers' social reality (see Howard and Lewis, 2012). Since television conveys "simulations of everyday situations," and since it shares similar characteristics of real-life events (e.g., sound and sight), vicarious experience via television may become a part of our social experience and serve as a basis for social judgments such as racial attitudes and ethnic stereotypes (Fujioka 52). Previous research with adults and youth has examined the relationship between Black media representation and racial identity (see Gorham 229; Gordon 245; Ward 284). Youth-oriented research has established a connection among self-esteem, body image, and media (Gordon 245; Ward 284). As such, it is expected that the focus-group sessions conducted in this study will touch on all or some of these aforementioned areas of self-concept.

There is a concern that Black American youth may accept negative media stereotypes of Black people as valid, resulting in a negative impact on identity and self-esteem. Thus, this study provides a space to explore how positive representation potentially reflects a positive sense of self and community. In addition, research has shown that many other factors influence the media viewing habits of Black youth, including but not limited to knowledge of Black history and racial socialization.

This study adds to the existing body of literature by ascertaining specific uses and gratifications around African American young adult viewership and the film *Black Panther*, with consideration given to the film's influence on self-concept. Practitioners, researchers, and filmmakers can use this data to gain insight into the types of mass-mediated images that motivate African American young adult audiences and positively impact them, in addition to the types of imagery that illicit enjoyment for this demographic.

THEORETICAL FRAMEWORK: USES AND GRATIFICATIONS THEORY

This study employs uses and gratifications theory, which views the audience as purposive, goal-oriented, and motivated in their use of the media to meet certain needs and to achieve certain goals. For this study, all focus-group participants saw the film more than once, making the uses and gratifications they received from the film of particular interest to the researcher. Based on the literature review, there is an interplay between self-concept, racial attitudes, self-esteem, and media usage. Therefore, this study employs a uses and gratifications theoretical framework, with a specific line of inquiry around self-concept, personal association with characters, and social stereotypes.

Study Objectives

The current research is designed to explore the numerous ways in which African American young adult audiences use the media, specifically the movie *Black Panther*, to satisfy certain needs, achieve certain goals, and challenge social stereotypes around race and ethnicity. Specifically, this study's objectives are to discover:

1. In what ways do African American young adult viewing audiences relate to the characters in the movie *Black Panther*?

2. In what ways, if any, does the movie *Black Panther* influence the self-concept of the African American young adult viewing audience?

3. What function(s) (or other use) does the movie *Black Panther* serve in the lives of African American young adult viewers?

Method

Two focus groups were established in the greater Philadelphia, Pennsylvania, area to collect data for this study. Five self-identified African American individuals participated in session 1, and six self-identified African American individuals participated in session 2. Session 1 consisted of four women and one man. Session 2 consisted of four women and two men. These demographics provided valuable insight into the Black female audience. Both quantitative and qualitative researchers have acknowledged that focus groups provide breadth of scope and depth of opinions to any particular research topic (see Krueger and Casey 2009). Therefore, focus-group interviews were an appropriate way to explore the study's objectives.

The participants filled out a demographic questionnaire, where all participants noted that they saw *Black Panther* at least once. More than half of the participants had seen the film three times or more prior to the study. This was preferred, as the study sought to uncover the motivations behind the participants repeated viewership of the film through a uses and gratifications approach. In addition, participants were all young adults, ranging from eighteen to twenty-one years old.

After filling out the brief questionnaire, the participants watched the movie, and then engaged in a facilitated discussion led by the researcher. Discussion questions specifically addressed self-concept and the participants' perception of representation in the film, with a focus on social stereotypes around race and ethnicity. Data along the lines of gender was expected due to the heavy female participation in the study and the gendered dynamics throughout the film—including an all-female warrior squad (the "Dora Milaje" led by Danai Gurira's Okoye).

In order to adhere to the ethical requirements for social scientific inquiry using human participants, the researcher used consent forms that allowed participants full permission not to answer questions that made them uncomfortable. The participants were granted full anonymity in all published reports and they were reminded that they could withdraw from the discussion at any point in time. Each session was audio-taped and conducted by the researcher who transcribed details of the focus group sessions. In order to ensure the participants' privacy and confidentiality, subjects were given aliases.

Qualitative Line of Inquiry

The lines of questioning in each of the two sessions were designed to take a subjective approach in addressing the three objectives previously outlined. This approach allows for dialogue on issues within and across the African American community in order to create a baseline of audience research that promotes further study on the impact of representation on Black young adult audiences (Howard and Lewis 124).

The first line of questioning regarded the participants' feelings of personal relationship to the characters. The second line of questioning inquired about the participants' observations around the ideologies depicted in the film, specifically in relation to oppression and racism. The third line of questioning addressed perceptions and/or assessment of social issues within the film. Specifically, the participants' perceptions of what they believe the film conveys about race, gender, and society. Finally, the participants were asked if there was anything they would have liked to add that they did not get a chance to discuss during the session.

Thematic Analysis

The transcribed conversations from each session were coded using thematic analysis (see Boyatzis 1998). Thematic analysis facilitates identifying, analyzing, and reporting patterns (themes) within data (Braun and Clarke 2006). Beyond categorizing and describing data, thematic analysis provides a more comprehensive and nuanced account of meticulous themes, or a group of themes, within the data. Specifically, this might relate to a specific question or area of interest within the data (which this research seeks to explicate) or to a particular "latent" theme across the whole or majority of the data set (Braun and Clarke).

Results

Themes emerged in the analysis of participants' responses. Themes were extracted by coding and collating initial codes examined through the transcription of the data, then allocating said codes to larger themes. The themes that emerged from the data, include: (a) multiplicity of Blackness (including a varied representation of Blackness); (b) messages of empowerment (including both community and self-empowerment); and (c) a healthy sense of self (including representations of pride and confidence).

Uses and Gratifications theory allows scholars to reveal what motivates people to use certain media in their daily life. These themes help illuminate the uses and gratifications associated with African American young adult audiences' viewership of *Black Panther* as well as their motivations for originally seeing the film in the first place, then repeatedly viewing the movie thereafter. This is important because of the large female viewing audience, and the large Black viewing audience—both outside of the norm for a superhero movie. According to the box office tracking company ComScore and Screen Engine, a higher percentage of women attended *Black Panther*'s opening weekend ("Theatrical"). Women represented 45 percent of the film's audience, which is less than the average moviegoing population but more than the typical female turnout for a superhero movie. The average superhero movie (many of which are led by mostly male characters) draws a 62 percent male audience, though *Black Panther* and *Wonder Woman* (2017) have unsettled that trend (Huddleston Jr.). In addition, in the US, 37 percent of the movie's overall audience was African American, which is well above the norm where the average movie audience is about 15 percent African American (Huddleston Jr.). Therefore, this study can shed light on the African American and female audiences' motivations to see *Black Panther*, outside of the simplistic notion that it featured a predominantly Black cast and a Black superhero. The findings of this research provide insight into the influence of media representation on Black self-concept, while also addressing ideas of community and the relationship between representation and movie-going motivation as it relates to African American young adult audiences and media images.

THEMES

Theme A: Multiplicity of Blackness (Including a Varied Representation of Blackness)

One of the most pervasive and prevalent themes to emerge was how *Black Panther* reflects the multiplicity of the Black experience (including ideologies, ethnicities, and family upbringing). This theme represents participants' responses around the ways in which the movie provided a nuanced representation of the Black community, as well as the ways the film challenged dominant stereotypes around race, ethnicity, and gender. This varied representation of Blackness allowed participants the ability to relate to the nuance of the characters in the film, which breaks away from the one-dimensional iconography historically presented in film. This theme addresses the first research question; *In what ways do African American young adult viewing audiences relate to the characters in the movie* Black Panther? Some of the responses reflected a clear appreciation for the representation of diverse family upbringing. A number of respondents reflected on the differences between T'Challa (Chadwick Boseman) and Killmonger (Michael B. Jordan). Chase noted, "You have one man growing up with his father, having his father guide him. Then you have the other one growing up without his father, and not knowing where he came from." Another participant, Brent, also related to Killmonger along the lines of familial upbringing. Brent said,

> I can relate to him [Killmonger], too, a little bit because how he learns as he goes along. So, like I said, I came from a single parent home, but my mom did a great job. But she had other things to do, so I had to learn a lot of stuff as I went along. So that's one thing I could relate to him.

Brent continued, "I didn't seek no revenge or nothing like that, but it was like . . . growing up I came from a single parent home. So, my pop wasn't really there. You felt his pain and his perspective." Participants unanimously agreed that they could understand, if not relate to, the ideologies of both Killmonger and T'Challa. They empathized with Killmonger, due to his familial upbringing, but they did not agree with his brutal revenge and violent tactics. Abby stated:

> I understand Killmonger. I think he's for his people just like T'Challa is, but he knows what they have and what they're capable of and that it can help the rest of the world. And that was his intent. He probably didn't go about it the perfect way, but that was his intent. And I understand T'Challa protecting what they have.

In addition to a nuanced reflection of ideologies, in which participants could empathize with or relate to responses also reflected an appreciation for the ways in which the film inspired them to think more deeply about who they were in relation to their ethnicity and ancestral background. Abby stated, the film "inspired me to go deeper into that [my history] and also look elsewhere, because I'm not just only Jamaican. So yeah, it really did inspire me." Violet reiterated this notion:

> I think it also inspired me to start the dialogue about the diaspora, because of course the beef between T'Challa and Killmonger had a lot to do with him being raised in Africa, and then also him [Killmonger] being American. So, I think it also inspired, I hope a new culture of people, to have a conversation with our brothers and sisters who come from Africa, you know what I'm saying? Because I feel like there's also tension, you know what I'm saying? That movie actually depicted a real tension between African natives and the people who were born here. So, I was inspired to probably start a dialogue with people, you know what I'm saying? That know their actual ancestors and their culture, to move forward as one instead of kind of divided.

Thus, not only did the film depict the multiplicity of the Black community (African Americans, the Diaspora, and Africans) or what it means to be Black, but it also provided a catalyst for Violet to engage in conversations with Black people who are ethnically different from her. Many participants commented on the varied representations of ethnicity but also the varied ideologies and perspectives of the characters, where Blackness was not stereotyped or confined to a rigid, singular representation. The film did not just depict the toxic masculinity of Killmonger; it also depicted T'Challa, who did not represent an extreme version of Black masculinity. Abby notes, "So I'm team T'Challa because he's the protagonist of course in the movie, but like you said, I also kind of see Killmonger's perspective, because you relate to the African American standpoint of it. Like how his dad said 'We're lost.' So, I thought that part . . . You relate to that as an audience-goer, but at the same time of course, he was very radicalized, more so of an extremist."

Theme B: Messages of Empowerment (Including Both Community and Self-empowerment)

This theme represents participants' responses around how the characters, plot, and storyline inspired them to "give back" to their community. This theme also represents feelings of empowerment around their self and their community invoked by the film. This theme addresses research question 1 (*In what ways, if any, does the movie* Black Panther *influence the self-concept of the African American young adult viewing audience?*) And research question 2 (*What function[s] [or other use] does the movie* Black Panther *serve in the lives of African American young adult viewers?*)

A sense of responsibility and community was prevalent across this theme. The film seemed to inspire a sense of community in real life, but it also represented the strength of community as depicted through the Wakandan society. Violet noted, "I think that's the part that I liked the most, was the communal feel that was across just everywhere, you know what I'm saying? Because Twitter and Instagram, you're talking with people from just different parts of the world, and just seeing how everybody felt the same exact way." Chase elaborated on this point, "I mean, it sparked a whole empowerment, like Black empowerment movement."

Chad also appreciated the way that the film allowed the viewer to break free of intergenerational trauma. Chad notes that a major lesson learned from the movie was "Don't let your father's mistakes define you; it was like his son was letting his past define him, and I feel like that happens in our communities a lot because we look to our elders." This respondent appreciated the tension between T'Challa and his father as a way to show that T'Challa did not have to make the same mistakes his father did. T'Challa could choose a different direction for his life and his community, and he ultimately did choose a different path than that of his father. Participants also felt empowered by the representation of women in the film. Nola stated:

> I feel like it [the film] signified a lot about the relationship between black men and black women. I feel like a lot of times the role that black women play is just helping the black man keep himself together in general. And so I felt like that scene where she was about to kill him, her man or whatever, and then he said, "You would kill me?" And she said, "For Wakanda I would." And he literally just said, "Forget it." And that was it.

Discussants also noted an appreciation for the way in which the women in the film did not conform to stereotypical physical representations of femininity. In one scene, a bald character, Okoye, must put on a wig as a disguise in order to enter a casino. In response to this scene, Julie stated, "And the woman was talking about how she thought it was a disgrace [to put on a wig]. And I thought how comfortable that she really was with herself and how she looked. Putting on a wig was something that she didn't need. She was so comfortable with how she was against how people view how women look." Thus, the film showed that Okoye was completely confident with her bald appearance and this is something that is not traditionally represented as a hairstyle of choice for women in film. Tonya elaborated on the way in which the representation of women was a tool of empowerment:

> I also wanted to piggyback what you said about women. I like that it really . . . I don't know what word I want to use, but it kind of brings out the good in Black women because I know we're so degraded. But Black women are so degraded often. So to kind of show that they have all these strengths, these powers, and for them to be one of the main characters, I felt . . . Me personally, I felt very appreciative of it. It gave me new hope and stuff. And I felt like black women were looked at differently. Even when I go on Instagram, and I see those two characters [Okoye and Nakia (Lupita Nyong'o)], they're killing it, people are supporting them 24/7, and a lot of women are starting to rock their natural hair, and just so many different things, and just their own beauty.

Jazmine noted, "I think just seeing how Black women were the generals, and they were the leaders to protect the king. So that was just yeah. The representation for the women in the movie was spectacular."

Theme C: Healthy Sense of Self (Including Representation of Pride and Confidence)

This theme represents participants' responses around the ways in which the film inspired an emotional or personal connection to the film, such as a stronger sense of self. This theme addresses research question 3 (*What function[s] [or other use] does the movie* Black Panther *serve in the lives of young adult African American viewers?*) This theme also addresses research question 2 (*In what ways, if any, does the movie* Black Panther *influence the self-concept of the young adult African American viewing audience?*)

Participants showed an appreciation for the film's ability to instill a sense of pride as well as confidence. This notion is best represented in following exchange:

> RESEARCHER: I know you said you felt inspired, but does the film spark any sense of positive emotions after you see it? What are the positive emotions that you feel?

JOHN: I mean, as soon as I walked out the movies, I was like, "I'm the stuff." Like, move out the way. That's just how I felt.

RESEARCHER: So, you felt proud?

JOHN: Yeah, I felt so proud of the movie, especially because there were the African cultures shown, and just especially how everyone reacted to it. It was like, "Yeah, those are my people."

RESEARCHER: Anybody else?

VIOLET: Yeah, I know I completely agree, and every time I watch the movie, I always feel like I need to go do something.

Another participant, Abby, echoes this connection to a positive sense of self inspired by the movie when she states, "So yeah, it [the film] really did inspire me, and it made me proud to be Black pretty much." The participants appreciated the film's display of confidence in the characters. Dre, particularly felt a connection around the idea of confidence as a positive character trait, "I definitely like the confidence within the movie, and everybody pretty much pitches in for one major goal." As Dre explains, he connects this sense of confidence to the larger idea of Black media representation.

DRE: And even with Killmonger, yeah, it's negative. But his confidence is remarkable.

RESEARCHER: Okay.

DRE: So even though it wasn't in the best light, he [Killmonger] believes in himself and he's very sure of himself. And most of the time you don't really see that all the time with us. We tend to . . . whenever we boast about whatever we're proud of it tends to be looked at as you're better than that person. But in reality, we don't ever get the chance to really express that.

RESEARCHER: Okay.

DRE: It was like even though he was the enemy . . . he was still likable. And people appreciated his confidence.

RESEARCHER: You could still relate to him and understand where he was coming from?

DRE: I feel like representation of African Americans who are powerful and have that is necessary, especially for younger kids to see that it's possible to do stuff. So, I think it was cool to have the aspect of Killmonger from Oakland and then Africa, because there are a lot of African Americans in poverty, and there are also a lot of African Americans who have wealth.

Later in the session Dre connected back to this sense of confidence as it relates to African American history:

Being in slavery, being in bondage, having to be enslaved. It was a powerful thing, and that just goes back to his confidence. Even at the end he [Killmonger] realizes everything, he realizes he wrong . . . or whatever, but that was the one moment where him and T'Challa could connect. . . . So that was powerful. I feel like I left inspired, wanting to learn more.

DISCUSSION/CONCLUSIONS

As demonstrated throughout this chapter, African American young adult responses to *Black Panther* are diverse. Uses and gratifications theory provides a strong framework to explain how this particular film functioned in the lives of a sample of African American young adult viewers by eliciting feelings of empowerment, pride, and confidence. Participants also enjoyed the film's varied depictions of Blackness, including the representation of the continent of Africa and the varied experiences of Black Americans. For theme (a) *Multiplicity of Blackness*, participants commented on how the film included characters with varied familial upbringings, such as Killmonger, who was raised by a single father, and T'Challa who was raised by both parents. In this way, the film challenged dominant and often negative stereotypes of the Black community by showing nuanced experiences of Black people. Participants unanimously agreed that the film was a healthy and positive representation of Black people, including the depiction of Africa. Participants also felt as though the representation of Black women challenged dominant narratives of Black beauty. Particularly, the confidence of the bald character Okoye, who was a strong female warrior.

Due to the implementation of an interpretive research design, this chapter provides a baseline of knowledge about a sample of African American young adult viewers on Black media presentation, media as it relates to a healthy sense of self, and how film can inspire a call to action in a minority community. In addition, this study sheds light on the motivations of the African American population watching this film multiple times, allowing the researcher to gain insight into the phenomena of a large Black and female viewing audience of a superhero movie.

It is apparent from this study that *Black Panther* cannot simply be dismissed as just another superhero movie. The film, as indicated by the research participants and its box office success, represents an iconic cultural moment in film history. Based on the comments of the participants, depictions of the Black experience in the film are refreshing and long overdue.

A few participants stated that the film inspired them to act or "do something" as it relates to giving back to their community and challenging themselves to strive for more. The participants' responses indicated an appreciation for the varied ideologies depicted in the film through the main characters Killmonger and T'Challa. The viewers were also very aware of the toxic masculinity depicted through Killmonger, but they appreciated the film's sense of connection to the nuanced perspectives of the Black community.

The film did not seem to simply depict characters that were marketable to a mainstream audience. In addition, it did not shy away from dealing with intergenerational trauma, racism, and the world's racialized history. As such, critiques that the film was white-washed or inauthentic did not manifest in any of the data. Thus, producers and writers of the film largely rejected many stereotypes regarding ethnicity, gender, gender presentation, and gender roles. Consequently, this sample of African American young adult viewers remained interested and committed to the film, as all participants saw the film more than once. Most viewers in this sample saw the film three or more times before participating in this study. Participants shared that the film appealed to aspects of their identity, such as inspiring them to connect to or learn more about their ancestral background. Participants expressed that the film is reflective of their personal experiences and that they could relate to situations that specific characters encountered, thus motivating this audience to watch the film and appreciate what it represented. This finding is similar to other Black viewing audience research data (see Howard and Lewis 122). Overall, the film provided a sense of empowerment and pride across the Black community, which were threaded through all three themes that emerged from the dataset. Finally, this research illuminates the notion that young Black adults positively benefit from media that reimagines the future and past from a position of power, not solely from the dominant standpoint of Black oppression or dominance. Media content that challenges stereotypical narratives of Africans and African Americans leads young Black viewers to engage more with their community, think deeply in terms of solidarity, and reflect positively on their own race.

FUTURE RESEARCH

First, the researcher would have liked a larger sample of participants upon which to draw conclusions. This chapter is not generalizable beyond the sample studied. Further research is needed with larger and more diverse samples of Black young adult viewers. Also, future research adjusting for a range of figures from which to categorize participants, such as having a background of low income, middle class, or upper middle class would be beneficial. The participants self-identified as Black or African American, which was not based on any predetermined categorizations of numerical value. Thus, the researcher has no way of determining if the participants were mixed race or from various Black ethnicities. Future studies should clarify class categories and set out to assess a range of social classes to more accurately assess Black young adult television viewing audiences. Listening to the voices of people who have been historically misrepresented in US popular culture has many implications. For example, the data did reveal possible "tension" or conflict between the experiences and perspectives of Black American and African peoples. Respondents acknowledged that this "tension" as a variable might influence cross-cultural communication, either positively or negatively. This is an area which future research should explore. The degree to which varied experiences across the Black diaspora is addressed in media programming would enhance cross-cultural communication, self-concept and esteem, as well as the production of media content.

Note

1. For the purpose of this study, Black and African American are used interchangeably. These terms denote Black people in America who are descendants of enslaved Africans. Where the researcher refers to Black people from Africa, the terminology used is African or a particular ethnicity, such as Ethiopian or Nigerian.

Works Cited

Adams-Bass, Valerie N. et al., "Measuring the Meaning of Black Media Stereotypes and Their Relationship to the Racial Identity, Black History Knowledge, and Racial Socialization of African American Youth." *Journal of Black Studies*, vol. 45, no. 5, 2014, p. 367.

Boyatzis, Richard E. *Transforming Qualitative Information: Thematic Analysis and Code Development*. Sage, 1998.

Braun, Virginia, and Victoria Clarke. "Using Thematic Analysis in Psychology." *Qualitative Research in Psychology*, vol. 3, no. 2, 2006, pp. 77–101.

Burroughs, Todd Steven. "Black Panther, Black Writers, White Audience: Christopher Priest and/vs. Reginald Hudlin." *Fire!!!*, vol. 4, no. 2, 2015, pp. 55–93.

Colan, Gene. *Panther's Prey*. no. 1, Marvel, Sept. 1990.

Davies, John J., and Douglas A. Gentile. "Responses to Children's Media Use in Families with and without Siblings: A Family Development Perspective." *Family Relations*, vol. 61, no. 3, 2012, pp. 410–25.

Fujioka, Yuki. "Television Portrayals and African-American Stereotypes: Examination of Television Effects When Direct Contacts Is Lacking." *Journalism & Mass Communication Quarterly*, vol. 76, no. 1, 1999, pp. 52–75.

Gillis, Peter. *Black Panther: Cry the Accursed Country!*, no. 1, Marvel, 1 July 1988.

Gordon, Maya K. "Media Contributions to African American Girls' Focus on Beauty and Appearance: Exploring the Consequences of Sexual Objectification." *Psychology of Women Quarterly*, vol. 32, no. 3, pp. 245–56.

Gorham, Bradley. "Stereotypes in the Media: So What?" *Howard Journal of Communication*, vol. 10, no. 4, 1999, pp. 229–47.

Howard, Sheena and Michelle Lewis. "African American Lesbians Watching the L Word." *Sexual Minority Research in the New Millennium*, edited by Todd G. Morrison, Nova Science Publishers, 2013, pp. 107–25.

Howard, Sheena C. *Encyclopedia of Black Comics*. 1st ed., Fulcrum Publishing, 2017.

Huddleston, Tom, Jr. "An Especially Diverse Audience Lifted 'Black Panther' to Record Box Office Heights." *Fortune*, 22 Feb. 2018, fortune.com/2018/02/21/black-panther-record-box-office-diverse-audience/.

Kirby, Jack. "Black Panther," vol. 1, Marvel, 5 July 1977–79.

Krueger, Richard A. and Mary Anne Casey. *Focus Groups: A Practical Guide for Applied Research*. Sage, 2009.

Piotrowski, Jessica Taylor. "Adolescents, Race, and Media: Commentary on Adams and Stevenson." *Racial Stereotyping and Child Development*, edited by Diana T. Slaughter-Defoe, Karger, 2012, pp. 47–51.

Priest, Christopher. *Black Panther*, vol. 3, Marvel, 1998.

Riesman, Abraham. "The Man Who Made the Black Panther Cool: Christopher Priest Broke the Color Line at Marvel and Reinvented a Classic Character. Why Was He Nearly Written out of Comics History?" *New York*, vol. 51, no. 2, Jan. 2018, pp. 70–73.

Theatrical Market Statistics. Motion Picture Association of America, 2016, www.mpaa.org/wp-content/uploads/2017/03/MPAA-Theatrical-Market-Statistics-2016_Final-1.pdf.

Thomas, Roy. "Jungle Action." *The Black Panther*, no. 5–24, Marvel, 5 July 1972.

Tompkins, Joseph. "Woke Hollywood? The Marketing of Black Panther." *CounterPunch.org*, 28 Mar. 2018, www.counterpunch.org/2018/03/30/woke-hollywood-the-marketing-of-black-panther/.

Ward, L. Monique. "Wading through the Stereotypes: Positive and Negative Associations between Media Use and Black Adolescents' Conceptions of Self." *Developmental Psychology*, vol. 40, no. 2, 2004, pp. 284–94.

Williams, Tommy. "Ryan Coogler Talks about the Pressures of Making BLACK PANTHER 2." *GeekTyrant*, 7 Nov. 2018, geektyrant.com/news/ryan-coogler-talks-about-the-pressures-of-making-black-panther-2.

Section 2

BEYOND COMIC BOOKS

Introduction

BEYOND COMIC BOOKS

IAN GORDON

From the moment that comics became a highly commercial form, they have existed off the page. Scholars like Roger Sabin (2003) and Christina Meyer (2019) have shown that two important nineteenth-century forerunners, Ally Sloper in the UK and the Yellow Kid in the US, had numerous incarnations in a variety of goods and services. Likewise, within three years of his first appearance in *Action Comics* 1 (June 1938), Superman appeared in comic strips, a radio serial, in animated form and in licensed toys and clothing for children (Gordon 2017). That comics characters, and superheroes in particular, transcend comic books is nothing new or novel. Shawna Kidman has noted that the comic book well has been historically tapped in this way many times (2019). She suggests, however, that unlike other commonplace streams of adaptation and licensing (book to film, for example), "the aggressive, consistent, and particular way in which comic books extend into other media texts and cultural goods is unique" (2). Nowhere is this rapacious tendency seen more than with the medium's most culturally synonymous content—the superhero. That said, the history and character of the strategies that attend this development remain somewhat understudied. As such, this section traces some of the ways that superheroes have come to exist beyond the page with some close examination of the way characters move from page to screen, the function of intellectual property (IP) rights in broadening the range and type of ways that superheroes are marketed to audiences, and the ways that audiences respond.

Superman had set the superhero ball rolling, and what followed for the Man of Tomorrow, rather appropriately for the moniker, was the kind of transmedia franchising that is now matter-of-course to modern audiences. The abundant "array of goods and services featuring Superman meant that the character was understood in part through acts of consumption" (Gordon 144) and this has become true of a great number of superhero characters since. What has changed are the qualities of this consumption and specifically its calculated coordination leading into the now aggressive expansion observed by Kidman. Some of this type of coordination was once more presaged by Superman, whose familiar radio serial opening carried over to his 1952 television series *The Adventures of Superman*. Superheroes more broadly, however, would experience a kind of cultural lacuna as the 1950s wore on (see Baker), and when their time came again in the 1960s there was a sense of needing to cash in before the bubble burst once more. The perceived fragility of the comics market informed, if not perhaps a more scattergun approach to rights and licensing, certainly a more frantic one that envisioned greater life for its characters off the page. This was certainly Stan Lee's and Martin Goodman's ambition at Marvel. A series of ads in *Variety* in the 1970s promised the Marvel superheroes "potential for outrageous stardom." The imperative to profit from these characters through as many revenue streams as possible seemed to dismiss any misgivings about curation.

Ideas around synergy and the more deliberated and targeted use of these superhero characters off the page would come more to the fore as the corporate structure of the United States shifted, its copyright laws were updated, and the creators of these characters challenged the work-for-hire practices that denied them ownership or often even recognition for their works (see Adams). Superheroes were someone's property, and with property comes stewardship. If not the property of their creators, they were the IP of Marvel and DC or the conglomerates that would acquire them. As notions of stewardship took hold, a more coordinated approach to licensing tentatively emerged with signs of this evident in Marvel's toy licensing in the 1980s. The *Secret Wars* event series, for example, was part of a deal with Mattel to launch a new toy line (see Bainbridge). The development of specialty comics stores, fan networks, and convention circuits during this period also marked the more coordinated consumption of superheroes from the bottom-up, paving the way for greater fan/industry interaction and eventually even laying the groundwork for the off-brand DIY superheroes discussed here by Teiwes.

A 1996 bankruptcy would waylay Marvel's progress on the coordinated dispersal of its superheroes off-page as its rights and licenses became the focal point of tumultuous legal proceedings. Just a few years prior, however, their "distinguished competition" DC comics had become a subsidiary of a new conglomerate, Time-Warner, whose horizontally integrated structure supported greater curation and coordination of its superheroes' multimedia circulation. An Emmy nomination for *Superman: The Animated Series*, produced by Warner Bros. and broadcast on their WB television network, was illustrative of this model's success and can be seen to reinforce Kidman's observation of how shifts in the media industry "enabled the resurrection of comics in quality media of the 1990s" (13). This resurrection would accrue to the carefully plotted multimedia ventures of the DC superheroes as they were selectively deployed under

"Bat-embargoes" and "no tights, no flights" rules. The resurrection (particularly in animation) would even, as Liam Burke details, precipitate the coalescence of the Marvel Cinematic Universe, which has since become the standard-bearer of coordinated superhero adventures beyond comic books ("Sowing the Seeds"). What follows in this section, then, casts light on the trajectory of superheroes as near-constant comic book émigrés with long transmedia histories. In particular, the chapters in this section enrich a contemporary scholarly discussion of how the extra-comic book affairs of superheroes have shaped not only our cultural engagement with them as archetypes but have, at the same time, charted the story of our continually concentrated mediascape as well.

Works Cited

Burke, Liam. "Sowing the Seeds: How 1990s Marvel Animation Facilitated Today's Cinematic Universe." *Marvel Comics into Film: Essays on Adaptations since the 1940s.* McEniry et al., (Eds.) McFarland, 2016. 106–17.

Gordon, Ian. *Superman: The Persistence of an American Icon.* Rutgers University Press, 2017.

Kidman, Shawna. *Comic Books Incorporated: How the Business of Comics Became the Business of Hollywood.* University of California Press, 2019.

Meyer, Christina. *Producing Mass Entertainment: The Secret Life of the Yellow Kid.* Ohio State University Press, 2019.

Sabin, Roger. "Ally Sloper: The First Comics Superstar?" *Image and Narrative,* no. 7, 2003.

Chapter 6

ANIMATING SUB-MARINER AND AQUAMAN

Generational Taste and the Moral Panic of the 1968 Television Season

DJOYMI BAKER

In the 1960s, moral panic about violent superheroes extended beyond comics into television. The controversy came to a head in 1968, when superheroes became one of the dominant genres in the children's Saturday morning animation slot on US television. The objections of commentators famously focused on violent content and perceived negative impact upon young viewers. This chapter uses the case studies of the two aquatic superheroes Namor the Sub-Mariner and Aquaman—who appeared in the syndicated series *Marvel Super Heroes* (1966) and *The Superman/Aquaman Hour of Adventure* on CBS (1967–68) respectively—to argue that underlying the calls to rein in superhero shows was a sharp divide in generational taste around genre and aesthetics, a split strongly informed by adult nostalgia.

In the 1960s, the superhero was frequently singled out as the epitome of bad children's television. The roots of the furore could be found a decade earlier in Frederic Wertham's infamous *Seduction of the Innocent* of 1954, which decried the negative influence of violent superhero comics upon the young (Higgins 6–10; Wertham 359).[1] Beyond comic books, Wertham was hopeful about the potential of television but noted that the children's programs most favored by parents were being axed, while violent shows continued (369, 383). A Senate Subcommittee on Juvenile Delinquency was held in 1954 and looked at comics and television as contributing factors (Leach). The negative publicity led to the foundation of the Comics Code Authority that year (Bongco 2–4), while television tried to appease the critics by adding what it argued were semieducational elements to contentious programs (Art 155). It was also in 1954 that *TV Guide* noted comic books were increasingly being adapted to television, though their commentary conflated comic strips and comic books, with the former supplying the bulk of adaptations ("Straight from the Drawing Board" 16–17).

Either way, Wertham was concerned by this development, writing: "Television has taken the worst out of comic books, from sadism to Superman . . . The greatest obstacle to the future of good television for children is comic books and the comic-book culture in which we force children to live" (381, 383). By 1961, the new chairman of the Federal Communications Commission (FCC), Newton Minow, famously declared that television was "a vast wasteland" and demanded better programs for children (Minow and MaLay 188, 189–91, 195).

The antiviolence sentiments of the 1960s brought the debate into public focus once more. Writing in the late 1960s, Stanley Cohen argued that a moral panic can occur when anxieties around a perceived threat to the social order gain traction in public discourse in an increasingly hyperbolic manner (1, 226). Moral panic often arises around shifts in media practices and can channel broader cultural unease. The direct adaptation of Namor from the *Sub-Mariner* comic books and the transmedia expansion of the Aquaman character into new animated TV stories in the mid-1960s emerged in the context of revived and heated debates around the moral influence of stories upon children. Cohen notes, "Successful moral panics owe their appeal to their ability to find points of resonance with wider anxieties" (xxxvii). The 1960s are often seen as a prime example of this confluence. David Perlmutter suggests "the King and Kennedy assassinations, the war in Vietnam, and the rise of social protest groups such as ACT" (Action for Children's Television) were broader social factors that contributed to "a change in the censorship atmosphere that severely limited the artistic mobility of television animation" (Perlmutter 123; Hendershot 27). In the wake of the Robert F. Kennedy assassination, Jack Gould at the *New York Times* noted increased concern over television violence but was also mindful that television was becoming "the scapegoat for society's ills. When youngsters know of elder brothers or fathers fighting in Vietnam, who can blame them for concluding that deadly violence is part of society's mainstream?" (Gould, "TV: Violence" 91). The sublimation of wider anxieties into the domain of children is reflected in the popular press of the era, in which the television superhero played a primary role. In a period of moral panic, concern becomes focused on stereotyped "folk devils" who "embody" broader social concerns and become subjected to increasingly exaggerated claims of social harm (Cohen xxvi, xliii). In the mid-to-late 1960s, television's animated superheroes became the latest of these "folk devils."

By March 1968, *TV Guide* was positively alarmed by the overwhelming number of what it called "weirdo" superheroes that season (Higgins 6–10). When the Children's Television Workshop (CTW) was announced in March 1968, Gould at the *New York Times* pointedly titled his article "Aquaman vs. The Alphabet" (D29). Troubled by the long hours children were spending watching television, the CTW aimed to shift more of those hours to educational purposes.

Although the article's title is clearly a case of convenient journalistic alliteration, it nonetheless suggests that the educational content that CTW hoped to bolster was perceived as being at war with its designated other: superhero animated programs. Aquaman here serves as the metonym for superhero television as a whole and its negative cultural associations in the context of the 1968 debates.

"DISTURBING" LIMITED ANIMATION

Central to the concerns about superhero animations in the mid-to-late 1960s was nostalgia for older animation and a prevailing feeling that newer animations had lost their way. In a review of the 1967 schedule of superheroes, the *New York Times* lamented that "contemporary TV cartoons recently have abandoned their traditional realms of fairy-tale fantasies or folklore beast fables and now are caricaturing the tired clichés of live television shows," singling out *Aquaman* as a prime example of this trend among the broader "orgy of cartoons" on Saturday mornings (Diehl 125). The choice of Aquaman would seem somewhat ironic, given that the superhero was based—if extremely loosely—on the ancient Greek myth of Atlantis. This suggests part of the issue was not whether the story's source could be found in a traditional tale, but rather how it had been adapted. Back in 1954, Wertham noted that television was adapting classic works, but in a "mutilated . . . comic-book form" that robbed them of any cultural worth (Wertham 381). For Wertham, television had failed to move beyond comics and their perceived shortcomings. This remained the prevailing view into the 1960s. It is difficult to support Diehl's assertion that stories based more closely on classics from literature, myth, and fairy tales were really the "traditional realm" of cartoons (125). What seemed really at stake was not the mythic or folkloric source of inspiration, but rather more broadly the fact that the new television animations of the 1960s simply were not the same as the old theatrical animations that the adults knew and loved.

Indeed, the aversion to superhero animations rested partly on a fondness for the older Warner Bros. cartoons in both content and style, an aesthetic divide most famously summed up by Chuck Jones in 1967 when he said television's limited animation was really just "illustrated radio" (quoted in Diehl 125; Sullivan). As Maureen Furness notes, "full animation employs constant movement with a minimum of cycles," while by contrast limited animation uses minimal movement or extensive use of cycles (133). In his *New York Times* article, Diehl lamented that the limited animation style being used on television was "disturbing to the Disney-oriented adults" (125). The taste cultures inherent in the resistance to the change in television animation are made clear in the illustration to the *TV Guide* article: Mickey Mouse is left alone to confront an advancing horde of superheroes, with Aquaman, Sub-Mariner, and their cohorts lead by Thing from Hanna-Barbera's *Fantastic Four* (1967–68). Mickey's animal colleagues, among them Daffy Duck and Bugs Bunny, flee in horror (Higgins 6). The *TV Guide* stand-off between the Disney and Warner Bros. cartoons against the new animated superheroes made it clear that while adults were concerned about superhero violence, more broadly, they were also disturbed by a generational changing of the guard in both content and form, such that nostalgia, aesthetic taste, and moral panic became intertwined in the debates.

The industry at the time seemed to believe children would either be unable to tell the difference between full and limited animation or would simply not care regardless (Mittell 65–6). Bill Hanna of Hanna-Barbera Productions explained the new approach to television animation: "Disney-type full animation is economically unfeasible for television, and we discovered that we could get away with less" (quoted in Diehl 125). The production challenges were such that for some time it had even been assumed that animation simply was not going to be possible on television (Grossman 343, 345). Hanna found that limited animation could be used, with "repeated cycles of action and selected area animation" (Hanna quoted in Diehl 125). Others soon followed suit. Both Filmation's *Aquaman* and Grantray-Lawrence Animation's *Sub-Mariner* used variations on the limited animation techniques that Diehl found so "disturbing" (125). Furniss suggests "people tend to label limited animation as relatively bad because it looks 'easier' to do than full animation, the perception of worth being tied to a work ethic, or perhaps the value of labour" (138). *Sub-Mariner* and *The Marvel Super Heroes* program used a form of limited animation called "xerography," in which the original comic book artwork was photocopied and then simplified for the television adaptation (Morton 354–55). In a 1966 interview, Grantray-Lawrence Animation's Bob Lawrence argued that Marvel's artwork already captures a sense of movement and action in the frame: "The characters don't actually move, and yet their actions seem to flow . . . [W]e wanted to retain this flow" (quoted in McGrath). They were also keen to harness existing Marvel readers without changing the aesthetic too greatly (McGrath). The distributers played up this fidelity angle, emphasizing that the show contained "the same superhero artwork as in the MARVEL comic books" (Beck).

The distributers' claims that the show had "Sensational Animation" (Beck) was not shared by contemporary or later reviewers. Indeed, Hal Erikson argues that to call *The Marvel Super Heroes* animated at all was somewhat of a stretch given that movement was often only suggested through "camera pans and hand-jiggled cut-outs" (Erikson 529; Morton 358).[2] At its fanciest, the animation would stretch to "moving mouths and flailing hands" (Burke 107). The fully animated title sequence for *Sub-Mariner* depicting the superhero leaping out of the water and diving back in was the most fully animated movement of the entire series. It also featured a catchy theme song penned by Jack Urbont, in which the pitch of the final phrase, "prince of the deep," was suitably resonant (Burlingame; Vinson). The contrast between the formal qualities of the title sequence and the program itself are such that in this instance, the title sequence does not fulfill one of its traditional roles as an advertisement for what viewers can expect of the program itself (Spigel, "Back to the Drawing Board" 32; Baker 110–11). Despite Lawrence's claims that aesthetics and the fan audience were responsible for the limited animation, the scant $6,000 budget per segment was the most likely driving force (Perlmutter 106). Child viewers and intergenerational comic book fans were not seen as discerning enough to require a higher budget.[3]

Over at Filmation, *Aquaman* had more animated movement, but costs were kept down with the repetition of stock sequences. Producer Lou Scheimer explains that they would take scenes and use them "over and over and over in different situations," such as swimming sequences, throwing water balls, and large schools of fish (Brosnan). Chuck Jones may have legitimately held his aversion to such limited animation techniques, but his own Warner Bros. cartoons also make use of repetition.[4] Beyond the quality concerns, labeling limited animation on television "disturbing" suggests the aesthetic debate was linked to more serious anxieties around spectatorship (Diehl). Cartoons were now seen almost exclusively as the province of children who needed protection from unsuitable content and—it would seem—style as well.

SUPERHERO ANIMATION AND THE CHILD AUDIENCE

The idea of children's viewing as a distinct practice in need of surveillance predated the superhero animation skirmish of the mid-to-late 1960s, but it was a scheduling change that brought the shows into particular focus. By the time *The Superman/Aquaman Hour of Adventure* first aired in 1967, cartoons were concentrated in a Saturday morning block on all three networks and appeared only rarely elsewhere (Mittell 59). As Jason Mittell notes, "cartoons were now culturally defined as a genre whose primary audience was children" (59, 67). This shifting perception brought animation under heightened scrutiny in a decade in which "children's viewing pleasures" attracted ever-increasing attention by adults (Spigel, *Welcome* 209; Mittell 59). Underlying the concern around children's viewing was the perception of childhood as a time of innocence that required protection (Lury 307; Spigel, *Welcome* 186–95; Cook 9, 27). Children's culture is a site of negotiation and conflict around adult notions of what children want and need (Cook 12–15, 81, 145; Mittell 75). Indeed, Lee

Edelman argues that the child signifies "the future of the social order," such that the cultural image of childhood is fundamentally based on adult values and fantasies rather than "the lived experiences of any historical children" (11, 25). Once cartoons were seen as children's programs rather than intergenerational fare, there was a renewed drive to bring them in line with adult sensibilities around childhood.

Superhero animations in particular became the focus of the antiviolence campaigns in the mid-to-late 1960s that were often really about generational taste. Fredric Wertham emphasized that television was only one of many negative influences on children, but he was nonetheless particularly critical of animated violence (Higgins 10). This moral debate set different animators against one another, with David DePatie and Friz Freleng arguing in 1967 that the problem with television's cartoons lay in the fact that "[r]ight now they want the blood, guts and gore that are inherent in the 'supers,'" and Bullwinkle creator Bill Scott complaining about "gratuitous violence" (quoted in Diehl 125). In the same year, Joseph Barbera complained that Hanna-Barbera was compelled to do "out-of-this-world hard action," namely, "comic-book fiction, super heroes, and fantasy. Not out of choice . . . It's the only thing we can sell to the networks" (quoted in Brown 248). Animated superhero television programs were in their ascendency.

The syndicated *Marvel Super Heroes* animation of 1966 capitalized on the success of Marvel comics in that decade, which distributors Krantz Films claimed had 60 million readers, such that "Marvel Super-Heroes will practically sell themselves!" (Beck). However, the real aim of the adaptation was as a promotional "loss-leader" to increase the value of Marvel in preparation for its sale, and *The Marvel Super Heroes* program ran for only one year before its Grantray-Lawrence Animation team was reassigned to the higher-budget ABC network show *Spider-Man* in 1967–70 (Morton 354–55). *The Marvel Super Heroes* nonetheless coincided with the animated superhero boom on television that year, spearheaded by Fred Silverman's vision for a "superhero morning" over at CBS beginning with Filmation's rotoscoped *New Adventures of Superman* (1966) (Silverman, quoted in Perlmutter 67, 131; Grossman 363). Silverman's gamble lifted CBS from third into first place in the ratings (Grossman 352).

Animation company Filmation built on the 1966 success of *The New Adventures of Superman* at CBS and expanded the format the following year with *The Superman/Aquaman Hour*. Just as they had done with *Superman*, Filmation brought over writers from the *Aquaman* comic book such as Bob Haney to work on the television show (Perlmutter 131). Michael Swanigan and Darrell McNeil note that this resulted in segments reasonably close in tone to the comic book at that time but relatively simplistic given the short run-time of only six and a half minutes (14). Keen to replicate the success of *Superman*, which kept a fantasy focus and deliberately refrained from commenting on contemporary politics, *Aquaman* followed suit with its fantastic marine/human hybrid foes and brief adventure format (Perlmutter 131).

Superhero animations were criticized for this adventure focus and their subsequent perceived lack of age-appropriate comedy. For reviewer Robert Higgins, writing in 1968, this made the recent batch of animated superheroes inferior to earlier comedic animation (10). For its part, *Aquaman* introduced the new character Tusky the walrus specifically for "comedy relief" for children (Swanigan and McNeil 14). For example, Tusky plays hide and seek with the seahorse Imp at the beginning of "To Catch a Fisherman" and then claps his flippers in delight when the Fisherman is caught (figure 6. 2). Tusky subsequently appeared in issue 36 of the *Aquaman* comic book in December 1967. Seahorses Imp and Storm were given greater prominence on the television program and, unlike their comic book equivalents, distinct personalities to appeal to younger viewers. *Aquaman* thereby combined the new trend for adventure superheroes with the older animated tradition of "cute little humanized animals" that reviewers thought preferable for children (Windeler 53; Diehl 125; Higgins 6).

Comedy was itself a matter of generational taste, in that the aesthetic limitations of superhero animations that adults complained about were instead enjoyed for their comedic value by teens and young adults. The *New York Times* reported that *The Marvel Super Heroes* on local station WOR-TV was "bringing happiness and escape to the college campus (so they say)" (Dougherty 142). Indeed, WOR-TV actively promoted the show along these lines, claiming "what with Pop-Art, Op-Art and Camp riding high . . . and the big, big boom in comic books" with "high school and college clubs," superhero comics on TV would be the next big thing (WOR-TV). *Sub-Mariner* was ostensibly more serious in tone than *Aquaman*, reflecting Namor's status as the earliest ambivalent superhero, "situated in that liminal zone between friend and enemy" (Curtis 83; Coogan 73). In the television show, Sub-Mariner most often battles Atlantean villains such as Krang and Attuma, but also clashes with humans in the episode "To Walk amongst Men!" Despite Namor's solemn demeanor, upon the release of *The Marvel Super Heroes* in 1966 the program was seen by *Variety* as tapping into camp humor specifically aimed at teen and young adults' nostalgia for the comic books of their youth, with particular appeal to the college set (Mor; Baker 50–51). As Susan Sontag explained in her 1964 essay, camp celebrates "artifice and exaggeration" and disregards "ordinary aesthetic judgment" (275, 286). For example, in the *Sub-Mariner* episode "The Start of the Quest," a thought bubble from the comic book is edited and transformed into a monologue, as Namor proclaims to an otherwise empty dungeon: "Namor the First, bound and helpless! And yet I shall escape! I shall regain my throne! I

Figure 6.1. Tusky ("To Catch a Fisherman").

must be true to my destiny!" (Lee and Austin 5). The adaptation of a comic book thought bubble into a television soliloquy, combined with John Vernon's deep voicework as Namor, make the superhero's characteristic pomposity comically pronounced in this scene. The extremely limited "xerography" animation of *Marvel Super Heroes* also emphasizes its aesthetic artifice, in the dungeon scene consisting merely of a camera zoom, animated lip movement, and periodically repeated water bubbles. The much-derided constraints of limited animation in programs such as *Marvel Super Heroes* were identified as its very attraction for older children and college students. This demonstrates the generational divide around animation yet also indicates that a degree of intergenerational viewing persisted.

Despite the grumbles among adult critics, the objections to superhero animation were tempered by a fondness for older characters from their own youth. Robert Windeler at the *New York Times* suggested that while most television superheroes were unacceptably violent, at least "old favorites" such as Superman did not "annihilate" enemies: "[H]e merely sends them back where they came from" (53). Filmation continued this approach with *Aquaman*. In "Treacherous Is the Torpedoman," Aquaman saves the life of the Torpedoman from a weapon intended to defeat Aquaman himself, saying "[H]e may be our enemy, but I can't let him die." Indeed, it was *Superman/Aquaman*'s producer Allen Ducovny who suggested in 1968 that the earlier theatrical animations, many of them subsequently broadcast on television, were often more violent than newer shows (Higgins 10). The difference, he argued, was that older titles—such as Hanna-Barbera's 1940 creation *Tom and Jerry*—held nostalgic appeal for adults that blinded them to their true content (Higgins 10). *Sponsor* magazine similarly pointed out that despite support for older cartoons of "the good old days," characters such as Tom and Jerry "have literally been beating each other's brains out" for decades ("Last flight" 36). What really lay at the heart of the debate were not the levels of violence per se, but rather shifting generational tastes and changing cartoon spectatorship.

A NEW ERA

Marvel Super Heroes lasted just the one season in 1966 before the team moved on to the more fully animated *Spider-Man* in 1967–70. *The Superman/Aquaman Hour of Adventure* changed to *The Batman/Superman Hour* on CBS the following season in 1968, with the *Aquaman* segments repackaged together in a standalone show. While the Saturday morning kids' slot had been dominated by superheroes and action shows, by 1968 CBS committed to putting 50 percent comedy in place in their new line up (Windeler 53; "Last flight" 39–40). This was ostensibly to satisfy children's tastes (Windeler 53), and in turn protect $50 million in advertising revenue ("Last flight" 36). Nonetheless, contemporary reviews, debates and protests make it clear that adult sensibilities were the primary driving force in the shift in genre focus. NBC for its part responded to the controversy by putting in place a three-stage plan beginning in 1968 (Leach 127). The first phase "looked to the removal of programs that might include . . . elements of violence . . . and replacement with series emphasizing fantasy and natural history" (quoted in Leach 127; see also "Last flight" 38). Reflecting later in 1973, NBC attorney Howard Monderer told the FCC that "the response from children has been a decline in interest . . . Viewing NBC on Saturday morning has declined since 1968 by about 25 percent" (quoted in Leach 181). Monderer felt this indicated that children simply did not want the kind of changes that Action for Children's Television and other concerned adults thought best (Leach 181). ABC was slowest to act but similarly overhauled its programming (Grossman 353).

Writing for the *New York Times* in July 1968, Robert Windeler notes, "Protests by parents and educators have caused the networks to reevaluate programming and substitute less violent half-hours for the 'zap-pow' superheroes" (53). Norman Prescott, producer of Filmation's *Superman/Aquaman*, proclaimed in 1967: "This is the era of the super-hero" (quoted in Diehl 125). Superheroes had successfully moved beyond the comic book to dominate children's television. By 1968, Prescott admitted their time was over: "They were just about exhausted anyway, everybody was doing the same thing . . . But it was the recent wave of antiviolence which really killed them off" (quoted in Windeler 53).

In 1969, a new study examined violence in the 1967–68 television season (Gould, "Of Scapegoats" D19). Discussing the study, Jack Gould criticized Saturday morning content but nonetheless returned to a point he had made the previous year, that "picking on TV alone is a national cop-out for the failure of adults to do what they can to set an example" in the real world (D19). Broader concerns about violent upheavals of the late 1960s had been channeled into a moral panic around television and animated superhero "folk devils" in particular. Despite Gould's own concerns about scapegoating, when the new fall television schedule was released for 1969, he was pleased to see that "the sadistic pow to the kisser did not seem quite so apparent" in the toned-down Saturday morning content ("TV Review" 83). The pressures of 1968 resulted in greater internal censorship that would only increase into the 1970s (Perlmutter 123; Grossman 353, 358).

Comic book adaptations on television in the 1960s such as *Sub-Mariner* and *Aquaman* nonetheless paved the way for more ambitious screen adaptations in subsequent decades that were increasingly pitched to an intergenerational audience (Burke 106–7).[5] Indeed, Liam Burke argues that today, "animation is not so much the missing link, but rather the forgotten bridge between the comics that are respected as the source text and the excitement that greets each new blockbuster movie" (116). The prospect of a mainstream superhero renaissance on screen would have excited children in the 1960s, but it would certainly have alarmed many of the adults. Gould lamented that the animations of the 1969 season may have been less violent, but the shows still seemed like "junk bereft of style, professional competence, touches of humor or any evidence of an inclination to raise standards of substance" ("TV Review" 83). In other words, with the violence debate momentarily defused, what remained was the same underlying problem around generational taste, genre, and aesthetics that had informed the controversy all along. It was not really a case of "Aquaman vs. The Alphabet," but rather "Aquaman vs. The Adults."

Notes

1. As Andrea Friedman notes, Wertham's book tapped into parental concerns in the 1950s that young boys in particular were in danger of becoming either too soft for a looming war with the Soviet Union or conversely too violent to have in the home (203; Rifas 12). As this chapter will demonstrate, heated discussions about the animated superhero programs of the 1960s focused primarily on violence. More broadly, the gendering of both the animated superhero programs and their reception warrants further study.

2. Thomas Lamarre calls this style the "tendency to move the drawing rather than to draw the movement" (335–36).

3. Many Marvel readers and later even Stan Lee would "disown" the show (Perlmutter 106), but it remains part of popular culture history (Ndalianis 282).

4. Sammond suggests this was simply a case of professional rivalry with a competitor.

5. The revivals also saw periodic resurgences of concern, such as *Mister Rogers Talks with Parents about Superheroes* in 1980 (Grossman 132; Neville).

Works Cited

Art [sic]. "Captain Video." *Variety*, 13 Jul. 1955. *Variety Television Reviews, Vol. 5, 1954–1956*, edited by H. H. Prouty, Garland, 1989–1991.

Baker, Djoymi. *To Boldly Go: Marketing the Myth of Star Trek*. I. B. Tauris, 2018.

The Batman/Superman Hour. CBS, 1968.

Beck, Jerry. "The Marvel Super-Hero Cartoons (1966)." *Cartoon Research*, 30 Mar. 2013, cartoonresearch.com/index.php/marvel-super-heroes-1966/#prettyphoto[2061]/0/.

Bongco, Mila. *Reading Comics: Language, Culture, and the Concept of the Superhero in Comic Books*. Routledge, 2014.

Brosnan, Michael, director. *Aquaman: The Sovereign of the Seas. The Adventures of Aquaman: The Complete Collection*. Warner Bros. Home Entertainment, 2007.

Brown, Les. *Television: The Business behind the Box*. Harvest, 1971.

Burke, Liam. "Sowing the Seeds: How 1990s Marvel Animation Facilitated Today's Cinematic Universe." *Marvel Comics into Film: Essays on Adaptations since the 1940s*, edited by Matthew J. McEniry, Robert Moses Peaslee, and Robert G. Weiner, McFarland, 2016, pp. 106–17.

Burlingame, Jon. "The Marvel Super Heroes Songs: The Inside Story." *The Film Music Society*, 14 Jul. 2015, www.filmmusicsociety.org/news_events/features/2015/071415.html?isArchive=071415.

Cohen, Stanley. *Folk Devils and Moral Panics*. Routledge, 2011.

Coogan, Peter M. *Superhero: The Secret Origin of a Genre*. MonkeyBrain, 2006.

Cook, Daniel Thomas. *The Commodification of Childhood*. Duke University Press, 2004.

Curtis, Neal. *Sovereignty and Superheroes*. Manchester University Press, 2016.

Diehl, Digby. "On Saturdays, Super-Heroes and Talking Animals." *New York Times*, 5 Mar. 1967, p. 125.

Dougherty, Philip H. "Advertising: How to Be First on the Block Just Watch the TV Commercials That Appeal to Kids." *New York Times*, 8 Jan. 1967, p. 142.

Edelman, Lee. *No Future: Queer Theory and the Death Drive*. Duke University Press, 2004.

Erikson, Hal. *Television Cartoon Shows: An Illustrated Encyclopedia, 1949 through 2003*. Vol. 2, McFarland, 2005.

The Fantastic Four. ABC, 1967–68.

Friedman, Andrea. "Sadists and Sissies: Anti-pornography Campaigns in Cold War America." *Gender & History*, vol. 15, no. 2, 2003, pp. 201–27.

Furniss, Maureen. *Art in Motion: Animation Aesthetics*. John Libbey, 1998.

Gould, Jack. "Aquaman vs. The Alphabet." *New York Times*, 24 Mar. 1968, p. D29.

Gould, Jack. "Of Scapegoats and Headlines." *New York Times*, 13 Jul. 1969, p. D19.

Gould, Jack. "TV Review: Fewer Pows and Sockos of a Saturday Morn." *New York Times*, 8 Sept. 1969, p. 83.

Gould, Jack. "TV: Violence as a Program Staple Prompts Concern." *New York Times*, 10 Jun. 1968, p. 91.

Grossman, Gary H. *Saturday Morning TV*. Arlington House, 1987.
Haney, Bob, and Nick Cardy. *Aquaman*. No. 36, DC Comics, 1967.
Hendershot, Heather. *Saturday Morning Censors: Television Regulation before the V-chip*. Duke University Press, 1999.
Higgins, Robert. "Mickey Mouse, Where are You?" *TV Guide*, 23 Mar. 1968, pp. 6–10.
Lamarre, Thomas. "From Animation to Anime: Drawing Movements and Moving Drawings," *Japan Forum*, vol. 14, no. 2, 2002, pp. 329–67.
"Last Flight for the Animated Horrors?," *Sponsor*, vol. 22, no. 5, 1968, pp. 36–41.
Leach, Alan Lyon. "Commercialism and the Quality of Children's TV Programs: An Analysis of Responses to the Proposals of Action for Children's Television, February 1970 to January 1973." Ohio State University, 1973.
Lee, Stan, and Adam Austin. *Sub-Mariner and the Incredible Hulk: Tales to Astonish*. No. 70, Marvel Comics, 1965.
Lury, Karen. "The Child in Film and Television: Introduction," *Screen*, vol. 46, no. 3, 2005, pp. 307–14.
The Marvel Super Heroes. First Run Syndication, 1966.
McGrath, Ron. "A MARVELous TV Season." *The World of Comic Art: The Historical Journal of Comic Art and Caricature*, vol. 3, 1966/7. Cartoon Research, http://cartoonresearch.com/index.php/marvel-super-heroes-1966/#prettyphoto[2061]/2/.
Minow, Newton N. and Craig L. MaLay. "Address to the National Association of Broadcasters, May 9, 1961." *Abandoned in the Wasteland: Children, Television, and the First Amendment*. Hill and Wang, 1995, pp. 185–96.
Mister Rogers Talks with Parents About Superheroes. PBS, 1980.
Mittell, Jason. *Genre and Television: From Cop Shows to Cartoons in American Culture*. Routledge, 2004.
Mor [sic]. "Marvel Super-Heroes." *Variety*, 26 Oct. 1966. *Variety Television Reviews, Vol. 9, 1966-1969*, edited by H. H. Prouty, Garland, 1989–91, n.pag.
Morton, Drew. "The Unfortunates: Towards a History and Definition of the Motion Comic." *Journal of Graphic Novels & Comics*, vol. 6, no. 4, 2015, pp. 347–66.
Ndalianis, Angela. "Enter the Aleph: Superhero Worlds and Hypertime Realities." *The Contemporary Comic Book Superhero*, edited by Angela Ndalianis, Routledge, 2009, pp. 270–90.
Neville, Morgan, director. *Won't You Be My Neighbor?* 2018.
The New Adventures of Superman. CBS, 1966.
Perlmutter, David. *America Toons In: A History of Television Animation*. McFarland, 2014.
Rifas, Leonard. "'Especially Dr. Hilde L. Mosee': Wertham's Research Collaborator." *International Journal of Comic Art*, vol. 8, no. 1, 2006, pp. 17–44.
Sammond, Nic. "Review: Sound in Hanna-Barbera." *Journal of Videographic Film & Moving Image Studies*, vol. 5, no. 3, 2018, http://mediacommons.org/intransition/sound-hanna-barbera.
Sontag, Susan. *Against Interpretation and Other Essays*. Eyre and Spottiswoode, 1967.
Spider-Man. ABC, 1967–70.
Spigel, Lynn. "Back to the Drawing Board: Graphic Design and the Visual Environment of Television at Midcentury." *Cinema Journal*, vol. 55, no. 4, 2016, pp. 28–54.
Spigel, Lynn. *Welcome to the Dreamhouse: Popular Media and Postwar Suburbs*. Duke University Press, 2001.

"Start of the Quest, The." *Sub-Mariner, The Marvel Super Heroes*, directed by Clyde Geronimi and Sid Marcus, written by Stan Lee, season 1, episode 2, Grantray-Lawrence Animation and Marvel Enterprises, 1966.

"Straight from the Drawing Board: More Comic Strip Characters Head toward Television." *TV Guide*, 13 Nov. 1954, pp. 16–17.

Sullivan, Patrick. "Sound in Hanna-Barbera." *Journal of Videographic Film & Moving Image Studies*, vol. 5, no. 3, 2018, mediacommons.org/intransition/sound-hanna-barbera.

The Superman/Aquaman Hour of Adventure. CBS, 1967–68.

Swanigan, Michael, and Darrell McNeil. *Animation by Filmation*. Blackbear Press, 1993.

"To Catch a Fisherman." *Aquaman, The Superman/Aquaman Hour of Adventure*, directed by Hal Sutherland, written by Bob Haney, season 1, episode 36, CBS, 1967.

"To Walk amongst Men!" *Sub-Mariner, The Marvel Super Heroes*, directed by Clyde Geronimi and Sid Marcus, written by Stan Lee, season 1, episode no. 7, Grantray-Lawrence Animation and Marvel Enterprises, 1966.

"Treacherous Is the Torpedoman." *Aquaman, The Superman/Aquaman Hour of Adventure*, directed by Hal Sutherland, written by Bob Haney, season 1, episode 14, CBS, 1967.

Vinson, Elizabeth. "Copyright Ownership—Even Iron Man Couldn't Protect the Work for Hire Doctrine from Third-Party Infringers." *SMU Law Review*, vol. 70, no. 1, 2017, pp. 221–28.

Wertham, Fredric. *Seduction of the Innocent*. Museum Press, 1954.

Windeler, Robert. "Violence in TV Cartoons Being Toned Down; Saturday Programs for Children Turn toward Comedy Adventure, Science Fiction Shows on Fall Schedules." *New York Times*, 20 Jul. 1968, p. 53.

WOR-TV. "*The Marvel Superheroes*." Press Kit, 1966. *Tellshiar: Marvel Comics Collectibles Resource Center*, 29 Dec. 2014, tellshiar.com/blog/previous/2.

Chapter 7

THE *TOY BIZ* OF SUPERHEROES

Superhero Action Figures

JASON BAINBRIDGE

INTRODUCTION

On January 3, 2003, the X-Men's long struggle to be treated like human beings failed. In the 2003 *Toy Biz v. United States*, Judge Judith Barzilay of the United States Court of International Trade held that for the purposes of tariffs, Toy Biz's action figures of the Marvel superheroes, along with their friends and foes, were toys, not dolls, because they represented "nonhuman creatures." The decision also excluded Spider-Man, members of the Fantastic Four, and even Daredevil's perpetual nemesis the Kingpin from being classified as human.

The action was motivated by import taxes imposed under the Harmonized Tariff Schedule which distinguished between two categories of action figures: dolls, which are defined to include human figures and thereby attract higher duties, and toys, which included the aforementioned "nonhuman creatures." During the case, more than sixty action figures of superheroes and supervillains were examined, from Toy Biz's X-Men, Fantastic Four, and Spider-Man toy lines. Finding in Toy Biz's favor halved the tariff rate for the company, from 12 to 6.8 percent tax (Iglesias) and granted Toy Biz reimbursement for all import taxes previously charged. While the Harmonized Tariff Schedule was later amended to eliminate the distinction between dolls and other toys, by placing them both in the same category, the decision prompted widespread concern and discussion in the fan community (Daily). The fans thought that it was ironic that the owners of Marvel superheroes, who had always maintained that the Marvel Universe was the world outside your window, essentially went to court to argue against this connection to reality—and against the humanity of some of their greatest characters ("No Time for Mutants").

In the face of such backlash, Marvel took the opportunity to restate their definition of superheroes being "living, breathing human beings—but humans who have extraordinary abilities." As such, Marvel concluded that Judge Barzilay's "decision that the X-Men figures indeed do have 'nonhuman' characteristics further proves our characters have special, out-of-this world powers" (quoted in King). Of course, the case was motivated by Toy Biz wanting a lower tariff rate. But it still provides a fascinating example of the challenges facing media properties like superheroes as they move across different delivery platforms—and the impacts such movement can have on their function and understanding.

Today, it's almost a cliché to say that the enormous success of the Marvel Cinematic Universe (MCU) franchise has made the superhero a truly transmedia phenomenon. Superheroes proliferate across film, television, games, books, theme parks, and toy shelves to such an extent that most are better known through their adaptations and intertexts than their source materials, the comic books themselves. This web of intertexts that surrounds, informs, and extends superhero texts across these different media platforms are all examples of *paratextuality*. As Gerard Genette explains, "a text is rarely presented in an unadorned state, unreinforced and unaccompanied by a certain number of verbal or other productions . . . These accompanying productions, which vary in extent and appearance, constitute what I have called elsewhere the work's *paratext*" (1, emphasis added). In regard to superheroes, these paratexts include posters, trailers, reviews, interviews, and, most importantly for this chapter, toys like the action figures produced by Toy Biz.

This chapter explores the often-symbiotic relationship between superheroes and toys, tracing the enormous impact the toy industry has had on superhero comics and the narrative evolution of superheroes into transmedia franchises. It follows media theorist Jonathan Gray's argument that "a proper study of paratexts . . . [should] challenge the logic of 'primary' and 'secondary' texts, originals and spinoffs, shows and 'peripherals'" (175). Just as Gray contends that paratexts "often play a constitutive role in the production, development, and expansion of a text" (175), this chapter demonstrates how important the toy industry has been to the definition, evolution, and survival of the superhero today.

BEN COOPER, MEGO, AND THE TRADEMARKING OF SUPERHERO

Superheroes largely remain the product of two companies, DC Comics (a division of AT&T's Warner Media) and Marvel Comics (a division of Disney). This is partly because the word "superhero" (along with "supervillain" and any variations thereof) is jointly claimed by DC and Marvel as a trademark in the United States. While it is widely known that DC and Marvel applied for joint registration of the superheroes mark for comic books in July 1979 (with the mark being registered for use in comic books from November 1981 and remaining active today), what is less well known is that the trademark claim itself was initiated through a complicated process of competing claims that did not originate from the comics companies at all—but from a costume company and a toy company, respectively.

Superheroes are *toyetic*: media properties capable of being merchandised across a range of licensed tie-ins such as games, novelties, and toys. While this might suggest a reductionist view of merchandising related only to "toys"—like the Mego Corporation's World's Greatest Superheroes (abbreviated to WGSH) toyline—in practice, toyetic potential can be found in any merchandise with some element of "play" value. This includes items like food and clothing, such as Ben Cooper's range of Halloween masks and costumes discussed further below.

If we define merchandising as the *materiality* of licensing (an extension of screen and literary texts into physical paratexts), then being *toyetic* is the interactive "make-and-do" aspect of merchandising, encouraging audiences to play with aspects of the media text: acting out narratives or creating new adventures or stories. Dan Fleming calls this "textual phenomenology" (11), where he suggests "a great deal [is] going on when a child plays with the toy" (15). So, being toyetic becomes an immersive practice where the "player" can customize textual content. While the term "toyetic" does not appear in any literature before 1977—where it is generally assigned to former president of the Kenner toy company, Bernard Loomis ("Interview")—the concept certainly existed long before being named as such. Indeed, in a world where technology could not capture superheroes' abilities to the extent seen in comic books, media theorist Henry Jenkins explicitly imbues toyetic play with the qualities of digital culture. He notes that "action figures provided this generation with some of their earliest avatars, encouraging them to assume the role of a Jedi Knight or an intergalactic bounty hunter, enabling them to physically manipulate the characters to construct their own stories" (Jenkins 147).

During the 1960s, Halloween costume maker Ben Cooper similarly recognized the toyetic potential of superheroes when the company licensed a range of properties from both DC and Marvel (Petty). They applied for the registration of "SUPER HERO" as a name for the line in April 1966, and it was published for opposition in December 1966. Extraordinarily, neither DC nor Marvel opposed the application, and the trademark "SUPER HERO" was granted to Cooper on March 14 1967 for use on masquerade costumes alongside the marks FAMOUS HEROES and GREAT HEROES (US Reg. No. 0825835).

By November 1972, the Mego Corporation (following in the footsteps of the Ideal Toy Company) similarly recognized the toyetic potential of superheroes.

Mego licensed characters from DC and Marvel and sought to promote the line under the WGSH trademark for a line of eight- and twelve-inch dolls with soft-cloth costumes. Ben Cooper filed an opposition to that registration in December 1973 and sought to register the plural SUPER HEROES (Opposition No. 55,127, 6 Dec. 1973), but the examiner suspended all further action on the SUPER HEROES registration until the opposition was decided. Rather than continue proceedings, Mego assigned its interests to DC and Marvel jointly in December 1975.

By 1975, DC and Marvel were both receiving more revenue through licensing than through their declining newsstand comic book sales (Wright 259), direct distribution to specialty stores still being in its infancy at this stage (Rhoades 264). This means that as early as 1975, both DC and Marvel were experiencing more success through their paratexts than the source texts (the comics). Faced with the comic companies' united opposition, Ben Cooper withdrew its opposition to the WGSH mark. This decision, along with a series of efforts by DC and Marvel together and individually over the preceding years to trademark superheroes for various products, meant that the two companies had joint control of the term "superhero," and all because the Mego toy company had pursued the mark (US Reg. No. 1080655, 27 Dec. 1977).

In practice, neither company waits for actual commercial use of "superhero" before raising an objection. They monitor trademark registration applications, request an extension of time to file an opposition (rather than incurring the expense of a formal opposition), and make their displeasure publicly known to start settlement discussions. Confronted with such pressure, applicants often abandon their applications, effectively creating this superhero duopoly (Petty 742–47). And the value of this decision is understandable when one considers that Marvel, with ownership rights to over five thousand superheroes, was purchased by Walt Disney for $4.3 billion in 2009.

SUPER POWERS AND R & D

The Mego Corporation closed in 1984 and with sales flagging on their iconic *Star Wars* toyline, the Kenner toy company pursued and were awarded master toy licensing rights for DC's stable of superheroes. Their *Super Powers Collection* commenced with a twelve-figure line-up packaged with minicomics that included the trinity of Superman, Batman, and Wonder Woman. It then broadened out to include their allies in the Justice League, their enemies, original creations, and denizens of Jack Kirby's Fourth World throughout subsequent series in 1985 and 1986. Thirty-three figures, several vehicles, and a Hall of Justice playset were ultimately produced. The line was supported by a change in name, focus, and design for Hanna Barbera's long-running *Super Friends* cartoon series together with a number of merchandising tie-ins (Rossen).

The toyline highlighted action features "unique" to each figure's "super power," where you could squeeze Superman's legs together to make him punch, extend Plastic Man's neck, or make Robin karate chop. But of more interest for this chapter, the *Super Powers* toyline serves as an early example of research and development, where a paratext is used to test ideas that then find their way into other texts. This occurred both diegetically (in the fictional story world of the superheroes) and extradiegetically (in terms of the real-world creators of these superheroes).

Diegetically, the *Super Powers Collection* (further supported by cartoon and merchandising paratexts of its own) served to popularize Darkseid and Jack Kirby's Fourth World characters as enemies (and allies) for the Justice League. It also made Teen Titan's Cyborg a member of the Justice League of America for the first time. These were ideas that carried over into the DC comic texts (most notably in Geoff Johns's "New 52" relaunch of the Justice League) and the Zack Snyder *Justice League* film (2017), both of which featured Cyborg as a founding member of the League—and Darkseid (and his forces) as the first villains they face.

Extradiegetically, the *Super Powers Collection* also highlighted alternative revenue streams that brought greater recognition for comic artists, both visibly and financially. The card art made people familiar with Spanish artist José Luis García-López's iconically sparse designs that were featured in DC's 1982 licensing style guide. Most important, it also provided artists with more royalties than they ever received for their comics work, including Jack Kirby (for redesigning his Fourth World characters), George Pérez (for his design of Cyborg and redesign of Superman villain Lex Luthor), and Ed Hannigan (for his redesign of Superman villain Brainiac) (Rossen). Notably, Kirby received some of the only royalties of his career for this work. This pattern of visibility and/or royalties continued for comic book creators as their characters were regularly adapted during the resurgence of superhero movies and television series from 2008 on.

SECRET WARS—ONE UNIVERSE

Envious of the success of Kenner's *Super Powers* and fearing that superheroes may become the next big thing, rival toy company Mattel partnered with DC's comic book rival Marvel to produce a toyline called *Secret Wars* (the name was chosen when Mattel's market testing revealed kids reacted positively to the words "secret" and "wars") (McLaughlin). Much as Kenner had licensed DC superheroes to support *Star Wars'* flagging toy sales, Mattel licensed Marvel characters in case their *Masters of the Universe* line faltered. But Mattel was concerned that recognition of the Marvel superheroes, outside of Spider-Man and the Hulk, was not as strong as the DC stable and asked Marvel to produce a comic to support the toyline (McLaughlin).

Marvel's then editor-in-chief, Jim Shooter, describes the origin of the *Secret Wars* comic this way:

> I offered an idea that was suggested by a dozen or so correspondents—usually younger ones—in the fan mail every day: one big, epic story with all (or many) of the heroes and villains in it. Everyone agreed . . . To this day, when I go to conventions, I'm asked to sign many, many copies. Lots of people tell me that *Secret Wars* is what first got them into comics. Makes sense. The idea came from the fans.

Written by Shooter, illustrated by Mike Zeck and Bob Layton, and inked by John Beatty, *Marvel Super Heroes Secret Wars* was a twelve-part miniseries, line-wide event bringing many of Marvel's premier superheroes and supervillains together to fight for the pleasure of a cosmic being known as The Beyonder on a distant planet called Battleworld. Largely structured around a series of fights to sell the toys, *Secret Wars* introduced new characters, brought She-Hulk into the Fantastic Four, and gave Spider-Man a sentient black costume that would later become the fan-favorite supervillain Venom.

Unlike *Super Powers*, the *Secret Wars* toyline had a number of design limitations largely born of a manufacturing push by Mattel to reuse molds to save money. As a result, the toyline was relatively unsuccessful; eight figures were released in series one with a few vehicles and one playset, but series 2 was cut to five releases with the additional three only being released in Europe (Iceman, Electro, and Constrictor who never actually appeared in the comic series).

In contrast, the comic series—and more particularly the ramifications of the series for the wider Marvel Universe—set up a successful storytelling model. Line-wide "mega" crossovers that draw in multiple titles have consistently featured as part of Marvel's release slate ever since and very much set the narrative direction for the interconnected nature of the Marvel Cinematic Universe. This storytelling model is as follows: multiple franchises (like Thor, Captain America, Iron Man, etc.) build to an interconnected event (like *Avengers: Infinity War* (2018) and *Avengers: Endgame* (2019)). The model was also reproduced less successfully by the aforementioned DC Extended Universe's *Justice League*. Once again, this is a storytelling model that originated outside the comic industry and was instead driven by the toy industry's desire for an "event" title to promote their accompanying toyline.

THE TOY BIZ

The final case study of toy/comic symbiosis is perhaps the most important. It begins in 1989 with millionaire businessman Ron Perelman's purchase of Marvel for $82.5 million from Marvel's then-owners New World Pictures. By 1991, Marvel was listed on the stock market and making acquisitions that cost Marvel a reported $700 million, including a 46 percent share in a toy company called Toy Biz. In exchange for this 46 percent share, the deal gave Toy Biz "exclusive, perpetual, royalty-free licenses" for Marvel characters (Lambie).

Marvel appeared to experience enormous growth during the 1990s, particularly off the back of titles like *Spider-Man*, *X-Men*, and *X-Force*, thanks to the speculator boom where collectors purchased multiple copies of individual issues as investment pieces. It was valued at over $1 billion on the market—but was likely overinflated—for from 1993 on, comic and trading card revenue declined by as much as 70 percent. The speculator bubble had burst and Marvel's stock value collapsed from $35.75 each in 1993 to $2.375 each in 1996. By 1995, Perelman was already confronting the collapsing bottom line by extending Marvel into new areas, setting up a film venture (Marvel Studios) and planning to buy the remaining shares in Toy Biz and merge it with Marvel (so Marvel would effectively become a comic, toy, and trading card company) (Norris). Marvel's shareholders resisted and Perelman filed for bankruptcy in an effort to reorganize Marvel without the shareholders' consent. This led to a protracted two-year struggle for control between various board members.

Ultimately, the merger with Toy Biz did go ahead following a lengthy court case, but in a very different way to what Perelman had envisaged. He was ousted by two Toy Biz executives who'd been on Marvel's board since 1993: Isaac "Ike" Perlmutter and Toy Biz's CEO Avi Arad (Rosenberg 295). ToyBiz, the toymaker, had effectively raised the money to purchase Marvel Comics, the comic company—forming Marvel Entertainment, Inc. and bringing the company out of bankruptcy as a result. Part of this restructure involved the formation of various holding companies for parts of the company, one of which was Marvel Characters, Inc.—the licensing wing of Marvel Comics containing all the IP rights of their characters. Not surprisingly, Toy Biz were keen to protect their "exclusive, perpetual, royalty-free licenses" and saw the best way of doing that as taking control of the company (Williams).

Arad's original portfolio had been overseeing the production of Marvel action figures at Toy Biz. He gained a 10 percent share as part of Marvel's 46 percent acquisition of Toy Biz in 1993 and replaced Stan Lee as head of Marvel Films, serving as executive producer on Fox's animated *X-Men* series (1992–97)—as well as brokering a deal with 20th Century Fox to make an X-Men movie that spawned its own franchise (Raviv). Subsequent funding from the Merrill Lynch bank in 2005—$525 million over seven years with Marvel's superheroes held as collateral—provided Marvel with the cash reservoir to buy back the rights to many of their characters and launch the Marvel Cinematic Universe. This paved the way for Disney's purchase of Marvel for $4.3 billion in 2009.

TOWARDS A "TOYESIS" OF SUPERHEROES

Arad had previously worked on Bandai/Tonka's *Gobots*, a set of transforming robots rivaling the better-known *Transformers*. To build the brand, Arad had adopted a three-pronged transmedia marketing strategy Marvel itself had developed with toymaker Hasbro for their *G.I. Joe* and *Transformers* brands back in the 1980s. This involved synchronized releases of comics, toys, and cartoons, where each would serve to promote (and in some cases enrich and deepen) the others. Under Arad's leadership, this transmedia marketing strategy started being replicated by Marvel again in the 1990s. Here it was a triad of Marvel comics, Fox Cartoon television series, and Toy Biz action figures. Indeed, to a large extent the latter MCU (commencing with *Iron Man* in 2008) was bound by this series of licensing decisions that Marvel (and Arad) made in the mid-1990s, including licensing the X-Men and Fantastic Four to Fox, and Spider-Man to Sony (in 1999). This meant that when Marvel Studios moved from character licensing to self-financing their own films (commencing under David Maisel in 2004) they had a greatly reduced slate of characters with which to work, mostly comprised of character rights that had reverted back to them because of nonproduction. These were largely *Avengers*-related (as with Iron Man, Captain America, and Thor) or characters deep in their back catalogue who had never been optioned before (as with the Guardians of the Galaxy).

With some of their most successful (and recognizable) characters excluded from the MCU, Marvel Studios once again relied on this three-pronged transmedia marketing strategy in the 2000s to build recognition for their characters—a triad of comics, associated cartoons and toylines (produced by Hasbro). In this way, when the relatively obscure Guardians of the Galaxy were being made into a movie, a new comic book series (written by Brian Michael Bendis and drawn by Steve McNiven) and a boxed set of action figures from Hasbro were released in the lead-up to the film, and the characters later guest-starred on the cartoon series *Avengers Assemble* (2013–19). This means that while Guardians' character Rocket Raccoon first appeared in 1976, the three-pronged strategy allows audiences to come to Rocket through the comics, the toys, the film, or via his cartoon appearances. As a result, Rocket becomes deliberately multi-origined, textually ambiguous, and at home across multiple media platforms. Most importantly, he becomes *known*.

To describe these complex textual relationships, the notion of "toyesis" (Bainbridge 2015) has been referred; a kind of reverse toyetics where these paratextual relays erase a text's origins to the point that they become truly multi-origined. They are thereby capable of more easily flowing across media platforms, generating the production of more media texts around them. The word is modeled on the relationship between kinetic (relating to or resulting from motion) and kinesis (motion itself). Whereas toyetic implies a one-way adaptation from screen/literary text to physical paratext (through merchandising), toyesis implies movement both ways across platforms to the point that the distinction between different texts becomes obscured and therefore less important. The exposure of and familiarity with a character like Rocket Raccoon is a demonstration of toyesis at work; paratextual relays that obscure the textual origins of superheroes, making them seem truly multiplatform, multiorigined, transmedia characters that flow from screen to material media and back again, capturing audiences as they move across each delivery platform.

Gray viewed toys as important paratexts because they "represented to many that media worlds could and should be somewhat *inhabitable*" (187). However, as Jackson notes, both children and adults increasingly seek out another type of play experience; toy sales are "decreasing" in part because of changes in the marketplace and "the fact that consumers are more likely to bypass the toy store for the computer store. Digital devices have become the mainstay of modern play [and] . . . In computer and video game scenarios, the element of control that was so essential to early play patterns is taken away" (144). Jackson therefore sees the distinction in play in the following way: "classic toys—which developed in the Industrial Age—taught *control and creation*, electronic toys—emblematic of the Information Age—teach *adaptation*" (144, emphasis added). These two different types of play also create different understandings of life: "In traditional play, children could be masters of their own fates, learning to control their roles in life . . . [whereas] digital play creates a sensation of the randomness of life" (Jackson 144).

Toys prefigured the superheroes' embrace of convergence culture and transmedia storytelling engendered by digital technology. Now, digital devices compete with and cannibalize traditional toy sales. But at the same time, they help prolong the life of licensed properties through digital special effects, digital technologies, and digital recording, meaning that they are creating new markets for toys as well—with examples including toylines based around gaming properties (including the Marvel Gamerverse), Hasbro's *Transformers* Studio Series toys based on the CGI Michael Bay *Transformers* films (2007–), and Hasbro's own Marvel Legends figures based on the MCU actors and designs. In this way, digital development both competes with and complements the ongoing process of toyesis, generating the potential to sell multiple versions of Captain America action figures for example, each "known" to the audience through a different medium (comics, games, cartoons, film, sequel, etc.) even as it further obscures the textual origins of the underlying property.

CONCLUSION

The important role the toy industry has played in superheroes' expansion across the mediasphere has been relatively underrepresented in studies of the MCU to date. This chapter lays out a case for greater consideration and appreciation of the toy industry's impact on both the comic industry and the wider public perception and recognition of superheroes. The four case studies presented show that the licensing decisions of the toy industry have in many ways shaped audiences' understanding of superheroes as much as, if not more so than, the comic industry ever has. They have helped define the superhero as a recognizable brand, allowed for research and development around superhero teams, villains, and creator recognition, built new and successful storytelling models, and reinvested back into the comic industry to aid its transition across multiple media platforms.

As for each of the toylines mentioned in this chapter, the Mego WGSH line, Kenner's *Super Powers* line, and even Mattel's *Secret Wars* line are all well-remembered by collectors and continue to sell well on secondary markets like eBay. *Super Powers* gained a commemorative line in 2014 (the thirtieth anniversary of the original release) by Kenner's rival Mattel. *Secret Wars* was similarly homaged with a small run of oversized reproduction figures by Gentle Giant in 2015. And Mego, homaged by many toymakers over subsequent years, formally returned to Target shelves in 2018 with a new line of figures, including DC superheroes. As for Toy Biz, following Toy Biz and Marvel's merger, it persisted as Marvel's main toy subsidiary and later "Marvel Toys" until 2007, the master toy license for Marvel Entertainment characters having been purchased by Hasbro for $205 million (for five years) in 2006 where it remains to this day.

Works Cited

Avengers Assemble. Disney XD, 2013–19.

Avengers: Endgame. Directed by Anthony and Joe Russo. Walt Disney Studios Motion Pictures, 2019.

Avengers: Infinity War. Directed by Anthony and Joe Russo. Walt Disney Studios Motion Pictures, 2018.

Bainbridge, Jason. "From *Toyetic* to *Toyesis*: The Cultural Value of Merchandising." *Entertainment Values: How Do We Assess Entertainment and Why Does It Matter?*, edited by Stephen Harrington and Christy Collis, Palgrave, 2017, pp. 23–39.

Daily, James. "Are the X-Men Human? A Federal Court Says No." *Law and the Multiverse: Superheroes, Supervillains and the Law*, 17 Dec. 2011. https://lawandthemultiverse.com/2011/12/27/are-the-x-men-human-federal-court-says-no/

Fleming, Dan. *Powerplay: Toys as Popular Culture*. Manchester University Press, 1996.

Genette, Gerard. *Paratexts: The Thresholds of Interpretation*. Translated by Jane E. Lewin, Cambridge University Press, 1997.

Gray, Jonathan. *Show Sold Separately: Promos, Spoilers and Other Media Paratexts*. New York University Press, 2010.

Iglesias, Matthew. "How Trade Policy Cost The X-Men Their Humanity." *Slate*, 29 Dec. 2011, https://slate.com/business/2011/12/are-mutants-human.html.

Jackson, Kathy Merlock. "From Control to Adaptation: America's Toy Story." *Journal of American and Comparative Cultures*, vol. 24, no. 1/2, 2009, pp. 139–45.

Jenkins, Henry. *Convergence Culture*. New York University Press, 2006.

King, Neal. "Fans Howl in Protest as Judge Decides X-Men Aren't Human." *Wall Street Journal*, 20 Jan. 2003, https://www.wsj.com/articles/SB1043013622300562504.

Lambie, Ryan. "How Marvel Went from Bankruptcy to Billions." *Den of Geek*, Apr. 17, 2018, https://www.denofgeek.com/movies/how-marvel-went-from-bankruptcy-to-billions/.

Loomis, Bernard. "Interview." *Rebelscum* with D. Martin Myatt, 13 Dec. 2001, http://www.rebelscum.com/loomis.asp.

"No Time for Mutants." *USC Annenberg Online Journalism Review*, 22 Jan. 2003, http://www.ojr.org/ojr/spike/1043234172.php?__cf_chl_managed_tk__=pmd_kaQgZLwdQOXzij2gLtekdglv23O_5cQoFfOe.mj7OLQ-1633417563-0-gqNtZGzNAuWjcnBszQNR.

McLaughlin, Jermaine. "An Oral History of Marvel's *Secret Wars*: The Iconic Crossover That Started It All." *Syfy*, 4 Mar. 2019, https://www.syfy.com/syfywire/marvel-secret-wars-oral-history.

Norris, Floyd. "Marvel Proposes a Merger with Toy Biz." *New York Times*, 29 Apr. 1997.

Petty, Ross D. "The 'Amazing Adventures' of Super Hero." *The Trademark Reporter: The Law Journal of the International Trademark Association*, vol. 100, no. 3, 2010, pp. 729–55.

Raviv, Dan. *Comic Wars: How Two Tycoons Battled over the Marvel Comics Empire—and Both Lost*. Broadway Books, 2002.

Rhoades, Shirrel. *A Complete History of American Comic Books*. Peter Lang Publishing, 2008.

Rosenberg, Hilary. *The Vulture Investors*. John Wiley and Sons, 2000.

Rossen, Jake. "Breaking the Mold: Kenner's *Super Powers Collection*." *Mental Floss*, 9 Feb. 2017, https://www.mentalfloss.com/article/92022/breaking-mold-kenners-superpowers-collection.

Shooter, Jim. "Secrets of the *Secret Wars*." *Jim Shooter*, 4 Apr. 2011, http://jimshooter.com/2011/04/secrets-of-secret-wars.html/.

Super Friends. ABC, 1973–86.

Toy Biz v. United States, Court No. 96-10-02291, *United States Court of International Trade*, 3 Jan. 2003.

Transformers (Film Series). Directed by Michael Bay. Dreamworks Pictures, 2007–9 and Paramount Pictures 2011–.

Williams, Trey. "How Marvel Bounced Back from Bankruptcy to Become Hollywood's Biggest Brand." *The Wrap*, 29 Apr. 2018, https://www.thewrap.com/how-marvel-went-from-bankruptcy-to-hollywoods-most-successful-franchise/.

Wright, Bradford W. *Comic Book Nation: The Transformation of Youth Culture in America*. Johns Hopkins University Press, 2001.

Zack Snyder's Justice League. Directed by Zack Snyder, Warner Bros. Pictures, 2021.

Chapter 8

FROM COMIC BOOKS TO COURTROOM

Unmasking the Intellectual Property behind the Superhero

MITCHELL ADAMS

> [W]e're going to need some law books. With pictures this time.
> —HARVEY BIRDMAN, ATTORNEY AT LAW

After eighty years of being the man of steel, no other superhero has fronted the courtroom like Superman. Since the first appearance of Superman in 1938, many creators have sought to control the use of their comic book characters. Moving beyond the pages of their comic book covers, superheroes have increasingly become the subject of protection under intellectual property (IP) regimes, including the copyright and trademark systems (Adams 92). Control of these fictional characters via these IP regimes has been instrumental to the publication of comic books, merchandizing activities, and more recently film and television adaptations. In particular, Marvel and DC, for decades, have fiercely protected the IP in their superheroes—inside and outside of the courtroom. The cumulation of their efforts has helped forge the law to protect individual fictional characters.

Commentators have long argued that the law silently shapes cultural forms (Gains 208). However, the inverse has also likely occurred. Superheroes over time have gone beyond their native comic strips and helped shape the contours of the law. This chapter will trace the ways Marvel and DC have used the law as a tool to build their franchising empires—with particular attention made to the IP regimes used in protecting their catalogue of fictional characters. It will comment on how superheroes have influenced the law and concepts of IP with a focus on copyright and trademark rights.

IP law allows individuals and corporations to benefit from their creative endeavors or investment emanating from creations of the mind (Munzer 168). In particular, the copyright system protects original creative expressions, including original artistic, musical, dramatic and literary works, and other works of authorship (17 USC § 102(a)). Protection affords the owner exclusive economic rights to reproduce and commercialize these works (17 USC § 106). Copyright also necessarily limits the ability of others to make use of these works in new and imaginative ways, without licensing or approval.

The trademark system, on the other hand, is not concerned with rewarding creators for original expressions but rather protecting consumers from confusion in the marketplace (Munzer 169). This involves protecting distinctive words, signs, images, and logos that identify the source and origin of goods and services. Owners of registered trademarks are protected against the unauthorized use of their marks, or marks that are similar, giving them the exclusive right to exploit their distinctive indicia (15 USC § 1114).

Historically, copyright has protected comic books as a whole, as either artistic works or literary works. This practice has shifted over time, with content creators seeking protection for the individual characters and associated attributes, using the copyright system to exert control and prevent others from exploiting similar characters (Helfand 626–27). More recently, DC and Marvel have led a push away from the copyright system for protection and towards trademark registration, augmenting IP law to exploit and control individual superhero characters in increasingly critical merchandising activities (Helfand 627). It is no coincidence that the increased focus on trademark protection and registration activity correlates with the introduction of transmedia versions of Marvel and DC's characters (Adams 92).

LEGAL BASIS FOR PROTECTING SUPERHEROES IN COPYRIGHT

After the first appearance of Superman in *Action Comics* 1, copyright battles ensued. More often than not relating to the protection of the character itself—fighting off alleged imitators. Although there have been cases in the United States relating to the ownership of Superman, the influential legal precedents were cases involving alleged mimics of Superman that DC argued sailed too close to the wind of their beloved character. These cases helped to silently shape the law regarding the IP protection of fictional characters.

Traditionally, copyright has protected the literary and artistic works that make up comic books or graphic novels (Helfrand 629). The justification for providing protection is to ensure authors regain a fair return on their efforts in adding to an ever-growing popular culture (Schreyer 52). Copyright law provides exclusive protection where the original work of authorship is fixed in a tangible material form (17 USC § 102(a)). However, the law does not grant protection to mere ideas, themes or concepts (*Sega Enterprises Ltd. v. Accolade, Inc.* 1526).

In exchange for the author's creative efforts, copyright law provides certain exclusive rights in their work. The fundamental right is to prohibit others from copying their work. However, the right granted is not absolute. Copyright law places a limit on the author's monopoly, ensuring protection expires and allows the work to become part of the public domain. Limiting the duration of copyright protection ensures that the public's interest in the public domain is balanced against the interest of creators to commercialize their original works (Foley 928).

Lesser known is that copyright can also protect the individual characters featured in the covers of a comic book. Over time, copyright law recognized that original expression of distinctive fictional characters could attract protection (Helfand 624, 632). Courts first determined that in order to obtain protection, a fictional character had to display sufficient original details (*Nichols v. Universal Pictures* 121). The more developed, the greater protection afforded (*Nichols v. Universal Pictures* 122–23). Therefore, a person would infringe the copyright in a fictional character if it exactly mimicked the character from a pre-existing work.

The courts soon expressed concern about authors gaining a monopoly over characters, as this was out of step with the goals of copyright law (*Nichols v. Universal Pictures* 121). The courts subsequently took a more restrictive approach to the copyright protection of a character appearing in a work. In the case of *Warner Bros. Pictures v. Columbia Broadcast Systems*, the United States Ninth District Court held that a character could only achieve copyright protection where the character constituted "the story being told" and could not be a "mere vehicle" for telling the story (950). The court reasoned that "It is conceivable that the character really constitutes the story being told, but if the character is only the chessman in the game of telling the story he is not [protected by copyright]" (*Warner Bros. Pictures v. Columbia Broadcast Systems* 950). This restrictive approach left most characters unprotected by copyright (Deamer 440).

Later judges declined to follow this approach, and the next shift came from the courts considering those characters depicted visually (Schreyer 59). Comic characters were regarded as more easily protected under copyright law (Helfand 633). Visual embodiments of characters were considered entitled to protection independent of their literary attributes: "A comic book character, which has physical as well as conceptual qualities, is more likely to contain some unique elements of expression" (*Walt Disney Prods v. Air Pirates* 755). Courts seemed to accept this statement without question (Deamer 441). Therefore, not all characters were treated equally under the law when it came to qualifying for copyright protection.

While the courts were formulating copyright principles to deal with fictional characters, Superman was soaring outside the bounds of his comic and silently shaping the law in DC's battles against Wonderman, Captain Marvel, and The

Greatest American Hero. These cases not only fortified DC's market position over the decades but also helped to influence the law itself; strengthening the entitlement of any comic book character to protection under copyright law.

The first was the copyright infringement case of Superman against Wonderman in *Detective Comics, Inc. v. Bruns Publications, Inc.* (432). The court here held that only specific details or expression of a character could enjoy legal protection and the archetype of a superhero is an idea that could not be protected against copying (433). For DC, this meant they could only prevent others from using characters portraying any of the feats of strength or powers performed by Superman or those closely mimicking his costume or appearance (*Detective Comics, Inc. v. Bruns Publications, Inc.* 433). This decision became a precedent and influenced the courts in not only subsequent Superman cases but also in the development of the law protecting fictional characters. In this instance, the attributes and antics of Superman and Wonderman were held to be too similar, and thus Bruns Publications were held to have copied. The court's comparison highlighted:

> Each at times conceals his strength beneath ordinary clothing but after removing his cloak stands revealed in full panoply in a skintight acrobatic costume. The only real difference between them is that "Superman" wears a blue uniform and "Wonderman" a red one. Each is termed the champion of the oppressed. Each is shown running toward a full moon "off into the night," and each is shown crushing a gun in his powerful hands. "Superman" is pictured as stopping a bullet with his person and "Wonderman" as arresting and throwing back shells. Each is depicted as shot at by three men, yet as wholly impervious to the missiles that strike him. "Superman" is shown as leaping over a twenty story building, and "Wonderman" as leaping from building to building. "Superman" and "Wonderman" are each endowed with sufficient strength to rip open a steel door. Each is described as being the strongest man in the world and each as battling against "evil and injustice." (*Detective Comics, Inc. v. Bruns Publications, Inc.* 433)

In a true act of balancing good and evil, the court had to also reconcile the grant of a monopoly against the interest of the public in creative expansion (Foley 928). The court was not prepared to grant DC protection over any character with the general attribute of a super powered being or a mere character of a "'Superman' who is a blessing to mankind" (*Detective Comics, Inc. v. Bruns Publications, Inc.* 434).

After twelve years of litigation, the United States Court of Appeals for the Second Circuit handed down their judgment in the next infringement case of Superman against Captain Marvel. In *National Comics Publications v. Fawcett*

Publications, the Court of Appeals upheld the lower court's finding that Fawcett copied the comic strips which appeared in *Actions Comics* and had done so with a degree of detail similar to that found in *DC v. Bruns* (597). A finding of copyright infringement resulted in Fawcett Comics cancelling all of its superhero related publications.

Not all cases were successful. In the later copyright infringement case of *Warner Bros. Pictures v. American Broadcasting Companies*, Superman was found to be susceptible to more than just Kryptonite (236). In the battle of Superman against The Greatest American Hero, the proprietors of Superman were unsuccessful in restraining the exploits of a cape-wearing superhero (*Warner Bros. Pictures v. American Broadcasting Companies* 243). The Second Circuit found that The Greatest American Hero was "not sufficiently similar to the fictional character Superman, the hero of comic books, television, and more recently films" (243). The court established this because the exploits of the alleged infringing superhero were one of a bumbling everyday man—akin more to a parody of the last son of Krypton (243).

After a trilogy of twentieth-century infringement cases, further incremental change surprisingly came with a battle over the Batmobile. The courts' previous approach to the original and consistent features of a character paved the way for protecting the Batmobile under copyright law. In *DC Comics v. Towle*, the Ninth Circuit court held that the Batmobile was eligible for protection as it displayed "a series of readily identifiable and distinguishing traits . . . recognizable because it contains bat-like motifs, such as a bat-faced grill or bat-shaped tailfins in the rear of the car, and it is almost always jet black" (967). Additionally, the court said that the creative elements that were incorporated into the Batmobile are separately identifiable and are capable of protection as they exist independently from the utilitarian aspects of the car (*DC Comics v. Towle* 968).

LEGAL BASIS FOR PROTECTING SUPERHEROES IN TRADEMARKS

Trademark law protects, *inter alia*, any word, name, symbol, figures, shapes, colors, or any combination thereof that identifies goods or services offered by a particular person or company (Munzer 168). These elements or "signs" help consumers to distinguish between goods and services that may come from different traders. Protection is enabled when the owner applies to register the sign as a trademark. Over time, Marvel and DC have made applications to register their superheroes and aspects of these characters as trademarks around the world (Adams 92).

Protection of a superhero character under trademark law is limited to the extent that the superhero or an aspect of the character functions to identify

Figure 8.1. Drawings from DC trademark application (United States Trademark registration nos. 1235769, 125674, and 1262504).

the source or origin of goods or services (Helfand 636). The establishment of a property right in a fictional character under trademark law is not possible when merely registering an image of a character as a trademark. Trademark law does not recognize the superhero's image outright; more accurately it is in the continued efforts of the owner to use the image as a source identifier that allows for protection (*In re DC Comics, Inc.* 1052). Hence, this is why Marvel and DC vigorously incorporate their characters and associated attributes into products such as toys, clothing, confectionery, and backpacks to maintain their trademark registrations (Gordon "Refiguring Media" 326–32). Furthermore, trademark registrations facilitate the commercialization of these characters with merchandising licensing ventures, allowing others to apply the characters on goods and services.

Trademark law is a familiar terrain for DC—having defended the right to protect their characters using the trademark system. In 1975, DC was able to again influence the progression of law when they sought to register drawings of three characters, Superman, Batman, and Joker, as trademarks for toy dolls (see figure 8.1).[1] DC safeguarded their application for trademark registration after an initial rejection. The United States Trademark Office initially considered the drawings naturally directed the attention of consumers to the appearance and purpose of the goods, being Superman, Batman or Joker toys (*In re DC Comics Inc.* 1042). Therefore, the drawings were "*so descriptive that they are not trademarks*" (*In re DC Comics Inc.* 211 USPQ 837). The United States Court of Customs and Patent Appeals court overturned the decision and held that DC's drawings were not descriptive of toy dolls and that "a trademark design can be embodied as a product, and marketed as such, without that design necessarily being denied trademark status" (*In re DC Comics Inc.* 1047). Once more, DC facilitated continued protection of the characters beyond their comic book covers, now under trademark law; a tactic that subsequently formed the basis of worldwide licensing.

Trademark registration affords the owner an exclusive right to stop others from using these attributes or signs in the course of trade without permission. The ultimate goal for trademark law is to protect the purchasing public from being confused with a product with a similar named or branded product from a different source (Helfand 635). An illustration of this is when considering counterfeit goods bearing a similar image of a Marvel or DC character. In these cases, the goods do not emanate from an authorized source and could be of inferior quality to the detriment of the consumer. Trademark law facilitates the true owner to control the flow of goods in the marketplace. Equally, trademark law also incentivizes Marvel and DC to maintain high levels of quality over its products and services (Helfand 635).

Trademark law was uniquely called upon in the 1980 superhero infringement case of *DC Comics v. Filmation Associates*. The United States Southern District Court of New York compared DC's characters Aquaman and Plastic Man to the defendants Manta and Superstretch characters appearing in the television show *Tarzan and the Super 7* (1275–76). The court first established that the protectable "ingredients" included character names, nicknames, physical appearance, and costumes but not their physical abilities or personality traits (1277). The latter intangible qualities could not constitute a symbol in the minds of the public to help convey source information. Ultimately, Filmation was found to have infringed the trademark rights of DC as the characters were considered too similar in appearance and that consumers were likely to be confused as to whether such characters were associated with DC Comics or not (1279).

While a superhero's name, image, or physical attributes may be protectable components under trademark law, in the end, and of importance to Marvel and DC is in the assertion of their rights. This means being able to beat their chests while waiving cease and desist letters at any competitors who dare come close to their superhero characters.

DC is not alone in asserting its rights; Marvel has also found creative ways to use IP law to gain a competitive advantage. An example of Marvel's chest-beating is the US trademark registration for the color "bright green" for use on the skin and eyes of super human character toys (United States Trademark registration no. 2834185). The trademark was filed on July 3, 2003, and coincided with the release of the 2003 Hulk motion picture. The trademark was specified as the application of the color to include the entire figure except for the hair, mouth, and shorts, as indicated in the figure below (figure 8.2).

Figure 8.2. Marvel Comics color trademark (United States Trademark registration no. 2834185).

Color trademarks such as these have remained a controversial subject in IP and in a likely effort not to offend, Marvel restricted the registration to cover the goods: "super-human character toys and playthings" (United States Trademark registration no. 2834185). Although on first glance, the registration looks overly oppressive in restricting other toy makers in using the color green, the trademark is likely unenforceable.

For an even more controversial example, Marvel and DC have jointly registered the words "SUPER HEROES" and "SUPER VILLAINS" as trademarks around the world for a variety of goods and services.[2] Perceived as a highly restrictive registration, both companies have previously failed to enforce the trademark in countries like the UK (*The Telegraph*).

THE SHIFT FROM COPYRIGHT PROTECTION TO REGISTERED TRADEMARKS

As noted in the preceding discussion, trademark and copyright principles apply to and protect different aspects of a comic book (including any enclosed characters) and are not mutually dependent. However, an important point to note is that trademark rights in a superhero character may be owned and enforced even if copyright protection in the character has expired or is lost. Unlike copyright, the benefit of trademark protection is that it can potentially continue indefinitely as long as Marvel and DC keep paying renewal fees.[3] Equally, the same applies if the superhero character is no longer being published in comic books.

Even so, trademark law does require Marvel and DC to continually convey its characters to the consuming public to maintain its registered trademarks in their superheroes. When a superhero becomes an indicator of source information, its owner has a greater imperative and burden to oversee all character-related uses, as any unfavorable use may damage the underlining protection afforded to the owner (Helfand 627). It is for these reasons that Marvel and DC are, more often than not, likely to use trademark law to circumvent what copyright law would allow under its defenses to infringement.

Commentators have argued that there has been a convergence of copyright and trademark law that has produced an "impenetrable shield" for characters such as superheroes (Helfand 641). From the 1970s, there has been a growing imperative for character owners such as Marvel and DC to seek stronger protection for their creations (Helfand 634). DC, in particular, led this charge with fears of Superman about to enter the public domain and lose copyright protection.[4] At the same time, there was a growth in opportunity for DC to merchandise Superman's image (Helfand 643).

The convergence became apparent during the 1980s in the infringement case of *DC Comics Inc. v. Unlimited Monkey Business*. The court in this case found that the defendant's use of similar costumes of Superman and Wonder Woman, balloons featuring the characters, use of the "Superman" name in advertisements, and use of similar characters in "skits" performed by their employees violated DC's rights under both copyright and trademark law (115–16). The court noted that harm occasioned by the defendant "tarnishes the 'all-American' image that the plaintiff has labored to create and to preserve" and the "Superman and Wonder Woman [trade]marks have acquired outstanding celebrity . . . as unique distinctive marks symbolizing the extensive goodwill associated with the public image of this hero and heroine" (115–16). In both instances, the court melded principles from copyright and trademark law finding in favor of DC (Helfand 648).

The convergence of copyright and trademark protection has caused alarm for some commentators. A convergence of IP principals for characters can indeed undermine the public policies upon which trademark and copyright law are founded on (Calboli 25; Helfand 652–55). The most notable problem is that attaching exclusive copyright protection while retaining a trademark's indefinite term of protection, Marvel and DC can then prevent unauthorized uses of a character in perpetuity (Helfand 654). This, in effect, could prohibit the character from falling into the public domain. However, Marvel and DC could only assert protection where the unauthorized use of the character is serving an identifying function and leaves the consumer confused as to the origin of the goods or services, as was found in *DC Comics v. Filmation Associates* (1275–76).

Notwithstanding the protection on offer, after the case of *Warner Brothers Pictures Inc. v. Columbia Broadcasting Co* in 1954, copyright appeared to fall out of favor for protection (Gaines 212). Copyright is not as flexible—unable to simultaneously protect the comic book title and character like a trademark registration can. In the United Kingdom, a trademark protecting a character's name could guard against any unauthorized use of an image recognizable as the character, even if the image is not protected as a trademark (*Hearst Holdings Inc. and another v. AVELA Inc. and others*).[5] With transmedia expansion of superhero characters beyond their native comic book strips, trademarks become increasingly important where the characters become the capital in the marketplace.

The consuming public purchases entertainment products based on the brands associated with such products. For Marvel and DC, the brands are the superhero characters. Thus, Marvel and DC's superhero characters become the crown jewel of IP rights for motion pictures, television, theme parks, and merchandising. Registered trademarks, therefore, became the critical legal tool that facilitates Marvel and DC's continued expansion.

Moreover, for Marvel and DC, registered trademarks prove to be a very effective IP right. Trademarks unapologetically stand for market expansion and control (Gaines 211). This was exemplified in the situation of Captain Marvel's name being changed to Shazam. After their defeat to DC in court, Fawcett Publications shut down their superhero comic department, allowing Captain Marvel to remain out of print for nearly two decades. Marvel saw an opportunity and in 1967 registered the name "Captain Marvel" as a trademark for a different character (United States Trademark registration no. 0892487). In 1972, when DC licensed Captain Marvel from Fawcett to revive the superhero, DC had to change the name of the publication to "Shazam" to avoid an infringement suit. Then when DC rebooted its entire comic line in 2011, it finalized the transformation and changed the name of the character from Captain Marvel to Shazam. This demonstrates the primacy of exacting market control using rights under trademark law.

As superheroes become more ubiquitous in popular culture, merchandising efforts continue to complete the robustness of the protection offered to superhero characters (Helfand 626–28). Trademarks tie characters together alongside multiple media incarnations, which appear to be mutually reinforcing, creating stronger protection (Gordon *Superman* 170). Generally, copyright is identified as the area of law to prevent unauthorized use of a character; trademarks are now increasingly being relied upon as a mechanism to control a character's use either as entertainment or merchandise products beyond their original comic book.

A NEW STATUS QUO?

Over time, trademark protection has appeared to dominate. Since the release of the 1978 Superman film, the approach of both Marvel and DC in protecting their superheroes has been to rely on trademark law. Applications for trademark protection has increased both in the United States and internationally for goods and services beyond comic book publication (Adams 96–97). Such proliferation illustrates that transmedia expansion has primarily driven the change. Not only are film and television titles being protected, but there has been an increase in protecting standalone characters and aspects of their image (Adams 94). Batman and Superman alone are the subjects of over 650 and 500 trademark registrations, respectively.

Trademark applications and registrations have shown that superhero characters do function as a "brand" or a "brand narrative" (Gordon *Superman* 170). Marvel and DC both file trademark applications to coincide with new television and film products (Adams 92). The more that this occurs, the protection becomes considerable, with recognition and use bolstering the IP protection. DC and Marvel's use of trademark law also represents a reach and influence far beyond the comics books and into the law itself, generating particularly robust and at times too strong protection for their superhero characters.

CONCLUSION

Although Superman remains invulnerable to bullets, he is not invulnerable to entering the public domain. The character as depicted in the *Action Comics* 1 (1938) is due to enter the public domain in 2033 (Sergi 208, 214).[6] However, even if entering the public domain, this would not permit others to sell goods or services bearing a similar name, image, or "S" insignia of Superman—the registered trademarks of these elements are likely to last forever.

Transmedia expansion has led to a proliferation of merchandising activities. As a result, Marvel and DC have come to use IP law as a mechanism of control over their superheroes. Given the expansion in superhero film and television franchises, the protection of a superhero's unique identity and image has become the focus of lawyers. In this way, comic book superheroes have moved beyond the pages of their comic books and silently shaped the way the law views concepts of IP and the bounds of what is capable of protection under copyright and trademark law. In short, superheroes have informed the law, even when it is not enforced.

The use of the law as a mechanism for such control has arguably created mutant IP rights that would rival even Professor X's powerful X-Men. DC and Marvel have, at various times, used copyright and trademark laws to prevent other companies from using competing characters. Surprisingly, both companies in the past have even joined forces to control the use of the word "superhero." At its core, IP law provides a framework that corporations use to allow access to their products in affording exclusive rights to their owners, to the exclusion of others. This has become no different for superhero characters.

Notes

1. See United States trademark nos. 1235769, 125674, and 1262504.

2. See United States trademark application nos. 0825835, 73384592, 77732560, 78356610, 73011796, 73222079, 72243225; Australian trademark application no. 347141; Canadian trademark no. 494962; Chile trademark application no. 709338 and 1196369; Denmark trademark no. VA197904094; European trademark application no. 3357621; Spanish trademark no. M0924589, M0924588, M0924586, M0924584, M0924585, M0924590, and M0946005; French trademark no. 1583843; Mexican trademark application nos. 119850466347, 119850466348 and 119850466350; and New Zealand trademark application nos. 130115, 130119, 130118, 130116, 130120 and 130114.

3. Registration of a trademark may be renewed for periods of ten years.

4. At that time Superman was due to fall into the public domain in 1990 under provision of the Copyright Act 1909 that granted a term of copyright protection for fifty-six years.

5. The England and Wales High Court held in this case that the use of the image of Betty Boop dressed as a cowgirl infringed the registered trademark for the words BETTY BOOP, even though the words did not appear on the product. The court regarded Betty Boop to be so well known and enjoyed such a significant reputation that it ultimately enhanced the distinctiveness of the registered trademark. The court reasoned that infringement was made out as the consuming public upon seeing the image would inevitably perceive the words "Betty Boop."

6. Depictions of Superman with additions of later developments of expression, for example, heat vision, are likely to remain protected under copyright for some time (*Silverman v. CBS Inc* 1344).

Work Cited

Adams, Mitchell. "The Secret Commercial Identity of Superheroes: Protecting the Superhero Symbol." *The Superhero Symbol: Media, Culture and Politics*, edited by Liam Burke, et al., Rutgers University Press, 2019, pp. 89–104.

"Businessman Wins Battle Against Marvel and DC Comics to Use 'Superhero' In Book Title." *The Telegraph*, 25 May 2019, https://www.telegraph.co.uk/news/2016/05/25/businessman-wins-battle-against-marvel-and-dc-comics-to-use-supe/.

Calboli, Irene. "Overlapping Copyright and Trademark Protection: A Call for Concern and Action." *Illinois Law Review Slip Opinions*, vol 25, 2014, pp. 25–34.

C.C.P.A. *In Re DC Comics, Inc.* vol 689, 1982, p. 1042.

DC Comics Inc. v. Cheqout Pty Ltd. 2013, p. 478.

DC Comics Inc. v. Crazy Eddie, Inc., Aka U.L.S., Inc., And Edward Antar. Vol. 205, 1979, p. 1177.

Deamer, Michael. "DC Comics v. Towle: Protecting Fictional Characters Through Stewardship." *Berkeley Technology Law Journal*, vol. 32, 2017, p. 437.

Foley, Kathryn. "Protecting Fictional Characters: Defining the Elusive Trademark-Copyright Divide." *Connecticut Law Review*, vol. 41, no. 3, 2009, p. 928.

Gaines, Jane. *Contested Culture*. Netlibrary, Inc., 1999.

Gordon, Ian. "Refiguring Media: Tee Shirts as A Site of Audience Engagement with Superheroes." *The Information Society*, vol. 32, no. 5, 2016, pp. 326–32.

Gordon, Ian. *Superman: The Persistence of An American Icon*. Rutgers University Press, 2017.

Hearst Holdings Inc. And Another v. AVELA Inc and Others. 2014, EWHC(Ch), p. 439.

Helfand, Michael Todd. "When Mickey Mouse Is as Strong as Superman: The Convergence of Intellectual Property Laws To Protect Fictional Literary And Pictorial Characters." *Stanford Law Review*, vol. 44, no. 3, 1992, p. 623.

Marvel Characters Inc. v. Gary Charles. 2011, p. 92.

Munzer, Stephen R. *New Essays in The Legal and Political Theory of Property*. Cambridge University Press, 2001.

N.D. Ga. *DC Comics Inc. v. Unlimited Monkey Business*. vol. 598, 1984, p. 110.

9th Cir. *DC Comics v. Towle*. Vol. 802, 2015, p. 1012.

9th Cir. *Sega Enterprises Ltd. v. Accolade, Inc*. vol. 977, 1992, p. 1510.

9th Cir. *Walt Disney Prods. v. Air Pirates*. vol. 581, 1978, p. 751.

9th Cir. *Walt Disney Products v. Air Pirates*. vol. 581, 1978, p. 751.

9th Cir. *Warner Bros. Pictures v. Columbia Broadcast Systems*. vol. 216, 1954, p. 945.

Schreyer, Amanda. "An Overview of Legal Protection for Fictional Characters: Balancing Public and Private Interests." *Cybaris Intellectual Property Law Review*, vol. 6, 2015, p. 49.

2d Cir. *Detective Comics Inc. v. Bruns Publications Inc*. vol. 111, 1940, p. 432.

2d Cir. *National Comics Publications, Inc. v. Fawcett Publications, Inc. Et Al*. vol. 191, 1951, p. 594.

2d Cir. *Nichols v. Universal Pictures Corp*. vol. 45, 1930, p. 119.

2d Cir. *Warner Bros., Inc. v. American Broadcasting Companies, Inc*. vol. 720, 1983, p. 231.

S.D.N.Y. *DC Comics Inc. v. Powers*. vol. 465, 1978, p. 843.

S.D.N.Y. *DC Comics v. Filmation Associates*. vol. 486, 1980, p. 1273.

S.D.N.Y. *Silverman v. CBS Inc*. vol. 635, 1986, p. 1344.

Sergi, Joe. *The Law for Comic Book Creators: Essential Concepts and Applications*. 1st ed., McFarland & Company, 2015.

TTAB. *In Re DC Comics*. vol. 211, 1981, p. 834.

Chapter 9

CAPES, TIGHTS, AND MOTHERSHIPS

Superheroes and New Transmedia Star Systems

CORMAC McGARRY

Superheroes have moved beyond the realm of comic books to become transmedia stars in their own right. As Mitchell Adams notes in "The Secret Commercial Identity of Superheroes," the intellectual property (IP) of superhero characters represents a highly valuable commodity that is jealously guarded by its rights holders (89). Indeed, the commercial and economic value of superhero IP is such that Ben Fritz and Stephen Metcalf have suggested that superhero characters have supplanted traditional star performers as the bedrock for successful film franchises (64; "How Superheroes"). While there may be some measure of hyperbole to Metcalf's claims that "superheroes have made movie stars expendable" and that a "business once ruled by star power is now dominated by intellectual property" ("How Superheroes"), there is also a kernel of truth here that befits further scrutiny. At a cursory glance, it can be observed that while actor star power has not been entirely eclipsed by that of IP, the presold capital for which traditional star power was originally valuable can now be equally, or even more readily, aligned to different forms of IP—particularly, as Fritz and Metcalf note, the superhero. This chapter thus examines the extent to which superhero IP has not so much torn down the existing structures of stardom but rather stepped into them in an appropriately transformative fashion.

Metcalfe's and Fritz's logic can be seen quite straightforwardly when looking at the behavior of media conglomerates as the so-called "streaming wars" kicked off in earnest. Whereas Apple's streaming platform was promoted by foregrounding star-headlined shows (with the likes of Jennifer Anniston), the Disney+ streaming service focused on IP and leaned heavily into superhero shows that would tie into its Marvel Cinematic Universe (MCU).[1] What is also significant about Disney's strategy is that, in leveraging its superhero IP in this way, the MCU can also be seen to reflect a repositioning of blockbuster cinema from end product to transmedia "mothership," especially as it becomes an anchor for a number of series for the Disney+ service.[2] This chapter contends that the transmedia approach taken in leveraging superhero IP, by Disney and others, is critical to the ability of that IP to function as a star system for its rights holders, transitioning the once comic book-bound superhero from four-color figure to a vast multimodal image producer.[3]

The chapter specifically addresses the concept of "superhero star" development by examining the transmedia franchise Marvel Rising. This project foregrounds some of Marvel's newer or lesser-known superheroes, including Ms. Marvel (Kamala Khan), Ironheart (Riri Williams), and Miss America (America Chavez). Importantly, by examining how Marvel Rising has been conceived and deployed as a franchise canonically separate to the MCU but which is nonetheless subordinate to its needs, this chapter outlines how superhero stardom is being used to lead novel strategies of transmedia stewardship as patterns of film, television, and streaming consumption undergo fundamental realignments. By blending star studies with Jason Mittell's framework for centrifugal (outward, event-based) versus centripetal (inward, character-focused) transmedia systems, this chapter analyzes how the Marvel Rising franchise can be seen as a development ground cultivating presold interest in superhero star personas in key demographics (young, female, Black, Latinx), while also providing multiple consumer entry-points and potential "thresholds" for these superhero upstarts to be become the prime movers of a superhero star system.

THE SUPERHERO STAR SYSTEM

The concept of stardom and a system of star production has been primarily explored through studies of the Hollywood film industry. As Paul McDonald succinctly expounds, the Hollywood star system functioned through the generation of star images or star personas, which were intertextual constructions that amalgamated a performer's film appearances with their publicity, promotion, and a curated image of their public and private lives. This produced a persona or "star image" that could not only be used to presell a film to an eager audience, but as a kind of collateral that could get a picture made in the first instance. McDonald explains that a star image could be marshaled as "a form of capital, [...] a form of asset deployed with the intention of gaining advantage in the entertainment market and making profits" (5). Stars held a unique place not only through the performative labor of their work onscreen, but as a valuable commercial "asset for the production company" (11). In this regard, traditional star performers had dual value. They were, on the one hand, a form of hired labor employed to perform the role of a scripted character, and on the other, they functioned as an investment, "a guarantee, or a promise, against loss" (Dyer, *Stars* 11). As such, the symbolic capital of a star's popularity and reputation could be routinely exchanged for economic capital at the box office. The capacity of a star to generate great reserves of symbolic capital that could be converted to monetary profit can be thought of as a measurement of "star power." Film producer Mark Damon summed this effect up well in an anecdote to Vanity Fair about bringing Justin Timberlake to a Cannes event to shore up foreign presells for the in-development *Spinning Gold* film. Damon observed that by "having [Timberlake] in Cannes hosting an opening-night party, we felt the publicity there would be enormous and help us achieve the number that we wanted to in the territories we sold—and then it did" (Goldstein). This kind of star power has become a crucial economic component of film production and the manufacture of stars through a system of star production has become equally vital.

The approach to superhero star production shares much common ground with the generation of traditional star images. In fact, this approach is something that has already been touched on above—the construction of an intertextual image. Richard Dyer notes that star images "are always extensive, multi-media, and intertextual" (*Heavenly Bodies* 3). McDonald puts it in plainer terms, noting that "[s]tars appear in films and other forms of media that cumulatively form the images of stars" (5). This cumulative construction through a series of intertexts suggests the power of star images can be leveraged for vast transmedia potential. McDonald describes that "the images of stars [are] constructed across various categories of texts, including not only a star's film appearances, but also forms of publicity and promotion" (6). This form of transmedia extension, now all but ubiquitous, is distinguished by Jonathan Gray as a paratextual framing which works to control entry to the text (in this case, a star image) and "to police certain reading strategies" between "the gaps of textual exhibition" (23). Jason Mittell describes such framing paratexts as part of transmedia's "complex intertextual web" (293). One advantage of using superhero IP in the mode of star personas, as this chapter will outline, is that they often come preloaded with such intertextual webs. These webs can then be marshaled to perform the functions of paratextual framing necessary for star production and promotion.

The superhero star carries forward many of the basic functions of traditional star performers, though with some caveats and some additional boons. In terms of the pure economic value of an intertextually constructed star image, that is, the part of a star that functions as "capital" and "asset," the superhero star as IP easily slips into this. What is lost falls on the side of labor. The superhero star requires embodiment in ways traditional star performers do not. This is the most obvious point of departure. Whereas the traditional star image is cultivated around a single living performer, the superhero star image has no single performer on which it is contingent. This opens it up to an extended transmedia potential with new forms of value, but it may also call for particular trade-offs over how the star image is embodied and what strategies are available to it in the accumulation of star power. Examining the point of origin of a star's intertextual image proves highly illustrative of the extent to which superheroes are capable of stepping into the existing structures of stardom and where differences in function and value begin to arise.

In trying to locate the originating instance of each type of star image, a number of key differences and trade-offs immediately come to the surface. By "originating instance," the chapter is referring to the source of a star image and the main focal point around which star power is accumulated and invested. As pointed out above, traditional star images are dependent upon their performers. In the absence of these performers, the star image cannot be easily extended.[4] Ryan Gosling, for example, is the baseline instance of Ryan Gosling's star image. Without Gosling's continued performance, the ability of his star image to circulate and accumulate star power is sharply curtailed.[5] In this way, traditional star images can be seen to be fundamentally attached to performers as the primary engines of their development. This is not the case with superhero stars, which tend to be more complex in terms of their source. Such complexity prevents a one-to-one comparison of originating instances and arises from the image of the superhero star not being contingent upon any given performer. The star image of Batman, for example, does not fold back singularly into Michael Keaton or Christian Bale or even into *Detective Comics* 27. The star image of Batman, and his star power, aggregates from each of these instances and none are able to hold it exclusively. There is no unitary source for a superhero's star image, though one can suggest that a superhero's comic book canon could be taken as a collective primary source for the image.[6] This canon, as a rich serial history, often provides what Mittell describes as a "complex intertextual web" (293) that can retroactively be put to work as an engine for the aggregation of star power. The difference in image construction and the accumulation of star power is made clear here. Where the star power of traditional images collapses back into a contingent performer as its primary engine, the star power of superheroes cannot be collapsed back into a singular source because one has never existed for it. Thus, while both images accrue star power cumulatively, they do so in different ways. Traditional star power is driven by the performer's extension of their own image through a "coherent continuousness" (Dyer, *Heavenly Bodies* 10), while superhero star power is generally derived from a more diverse image that is always already dispersed and drawn into association ex post facto.

This difference in the image construction and accumulation of star power also highlights some of the additional trade-offs between the two star types. While traditional performers, as the main drivers of their image, can have star-making turns on the backs of single pictures, the superhero stars pointed to by Fritz and Metcalfe have required much longer gestations. A notable exception here is the character of Superman. Ian Gordon notes that a quick expansion into radio, animation, and television marked a relatively rapid star turn which saw the character swiftly transfigured into "something larger than simply a comic book superhero" (6–7). While other superheroes such as Wonder Woman and The Incredible Hulk enjoyed periods of notoriety through prime-time television, the star-making of superheroes has generally required multiple outings. Liam Burke details this in relation to Marvel—now a household brand, but which had "struggled to realize its characters in other media" prior to "the success[es] of the 1990s" ("Sowing the Seeds" 106). Burke makes the point that Marvel's range of animated series during this time period was critical as a stepping stone in taking its superhero characters into the mainstream and setting up the later success of the MCU. He notes, quoting Robert Stam, that "diverse prior adaptations can form a larger, cumulative hypotext that is available to the filmmaker who comes relatively 'late' in the series" (Stam 66). Burke cites, as an example, Bryan Singer's commentary on the value of the *X-Men* animated series (1992–1997) in having built up greater public awareness of the characters ahead of their first feature film installment ("Sowing the Seeds" 106). The value of this larger hypotext can be couched in terms of a cultural capital which, preexisting in the dispersed image of the superhero, can kickstart the accumulation of greater star power and protect this star power from being cannibalized by the images of stars who step into superhero roles.

The particular lineage of superhero star images as having typically passed through animation on their way from comic books to the silver screen might have a particular importance in this regard. Burke, contextualizing John Semper's insights on *Spider-Man: The Animated Series* (1994–98), notes that "these animated series did not have the benefit of successful audiovisual versions of the heroes to guide the adaptations" ("Sowing the Seeds" 112). This could, however, also be seen as having a double effect. With no real successful audiovisual versions of the characters being widely appreciated and the often-obscured identity of performers within animation, the cultural capital accrued by these series could be understood to be invested primarily in the images of the superheroes themselves. Thus, not only would these series provide a blueprint to future feature adaptations, but the superhero characters of these features could rise to stardom on the back of a cultural dividend that they did not have to share with their performers. What is more, that dividend essentially becomes reinvested by the performances of traditional stars in superhero features as they continue to add to the cumulative hypotext. This is a phenomenon that the Marvel Rising franchise examined later in the chapter aims to replicate. The slow maturation of such cultural dividends does, however, make quite clear that a central trade-off of the superhero star is rooted in the additional time required for development. A study of *Marvel Rising* shows that new transmedia strategies are being employed by conglomerates, such as Disney, to decrease the gestational length of these cumulative hypotexts in order to more expeditiously transfigure their superhero IP into profitable star personae. In order to best understand how these transmedia strategies operate, it is first necessary to outline one further core difference between traditional star performers and superhero stars. I categorize this as a tension between the monopoly value of a star image and its *threshold value*.

THE MAXIMUM OCCUPANCY OF A MASK

Janet Staiger explains that "[e]conomically, the star may be thought of as a monopoly on personality" (104). She suggests that a star's "unique qualities [...] permit a company to declare the merchandising of an exclusive product" and that the star thus becomes "a means to differentiate product to achieve monopoly profits" (104). The individuality of a star performer, say Tom Hanks, provides differentiation by virtue of there being only one Tom Hanks. The singularity of that star persona's originating instance enables a monopoly value. Essentially, because there are no other "Tom Hankses" available to the market, as long his star image maintains some symbolic capital (prestige, reputation, or recognition of uniqueness), there is nothing to prevent or dilute its conversion into substantive economic capital. Audiences are attuned to this monopoly such that there is an understanding of going to see a "Tom Hanks picture." Thus, Tom Hanks alone embodies his monopoly value. His star image can therefore be seen to provide market differentiation for the film and raise its potential for profit. This monopoly value reflects the ability of star power to function as the "guard against loss" discussed earlier (Dyer, *Stars* 11). Over time, a number of superhero star personas have achieved this level of differentiation too. Audiences will understand and respond to the idea of going to see a "Batman film," for example. A similar kind of monopoly value is in play here.

There are, however, some key differences with the superhero star image that can potentially undermine its monopoly value. This is where the star's originating instance comes in. Although, like the superhero star, a traditional star persona is not a real person but an intertextual and mediated image; that image always folds back singularly into its performer where the cumulative hypotext of the superhero star prevents this action. As Paul McDonald notes, the intertextual construction of the star persona is "taken to stand in for the person" (6). For traditional star performers, this stand-in is singular and unable to be stepped into. It has a maximum occupancy of one and is completely tied to the performer who generates the image. This maximum occupancy is critical to their monopoly value as it singles them out in their uniqueness. Superhero stars, on the other hand, are already uncontingent intertextual constructions. As such, they can have their star image—their stand-in—stepped into by any number of simultaneous performers in any of the intertexts that make up that construction. The tights and masks of superhero stars have no maximum occupancy. They can be *manifoldly embodied*. The star image of the Flash, for example, can be simultaneously stepped into by both Ezra Miller (*Justice League*, 2017) and Grant Gustin (The CW's *The Flash*, 2014-2023). This is the kernel of an extended transmedia potential that enables the threshold value detailed below. It does, however, carry the risk of diluting the monopoly value of the superhero star, since manifold embodiment reveals the always artificial nature of the superhero star's monopoly value. Manifold embodiment can threaten the monopoly value of the star image because it enables heterodox meanings—which is to say, because a superhero star can be inhabited by several performers at the same time, each iteration potentially creates a number of different meanings that can disrupt the status quo of the image or prevent one from forming altogether. In context, this means that while Ezra Miller and Grant Gustin both embody a same and single referent in the Flash, they each develop meanings for that referent differently.

This heterodoxy (the branched meaning of a single referent) has largely been seen as a risk to the monopoly value of the superhero star and the market differentiation it provides. This pertains especially to any simultaneous heterodoxy in which multiple versions of the character are in play at the same time. As such, IP holders have usually favored limiting this potential risk by constraining how the superhero star image is stepped into. These constraints have been visible through a number of embargoes placed on where and when certain superhero characters could appear, thereby placing protectionist limits on the maximum occupancy of the superhero star image. The "Bat-embargo" is probably the most well-known of these. The embargo earmarked certain characters that were to appear only in Christopher Nolan's *Dark Knight* trilogy (2005-12) and the animated series *The Batman* (2004-8). Paul Levitz, then president and publisher of DC Comics, explained to the *World's Finest* fan-site that "[p]roducts work better when they have a single outlet. As a company (in this case, DC) you don't want to oversaturate your market" ("The Embargo"). This echoes Janet Staiger's explanation of monopoly value. As further explained on *World's Finest*, the embargo was seen as serving the function of preventing audience conflicts and confusion between concurrent iterations of a character ("The Embargo").

The perceived wisdom here being that the embargo prevented the company from having to differentiate characters from themselves, thus enabling the star image of the IP to hold an artificial, but no less profitable, monopoly value. While a number of petitions against the "Bat-embargo" attracted followings and criticized the implication of audiences' naivety, the policy remained and was replicated for other DC Comics superheroes.[7]

Such embargoes neatly emblematize the tension between preserving the monopoly value of a character or gambling whether investment in the wider and more diverse threshold value of the star will bear greater fruit. Conglomerates have traditionally backed the more conservative approach to preserve monopoly value. As Staiger and Dyer have set out, it is a more established guard against loss. However, as patterns of consumption have changed and industries around streaming and videogames have risen to challenge and outperform Hollywood, conglomerates have demonstrated a greater willingness to allow its superhero stars to be manifoldly embodied in order to exploit the threshold value of its IP. In this regard, superhero characters have been at the forefront of shifting conceptions about the most profitable ways to tap into a star's capital.

I propose the concept of *threshold value* as a framework for understanding how the superhero star, through manifold embodiment, can be exploited for capital without conforming to the more established logic of monopoly preservation. In contrast to monopoly value, which relies on the exclusivity of the star as something rare and carefully apportioned, threshold value takes advantage of stars whose images are drawn from diverse and multiple instances. These instances can then be used as the kind of transactive space which Gérard Genette has termed "the threshold" (2). While thresholds are by no means unique to superhero stars (all texts can be seen to have thresholds), the superhero star is specially gifted when it comes to the generation and systematization of them. Genette explains that the threshold should be considered a "'vestibule' that offers the world at large the possibility of either stepping inside or turning back. It is an 'undefined zone' between the inside and the outside" (2). Importantly, Genette outlines that the threshold is "a zone not only of transition but also of *transaction*" (2). The threshold, then, is both that paratextual space which Gray lays out as preparing our entry into the core text and policing our reading around it (23), in addition to functioning as a wider transtextual space of exchange. It is this latter and less-discussed mode which threshold value takes most advantage of, allowing for cultural dividends from different instances of a superhero to come together as a greater symbolic capital which can always be reflexively reinvested. This leads to what might be called "reflexive economies of scope" in which greater monetary profits could potentially be garnered than through constraining the same star to produce an artificial monopoly value.

In economics, economies of scope relate to efficiencies and profits made by increased variety through the diversification of existing product. The term "reflexive economies of scope" is suggested here to denote instances in which two or more such economies prosper from the diversification of the same product. They are thus mutually interlocked and can always potentially refer back to each other. By sharing a common threshold, reflexive economies of scope can vastly expand the potential for gross profit through a powerful cross-selling mechanism. In this way, reflexive economies of scope can be seen to fulfill what Derek Johnson describes as the "industrial promise of 'synergy,' where [notionally] the same content can dominate multiple markets and generate more value than the sum of its iterative parts" (67). These reflexive economies of scope are thus primed to exploit superhero stars who, having no maximum occupancy for their star image, can be put to diverse and simultaneous transmedia work which raises the potential for profit. Threshold value, then, reflects this ability to leverage a common threshold between instances of the star to perform this work. It is particularly supported by the new transmedia strategies which this chapter proposes are promoting superhero stardom. The Marvel Rising franchise is offered below as a case study in how these new transmedia strategies operate and how they look to take advantage of superheroes' innate threshold value to create the superhero stars referred to by Fritz and Metcalfe.

RISING TO STARDOM: MARVEL'S COEXTENSIVE TRANSMEDIA

The Marvel Rising franchise was a transmedia project launched in 2018 and consisted of a television film, several shorts and TV specials, two print comic book series, six motion comics, a series of music singles, and a toyline. The franchise focused on Marvel's newer or less-developed superhero properties in a number of important target demographics and skewed particularly towards young adult and preteen audiences. It represents, perhaps, Marvel's most considered transmedia effort outside of its cinematic universe. Importantly, the two have no diegetic connections, and the character instances of *Marvel Rising* are not canon within the MCU. They are either heterodox (different from an MCU counterpart) or have never had any noteworthy representations that might otherwise dominate familiarity. In spite of having no diegetic links, the chapter proposes that *Marvel Rising* is nonetheless subordinate to the needs of the MCU and is positioned to elevate select characters to superhero stardom by capitalizing on new transmedia strategies designed to maximize returns from threshold value. These strategies can be explained as a kind of *coextensive transmedia* that builds on Jason Mittell's concepts.

In his analysis of complex narration in contemporary television, Mittell outlines two frameworks of storytelling that he later extends to emblematize different kinds of transmedia systems. These systems provide an ideal context for the exploration of the threshold value, which this chapter proposes is the operative economic logic behind the development and success of superhero stars. Mittell outlines the contrasting characteristics of "centrifugal" and "centripetal" systems of transmedia storytelling (304, 311). Centrifugal systems, he notes, can be seen at work where "the ongoing narrative pushes outward, spreading characters across an expanding storyworld" (222). Mittell explains of the centrifugal system that it has "no single narrative center" and that "its richness is found in the complex web of interconnectivity forged across the social system rather than in the depth of any one individual's role in the narrative" (222). Disney's MCU can easily be seen to obey this kind of narrative flow in which "[s]ystemic logic trumps characters' actions" (222). A centrifugal system thus seems to suit the ideals of blockbuster franchises and more event-based storytelling.

Centripetal systems, on the other hand, contrast with this state. Mittell explains that centripetal systems reflect a model in which "narrative movement pulls actions and characters inward toward a gravitational center, establishing a thickness of backstory and character depth that drives the action" (223). This model is, perhaps, less conducive to cinematic franchises, which have typically traded on event-based spectacle. Mittell, whose focus is on television, offers the example of *Breaking Bad* (2008–13) as a stand-out model, noting how its narrative and limited transmedia tend to focus on character elaboration over plot or setting (311). Interestingly, Mittell observes of *Breaking Bad*'s centripetal transmedia that it focused on "secondary characters" (311). This chapter suggests that *Marvel Rising* could be considered such a centripetal system owing to its focus on building out backstory and depth for ancillary characters. Considering this, Mittell's models become very useful ways to think about how transmedia storytelling is being approached by content producers and how these models can be used to shed light on the operations of a potential superhero star system. It seems that media conglomerates have figured out how to deftly combine these transmedia models so that their synergy maximizes the potential for their IP's threshold value to return profits. This synergized transmedia model appears to have been largely tailor-made to develop and capitalize on superhero stardom. I propose the term "coextensive transmedia" as a descriptor of this model and suggest Disney's management of the Marvel Rising franchise illustrates its workings especially well.

The term "coextensive transmedia" is offered for this synergized model since, like the reflexive economies it aims to produce, it relies on shared referents. These referents (the intertextual stand-ins of star images), coextending over a common threshold, can thus easily be leveraged to lead, organize, and support a wide transmedia consumption. To achieve this state, coextensive transmedia employs Mittell's centrifugal and centripetal systems in orbit around each other. Much as is the case for traditional transmedia storytelling, coextensive transmedia is usually "unbalanced" (294). Mittell explains that this means there is "a clearly identifiable core text and a number of peripheral transmedia extensions" (294). Whereas traditional transmedia storytelling commonly privileges a core text as its narrative "mothership," a coextensive transmedia strategy would privilege a core *system*. Following the engrained economic logic of the field, this system tends to be the more event-based centrifugal system where film franchises are given priority. David A. Gross summarizes this logic, noting that "there is no more profitable business model than a successful theatrical release—creating the biggest pop culture event possible. It's the locomotive that pulls the entire train: merchandise, theme park licensing, other income" (quoted in Barnes). Coextensive transmedia places smaller centripetal systems in the service of this train, allowing the centrifugal system to draw on them for fuel. In doing so, coextensive transmedia can be employed to cut down the gestational length of the cumulative hypotexts required for superhero star power, the biggest stumbling block to profiting from their greater threshold value. The MCU and *Marvel Rising* exist in a coextensive formation where the former acts as a mothership that anchors and subordinates a smaller system geared towards character development and profile building for future superhero stars that the mothership might use.

For coextensive transmedia to cut down the gestational length of hypotexts, it must rely on two things: firstly, the superhero image's uncapped maximum occupancy (i.e., its potential for heterodoxy and manifold embodiment), and second, the transparent layering of a superhero's many heterodox instances. This transparent layering, or framing, serves an additional vital function as a hierarchy which upholds what Mittell has described as the commercial and "industrial edict" to protect the mothership (295). It allows the constituent systems to remain diegetically unrelated even as a common threshold is shared. This means that by simply being coextensive, the risk of introducing a "dud" into the main system is reduced as characters who fail to build significant star power can simply remain in the orbiting system. This allows orbiting centripetal systems to vastly and simultaneously expand the cumulative hypotext of a given superhero while functioning as safe development grounds that preserve the integrity of the mothership.

This safety allows for the time taken to create large hypotexts to be cut down and for conglomerates to shepherd through characters in key demographics with targeted centripetal systems instead of having to rely on star casting to generate enthusiasm. *Marvel Rising* is an excellent example of this.

Cort Lane, senior vice-president for Marvel Animation and executive producer of *Marvel Rising*, attested to this when he noted a strategic targeting of a young female audience.

> [We] have been observing that half our [MCU] box office is female of various ages. We've been watching in consumer products and in publishing. Certain female characters really pop as being relevant to women and girls, and so we saw there was an opportunity—a very clear opportunity, more than there ever has been—to do something that was more girl-targeted. (quoted in Damore)

Lane's comments underscore the position of *Marvel Rising* as a targeted system of character development in service to the MCU. As Lane notes, the box office return of a larger centrifugal system was clearly a conscious factor in the design of *Marvel Rising*. In a separate interview, Lane also notes the importance of developing content for this demographic "outside the feature films" (quoted in Trumbore). This reflects Mittell's observations of a commercial edict that requires the mothership to be protected and further reinforces *Marvel Rising*'s position as a character development system unconnected to the MCU but nonetheless in service of it.

Of *Marvel Rising*'s central cast, Ms. Marvel (Kamala Kahn) has headlined an eponymous Disney+ series and features as a main character in *The Marvels* (2023), while Ironheart (Riri Williams) debuted in the much-anticipated sequel *Black Panther: Wakanda Forever* (2022) and is set to follow Ms. Marvel in leading her own Disney+ series. Miss America (America Chavez), meanwhile, featured prominently in *Doctor Strange in the Multiverse of Madness* (2022). They each represent important target demographics where the MCU lacks star power (namely, queer characters and women from African American and Latin communities). By developing larger hypotexts for these characters, Marvel aims to foster the investment of a greater cultural dividend that will ensure their successful mothership entry. *Marvel Rising* has been positioned as a strategically timed vehicle for this and as such can be seen to put stock in the ability of the characters' threshold value to produce these cultural dividends. Notably, the franchise's main installments recapitulate the trajectory of superheroes passing through animation on their way to live action; in this case, both to cultivate the exclusive investment of the cultural dividend with the superhero image and as a further marker of difference that protects the mothership. For *Marvel Rising* to be successful in this coextensive role, it must also build in the layers of transparency discussed above. These are essential to the ability of the cumulative hypotext to provide star power for these characters.

Christine Geraghty notes that transparency allows for the potential to see through texts (or in this case, heterodox referents) and accounts for the effect of simultaneity as drawing on "understandings built up through time and knowledge" (195). Liam Burke, meanwhile, observes the related phenomenon of "flexible continuity" which has been a particular hallmark of serialized comic book superheroes and has allowed transmedia texts to cohere and amend themselves "around widely seen adaptations" ("Bigger Universe" 36). Such transparency and flexible continuities allow for heterodox instances of superheroes to become what Lincoln Geraghty has referred to as "transmedia signposts" that can direct audiences and function as "signifiers of [. . .] transmedia history [. . .] and objects of fan-cultural value" (117). For *Marvel Rising*, which aims to introduce future mothership stars, this transparent layering takes shape through heterodox versions of established mothership characters. Captain Marvel, Shuri, and SHIELD agent Daisy Johnson are among some of the signposts that enable transparent layering and the coextension of a threshold through which new stars can make the jump to the mothership. Their more rapidly developed cumulative hypotexts can be transacted for star power through this process. Daisy Johnson, in particular, is voiced by, and modelled after, her *Agents of S.H.I.E.L.D.* (2013–20) actor Chloe Bennett. This transparency allows for audiences to make connections between the two transmedia systems even as they are kept diegetically separate. While Johnson is perhaps not quite at the level of superhero stardom as Captain Marvel, both demonstrate threshold value as characters who can do simultaneous work in leading, organizing, and supporting reflexive transmedia consumption across systems. Additionally, their transparency as signposts allows for characters like Kamala Kahn, America Chavez, and Riri Williams to board the mothership more easily, having quickly built up larger cumulative hypotexts and secure cultural dividends as the anchors of centripetal systems devoted to their character development. Once successfully integrated, their star power can also function reflexively and drive movement between systems and potentially expand gross profits. Whereas superheroes earmarked for the silver screen may previously have been embargoed to protect their monopoly value, conglomerates are now recognizing that exploiting their threshold value may prove more advantageous.

Superheroes, then, have not dismantled Hollywood's longstanding star structures but have instead transformed them in a manner that has allowed once comic book-bound characters to ascend to the spotlight on their own merits. *Marvel Rising* has demonstrated the capacity of superheroes to produce a threshold value that can underpin stardom through new transmedia strategies. Superheroes, by their ability to be manifoldly embodied, can be used in coextensive transmedia systems where the previously presumed threat of their heterodoxy is mitigated by making them transparent signposts able to share thresholds that mobilize reflexive consumption and economies of scope. Such transmedia systems greatly cut down on the development time of the cumulative hypotexts needed for superhero stardom. Through coextensive transmedia, the potential of the superhero's threshold value is realized, and powerful cultural dividends can be quickly produced to propel them beyond comic books and into the limelight.

Notes

1. Disney+ notably promoted its launch with the announcement of several comic book-based properties that would tie into the MCU through established characters, thus reiterating the capital of IP as equal to or above traditional star power. Disney doubled down on this approach, announcing a second wave of uncast MCU tie-in shows at its D23 Expo in 2019.

2. The "mothership" is a term used to describe the core text that orders a hierarchy of transmedia extensions. It was coined by Damon Lindelof and Carlton Cuse in relation to the transmedia strategies of their TV series *Lost*.

3. It should additionally be noted that Warner Media's HBO Max service also leveraged comic book superheroes, both by highlighting its DC Comics IP in sizzle reels and through the creation of a promotional digital comic series.

4. Star images do not necessarily die with their performers. They can continue to circulate through their preexisting texts, but that circulation is difficult to expand without the performer. Technology enables some attempts to be made through what we might call *digital revenants*. James Dean, for example, is set to be digitally recreated to star in *Finding Jack*. However, the performative distinctions which often drive a star's monopoly value are not as easily recreated as their likeness, and thus this practice may not bear the same profits. This might also explain the limited effect of biopics in extending the star images of deceased performers.

5. Star images can become entangled as in the case of star couples such as "Brangelina" (Brad Pitt and Angelina Jolie). Such star couples tend to mutually extend each other's star images by their shared publicity. The disentangling of the images, however, largely sees star power repatriated to the individual performers respectively. This highlights the contingency of entangled images upon its constituent performers and points to the individual as the primary source of the star image. Whether the entangled image could emerge as a star image in its own right is debatable.

6. The vast majority of superhero stars are adaptations originally derived from serialized comic books. It is not impossible for superhero stars to have origins in other media or in single texts, but as the chapter *passim* points out, superhero stardom generally relies on having established intertextual networks to expedite their value. Thus, superhero stars without these networks to draw on may require long gestations which make them unviable as options for immediate or sustained turnover.

7. Character embargoes have previously applied at large to characters such as Aquaman and Wonder Woman. The CW Network's *Arrow-verse* and its prior DC shows like *Smallville* (2001–11) have also been affected by more limited embargoes.

Works Cited

Adams, Mitchell. "The Secret Commercial Identity of Superheroes: Protecting the Superhero Symbol." *The Superhero Symbol: Media, Culture, and Politics*, edited by Liam Burke et al., Rutgers University Press, 2020, pp. 89–104.

Barnes, Brooks. "Managing Movie Superheroes Is About to Get a Lot More Complicated." *New York Times*, 27 Dec. 2020, www.nytimes.com/2020/12/27/business/media/dc-superheroes-movies.html.

Burke, Liam. "A Bigger Universe: Marvel Studios and Transmedia Storytelling." *Assembling the Marvel Cinematic Universe*, edited by Julian C. Chambliss et al., McFarland, 2018, pp. 32–51.

Burke, Liam. "Sowing the Seeds: How 1990s Marvel Animation Facilitated Today's Cinematic Universe." *Marvel Comics into Film: Essays on Adaptations since the 1940s*, edited by Matthew J. McEniry et al., McFarland, 2016, pp. 106–17.

Damore, Meagan. "Marvel Rising: Secret Warriors EP Wants to Show 'Girls Kick Butt' Too." *CBR*, 22 Sept. 2018, www.cbr.com/marvel-rising-secret-warriors-cort-lane/.

Dyer, Richard. *Heavenly Bodies: Film Stars and Society*. 2nd ed., Routledge, 2004.

Dyer, Richard. *Stars*. BFI Publishing, 1998.

"The Embargo." *The World's Finest*, dcanimated.com/WF/sections/faq/.

The Flash. Performance by Grant Gustin. The CW, 2014–2023.

Fritz, Ben. *The Big Picture: The Fight for the Future of Movies*. Houghton Mifflin Harcourt, 2019.

Genette, Gérard. *Paratexts: Thresholds of Interpretation*. Translated by Jane E. Lewin, Cambridge University Press, 2001.

Geraghty, Christine. *Now a Major Motion Picture: Film Adaptations of Literature and Drama*. Rowman & Littlefield Publishers, 2008.

Geraghty, Lincoln. "Transmedia Character Building: Textual Crossovers in the Star Wars Universe." *Star Wars and the History of Transmedia Storytelling*, edited by Sean Guynes and Dan Hassler-Forest, Amsterdam University Press, 2018, pp. 117–28.

Goldstein, Gregg. "Cannes: Star-Studded Pre-Sales Events Lure International Buyers." *Variety*, 15 May 2014, variety.com/2014/film/markets-festivals/agents-find-new-expensive-ways-to-sell-movies-in-crowded-markets-1201178801/.

Gordon, Ian. *Superman: The Persistence of an American Icon*. Rutgers University Press, 2017.

HBO MAX Digital Comic, no. 1, DC Comics, June 2020.

Johnson, Derek. *Media Franchising: Creative License and Collaboration in the Culture Industries*. New York University Press, 2013.

Justice League. Directed by Joss Whedon, Warner Bros. Pictures, 2017.

Marvel's Agents of S.H.I.E.L.D. Performance by Chloe Bennett, ABC, 2013–2020.

Marvel Rising: Secret Warriors. Performance by Kathreen Khavari. ABC, 2018.

McDonald, Paul. *The Star System: Hollywood's Production of Popular Identities*. Wallflower, 2000.

Metcalf, Stephen. "How Superheroes Made Movie Stars Expendable." *New Yorker*, 9 July 2019, www.newyorker.com/magazine/2018/05/28/how-superheroes-made-movie-stars-expendable.

Mittell, Jason. *Complex TV: The Poetics of Contemporary Television Storytelling*. New York University Press, 2015.

Smallville. Performance by Tom Welling. The WB/The CW, 2001–11.

Spider-Man. Performance by Christopher Daniel Barnes. Fox Kids Network, 1994–98.

Stam, Robert. "Beyond Fidelity: The Dialogics of Adaptation." *Film Adaptation*, edited by James Naremore, Rutgers University Press, 2000, pp. 57–78.

Trumbore, Dave. "Cort Lane on 'Marvel Rising' and Bringing Superheroes to Life in Ways Never Seen Before." *Collider*, 24 Sept. 2018, collider.com/marvel-rising-cort-lane-interview/.

X-Men. Performance by Norm Spencer. Fox Kids Network, 1992–7.

Chapter 10

SUPER FANS OR TOXIC MADMEN?

Fantasy, Reality, and Marginalized Identities in Subversive "DIY Superhero" Indie Films

JACK TEIWES

Over the first two decades of the millennium, superhero cinema has rapidly ballooned from a sporadic genre at best to becoming the nigh-dominant model for movie blockbusters.[1] The 2010s saw the rise of the Marvel Cinematic Universe (MCU), an effectively unprecedented endeavor in both ambition and success,[2] encompassing twenty-three interconnected films over its first eleven years. The MCU rapidly developed a sprawling common diegesis that for the first time robustly reflected the ongoing "shared universe" model which has typically unified most superhero comic books produced under a single publisher, for well over half a century (Burke *Comic Book Film Adaptation* 63, 66; "A Bigger Universe" 40, 42–45, 47).

Less well known, however, is that alongside this newfound ubiquity for superhero films came a cluster of original low-budget, deeply unconventional superhero films, produced independently of Hollywood's studio system. Looking beyond comic book adaptation, these films took a subversive approach to the increasing popularity of the genre and mainstream image of superheroes. Conceived of individually rather than as part of any coherent aesthetic movement, six such movies were released over the course of as many years. They comprise the American productions *Special* (2006), *Defendor* (2009), *Kick-Ass* (2010), and *Super* (2010), as well as Australia's *Griff the Invisible* (2010) and China's bilingual *Inseparable* (2011).

This chapter argues that these constitute a small yet distinct subgenre of films definable through a very similar premise and key criteria that set them apart from the dominant comic-based superhero narratives. Each features a geeky lead character, portrayed as a socially "Othered" outsider with some form of implied neurodivergent cognition or otherwise vaguely defined mental health issue, who decides to adopt a superhero identity in an attempt to fight crime. Crucially, these narratives are always framed as occurring in notionally "real world" settings, wherein superheroes hitherto only exist as fictional characters.

Despite this concession to realism, however, each protagonist is contextually presented as though they are implicitly the first person who has ever attempted such a thing. This sidesteps any acknowledgement of the *actual* "Real Life Superhero" (RLSH) phenomenon of citizens dressing up in outlandish costumes to deter crime and perform community service (Iouchkov and Birch 56–64).

No interviews or commentary were found by the respective filmmakers indicating that they took any inspiration from (or had much prior awareness of) the relatively new RLSH phenomenon while making their films. Given the generally more violent and dramatic content of these movies, it would be a misnomer to describe their protagonists as fictionalized RLSH representations. Thus, to avoid confusion, I use the term "DIY Superhero." The "Do-It-Yourself" ethos both diegetically and extradiegetically describes not only the characters' paths to costumed vigilantism, but also the indie film nature of this subgenre.

This chapter will demonstrate how these films fundamentally take their intertextual genre cues from character dramas and black comedies more so than the action-adventure tropes of traditional comic-adapted superhero movies. The six films depict dysfunctional protagonists struggling with some sense of being marginalized or Othered, who seek redress via asserting a violent masculinity achieved through constructing superhero identities. Though heterosexual, cisgendered, and predominantly white men, these characters self-consciously do not measure up to the comic book alpha males they seek to emulate. This chapter will also unpack how these protagonists are framed in respect to fan culture and toxic masculinity, as the films implicitly question the appeal of masked vigilantism and violent heroism.

DEFINITIONS AND EXCLUSIONS

This chapter casts a wider net for the purposes of clarifying the framework and parameters of this research project. Many films were considered for inclusion, as a method of both testing, and refining, the criteria for classification.

A wealth of material exists for a broader project studying superhero-themed or inflected movies outside of the Hollywood system, or original superhero films that are not adapted from other media. Such is the case without even embracing wider definitions of "superheroes" that could encompass Mexican *Luchador* films or subsets of Japanese *Tokusatsu*, let alone unlicensed international movies that flout copyright on American superhero IP.

For the purposes of this chapter, however, the qualifying criteria for identifying a "DIY Superhero Film" requires the following:

1. An ostracized, socially dysfunctional, and/or cognitively atypical protagonist.
2. An ostensibly "realistic" diegesis in which superheroes or paranormal forces do not demonstrably exist.
3. The protagonist creates a vigilante alter-ego, at least attempting to conceal their "secret identity" by putting together an original superhero-themed costume.
4. Whether fully comprehending the facts or not, they attempt crimefighting despite not possessing superhuman powers, nor any technologically implausible/magical equipment.

DISQUALIFIED EXAMPLES

Many other unconventional superhero movies were considered, on the basis of generally being independent productions, featuring original superheroes with similar offbeat thematic or conceptual elements. Most were ultimately excluded for failing to meet all four qualifying factors (figure 10.1).

Disqualifications included films where protagonists in a seemingly "real world" setting nevertheless display actual superpowers (e.g., *American Hero* 2015) or fight crime without either powers or a costume (*Boy Wonder* 2010). Some involved protagonists with no atypical mental state (*Unbreakable* 2000), or feature superhero-themed delusions but no attempted crimefighting (*Paper Man* 2009). Others featured dysfunctional and nonpowered leads yet had fantastical settings in which superbeings and mad-science objectively exist (*All Superheroes Must Die* 2011), or where the revelation of a similarly strange milieu belatedly renders the nonpowered protagonist superhuman after all (*Zebraman* 2004). Alternatively, a hitherto seemingly delusional vagrant's suppressed superpowers actually do return, validating his fantastical backstory in a final twist (*Archenemy* 2020).

Some already disqualified films had additional thematic or stylistic incongruities with the proposed subgenre, being either outright comedies (*The Specials* 2000) or essentially vigilante crime thrillers, indistinguishable from the likes of *Death Wish* (1974) or any conventional action movie, were it not for some very token costume elements (*John Doe: Vigilante* 2014). Some films presented vigilante superhero tropes without subversion of their obsessive motivations, uncritically portraying lower-tech Batman-type heroes in earnest (*Bhavesh Joshi Superhero* 2018).

Figure 10.1. Theatrical release posers for many of the liminal and disqualified films considered, from: (L-R) *Bhavesh Joshi Superhero* (2018), *Birdman* (2014), *The Specials* (2000), *Sidekick* (2005), *John Doe: Vigilante* (2014), *Blankman* (1994), *Boy Wonder* (2010), *American Hero* (2015), *Vigilante* (2008), *Crimefighters* (2010), *Zebraman* (2004), *Hero at Large* (1980), *Hancock* (2008), *Paper Man* (2009), *Noise* (2007), *Joker* (2019), *Unbreakable* (2000), *Condorman* (1981), *All Superheroes Must Die* (2011), and *Archenemy* (2020).

Since my original research, the Academy Award–winning film *Joker* (Phillips 2019) has been released to acclaim, backlash, and moral panic over its contested political undertones, including over issues of toxic fandom and masculinity to be discussed later. Despite being (very loosely) based on arguably the most prominent villain character in the history of superhero comics, it is relevant to mention at this juncture, as the movie actually shares most of the qualifying tropes for the DIY Superhero subgenre.

Joker showcases a severely ostracized man with overtly stated (but unspecified) psychiatric disorders and no superhuman abilities, in the process of "empowering" himself through the use of a violent costumed identity, amidst an ostensibly realistic setting. However, the key factor, which discounts the film from inclusion, is that its protagonist, Arthur Fleck, does not model his colorful new persona as a superhero nor in any way aspire to be one.[3] Indeed, although diegetically framed by others as some form of vigilante or even revolutionary, the homicidal Fleck openly rejects these labels, embracing (vaguely defined) infamy instead.

LIMINAL EXAMPLES

Although still not satisfying all the DIY subgenre criteria, three antecedent films demonstrated sufficient generic density to merit brief mention.

Condorman (1981) features a comic book writer/artist who conducts espionage in the persona of his previously published superhero creation. Although nonpowered, the CIA builds him implausible laser guns and outlandish Batman-style vehicles. Additionally, Condorman fights spies rather than criminals and appears sane, albeit blithely risk taking.

Blankman (1994) portrays a tinkering inventor and Batman fan, seemingly on the autism spectrum, becoming a superhero to clean up his community. The spoof film includes a scene where he is mocked for wishing to speak to the police commissioner, as well as an ersatz Lois Lane love interest, tropes both common to the DIY subgenre. However, the movie's tone is broad comedy, and moreover Blankman invents impossible gadgets, effectively granting himself superpowers.

The film closest to qualifying is *Hero at Large* (1980), concerning a struggling actor who impulsively foils a grocery store robbery, while coincidentally still wearing a costume from his menial job promoting a *Captain Avenger* movie. A media circus and further crimefighting attempts ensue. The movie almost meets the criteria, featuring a wannabe superhero in a fairly realistic milieu.

However, the naïvely altruistic lead is not portrayed as observably neurodivergent, nor on society's fringes. Additionally, the disguise he opportunistically adopts is that of a preexisting fictional character (albeit only within the film's diegesis), rather than crafting his own unique superhero identity. Furthermore, very little of the film truly concerns vigilantism, being primarily a romantic comedy.

THE SUBVERSIVE SIX

In what seems to have been a cluster of parallel creative impulses without significant cross-pollination, it is difficult to find evidence of the six DIY Superhero filmmakers demonstrating notable self-awareness of their movies bearing such similarity to each other, let alone potentially pioneering or belonging to any subgenre per se. In a notable exception, *Super*'s writer-director James Gunn acknowledged that the almost-concurrently released (and higher profile) *Kick-Ass* shared broadly the same premise as his own film. Gunn also cited *Hero at Large* as the original "superheroes without powers movie" ("SXSW Premiere"). This instance of such awareness of potential subgeneric status however, appears to have been isolated.

Given their relative obscurity, and in order to discuss commonalities of theme and storytelling, the six qualifying films proposed as constituting such a subgenre require brief summarization (figure 10.2).

Special foregrounds lonely meter man Les Franken (Michael Rapaport), a single man approaching middle age with no evident family or friends, aside from the employees of a comic store. Les signs up for a clinical trial of a new antidepressant pill and begins hallucinating that he is developing various superpowers, including telepathy, levitation, and intangibility.

Ignoring his doctor's advice that he is experiencing a psychotic break and must stop taking the drug, Les fashions a crude, spray-painted superhero costume, using the feather symbol of the medication as his torso emblem. While he foils some purse-snatchings and attempted robberies due to believing he can telepathically detect petty criminals' intentions, there is also an implication that Les may be mistakenly assaulting some innocent people as well.

When the businessmen who developed the antidepressant ask him to stop wearing their logo while conducting illegal vigilantism, Les becomes convinced they are his supervillainous adversaries. After increasingly violent scuffles with them, Les ultimately realizes that he is indeed delusional and allows the drugs to leave his system, receiving aid from a woman with a stutter he has been awkwardly courting.

Defendor focuses on Arthur Poppington (Woody Harrelson), a homeless early-middle-aged man with apparent neurodevelopmental disorders,[4] who affects the gruff-voiced persona of Defendor. Wearing a cheaply made costume with a duct-taped "D" insignia, he assaults petty criminals with his

Figure 10.2. Theatrical posters for the six "DIY Superhero" films, from (L-R) *Special, Defendor, Kick-Ass, Griff the Invisible, Super,* and *Inseparable.*

grandfather's trench club, and low-budget gadgets he constructs such as glass jars filled with wasps.

Arthur "rescues" Kat, a crack-using sex worker, from exploitation by a corrupt policeman. He naively tries to get her clean, encouraging the young woman to become a writer "like Lois Lane." Instead, she manipulates his simple-minded nature into assaulting her abusive father, before arbitrarily identifying a real-life gangster and sex-trafficker as "Captain Industry." Arthur has been obsessively seeking this imaginary supervillain for years, whom he blames for his mother's death from a drug overdose. This quest stems from a childhood misinterpretation of the vague words of his grandfather, who had also taught him to read via comic books.

Arthur experiences the most realistic consequences for his vigilantism of any DIY Superhero protagonist: he is hospitalized, arrested, tried for assault, and subjected to psychiatric evaluation. Perhaps most notably, in his heroic final stand against the genuinely dangerous gangster designated as his nemesis, Arthur is fatally shot, being the only lead protagonist in any of these films to perish.

Kick-Ass received far greater cultural awareness than its stablemates, thus warranting less summary here of the movie's content than its context.

Something of an outlier in the group, it is the only film derived from an actual comic book, as opposed to an original narrative wholly of the filmmaker's own creation. However, it is "based" on a "source" comic codeveloped with (and released parallel to) the film's production, rather than preexisting in its entirety and subsequently being directly adapted. Moreover, the film iteration diverges from the concurrent comic version in certain elements of plot and tone.

While still an independently produced movie with a low budget by blockbuster standards, *Kick-Ass* cost more than the other five DIY films put together, received a much wider release, and was the only box-office hit. Nevertheless, it remains an example of a comic book movie self-defined "in juxtaposition to mainstream productions" (Burke, *Comic Book Film Adaptation* 44).

Ironically, despite being the most prominent example of the subgenre and inadvertently inspiring this research, *Kick-Ass* almost flunks the qualifying criteria. Although an emasculated, picked-upon geek, Dave Lizewski (Aaron Johnson) is motivated to become a costumed crimefighter largely as an altruistic outgrowth of his comics fandom. Although not portrayed with overtly indicated mental illness or other neuroatypicality, his determination to fight crime certainly appears compulsive, especially on persisting after initially sustaining severe injuries. The criteria more tidily applies to the brainwashed Hit-Girl and the sociopathic Big Daddy, effectively the film's secondary protagonists.

Conversely though, their existence also somewhat strains the "real world" criteria, as these other would-be superheroes display levels of competent lethality that, although using conventional weapons, stretches the bounds of credibility, as does Dave gaining a combat advantage from deadened nerves and metal plates in his skeleton, due to earlier injuries (Burke, *Comic Book Film Adaptation* 102). This slightly heightened milieu climaxes, as does the movie itself, via the use of a machine gun-mounted jet pack. However, if the preponderance of "generic distinction" can be used to identify outliers in the mainstream superhero genre (Coogan 30–40), *Kick-Ass* is stylistically and thematically so clearly cut from the same conceptual cloth as the other five DIY films that it certainly warrants inclusion in the subgenre by much the same token.[5]

Super depicts introverted short-order cook Frank Darbo (Rainn Wilson) becoming distraught when his wife, Sarah, a recovering addict, relapses and leaves him for local druglord Jacques, her boss at the strip club. In his grief and impotence, Frank prays to God and experiences a bizarre vision exhorting him to become a superhero, the Crimson Bolt.

Frank cobbles together a costume and attacks petty criminals like drug dealers, rentboy clients, and even people butting in line, violently cracking them over the head with a pipe wrench and hollering his catchphrase: "Shut up, crime!" It is mildly ambiguous whether Frank's visions could really be divine messages as he believes them to be, or simply the hallucinations of his seemingly unhinged mind. He is eventually joined by local comic store employee Libby, a young woman who insists on becoming Frank's amoral "kid" sidekick, Boltie. She ultimately demonstrates an even more bloodthirstily inept psychopathy than the Crimson Bolt, as well as harboring a fetishism towards their costumed identities that culminates in her raping Frank.

In the bloody climax, Frank rescues his would-be damsel wife, but Libby quite graphically dies in the process, and a coda reveals that Sarah ultimately leaves him again. He is content, however as she manages to stay sober this time and has four children with a kinder man than himself, while Frank learns to embrace life's positives.[6]

Griff the Invisible's titular protagonist (Ryan Kwanten) is a socially isolated young man bullied at his office job, but who at night patrols the streets in an impressively cinematic superhero costume, saving frightened women from being stalked by outlandish supervillains. Or does he. . . . ? We eventually come to understand that his costume really looks far more homemade, and the women he is trying to "save" are actually frightened of *him*, because the bad guys chasing them only exist in Griff's mind.

The theme of unfettered imagination forms the major subject of the narrative, as Griff falls in love with Melody, a similarly oddball young woman with poor social cues, who believes she could pass through solid walls with sufficient concentration. She asks to be his (uncostumed) sidekick and begins to participate in Griff's superhero fantasies, reinforcing the belief that his useless "inventions" actually work and sending him on fantasy rescue missions.

Griff's seeming inability to control these flights of fancy cause serious problems in his life, and his protective yet exasperated brother believes he needs "professional help," explaining that this behavior has got him in trouble before. Indeed, these current antics lead to Griff being detained by police for prowling, stalking, and voyeurism. He is let off with a warning against vigilantism yet soon gets himself fired for sneaking into his workplace at night, believing that he had invented a suit that could literally make him invisible.

Like *Special*, this film frequently visualizes the clear difference between the subjectivity of Griff's imagination and the objective reality of events, yet it is also similar to *Super* in not explicitly clarifying its protagonist's mental state. Griff could easily be interpreted as suffering from some form of dissociative break from reality, and/or being on the autism spectrum. Conversely, however, he could be read as a neurotypical individual who is voluntarily, albeit compulsively, refusing to grow out of playing "let's pretend" well into adulthood.[7]

Inseparable concerns the mental state of depressed office worker Li (Daniel Wu). So distraught over a recent miscarriage and resulting estrangement from his wife, he attempts to hang himself in his apartment, only to be stopped by his American neighbor, Chuck (Kevin Spacey).

Chuck encourages Li to funnel his rage and helplessness into becoming a superhero-themed vigilante, acting as his enabler/mentor-come-sidekick. Together they go after the corrupt manufacturers of tainted tofu and substandard baby formula, informed by the research of Li's wife Pang, a Lois Lane-like investigative journalist.

However, Li realizes that he is starting to experience hallucinations and visits a psychiatrist, discovering that he is suffering from what the film terms a "Brief Psychotic Disorder." Worse still, in a Tyler Durden-esque twist, Chuck is revealed to actually be a total figment of his imagination, and thus symptomatic of his condition.

Li spends the rest of the narrative wrestling with whether to take his medication, in the hopes of getting mentally well and repairing his marriage, or submit to Chuck's increasingly sinister demands to continue fighting crime. After a brush with the law over delusionally attacking an innocent man, Li ultimately chooses normalcy, takes his antipsychotic medication, and reunites with Pang.

SELLING A SUBGENRE [WHEN YOU DON'T KNOW YOU ARE PART OF ONE]

In analyzing how these DIY Superhero films can be assessed for subgenre status, it is helpful to also look beyond their direct textual overlap. Despite the small sample size, a significant commonality that supports their generic grouping can be observed though "circulation outside [their] performance in cinemas" (Ellis 31), in this case by examining how similarly these films were marketed.

This consideration of the intertextual relay (Lukow and Ricci 29) of how these six films were framed for their prospective audiences strengthens the case for this unintended unity, particularly regarding how their generic distinction from conventional superhero cinema was communicated. Using the paratexts of movie trailers, these films' promotional strategies demonstrate striking parallels in terms of genre positioning. All sought to frame their product as inherently subversive of, or even oppositional to, the solidifying hegemonic tropes of mainstream superhero blockbusters, rather than in any way attempting to hoodwink audiences by pretending to be conventional superhero narratives themselves.[8]

Signaling genre hybridity through editing choices was a key unifying strategy, with each of the films' respective trailers variously pivoting their demographic outreach by emphasizing intertextual elements. These juxtaposed their superhero imagery with dialogue, imagery and music choices suggestive of offbeat "arthouse films," psychological dramas, gritty vigilantism, slapstick action, and even romantic "date movie" tropes. In all cases, quirky and/or black comedy beats were highlighted, to a lesser or greater extent, indicating a shared marketing impulse to represent their films as having an inherently skeptical, even satirical approach towards traditional superhero cinema.

Even more striking are the parallel framings of their shared subgeneric narrative features, previously identified as their qualifying criteria. The trailers all emphasize their protagonists as socially othered individuals becoming nonpowered superheroes in a real world, intercutting other characters' reactions to the apparent absurdity and unprecedented nature of such an endeavor. These shoddy DIY superheroes are uniformly framed by the trailers' choices of footage, dialogue, and voiceover as having questionable sanity,[9] with some even using onscreen text to describe their characters as "delusional" or "a dreamer."

Perhaps fearing stylistic and content cues insufficient to clearly demarcate their films as generically distinct from their mainstream "parents," three of the films' trailers go so far as to include overtly indicative text taglines such as "Super[powered heroes] can suck it," "Love is the greatest superpower of all," and even "THIS IS NOT A SUPERHERO MOVIE."[10]

UNIFYING DELUSIONS?

When considered collectively, the six films reveal additional shared themes and tropes that further unify them as a subgenre. These stand beyond the seemingly coincidental similarities of premise that determine their qualifying criteria, or even the intertextual relay of parallel attempts to communicate these movies' genre positioning to prospective audiences via marketing. Although disparate in their individual approaches to shared subject matter, these films have more in common with each other, on deeper levels of conception and execution, than they do with the wider genre of superhero cinema.

All of these movies are at least semicomedic and are implicitly satirizing elements of the superhero genre, although unlike the three liminal examples discussed, they are not outright comedies or spoofs. This "dark dramedy" approach is key to the six films' differing strategies for establishing their realistic dieseses. Each narrative explicitly frames the notion of becoming a superhero "in real life" as inherently ridiculous, as though to suggest that a person *must* be "unbalanced" to even attempt it.

Contextually, this framing of each protagonist as variably suffering from actual or implied mental illness, other loosely defined cognitive issues or, at the very least, significant social maladjustment, feeds into the "othering" criteria. Indeed, part of the core premise of each film (to differing extents) is that these marginalized individuals all create superheroic identities as either some form of response to their atypical mental state or imply that the mere fact of actually carrying out the desire to do so serves as an indication of their skewed perceptions.

This, it should be noted, is a problematic narrative strategy as a common (even qualifying) theme linking all six films, it risks uncritically perpetuating stereotypes of neurodivergent individuals as especially prone to violence.[11] The issue is worsened by the fact that, despite their notionally realistic settings, most of the films give vague explanations at best of their respective DIY superheroes' psychopathology. Although sympathetic to their lead characters, these movies are not especially sensitive to social issues surrounding the representation of mental health and neurodivergences.

Regardless of how their differing psychological states are defined, their behaviors are largely similar. All of these characters to some extent or another reframe their lives and environments as a masculine superhero narrative, casting themselves as the righteous Campbellian protagonist of heroic destiny.

These would-be crime fighters are all shown as inexperienced with violence and unprepared for its reality, most finding themselves causing excessive harm, sometimes even towards undeserving targets. Conversely, they are also depicted losing or barely escaping from fights, sometimes being seriously injured by hardened criminals or even average civilians.

The logistical impracticality of vigilantism is also a running theme, with the difficulty of actually *finding* appropriate crime to target being portrayed as boring, frustrating, and wholly dissimilar to genre staples of webslinging across the city "on patrol" or being summoned by an image projected into the sky. Indeed, a gag shared by half of these films (*Defendor*, *Special*, and *Griff the Invisible*) has the DIY Superheroes referencing the famous Bat signal in attempting to offer their services to the police. They naïvely ask to speak to "the Commissioner," or compulsively refer to whichever officer they meet as commissioner, regardless of rank.

This foisting of stock comic book roles onto people in their lives works intertextuality on both a diegetic and extra-diegetic levels as, unlike in most mainstream superhero movies, Batman is referenced here as an explicitly fictional character, whose associated tropes are equally as well known as such to characters in these "real world" films as they are by the viewer. Such delusional projections also notably extend to the crucial superhero genre archetypes of the damsel-in-distress love interest, and the supervillain archnemesis.

Five of the six films' protagonists reframe a woman in their life as being in need of rescue,[12] regardless of whether she herself wants or requires intervention. Most view the woman in question as an object of romantic interest—again, regardless of reciprocation—some even specifically likening their love interest to Lois Lane by name, career, or both.

The "heroes" in all these films additionally fix upon an individual whom they view as their nemesis, assigning them supervillainous traits to varyingly deserved extents.[13] In both *Special* and *Defendor* the hero targets a genuinely bad man yet does so by projecting essentially imaginary personal connections onto them. None of these designated villains has a personal animus against the protagonist prior to being targeted by them, making the violence of their confrontations ultimately self-fulfilling narratives compulsively instigated by the "hero," not their "villain."[14]

In *Super*, the villain-grudge and damsel-rescuing tropes are closely tied. Frank "rescues" his wife from drug runner Jacques, whom she voluntarily left him for, despite being unaware that her situation became more dire in the interim. Just before Frank brutally stabs Sarah's exploiter to death in front of her, Jacques screams the line: "Do you think you're some kind of fucking hero? This is not about good and evil. This is about *I* had her, and you *didn't*. This is about she loved me more, because I am fucking *interesting*!"

Clearly, the film dramatizes competing narratives of male entitlement over a woman's agency at play, with the application of violence upon each other ultimately arbitrating who "wins" her in the short term.

FREAKS, GEEKS, OR PSYCHOS?

The issue of whether these DIY Superheroes act out of pro-social altruism, as they would see themselves, or should be regarded as ["mad"?]men locked in regressive, even toxic male power fantasies, is endemic to each of these movies. The subgenre plays with the question of whether even the *desire* to become a superhero may be inherently problematic.

This is most notably observable through a striking instance of an apparently coincidental case of highly specific parallel creative impulses, whereby five of the six films feature nigh-identical portrayals of the protagonist manifesting their alternate identity, not by evoking origin tropes, but rather an iconic scene from the canon of deranged vigilante cinema. In each case, the protagonist tries on their costume in front of a mirror, poses (typically pointing at their reflection), and rehearses dialogue they imagine makes them sound like a hypermasculine tough- guy (figure 10.3). *Kick-Ass* even directly quotes the famous line "Are you talkin' to me?"

The unflattering parallels raised by these evocations of *Taxi Driver*'s famous mirror scene should not be lost on us. Travis Bickle (Robert DeNiro) surely stands as the cinematic patron saint of isolation and toxic masculinity informing the actions of a delusional would-be vigilante. When asked in a promotional interview what his favorite superhero movie was, *Super*'s star Rainn Wilson wryly answered "Taxi Driver" ("SXSW Premiere").

Visually paralleling these men's attempts to be superheroes with Travis Bickle's notorious disconnection from reality serves as a key intertextual

Figure 10.3. Virtually identical scenes of rehearsing hypermasculine identities in the mirror, from: (L-R) *Taxi Driver*, *Kick-Ass*, *Super*, *Defendor*, *Griff the Invisible*, and *Inseparable*.

strategy in furthering their framing as mentally unwell vigilantes, rather than bona-fide heroes.[15] In terms of the intertextual relay of marketing, three of these five *Taxi Driver*-homaging mirror scenes were pointedly included in the respective films' trailers, highlighting a major intertextual link outside of the genre of mainstream superhero cinema, from which these films were clearly positioning themselves as distinct from, and commentative upon.

This collective invocation of Bickle across most of the DIY Superhero films clearly carries a shared implicit critique of the notion of becoming a costumed crimefighter in the real world. Perhaps by paralleling their protagonists to such an infamously toxic and isolated character, these filmmakers were attempting to imply not only some skepticism of the superhero genre itself, but even towards its fans in particular.

Benjamin Woo writes at length about the social construction of "nerd" and "geek" lifestyles and communities, and in doing so interrogates their stereotypes. He distills geeks' traditional representation as that of "straight, white, cisgendered men" (Woo, *Getting a Life* 12, 183, 186) of inferior masculinity and social skills, exhibiting inadequacy in finding sexual partners (9–10, 178), and prioritizing obsessiveness with their chosen fandom in lieu of "normal" social interaction, even to the extent of being suggestive of residing on the autism spectrum (15, 190–91, 196).

The coding of these protagonists' civilian identities as being not only variably dysfunctional in mainstream society and/or neurodivergent, but specifically as representative of broader geek stereotypes, is fundamental to their formulation as overlooked and emasculated misfits. The films' intertextual equation of the traditional superhero's secret identity, as the stereotypical "mild-mannered" pushover, with the real societal stereotype of geeky superhero fans being inadequately masculine introverts, is no coincidence. Moreover, this "loser" framing is utilized by all six films.

Les is socially isolated, has a low-prestige job which a woman openly mocks him for, and cannot summon the confidence to flirt with another whom he finds attractive; Arthur is homeless, has difficultly socializing, and is implicitly a middle-aged virgin; antisocial Frank is a doormat at work and home, sexually rebuffed by his wife who then leaves him for her drug dealer; Dave is a virginal comics nerd humiliated by muggers and schoolgirls; Griff is bullied at work and deeply awkward, especially with women; and suicidal Li is harangued by his female boss, while at home his marriage is falling apart.

Each of these men is portrayed as either a comic book reader or otherwise consuming some form of superhero media. While only Dave is portrayed as the fully fledged comic-geek stereotype, for each character there is a clear throughline of associating his personal/social inadequacy with the appeal to them of empowering masculine superhero narratives. This culminates in their underlying neurodivergences being portrayed as implicitly facilitating, through disinhibition, the creation of such an identity, and attempting to enact its associated tropes in reality.

Whatever consciously motivates their varying compulsions to "fight crime," they each assume an empowered alternate persona which they clearly feel self-actualizes their normally underwhelming masculinity through violence. By asserting dominance over aspects of their environment which induce a sense of powerlessness, their superhero identities make them feel better, special, or in control. When skeptically asked why he dresses as a superhero, dimwitted Arthur replies: "'Cause superheroes aren't stupid. They're not afraid. And when I'm Defendor, I'm not Arthur anymore. I'm a million times better than Arthur."

Ultimately though, and perhaps as products of their times, none of the films are willing to come down hard on the side of condemning their own protagonists. Griff, Frank, Dave, Les, Li, and Arthur are all portrayed as fundamentally decent, kind-hearted men, as though these ennobling characteristics should implicitly mitigate or otherwise override audience concerns over their socially aberrant enactment of violent superhero fantasies.

Moreover, to varying extents their respective movies all conclude on relatively upbeat notes. It is implied that their attempts to oppose those who would harm and exploit others were worthwhile, or at the very least pure in intention.

"Just the perfect combination of optimism and naïveté," as per Dave's overly self-aware narration in *Kick-Ass*. Some of the films even portray diegetic news media and/or grassroots activities as indicating that public sentiment supports the actions of these DIY Superheroes. It nevertheless seems difficult to infer any genuine endorsement of vigilantism, given each film's implicit critique of costumed crime fighting.

Perhaps instead, these ultimately valorizing portrayals of such characters, whose own narratives frame them as troubled and misguided, result more from a failure to creatively escape the gravitational pull of the parent genre's mainstream tropes altogether. Hollywood superhero leads are habitually coded as ultimately being morally in the right, often innately so. Attempting to totally defy this metanarrative pull via any truly downbeat endings repudiating their protagonists was eschewed, with even *Defendor*'s foolhardy death portrayed as a righteous Pyrrhic victory inspiring public memorials. While seeking generic differentiation from conventional superhero cinema, each film seems to want their subversive "hero" to have their intertextual cake and eat it too.

It must also be noted that, despite being framed as implicitly disadvantaged by their atypical mental states or social marginalization, all of the key protagonists in these films are heterosexual, cisgendered males,[16] and all but one are Caucasian.[17] By only scarcely stepping outside of the enduring geek stereotypes—which Woo cogently argues underrepresent the true diversity of fan demographics via cultural portrayals and academic study alike ("The Invisible Bag of Holding" 245–52)—these films' protagonists may be Othered, yet they undeniably retain significant privilege. As such, they do not ultimately stray too far from the type of demographic representation seen in the majority of traditional superhero images either.

CONCLUSIONS

Having made the argument for the identification of a subgenre, what then can we take from six such conceptually similar films manifesting in a burst of unintentional creative synergy between 2006 and 2011, almost perfectly parallel to the six films comprising the first phase of the MCU?

It may simply be a coincidence in the emerging zeitgeist, only seeming significant in hindsight. For while DIY Superhero films are awkwardly both oppositional to and yet still somehow inescapably celebratory of the genre they subvert, their writer-directors were surely responding to the gradual proliferation of disconnected superhero movies over the preceding decade, rather than the exponential yet interconnected expansion of which they stood on the cusp. These low-budget arthouse films interrogate and problematize the superhero genre and its fandom without any commentary on shared universes or corporatized transmedia strategies, clearly unaware of their own concurrence with an emerging pivot point in the mainstream genre's history.

Yet perhaps in doing so, the filmmakers were each in their own way using their genre-hybridized "real" superheroes to look beyond the swelling hegemony of comic book–derived characters and question what else the superhero concept can be used to express about society. Their shared juxtaposition of social alienation and psychological turmoil with the impulse to become instead a hypermasculine, even violent "hero" persona, inescapably suggests skepticism towards the appeal of these mainstream narratives, as well those who are traditionally enamored with them.

Granted, their respective subversions each fall short of fully undermining conventional superhero cinema, and conversely risk becoming (very skeptical) addenda to it. Yet when examined through this different lens as a quasioppositional subgenre, these six films cast a fascinating if unintentionally prescient light on troubling trends in contemporary fandom. Such considerations seem all the more relevant now, in a time when the superhero genre has never had greater mainstream appeal.

Given these issues, it is hard to imagine the DIY Superhero subgenre manifesting again unchanged in the 2020s or beyond, especially when reflecting on Woo's excellent analysis of the "battle going on for the soul of geek culture" (*Getting a Life* 189), and certainly not using such often blithely vague portrayals of neurodivergent characters. The rise of Alt-Right inflections in misogynistic and racist harassment across various fandoms has demonstrated that such behaviors are clearly rooted in a subculture of toxic masculinity (173–88, 198, 234).

Even though none of these six films' protagonists are portrayed as notably sexist nor racist, their framing as emasculated geeky men using (literal) masks of anonymity to assert their manhood through acts of violence would likely play very poorly today, in a climate where the darker corners of nerd culture are being viewed as places where "young men are radicalized into a particularly toxic form of misogynist and racist masculinity" (172). Not to mention that reportedly these "toxic fanboys" demographically encompass most of the perpetrators behind the escalation of mass shootings (177), fueled by the "aggrieved entitlement" born of "a fusion of that humiliating loss of manhood and the moral obligation and entitlement to get it back" (Kimmel 125). The thematic parallels are disquieting to say the least.

The DIY Superhero films represented a moment in time which has apparently now passed, yet it was an observably cohesive subgenre all the same. Were it to ever re-emerge in the foreseeable future, it might perhaps prove a fertile template for an even more subversive and socially relevant critique, not of geek culture in its true expanding diversity, but rather that of its putrefying vocal minority of intolerants. This self-styled vanguard of the toxic fan demographic, seeking to protect its imaginary homogeneous masculine purity from those it vilifies as interlopers and usurpers, may just find themselves parodied not as wannabe heroes, but DIY villains.

Notes

1. Demonstrated extensively in Burke's *The Comic Book Film Adaptation: Exploring Modern Hollywood's Leading Genre* (passim).

2. Although it can certainly be argued that the MCU is the first live-action shared universe to achieve such scale and success, it is far from the first. Nor, as Burke details, is it even the first attempt to adapt Marvel's comics to screen in such a unified fashion ("Sowing the Seeds" 106–17).

3. Ironically, despite being set in (a version of) the oldest superhero shared universe, *Joker* has the least generic density of, or reference to, superhero genre tropes of any film discussed here. Instead, it apes the Martin Scorsese films *Taxi Driver* (1976) and *The King of Comedy* (1982), featuring similarly isolated men with a shaky grip on reality. The narrative's lack of superhero genre iconography, even though actually including a pre-Batman Bruce Wayne as a character in the film, could be contextually inferred to imply the film takes place in a diegesis wherein superheroes do not yet exist as either real or even fictional figures. It seems just as likely, however, that director Phillips was simply far more interested in homaging Scorsese than Finger, Robinson, and Kane and colleagues.

4. Arthur's lawyer attempts to raise "a question of intellectual capacity" in his defense, and even a friendly employer describes him as both "a little slow" and "not quite all there upstairs." A court-ordered psychological evaluation assesses Arthur as presenting with apparent "FAS, ADD, depression, delusional megalomania, unable to anticipate consequences, serious lack of common sense, socially immature."

5. *Kick-Ass 2* (Wadlow 2013) has been excluded on the basis that the protagonist is no longer socially isolated, and that the heightened diegesis which almost rendered the original film liminal is exaggerated past this threshold in the sequel.

6. Although contextually the film would seem to suggest Frank abandons crimefighting at this point, strictly speaking, the narrative is ambiguous on the matter. His career as the Crimson Bolt is, however, referenced in something of an "easter egg" at the end of the superhero-horror film *Brightburn* (Yarovesky 2019), written by *Super* director James Gunn's brothers, in a (likely just satirical) retroactive play on the idea of superheroes inhabiting shared cinematic universes.

7. The latter was the stated intent of writer-director Leon Ford, as per his DVD audio commentary. However, this is altogether textually ambiguous in the film as presented. Such ambiguity is deepened towards the conclusion, when a disillusioned Griff appears to be able to voluntarily shut off his vivid imagination in an attempt to finally "grow up," only for the movie to conclude with an impossible scene of Melody falling through a solid door into his arms. Assuming that this does not literally happen in some last-minute detour of the film into magical realism, Griff's total surprise at this occurrence can only be interpreted as either an involuntarily shared hallucination between Griff and Melody, or an entirely subconscious re-engagement of his immersive imagination in a desperate attempt to undo their immediately preceding breakup.

8. With the exception of the additional (Hit-Girl-centric) shorter "teaser" trailer and television adverts focusing on action for the broader *Kick-Ass* marketing rollout, as well as the international trailer for *Inseparable*, discussed below.

9. This is more lightly indicated in the trailers for *Super* and particularly *Inseparable*, for which the full revelation of the hallucination scenes was evidently considered to be narrative "spoilers."

10. The latter is from the original Chinese trailer for *Inseparable*, which frames the film predominantly as a psychological drama. This ironically stands in marked contrast to the same movie's radically different and obfuscatory international trailer, being the only example found for any of these six films overtly attempting to pass itself off as anything approaching a conventional superhero narrative.

11. *Griff the Invisible* might be considered a partial exception, as the titular character only enacts his violent fantasies upon imaginary opponents, although his behavior does unintentionally terrorize the random women he imagines himself to be "rescuing." The only real physical altercation in the film features Griff quite helplessly being beaten up by his office bully, while out of costume.

12. Excluding *Inseparable*, which nevertheless frames the love interest character as a Lois Lane analogue, although she is not "damselled."

13. The villains in *Griff the Invisible* are imaginary, with the exception of an office bully, a nemesis whom Griff does not explicitly frame as a comic book villain, but does retaliate against, using his dubious "superhero inventions."

14. With the arguable exception of the Mafioso in *Kick-Ass* misattributing the actions of Hit-Girl and Big Daddy to the title character.

15. Ironically, despite taking pervasive cue from *Taxi Driver* and even including notable scenes featuring rehearsal and mirrors, *Joker* does not follow the DIY Superhero films' uniting impulse to specifically evoke DeNiro's "Are you talkin' to me?" mirror scene.

16. The female DIY Superheroes Hit-Girl and Boltie (and perhaps Melody) are notably coded as sidekicks, not leads.

17. Note that although Li is an Asian character, he is the protagonist of a Chinese film set in mainland China and thus is not contextually framed as an ethnic minority, which he likely would have been in an American movie.

Works Cited

Blankman. Directed by Mike Binder, Wife N' Kids films, 1994.

Burke, Liam. "'A bigger universe': Marvel Studios and Transmedia Storytelling." *Assembling the Marvel Cinematic Universe: Essays on the Social, Cultural and Geopolitical Domains*, edited by Julian C. Chambliss, et al., McFarland, 2018, pp. 32–51.

Burke, Liam. "Sowing the Seeds: How 1990s Marvel Animation Facilitated Today's Cinematic Universe." *Marvel Comics into Film: Essays on Adaptation since the 1940s*, edited by Matthew J. McEniry, et al., McFarland, 2016, pp. 106–17.

Burke, Liam. *The Comic Book Film Adaptation: Exploring Modern Hollywood's Leading Genre*. University Press of Mississippi, 2015.

Condorman. Directed by Charles Jarrott, Walt Disney Productions, 1981.

Coogan, Peter. *Superhero: Secret Origin of a Genre*. MonkeyBrain Books, 2006.

Defendor. Directed by Peter Stebbings, Darius Films, 2009.

Ellis, John. *Visible Fictions. Cinema: Television: Video* (revised edition). Routledge, 1992.

Griff the Invisible. Directed by Leon Ford, Green Park Pictures, 2010.

Hero at Large. Directed by Martin Davidson, Metro-Goldwyn-Mayer, 1980.

Inseparable [形影不离]. Directed by Dayyan Eng, Colordance Pictures, 2011.

Iouchkov, Vlad, and Philip Birch. "'Masked crusader': A Case Study of 'crime-fighting' Activities by a 'real-life superhero.'" *Journal of Criminological Research, Policy and Practice*, vol. 1, no. 2, 2015, pp. 56–64.

Joker. Directed by Todd Phillips, Warner Bros. Pictures, 2019.

Kick-Ass. Directed by Matthew Vaughn, Marv Films, 2010.

Kimmel, Michael S. *Misframing Men: The Politics of Contemporary Masculinites*. Rutgers University Press, 2010.

Lukow, Gregory, and Steve Ricci. "The 'Audience' Goes 'Public': Intertextuality, Genre, and the Responsibilities of Film Literacy." *On Film*, no. 12, 1984, pp. 29–36.

Special [aka *Special (RX) Specioprin Hydrochloride*]. Directed by Hal Haberman and Jeremy Passmore, Rival Pictures, 2006.

Super. Directed by James Gunn, This Is That Ambush Entertainment, 2010.

"SXSW Premiere" *Super*. This Is That Ambush Entertainment, 2010. Blu-Ray.

Woo, Benjamin. *Getting a Life: The Social Worlds of Geek Culture*. McGill-Queen's University Press, 2018.

Woo, Benjamin. "The Invisible Bag of Holding: Whiteness and Media Fandom." *The Routledge Companion to Media Fandom*, edited by Melissa Click and Suzanne Scott. Routledge, 2017, pp. 245–52.

Section 3

BEYOND THE UNITED STATES

Introduction

BEYOND THE UNITED STATES

LIAM BURKE

Exhaustive histories of superheroes often stretch back to the myths from around the world that inspire today's costume-clad adventurers. In his expansive book *On the Origin of Superheroes*, Chris Gavaler maps a global prehistory of superheroes that includes "Mesopotamia's first big superhero saga" Gilgamesh, the Pacific Island–hopping Maui, and the Egyptian god Horus, who "roamed Europe before settling in the Nile Valley" (18). However, the high-flying superhero that we recognize today is largely thought to have been codified by Depression Era comic book publishers in the United States as a four-color response to the challenges of Machine Age America (Fawaz 6; Highmore 124; Feiffer 9). This close connection between the superhero and the United States was solidified moving into the Second World War when a cadre of star-spangled superheroes was created by anti-isolationist creators hoping to hasten and support US involvement in the war effort. Duncan and Smith note that sixty-one patriotic comic book heroes were recruited by US publishers between 1940 and 1944 to fight Axis forces, including The Shield, Liberty Belle, and, of course, Captain America (250).

Many scholars describe the superhero as an urban update of the gunslingers and cowboys of the American West (Harvey 65; Fawaz 6). This vigilante myth has been criticized for promoting near-fascist fantasies that John Shelton Lawrence and Robert Jewett, expanding on Joseph Campbell, dubbed the "American Monomyth." Writing in their 2002 book Lawrence and Jewett suggest US audiences relish "depictions of impotent democratic institutions that can only be rescued by extralegal superheroes" (7–8). For example, superhero stories produced in the wake of 9/11 often seemed to conform to this reading of the superhero's ideological underpinnings. Conservative commentators suggested that Batman's use of extraordinary rendition and illegal surveillance to stop a terrorist in Oscar-winning film *The Dark Knight* (Nolan 2008) validated the Bush administration's oft-criticized War on Terror policies.

Lawrence and Jewett trace the emergence of the American monomyth back to the 1930s, when comic book superheroes first emerged, noting, "It would not be long before the American monomyth became a subculture of Planet Earth" (83). However, while superheroes became the mainstream comic book's defining content in the United States, around the world a more diverse array of genres proved popular. When overseas publishers did create superhero stories, it was often as a critique of the genre, and, by extension, perceived US cultural imperialism. For example, British publishers tended to produce comics in genres far removed from superheroes such as war books like *Commando*, girls' titles such as *Bunty*, and humor comics like *The Beano* and *The Dandy*. Chris Murray notes that when British creators did venture into the superhero genre, they tended to subvert the character through parodies like *Bananaman* and "in some instances offer a satirical critique of the genre and its politics" (3–4), as was the case in Grant Morrison's scathing superhero-as-celebrity comic *Zenith*.

US publishers did attempt to make up for the dearth of overseas superheroes by introducing internationally themed costumed crimefighters like the Batmen of All Nations, Soviet Captain America analogue Red Guardian, and the Canadian heroes Alpha Flight. Many of the international superheroes produced by US-based creators were developed using familiar conventions for depicting these regions that often perpetuated harmful stereotypes (Burke). Dittmer criticized Marvel's 1982 comic book crossover *Contest of Champions*, which featured internationally themed superheroes such as German electrokinetic Blitzkrieg, the magic carpet flying Arabian Knight, and Aboriginal Australian sorcerer Talisman. Dittmer notes how these overseas heroes never received dedicated comic books but argues that the presence of such nationally themed characters suggests a false equivalency that "elides the role of American power in producing its global hegemony" (21).

As this section charts, the global presence of superheroes began to evolve in the early 2000s due to a number of factors. Where once most US comics were made by creators based in the New York metro area (Duncan and Smith ix), digital communications technologies have made it easier for international creators to work with US publishers. Many of these overseas creators use this opportunity to create international superheroes for US publishers that avoid, even challenge, the stereotypes of the past (see Burke). Superheroes also gained wider visibility due to the unprecedented number of adaptations of comic books to movies, games, and TV shows since the turn of the millennia, inspiring publishers, studios, and broadcasters around the world to start making their own contributions to the now dominant superhero genre (see Uribe-Jongbloed and Espinosa-Medina). US creators have continued to produce international superheroes, but they have increasingily done so through consultation and collaboration with artists from these regions (see Golding). Digital technologies, including the web and user-friendly graphics software, also made it easier for amateur and independent creators to produce and distribute their own work with writers and artists around the globe creating their own local responses to the superhero archetype. These creators have proven successful at reconciling the US icon with local mythology and culture (see Santos), even using the superhero to address specific concerns and interests (see Humphrey). As Dittmer observed, "even if the superhero genre is primarily associated with the United States and carries the trace of its origins, it is nevertheless a resolutely transnational phenomenon whose appeal exceeds national borders" (5)

Responding to the international expansion of the superhero, scholars have begun to chart and analyze this now global archetype. Books such as Chris Murray's *The British Superhero* focus on a specific region while Rayna Denison and Rachel Mizsei-Ward's collection *Superheroes on World Screens* takes a transnational perspective. Widening the scope to include diasporic communities, Frederick Luis Aldama, who provides the introduction to this collection, has highlighted Latinx superheroes and creators across page and screen in his Eisner-Award winning work. From Australia to the Philippines, Colombia, and Senegal (via Wakanda), the contributions to this section seek to extend our understanding of how the superhero has gone beyond the United States to become a global icon.

Works Cited

Aldama, Frederick Luis. *Latinx Superheroes in Mainstream Comics*. University of Arizona Press, 2017.

Burke, Liam. "Apes, Angels, and Super Patriots: The Irish in Superhero Comics." *The Superhero Symbol: Media, Culture, and Politics*, edited by Liam Burke, Ian Gordon, and Angela Ndalianis, Rutgers University Press, 2020, pp. 231–52.

Denison, Rayna, and Rachel Mizsei-Ward, editors. *Superheroes on World Screens*. University Press of Mississippi, 2015.

Dittmer, Jason. *Captain America and the Nationalist Superhero: Metaphors, Narratives, and Geopolitics*. Philadelphia: Temple University Press, 2013.

Duncan, Randy, Matthew J. Smith, and Paul Levitz. *The Power of Comics: History, Form, and Culture*. Bloomsbury Publishing, 2015.

Fawaz, Ramzi. *The New Mutants: Superheroes and the Radical Imagination of American Comics*. New York University Press, 2016.

Feiffer, Jules. *The Great Comic Book Heroes*. Fantagraphics Books, 2003.

Gavaler, Chris. *On the Origin of Superheroes: From the Big Bang to Action Comics No. 1*. University of Iowa Press, 2015.

Harvey, Robert C. *The Art of the Comic Book: An Aesthetic History*. University Press of Mississippi, 1996.

Highmore, Ben. *Cityscapes: Cultural Readings in the Material and Symbolic City*. Red Globe Press, 2005.

Lawrence, John Shelton, and Robert Jewett. *The Myth of the American Superhero*. Wm. B. Eerdmans Publishing, 2002.

Murray, Chris. *The British Superhero*. University Press of Mississippi, 2017.

Chapter 11

WE NEED ANOTHER HERO

The Incompatibility of Superheroes and Australia

LIAM BURKE

Australia loves superheroes. Superhero movies such as *The Dark Knight* (Nolan 2008), *The Avengers* (Whedon 2012), and *Spider-Man: No Way Home* (Watts 2021) have topped Australia's annual box office. The country's most celebrated galleries and event spaces have hosted superhero exhibitions such as *The Art of the Brick: DC Comics* at Sydney's Powerhouse Museum, *Marvel: Creating the Cinematic Universe* at Queensland Art Gallery & Gallery of Modern Art, and the interactive exhibition *Avengers S.T.A.T.I.O.N.* in Melbourne's Central Business District. In fact, Melbourne's Docklands Stadium was even renamed Marvel Stadium when the Disney subsidiary purchased the naming rights in 2018.

Although the annexation of a major sports ground by a company synonymous with superheroes suggests a new level of pervasiveness, Australia has always demonstrated an interest in costume-clad adventurers. For example, in keeping with wider interest in American popular culture following the Second World War, there was a boom in local superhero comic books with titles such as *Captain Atom*, *The Phantom Knight*, and *The Crimson Comet*. However, as the leading scholar on Australian comics, Kevin Patrick, notes, many of these locally produced superhero comic books attempted to pass themselves off as US imports by affixing "Price in Australia" stickers to covers and ensuring that the heroes had American civilian identities. Describing Australia's Captain Atom, whose alter-ego was FBI agent Larry Lockhart, Patrick explains that "to cast the likes of Captain Atom as anything other than American would have tested the credulity of Australian audiences" (Patrick "Atoman" 286–302). More recently, Australia has served as the location for the production of superhero movies such as *Aquaman* (Wan 2018), *Shang-Chi and the Legend of the Ten Rings* (Cretton 2021), and *Thor: Love and Thunder* (Waititi 2022), while Australian actors such as Chris Hemsworth, Margot Robbie, and Hugh Jackman have slipped on capes, cowls, and claws to portray superheroes such as Thor, Harley Quinn, and Wolverine. Despite a ready local audience for superheroes and a tradition of producing superhero stories, Australian creators, on the page and screen, have rarely attempted to develop superpowered characters who were Australian and/or operated in a local setting. As US singer Tina Turner famously wailed on the soundtrack for Australian dystopic adventure film *Mad Max beyond Thunderdome* (Miller and Ogilvie 1985): "We Don't Need Another Hero."

This chapter will consider some of the reasons for the seeming incompatibility between Australia and the superhero. Drawing on one hundred interviews with superhero creators and fans at Melbourne comic book conventions the most frequently cited reasons for Australia's superhero drought will be organized and analyzed under three inter-related headings: National Identity, Cultural Cringe, and Market Differentiation.[1] Although many of the perceived obstacles to Australian superheroes are no longer relevant (and perhaps never were), the respondent interviews demonstrate how they still have potent purchase in Australian cultural life. This chapter will also consider how the comparatively recent emergence of local superhero writers and artists working for international publishers like Marvel and DC Comics is providing a corrective to outdated depictions of Australia. The analysis will conclude with an examination of how the Australian superhero TV show *Cleverman* surmounts many of the long-standing hurdles to Australian superheroes through a careful integration of superhero conventions and Indigenous mythology, suggesting a future direction for Australian superheroes.

Despite the dearth of Australian superheroes, 80 percent of the creators and fans interviewed for this study said that they would be eager to see more local superheroes on the page and screen. However, when asked to name existing Australian heroes, many respondents struggled to identify any and those that did tended to point to international examples like the DC Comics villain Captain Boomerang, who has been reworked as an antihero in the superhero movie *Suicide Squad* (Ayer 2016) and related media.[2]

Traditionally, Australian characters in international comics were rare. For example, while the "Batmen of All Nations" team-up from *Detective Comics* 215 (Jan, 1955) included Ranger from "Faraway Australia" he only received two lines of dialogue in the issue and was not included when the team reappeared two years later in *World's Finest Comics* 89 (July, 1957). This apathy vanished in the 1980s, which Geographer Alyson L Greiner identifies as the "decade of the 'Australian Invasion.'" Pointing to Outback heroes Mad Max and Crocodile Dundee, Greiner describes how "Representations of Australia in American cinema and broadcast media became much more commonplace" (186). Comic book publishers in the United States and United Kingdom also attempted to take advantage of the unprecedented interest in Australia. For example, in

Figure 11.1. Detective Comics 591 (October, 1988) in which Batman fights the "Aborigine."

1988: Batman fought the boomerang-wielding "Aborigine"; the UK's alternative comic book character Tank Girl roamed a postapocalyptic Australia with her kangaroo boyfriend; and even the X-Men moved their headquarters to the Australian Outback.

There were some local efforts during this time to create Australian superheroes, with the most successful example being *The Southern Squadron* by David de Vries and Glenn Lumsden. The superhero team was first published in the comics anthology *Cyclone!* in 1985 before receiving a dedicated title that was also republished in the US. Cover blurbs introduced the Southern Squadron as "Australia's own superhero trouble shooters!" The irreverent comic played upon distinctly Australian archetypes with team members such as the beer-swilling ocker Nightfighter or beast-like Dingo. However, despite wider interest in Australia during the 1980s, there were no sustained attempts to produce superheroes, and none of the local examples introduced during this time was identified by this study's respondents, who tended to point to Australian characters created by US publishers.

As stereotypical as international examples might be, with Australian creators unable or unwilling to provide local superpowered heroes, depictions of Australia in superhero stories were provided by overseas creators. As demonstrated by this study's responses, these international examples have also been influential in Australia, even while they perpetuate stereotypes that bear little resemblance to the lives of most Australians. For instance, when interviewed for this research *Cleverman* creator Ryan Griffen highlighted the little-known Avenger Manifold as an example of an Indigenous Australian hero, but cautioned, "[T]hese are superheroes that were created by people outside of Australia and they're just using either stereotypes or what they can quickly Google to help fuel the creation of the characters." Given the local enthusiasm for masked marvels it is important to consider: Why Australia has generally avoided creating native superheroes; How this shortfall has allowed certain stereotypes to go unchallenged; and where this seeming incompatibility is slowly being resolved.

NATIONAL IDENTITY

When asked about Australian superheroes for this project, creator of *The Crow*, American writer-artist James O'Barr identified costumed crimefighter the Phantom. When it was explained that the Phantom was not actually Australian, but the creation of New Yorker Lee Falk, the writer-artist replied, "It's kind of mystifying because he's forgotten about in the US." As Aaron Humphrey details in his contribution to this collection, although the purple spandex-wearing adventurer was an American creation, the Phantom was adopted by Australia following his introduction in the housekeeping magazine *Australian Woman's Mirror* in 1936. Despite appearing before Superman, the Phantom is not considered the first classical superhero by scholars like Peter Coogan due to the comic's jungle setting (182). However, as Kevin Patrick notes in his exhaustive study *The Phantom Unmasked*, the "factors that arguably militated against the Phantom's popular acceptance in his American homeland—such as his lack of superpowers, or recognizably American origin or setting— did much to enhance his international appeal." In keeping with wider resistance to American cultural imperialism, Patrick adds "Australians, it seemed, admired the Phantom because they saw him as the very antithesis of the American 'super' hero" ("Transplanted Superhero" 21–31). Drawing on extensive research with generations of Australian Phantom fans (or "Phans"), Patrick describes how his survey respondents gravitated to the character because he embodied "Australian" values. However, what are the tenets of Australian national identity that seem to resist the classical superhero?

As tourism scholar Sue Beeton notes, since Federation in 1901 Australian culture has often sought to forge a distinct identity by positioning the Australian bush and bushman as a "symbol of nationalism" (126). This tactic served to differentiate Australia from European idylls and urban centers by depicting Australia as a distant and often unforgiving rural landscape thinly populated by a hard-working and humble people. However, in an attempt to forge a distinct national identity, such cultural nationalism has implicitly endorsed colonialist images of Australia. This tradition has continued with many scholars pointing out how despite Australia being one of the most urbanized countries in the world today, local arts and culture often depict the nation as a "blank canvas" free from the restrictions of the modern world (Williams 301; Haltof 29; Greiner 186).

Created in the depths of the Depression as a response to the challenges of the Machine Age, superheroes are inescapably modern and urban. As Ben Highmore notes of these thoroughly modern marvels, superheroes are a "species that has adjusted to the modern city and overcome its obstacles" (124). Often considered the first classical superhero, Superman demonstrated this Machine Age resilience from his first appearance in *Action Comics* 1 (June, 1938) in which he hurdled a twenty-story building and outpaced an express train. Scottish comic book writer Grant Morrison argues, "Like jazz and rock 'n' roll" the superhero is also a "uniquely American creation" (29). Such US origins were part of the superhero's long-standing appeal in Australia, but it has also provoked wider concerns regarding cultural imperialism. For instance, one article published in the *Sydney Morning Herald* on December 28, 1948, "Are 'Comic' Books Harmful to the Minds of Young Readers?," warned "The language used in many of the comics on sale in Sydney shows an unmistakable United States origin" (2). However, as Kevin Patrick explains many of the superhero comics identified in the article were actually locally produced, albeit with American trappings ("Atoman"). Thus, almost from their inception, star-spangled, city-dwelling superheroes have clashed with traditions of Australian national identity such as the Outback, the bushman, and egalitarianism.

Beeton notes how in the pursuit of a distinct national identity near the end of the nineteenth century, Australian bush poets such as Banjo Paterson and Henry Lawson reworked European rural idylls by focusing on the countryside as "a living being to [be] conquered by living in it, not passively enjoyed" (127). Thus, the capacity to live in an inhospitable environment became central to Australian cultural nationalism, with the everyday celebrated as a heroic triumph. Despite the bush/Outback experience being out of step with the daily lives of most Australians, it has found an eager audience internationally with Australia often positioned for the "tourist gaze" (Urry 1). In his cross-cultural reception study of the Australian adventure film *Crocodile Dundee* (Faiman 1986), Stephen Crofts notes how US reviewers described how the film depicted Australia as a "lost frontier" with reviewers speculating that its stateside success owed much to it providing American audiences with a "primal innocence" they felt they had lost (161). US superhero comic books also participated in this representation of the Australian landscape as a frontier free from the stifling conformity of progress. For example, presaging the casting of Australian actor Hugh Jackman as Canadian character Wolverine in cinema, in *Uncanny X-Men* 230 (June, 1988) the X-Men's Rogue comments on her teammate's seeming suitability to the Australian Outback, "Wolvie loves this wilderness. It's as elemental as he is . . . country where you work to nature's schedule an' rules not some arbitrary man-made timepiece."

Many of this study's respondents echoed this wider perception of Australia. For example, Australian actor Eka Darville (*Jessica Jones*) perpetuated the urban/rural dichotomy, commenting, "Aussies have a very special connection with nature, because America has been so dominated there's not that kind of [connection to nature]. Every Aussie has grown up with snakes and spiders and all of these kinds of threats that make the natural world very real." Similarly, Australian comic book writer and publisher Darren Koziol explained how the comics he publishes under his company Dark Oz, "contain a lot of Australian themes and characters [. . .] The previous issue I did—the Ozploitation issue—was very popular, we got these American tourists stuck in the Aussie Outback playing up to all your usual stereotypes of everything in Australia wants to kill you." Koziol later added, "I actually wrote that story knowing I was going to San Diego Comic-Con, so I specifically aimed and designed it to play up to their ideas of Australia and to really captivate [US readers]." With the proven success of Outback-set Australian stories, there has often been little appetite among local or international creators to move these adventures to the urban environments where superheroes traditionally operate—with no buildings to leap in a single bound, how can a Superman test his mettle in the Outback? Nonetheless, this mythologized terrain does produce heroes of a different order.

Beeton notes how "even though most of today's Australians have little direct relationship with any Australian bushmen," the self-reliant and resourceful rural worker who overcame Australia's unforgiving landscape is still a "symbol of nationalism." She adds that the myth is "analogous to the pervasive legend of the American west and the notion of 'the frontier' in the American psyche" (128). This Western gunslinger is often considered the superhero's immediate antecedent (Harvey 65). However, as the Machine Age progressed the cowboy was increasingly out of step with contemporary US interests, with Ramzi Fawaz distinguishing the superhero from the Western gunfighter through the superhero's "mutually constitutive relationship to twentieth-century science and technology" (6). Thus, while US and Australian heroic types share frontier origins, US superheroes became modern, urban, and optimistic, while their Australian cousins maintained a rural tradition that prized stoicism, self-reliance, and rough pragmatism. Indeed, many of this study's respondents pointed to bushman descendants Mad Max and Crocodile Dundee when identifying local heroes but noted that these heroes did not fully align with the classical superhero, with typical responses including, "Australian superheroes would look like [wildlife expert parody] Russell Coight"; "like [wildlife documentarian] Steve Irwin or Crocodile Dundee. [Someone who] uses crocodiles as his power or something like that would be pretty cool," and "Could you imagine someone like Crocodile Dundee being a superhero with a cape?"

Part of the incompatibility between the superhero and the rural "battler" is the bushman's inability to accommodate what Morrison identifies as the "the transcendent element in the Superman equation": The secret identity (9). Sociologist Karina J. Butera notes of the "toughness, independence and resilience" of Australian masculinity and mateship that "overt displays of vulnerability or emotion are to be avoided" (269). The superhero's transformation from a mild-mannered civilian identity to a paragon of masculinity is widely considered a key convention of the genre and central to the superhero's appeal (Eco 15; Reynolds 12–16; Coogan 59–60). While the urban centers of US superhero stories allow these characters to hide out as reporters and playboy billionaires, the unrelenting rural experience of the bushman and his descendants does not permit such moments of vulnerability. Indeed, drawing comparisons with the anti-hero protagonists of 1950s' revisionist Westerns like *The Searchers* (Ford 1956), Rose Lucas describes Mad Max as "a superman who refuses to resume the costume of the ordinary (143). Indeed, Clark Kent wouldn't last five minutes in this mythic Outback.

Although traditional Australian heroic types are at odds with the superhero's vulnerable civilian identity, they also tend to resist the garishness of the costume-clad alter-ego. In his article "An Australian Superman" philosopher Damon Young imagines what might have happened if the infant Superman had landed in the Australian Outback rather than the cornfields of Kansas. Noting the centrality of the image of "tough, simple, hard-working diggers," "the Anzac legend of stoic mateship and silent sacrifice," and the celebration of "egalitarianism" to Australian national identity, Young concludes that his Australian Superman "is more likely to become a cautious provincial survivor than a messianic hero" (29–30). This democratic spirit still resonates in Australian cultural life and is often demonstrated through "Tall Poppy Syndrome,"

Figure 11.2 Cover of the "Ozploitation" issue of Australian comic *Decay* (April, 2016).

which journalist Peter Hartcher identifies as an "unspoken national ethos" that "no Australian is permitted to assume that he or she is better than any other Australian. How is this enforced? By the prompt corrective of levelling derision" (Booker). It is hard to imagine a taller poppy than the spandex-wearing popinjays who leap from the covers of US comics. In Young's Australian Superman the hero never adopts a public heroic identity. Accordingly, he avoids the tall poppy status that is so unpalatable to many Australians, including a number of this study's respondents. As Wonder Woman artist Nicola Scott summarized, "Our superheroes are like Mad Max. When I think of an Australian superhero I don't think of someone wearing spandex—that's a really American image."

Fans and creators interviewed for this study consistently pointed to the tenets of Australian national identity, including the Outback, bushman, and egalitarianism when describing local heroes, with many suggesting that these qualities were at odds with the urban, optimistic, and individualistic superhero. While these qualities were used to forge a distinct Australian national identity, these foundational myths do not align with the experience of many Australians who today live in one of the world's most urbanized countries. That Australian superhero fans struggled to imagine superheroes existing in an Australian context testifies to the hegemonic dominance of this particular brand of national identity. However, the resistance to Australian superheroes also points to a cultural cringe that still seems to haunt much of Australian art and entertainment.

CULTURAL CRINGE

The term "cultural cringe" was popularized by Melbourne-born critic and teacher Arthur Phillips to describe the presumed superiority of culture produced overseas (in particular England) compared to local efforts. Writing in 1950, Phillips described "a disease of the Australian mind," which he identifies as "an assumption that the domestic cultural product will be worse than the imported article" (299). Greiner, citing Stephen Alomes, suggests that such cultural cringe gives way to the "peculiarly Australian practice of 'knocking,' or constantly criticizing things Australian" (186) Indeed, despite broad enthusiasm for more Australian superheroes, many of this study's respondents ridiculed the possible results: "I can't imagine someone really Australian unless you get someone really bogan," "if they had a super-ocky accent, that would be hilarious," and "there was an Australian Deadpool [in cosplay] before. He had a cork hat, so something like that?"[3]

Kevin Patrick notes of one of the first Australian superhero comics, *Jo and her Magic Cape*, published in 1945, "the approach, widely emulated by subsequent Australian-drawn superhero comics, was a harbinger of what architect and social commentator Robyn Boyd denounced as the 'culture of Austerica.' Australian society, he argued, was 'mesmerized by the appearance of Americana,' but was only capable of producing an austere, threadbare imitation of American popular culture" ("Atoman" 290). Similarly, many of this study's respondents worried that local efforts could only offer attenuated avengers. Demonstrating the reach of US popular culture, one fan attending Oz Comic-Con dressed as Captain America cautioned, "Australian superheroes? You know what, no, because I think our superpowers would be like throwing drop bears and drinking grog. Unless you wanted a Captain Bogan? No, let's just leave it to the big boys, shall we?"[4]

Reflecting on the difficulties faced by Australian writers, such as the Jindyworobak Movement, to forge a unique culture, Phillips describes how when local authors use Australian imagery it "doesn't quite come off" as it heightens our awareness of the writer's process (299). Similarly, some respondents identified a tension between distinctly Australian elements being added to a character type so firmly associated with the US, "What about the accent? It probably just wouldn't sound right." However, Grant Morrison argues that "superheroes were nothing if not adaptable, and as they grew and multiplied across the comic-book pages of the Free World, they happily took on the flavor of their surroundings" (29). Many fans were eager for superheroes with such a local flavor, "I think an Australian superhero would be just like a normal superhero, but maybe with a bit more of a relaxed attitude." Phillips might have endorsed such a laid-back Australian superhero, as he concluded his analysis of cultural cringe with a call for Australian art to be "unselfconsciously ourselves" adding "the opposite of the Cringe is not the Strut, but a relaxed erectness of carriage" (302).

MARKET DIFFERENTIATION

Describing the superhero dominance of the US comic book industry in 2000, *Watchmen* artist Dave Gibbons remarked, "superheroes are a genre that has overtaken a medium" ("Comics and Superheroes"). Since then, this superhero dominance has spread to mainstream cinema, television, and video games. However, most entries in the superhero genre still tend to stem from the two big US publishers Marvel and DC Comics, making it difficult for creators from any country to introduce new costumed crimefighters. For example, Dark Oz publisher Darren Koziol who mainly publishes horror and science fiction titles suggested, "I don't think we get too many Australian superheroes because the market is already dominated by all your Marvel and DC superheroes." This sentiment was shared by Wolfgang Bylsma, the editor-in-chief of Australia's leading graphic novel publisher, Gestalt, "If you look at Marvel and DC, which most people describe as the 'big two,' that's where the majority of people buy their superhero comics from [. . .] there's just too much of it to really make enough noise with new titles." Thus, a pragmatic need for differentiation in an international and domestic market already clogged with costume-clad characters has also contributed to the dearth of locally produced Australian heroes.

Although the one hundred creators and fans interviewed for this study have helped articulate the existing reasons for Australia's seeming incompatibility with the superhero, they also hint at how these hurdles might be surmounted, if not quite in a "single bound."

FROM BUSHMAN TO CLEVERMAN

There have been frequent attempts to challenge the dominance of US superheroes in Australia. Kevin Patrick notes how in the 1960s, the first organized Australian comic book fan communities were raised "on local editions of overseas comics, as well as indigenous publications" and celebrated local achievement through fanzines like *Down Under*, whose editor, John Ryan, dismissed readers with a "single-minded devotion to Marvel Comics" as "fanatics" ("[FAN] Scholars" 31). Cosplayers have also sought to recover Australian characters created by international writers and artists. For instance, a 2017 exhibition at the Melbourne Museum, *Marramb-ik*, focused on Indigenous Australian superheroes created by and for Australia's First Nations Peoples. It featured the work of Indigenous cosplayer Cienan Muir who attends comic book conventions dressed as the DC Comics villain Captain Boomerang—a white Australian character who uses the Indigenous Australian tool to superpowered effect. Such cosplay reclaims the stereotypical Australian character, and as the museum notes explained, "Cienan believes the very act of cosplay shows that a person can dismantle the concept of shame, suspend judgement and eliminate intimidation."

While acknowledging that some Australian superheroes have appeared in international comics, *Cleverman* star Hunter-Page Lochard argued that "I think what's important now is that these characters start being created by Australian people." Traditionally, "all of American comics were created by a couple hundred people in the New York metro area" (Duncan and Smith ix). In recent years digital technologies have enabled international creators to shape these US icons, with Australians Tom Taylor, Nicola Scott, and David Yardin, who were interviewed for this study, working on high-profile US comics including X-Men, Wonder Woman, and Black Panther. Writer Tom Taylor argues that "there aren't enough Australian superheroes and there definitely should be more," and has based some of his US comics in Australia. For instance, in one Melbourne-set issue of the *Injustice: Gods among Us* comic (April, 2013) a local superhero attempts to assert Australian sovereignty in the face of a now-villainous Superman, but his powers are revealed to be a dull imitation of the Man of Steel, and he is quickly overpowered. This one-sided fight could be read as a metaphor for how US superhero comics dominate Australia, but it also points to the subtle influence Australian creators are now able to cast over an increasingly global comic book industry. Taylor's Superman does not touch down in an ersatz Outback, but an authentic depiction of urban Australia, with details specific to the writer's Melbourne. The success of these Australian creators helps to dismantle the stereotypes of an outdated national identity, while the endorsement of US publishers Marvel and DC Comics combats cultural cringe. Nonetheless, these are still US comics, but in 2016 local creators offered a significant contribution to the superhero pantheon that was unambiguously Australian: Cleverman.

Cleverman was created by Indigenous Australian writer Ryan Griffen, who, when interviewed for this research, described how following an afternoon playing Batman with his son he wanted to create something that his child "could connect to on a cultural basis [...] an Aboriginal superhero." The eventual television show, *Cleverman*, was first broadcast in 2016, and imagines an X-Men-like near future Australia in which mythological "Hairypeople" have re-emerged to take their place alongside humans. However, coexistence is not easy, with government agencies unwilling to recognize the Hairypeople (or "Hairies") as citizens and limiting their movements to a heavily-policed "Zone." Drawn into this conflict is Koen West, a reluctant superhero who has recently become the Cleverman, a conduit for Australia's First Nations Peoples to the Dreaming.[5] With a largely Indigenous Australian cast and crew, *Cleverman* successfully negotiates many of the perceived obstacles to Australian superheroes.

In keeping with superhero conventions, *Cleverman* is largely set in a generic cityscape (recognizably Sydney to locals), but it maintains a connection to Indigenous traditions. As creator Griffen explains, "We've used our culture, the Aboriginal culture, in different ways: To give one of our characters a story arc, [...] to create the creatures in our world, and we also used it for just opening up the spectrum of political issues." However, superhero genre conventions do not always align with cultural sensitivities, with Griffen describing how in developing the show "you'll hear a story beat that is amazing in the genre world and you really want to do it, but I'll be sitting in the room and I'll put my hand up and go, 'Well, we can't do that because of the cultural sensitivity [...].' And so you then need to figure out a way to create that story and adhere to the culture, but also what people expect out of genre." Through a commitment to First Nations Peoples and their culture, *Cleverman* does not offer the pale imitation of US superheroes that so many of this study's respondents feared, but rather it adapts the superhero to a local context.

Cleverman also avoids the cultural cringe that burdens much of Australian output, as it comes with tacit international approval: among the show's production partners is the US cable channel Sundance TV, the show's creature effects were provided by the Academy Award–winning Weta Workshop, and the cast includes recognizable international actors such as *Game of Thrones* star Iain Glen. However, the show is not merely reflective of growing Australian confidence, but is active in contributing to that confidence. For instance, when interviewed for this study prior to the show's premiere actor and musician Adam Briggs described how "growing up the only Indigenous superhero that I knew of was Bishop from X-Men," but Briggs believed that a superhero show like *Cleverman* demonstrated a greater "confidence," adding "things like this

Figure 11.3. *Cleverman #1* (September, 2017) cowritten by Ryan Griffen and Wolfgang Bylsma.

are only going to spark ideas and have kids writing their own stories, and finally putting themselves in these roles of being leaders." This confidence was evident when star Hunter Page-Lochard attended the Melbourne popular culture convention AMC following the show's well-received first season. The actor described how, "to be at a Con where I'm sitting next to [*Wolverine* comic book writer] Larry Hama and there's a Disney princess walking past me [voice actress Linda Larkin] and I've got a Cyborg [*Justice League* actor Ray Fisher] next door, it's like whoa, this is awesome. But the thing that's most awesome about it is little small me from Australia deserves to be here as much as they do."

In his essay "The Cultural Cringe" Arthur Phillips identifies a lack of distinct cultural traditions in Australia for prompting unfavorable comparisons between local artistic works and those produced overseas, "We cannot shelter from invidious comparisons behind the barrier of a separate language; we have no long-established or interestingly different cultural tradition to give security and distinction to its interpreters" (299). However, *Cleverman* makes use of Indigenous Australian culture to serve as a point of differentiation, with creator Ryan Griffen explaining "These are 60,000-year-old stories that have never been told in this sort of realm and that is what makes us unique, and that is what broadcasters around the world are looking for, something new, something different." Thus, the use of local mythology not only provides the show's creators with confidence, but also much-needed distinction in a crowded marketplace. For example, Gestalt editor-in-chief Wolfgang Bylsma was interviewed for this project in 2016. At that point Gestalt was primarily focused on horror and science fiction books. Bylsma believed that the comic market was saturated by superheroes, explaining "It feels like there's enough to go around already. But who knows? I mean, somebody might surprise you with something that absolutely knocks it out of the park." In 2017 Gestalt not only published the *Cleverman* tie-in comic book, but Bylsma cowrote the comic with series creator Ryan Griffen. Seemingly, the use of Indigenous Australian mythology was enough to rejuvenate the tired superhero genre and provide the necessary market differentiation for a local superhero.

Through a deft mix of Indigenous mythology and superhero conventions, *Cleverman* demonstrates it is possible to reconcile those tensions—national identity, cultural cringe, and market differentiation—that once kept Australia and the superhero apart, demonstrating that despite Tina Turner's protests: We Do Need Another Hero.

• • •

Postscript: This article was originally published in *Senses of Cinema* issue 89 (December 2018). Since that publication, Australian comic book writer Tom Taylor, who was interviewed for this study, has added another Australian superhero to the comic book pantheon: Thylacine. Thylacine is an Indigenous Australian superhero whose stealth powers are inspired by the large carnivorous marsupial thylacine, also known as the Tasmanian Tiger or Tasmanian Wolf. Taylor consulted with *Cleverman* creator Ryan Griffen and Indigenous Australian actress Shari Sebbens in developing the character, who first appeared in *Suicide Squad* 1 (February, 2020) published by DC Comics. Thylacine continues the strategy Griffen and his collaborators employed on *Cleverman*, reconciling the longstanding tensions between Australia and the superhero archetype through a use of Indigenous traditions. Furthermore, Taylor used his status as a writer on US superhero comics to challenge long-standing stereotypes about Australia. As Taylor explained of Thylacine and her first story arc in which she hunts Captain Boomerang across Australia, "It's very Australian. It's a way for people here in Australia to see people who aren't tropes—who aren't throwing another shrimp on the barbie or who aren't in Crocodile Dundee world. To show the rest of the world real Australians is really important so for that reason it would be great if Thylacine had a long future at the company" (Kembrey). Although *Cleverman* never received a third season, as the Thylacine example suggests, its influence continues past the life of the television show. Indeed, Australia may finally have found its heroes.

This research was conducted as part of the *Superheroes & Me* linkage project funded by the Australian Research Council.

Notes

1. The interviews for this study were carried out as part of the *Superheroes & Me* research project funded by the Australian Research Council. In 2016 attendees and guests at Melbourne-based comic book conventions, Supanova, Oz Comic-Con, and AMC participated in semi-structured interviews about superheroes and fan culture. Additional interviews were carried out at a preview screening of *Cleverman*, also in 2016. Unless otherwise indicated, all quoted interviews are from this research. This study's semi structured interviews adhered to the Australian Code for the Responsible Conduct of Research and received ethics clearance from Swinburne University of Technology.

2. As this study's interviews were largely conducted before *Cleverman* was broadcast, it is possible that respondents would have cited the character if the research had taken place following the broadcast of the television show's first season.

3. "Bogan" and "ocker" are Australian slang terms that are often used pejoratively to describe someone who is unsophisticated and/or working class.

4. "Drop Bears" are an Australian in-joke about a predatory koala that attacks people who do not have an Australian accent (i.e., tourists). "Grog" is an Australian slang term for alcohol.

5. The Dreaming is a central aspect of Aboriginal Australian spiritual beliefs. In Dreamtime, all life is part of a larger network that can be traced back to the great sprit ancestors of the Dreamtime.

Works Cited

Altman, Dennis. "The Myth of Mateship." *Meanjin*, vol. 46, no. 2, 1987, pp. 163–72.
"Are 'Comic' Books Harmful to Minds of Young Readers?" *Sydney Morning Herald*, 28 Dec. 1948.
Beeton, Sue. "Rural Tourism in Australia — Has the Gaze Altered? Tracking Rural Images through Film and Tourism Promotion." *International Journal of Tourism Research*, vol. 6, no. 3, 2004, pp. 125–35.
Booker, Nigel. "Our Colonial Columnist Continues to Deliver His Own Views and Opinions." *Riddle Magazine*, 18 Aug. 2018, riddlemagazine.com/antipodean-adventures/.
Butera, Karina J. "'Neo-Mateship' in the 21st Century: Changes in the Performance of Australian Masculinity." *Journal of Sociology*, vol. 44, no. 3, pp. 265–81.

"Comics and Superheroes" (Supplementary material on DVD release of *Unbreakable*). DVD. Touchstone Home Video, 2000.

Coogan, Peter M. *Superhero: The Secret Origin of a Genre*. MonkeyBrain Books, 2006.

Crofts, Stephen. "Cross-Cultural Reception Studies: Culturally Variant Readings of Crocodile Dundee." *Continuum*, vol. 6, no. 1, 1992, pp. 213–27.

Duncan, Randy, and Matthew J. Smith. *The Power of Comics: History, Form and Culture*. Bloomsbury, 2013.

Eco, Umberto. "The Myth of Superman." *Diacritics*, vol. 2, no. 1, 1972, pp. 14–22.

Fawaz, Ramzi. *The New Mutants Superheroes and the Radical Imagination of American Comics*. New York University Press, 2016.

Greiner, Alyson L. "Popular Culture, Place Images, and Myths: The Promotion of Australia on American Television." *Journal of Popular Culture*, vol. 35, no. 1, 2001, pp. 185–93.

Haltof, Marek. "In Quest of Self-Identity: Gallipoli, Mateship, and the Construction of Australian National Identity." *Journal of Popular Film and Television*, vol. 21, no. 1, 1993, pp. 27–36.

Harvey, Robert C. *The Art of the Comic Book: An Aesthetic History*. University Press of Mississippi, 1996.

Highmore, Ben. *Cityscapes: Cultural Readings in the Material and Symbolic City*. Palgrave Macmillan, 2005.

Kembrey, Melanie. "Suicide Squad Enlists First Indigenous Australian Character, Thylacine." *The Sydney Morning Herald*, 14 Apr. 2020.

Lucas, Rose. "Dragging It Out: Tales of Masculinity in Australian Cinema, from Crocodile Dundee to Priscilla, Queen of the Desert." *Journal of Australian Studies*, vol. 22, no. 56, 1998, pp. 138–46.

Morrison, Grant. *Supergods: Our World in the Age of the Superhero*. Jonathan Cape, 2012.

Patrick, Kevin. "Age of the Atoman: Australian Superhero Comics and Cold War Modernity." *The Superhero Symbol: Media, Culture, and Politics*, edited by Liam Burke et al., Rutgers University Press, 2019, pp. 286–302.

Patrick, Kevin. "(FAN) Scholars and Superheroes: The Role and Status of Comics Fandom Research in Australian Media History." *Media International Australia*, vol. 155, no. 1, 2015, pp. 28–37.

Patrick, Kevin. *The Phantom Unmasked: America's First Superhero*. University of Iowa Press, 2017.

Patrick, Kevin. "The Transplanted Superhero: The Phantom Franchise and Australian Popular Culture." *Superheroes on World Screens*, edited by Rayna Denison and Rachel Mizsei-Ward, University Press of Mississippi, Mississippi, 2016, pp. 19–35.

Phillips, Arthur. "The Cultural Cringe." *Meanjin*, vol. 9, no. 4, 1950, pp. 299–302.

Reynolds, Richard. *Super Heroes: A Modern Mythology*. University Press of Mississippi, 1994.

Urry, John. *The Tourist Gaze: Leisure and Travel in Contemporary Societies*. Sage, 1990.

Williams, Paul. "Beyond Mad Max III: Race, Empire, and Heroism on Post-Apocalyptic Terrain." *Science Fiction Studies*, vol. 32, no. 2, 2005, pp. 301–15.

Young, Damon. "An Australian Superman." *Island*, no. 137, 2014, pp. 27–30.

Chapter 12

WITHOUT SEEING THE DAWN

Monstrous (Super)Heroes and Philippine Myths in Mervin Malonzo's *Tabi Po*

MARIA LORENA M. SANTOS

"The specters of the past return, seeking justice"[1]—so warns the blurb for Mervin Malonzo's *Tabi Po*, an award-winning graphic novel from the Philippines. Set in the country's nineteenth-century Spanish colonial period, *Tabi Po* tells the story of a newborn *aswang*, a flesh-eating monster who comes to terms with his true nature when he crosses paths with a human woman and rape survivor who seeks vengeance against her oppressors. These two outsiders of Philippine society join forces in a vigilante quest set against the backdrop of the country's revolt against its colonizer. This chapter argues that Malonzo's text engages with the conventions of the superhero genre, both in the US and the Philippines, by reimagining marginal characters from the canon of Philippine nationalism as monstrous heroes. *Tabi Po* not only redefines the genre, but also the "heroic," in the Philippines by harking back to pre-Superman myths and revolutionary heroes. The graphic novel appropriates Philippine national hero and writer José Rizal and his characters to question the history of Western mythmaking in the country. Through the intertextuality of its narrative and illustrations, as well as its focus on liminal identities, the graphic novel *Tabi Po* both reconstructs and reclaims Philippine heroism and the Filipino superhero.

TABI PO AND THE SUPERHERO TRADITION IN THE PHILIPPINES

The heroes in Malonzo's *Tabi Po* implicitly talk back to the earliest Filipino superheroes from the superhero tradition in the Philippines, which began in the form of the post–World War II *komiks magasin* (or magazine) patterned after the "American cultural export" of comic books (Flores, "Comics Crash" 47). The Filipino superhero during these early decades "was very much attached to the classic American comic-book superhero script" (Gutierrez 348). Local characters could be identified with American counterparts, e.g., Mars Ravelo's Darna in the 1950s with Wonder Woman, and Captain Barbell, and Lastik Man in the 1960s with Captain Marvel and Plastic Man, although there were distinguishing Filipino characteristics. Comics scholar Emil Flores asserts that the Filipino-ness of these superheroes lay, not in the replication of Western art style, but in their origin stories: "[T]hey belong to the working class and receive their powers from magical objects handed down to them because of their humility and purity of heart" ("Comics Crash" 53). Anna Katrina Gutierrez identifies in these origin stories a Filipino metanarrative of "the triumph of the underdog," reflective of "the desire of a people to overcome persistent and pervading hegemony" (348). However, she argues that such triumphs are undermined by the colonial mentality in these early *komiks*' imagery, that is, in the fact that ordinary people gain power when they don "Americanised costumes" (Gutierrez 348).[2] Others, like Eleanor Sarah Reposar, identify at the very least a "strain of subversion and resistance against colonial rule" (428). Referencing earlier scholar Soledad Reyes's assertion that Filipino komiks used humor to commit "transgressive acts within the colonial system" (81), Reposar describes the "play on the phonetics of the [superheroes'] names" as "a kind of downplaying and spoofing of these same American characters" (429).

Paving the way for Malonzo's *Tabi Po* was the rise in the late 1990s and early 2000s of graphic novels in the Philippines and the emergence of new Filipino superheroes. Although these comics were still influenced by Western tropes, and many written in English for a middle-class audience, these superheroes were overtly grounded in "distinctly Filipino settings and themes" (Reposar 430). Arnold Arre's *The Mythology Class* (1999), for example, "integrated Philippine images and meanings with the American superhero comic book genre" by featuring creatures from Philippine myths and folklore (Gutierrez 349). Carlo Vergara's *Ang Kagilas-gilas na Pagsasapalaran ni ZsaZsa Zaturnnah* (2003) deliberately drew from the aesthetics and motifs of Western superhero comics, while at the same time subverting them by introducing a transsexual woman as a superhero whose Filipino gay lingo "destabilizes and undermines the dominant heterosexist, colonialist notions embedded in language" (Reposar 434).[3]

Malonzo's three-issue graphic novel is situated among superhero texts from later in the 2000s that more directly engage with Philippine postcolonial identity, such as Gilbert Monsanto's *Bayan Knights* (2008), Paolo Fabregas's *The Filipino Heroes League* or *FHL* (2011), and Arnold Arre's *Ang Mundo ni Andong Agimat* (2011). Exploring Filipino cultural identity in these superhero *komiks*, Flores highlights their appropriation of the American superhero concept, noting how they all "use history as a way of placing the superhero in [a] Philippine context" ("Up in the Sky" 15). The series *Bayan Knights*, literally "Knights of the Nation," manifests "a deliberate attempt to use Filipino motifs" and to "identify ... characters with Filipino nationhood," via the superheroes' names, origin stories, and Philippine-flag-inspired costumes ("Up in the Sky" 6). Flores sees *The Filipino Heroes League*, about an undermanned and underfunded organization faced with the problems of poverty-stricken Philippine society, "as a Third World deconstruction of superheroes in the vein of Alan Moore's *Watchmen*" ("Up in the Sky" 9). In *FHL*, the most powerful and wealthy Filipino superheroes leave the country, while the members of the League remain oppressed. Even in the fantasy world, Flores observes, "there is apparently no escape from Third World Reality" and "Filipino colonial history" ("Up in the Sky" 11). In contrast, Flores notes how *Ang Mundo ni Andong Agimat* follows a different template; written in conversational Filipino and featuring Filipino heroes from history, myth, and action films who are "not deconstructed Third World versions but are characters grounded on Filipino culture and elevated to superhero status," it serves as "a contemporary epic that attempts to examine the nation's history" ("Up in the Sky" 15).

Tabi Po also comes from a different mold. The graphic novel is written in Filipino and implicitly critiques the superhero myth as represented by Superman and his Filipino counterpart, Darna.[4] Its characters have no American parallels, wear no spectacular costumes, and their triumphs are balanced by pain and loss; as characters transported from Rizal's novels to an even darker story, their subversion is no longer just hinted at but directly expressed. *Tabi Po*'s writer Malonzo is the cofounder of Haliya, an independent comics group that aims to publish books that are "artist-centric, diverse in topic, intellectually arresting, and contractually fair" and which claim to be "mapping out the future of the form today" (Haliya Publishing). Published from 2014 to 2017, and winner of the 2015 National Book Award, *Tabi Po* builds on the superhero comics movement that questioned outdated (i.e., American) definitions of superheroes, particularly in the Philippine context. In more recent superhero tales, what is palpable is "the Filipino komiks creators' conscious or unconscious connection to the struggle for freedom" (Flores, "Up in the Sky"15). Like the three texts discussed by Flores, Malonzo's graphic novel features characters connected to the Katipunan, a revolutionary organization led by Andres Bonifacio, which opposed Spanish rule in the late 1800s. Accordingly, this chapter examines how *Tabi Po* uses Philippine history and mythology to contend with not just the imported American superhero, but also with two colonial periods of mythmaking in the Philippines: the Spaniards' demonizing of local beliefs and the Americans' alleged sponsoring of a Philippine national hero: José Rizal.

JOSÉ RIZAL AS FILIPINO (SUPER)HERO

In the Philippines, José Rizal is regarded as not just a national hero but as one of the greatest Filipinos who ever lived (Coates xviii). Represented as larger than life by many biographers, Rizal is lauded for his skills as a novelist, essayist, poet, doctor, scientist, polyglot, Renaissance man, and even lover. Both popular and academic texts depict or refer to him as a superhero. On social media and online art sites, one may find many renderings of him as a superhero, sometimes caped and flying, other times garbed in localized superhero attire, while the 2003 cover of Filipino historian Ambeth Ocampo's biography, *Rizal without the Overcoat* (1990), features said outerwear opening to reveal Superman's emblem (see figure 12.1). A 2011 speech by then President Benigno S. Aquino III, given on the 150th anniversary of Rizal's birth, contains the assertion that "Rizal was not *born* a superhero" [emphasis added]. Lasty, a planned graphic novel by Gerry Alanguilan is titled *The Marvelous Adventures of the Amazing Dr. Rizal* and features on its teaser cover a jet-pack-wearing Rizal (see figure 12.2).[5]

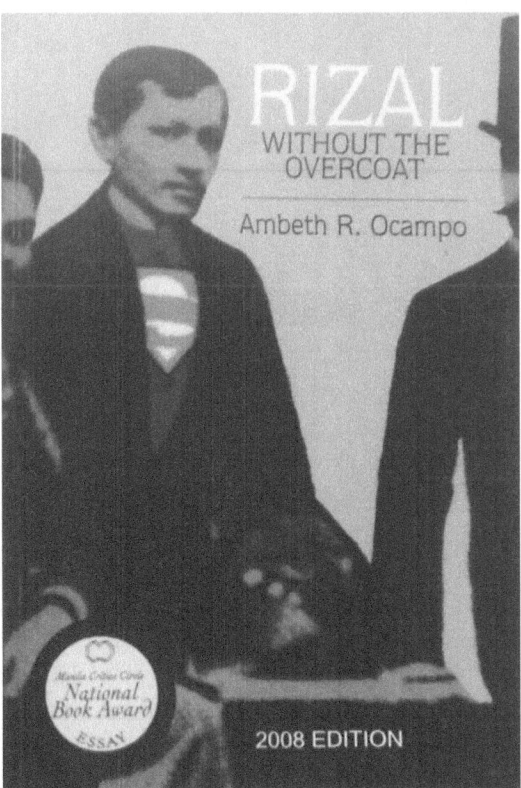

Figure 12.1. The cover of Ambeth Ocampo's *Rizal without the Overcoat*.

Figure 12.2. The cover of Gerry Alanguilan's *The Marvelous Adventures of the Amazing Dr. Rizal*. From the estate of Gerry Alanguilan.

The comic book *Tabi Po* draws from both the figure of Rizal as a homegrown hero—specifically from the local narratives and debates about his politics—and from the heroes and villains he created as a writer. A fan of Rizal, *Tabi Po* creator Mervin Malonzo used characters from the national hero's late nineteenth-century novels *Noli me Tangere* or "Touch Me Not" (1887) and *El Filibusterismo* or "The Subversive" (1891), which are abbreviated here as *Noli* and *Fili* respectively.[6] These texts played a pivotal role in Philippine political history, as they were scathing critiques of three hundred years of Spanish colonial rule (from 1521 to 1898) and its many social ills. The writing of these novels, which were banned by the Spanish government, along with Rizal's suspected involvement in revolutionary organizations, led to his exile and eventual execution. Today the novels are viewed as national epics and catalysts for the country's revolt against Spain.[7] The Rizal Law, or Republic Act No. 1425, passed in 1956, requires "the curricula of private and public schools, colleges and universities courses to include the life, works and writings of José Rizal, particularly his novels *Noli Me Tangere* and *El Filibusterismo*, in order to educate the students about the concept of nationalism."

The question of what kind of nationalism he was advocating relates to the controversy surrounding Rizal's status as national hero which, like the Filipino superhero tradition, is linked to American colonialism. While there is evidence that Filipinos chose Rizal to be their national hero in 1898, scholar Renato Constantino's labeling of him in 1969 as "An American-sponsored Hero" (4) continues to be influential. To support his assertion, Constantino cited President William Howard Taft's recommendation in 1901 that Rizal be named a national hero, as well as excerpts from Theodore Friend's book *Between Two Empires* about a meeting among American colonial officials and "some conservative Filipinos" who selected Rizal over Katipunan leader Bonifacio whom they deemed "too radical" (5). Historian Ambeth Ocampo claimed in 2011 that no record of such a meeting could be found (cited in Chua), but the pitting of "reformist Rizal" against "revolutionary Bonifacio" as rivals for the role of national (super)hero persists today.

In its consideration of real-world heroes who came before Superman, Chris Gavaler's *On the Origin of Superheroes* states, "Superheroes are revolutionists. They overthrow the natural order and establish themselves as our benevolent protectors" (9). Questions about Rizal's revolutionary leanings and the debate about whether he is truly representative of Philippine heroism extend to analyses of his novels' characters, some of whom feature as leads in *Tabi Po*. While Rizal was an advocate of institutional reforms through peaceful means rather than violent revolt, his novels *Noli* and *Fili* trace the transformation of privileged, Western-educated Crisostomo Ibarra into the subversive anarchist Simoun. In the first novel, Ibarra's idealistic plans for San Diego, a fictional town representing Philippine society, are thwarted by enemies among the abusive Spanish clergy and local authorities. In the second, Ibarra as a wiser and more cynical Simoun plans a violent attack on the government but fails because of conflicts both within himself and the revolution. Scholars and activists see Rizal's more seditious leanings in this transformed character. Simoun (as Simon) is only introduced in the third issue of *Tabi Po*, but a teaser at the end of this issue, states that, as in Rizal's novels, he will be the central character of *Tabi Po 2*.

Rizal's revolutionary tendencies and, thus, relevance as a (super)hero, are also evident in Elias, the protagonist of *Tabi Po*, who only plays a secondary role in *Noli*. In Rizal's novel Elias is a character with a mysterious past, an outlaw, and a fugitive who befriends Ibarra and later sacrifices himself to save the latter's life. The lines uttered by this character before his death are often quoted by those delivering patriotic speeches, as these were repeated by Rizal himself in his message to the youth on the eve of his execution: "I die *without seeing the dawn* brighten over my native land. You who have it to see, welcome it, and forget not those who have fallen during the night!" (Rizal, *The Social Cancer* 243, added emphasis). As a revolutionary and a martyr, Elias has been associated with the heroism and valor of Bonifacio as well as with the perceived revolutionary side of Rizal.

Additional information about Elias can be found in the chapter titled "Elias at Salome," which Rizal later excised from *Noli* to reduce publication costs (Acibo and Galicano-Adanza 157) and where his sweetheart, Salome, makes her only appearance. Elias visits Salome to tell her he cannot marry her, as he does not wish to involve her in his troubles. He urges her to leave her forest home, and she reluctantly agrees even as she describes their parting as leaving behind half of her life. As a female character, Salome has been read by scholar Epifanio San Juan Jr. as one with "relative control over her means of subsistence and her isolation" (37); she has "a latitude of activity, a degree of autonomy" (41) greater than that of the demure and upper-class Maria Clara, Ibarra's sweetheart who retreats to a convent, is raped there, and then commits suicide. Malonzo notably omits Maria Clara from the comic and makes Salome a central character in a retelling of the novel that extends what is now referred to as "the lost chapter," the missing chapter," or "Chapter X (Ex)." This chapter has been reinstated in modern editions of Rizal's *Noli* as part of the appendix or as chapter 25. Its presence, along with that of Salome, in various adaptations and reworkings like Malonzo's can be read as a problematizing of the binary of revolution and reform—in a sense, the brand of heroism—of Rizal and his novels.[8]

RECONFIGURATION OF FILIPINO (SUPER)HEROISM

Although it is not the first adaptation of this deleted chapter, *Tabi Po* is the first to make leads of Rizal's two marginal characters in comic book form: as morally ambiguous monsters and, arguably, as superheroes. In *Tabi Po*, Malonzo reimagines Elias as a supernatural creature, a powerful *aswang*, the Filipino equivalent of a ghoul or vampire. Salome, kept as a sex slave by Spanish friars, is portrayed as a woman whose misery and bloodlust give her a monstrous strength. They represent two of the fearsome creatures that the series' title may allude to: In the Philippines, there is a folk practice of saying "tabi-tabi po" ("Please move aside") as a sign of respect to potentially dangerous entities into whose territory one trespasses. Other key characters in the comic book are two *aswang*, Tasyo and Sabel, who take Elias under their wing to live among the humans in San Diego, Laguna. This fictional town is under the control of Spanish friars Padre Damaso and Padre Salvi, officials like the *Alperez* (a Spanish lieutenant-general), and the avaricious Chinese businessman Quiroga. Elias joins Salome in seeking revenge against those responsible for her misery, but trouble ensues when their killings, along with others committed by Tasyo and Sabel, are attributed to the revolution brewing on the outskirts of town.

Tabi Po and its interpretation of Rizal's characters have a complex relationship with both Filipino and US superhero traditions in that the comic book both draws from and subverts the conventions of these two traditions. Richard Reynolds, in *Superheroes: A Modern Mythology*, extrapolated seven superhero features or conventions from the origin story of Superman published in 1938 during the Golden Age of American comics. These are, in Reynold's order: "1. *Lost parents*," "2. *The man-god*," "3. *Justice*," "4. *The normal and the superpowered*," "5. *The secret identity*," "6. *Superheroes and politics*," and "7. *Science as magic*" (16). Flores reworked this typology for the Filipino superhero in his essay "The Concept of the Superhero in Filipino Films," identifying five key features: "*Parents* (or guardians), *Powers* (including costumes as symbols of superpowers), *Purity and Piety*, *The Private and the Public* (secret identities and public perception), and *Politics*" (29). The remainder of this chapter will examine *Tabi Po* in terms of how it reconfigures Reynold's and Flores's typologies and, by implication, the traditional superhero archetype on which the earliest Filipino superheroes were based.

The first two features of Reynolds's template, "*Lost parents*," and "*The man-god*" (16) are roughly equivalent to Flores's "*Parents*" and "*Powers*." Both Elias's and Salome's origins align with Reynold's typology more than Flores's: Not only are their characters "marked out from society" and reach maturity "without having a relationship with [their] parents" (16), but they are utterly alone, unlike many early Filipino superheroes who have at least one living family member. As for the second convention, Elias resembles American superheroes who are "like earthbound gods in their level of powers" (Reynolds 16). He has superhuman strength and recovers quickly from wounds but, unlike the Filipino superhero, he is not pure of heart nor granted his powers via a magical object because of this trait. The remaining features in Reynold's and Flores's typologies do not neatly fit with *Tabi Po*'s characters and conceit and are discussed in four subsections that relate to *Tabi Po*'s reconfiguration of these conventions.

THE ORDINARY AND THE EXTRAORDINARY, THE HEROIC AND THE MONSTROUS

In Reynold's template, the contrast between "*The normal and the superpowered*" relates to how "The extraordinary nature of the superhero will be contrasted with the ordinariness of his surroundings" (16). However, *Tabi Po* does not contrast the ordinariness of the Philippine setting with the extraordinary powers of the *aswang*. Instead, it interrogates what is normal in this setting—what is deemed monstrous and heroic in *both* the ordinary and the extraordinary, thus blurring the boundaries between these categories.

When the story begins, Elias and his mentors at first attempt to appear ordinary. They lie low by eating those who would be least missed: poor farmers and town outcasts. Later, however, they target the prominent Padre Damaso, whose sermons anger them. Damaso threatens death to sinners and heretics whom he says will be killed by the *dimonyo* (demons) and *aswang*; in giving them this name, Damaso constructs the *aswang* as monsters for his own political ends—to frighten the Filipino townsfolk and keep them in line. In Rizal's novel, Damaso is an abusive friar who fathers Maria Clara by raping her mother; in Malonzo's graphic novel, he chains Salome to a bed where he and other men molest her. Thus, Damaso is represented in *Tabi Po* as the demon he condemns for feasting on human flesh. Malonzo uses this character to address Spanish appropriation of local mythology as a form of colonial control—to suppress political dissent, keep Filipinos within easy-to-manage towns, and discourage contact with rebels. But Malonzo also depicts the ferocious Tasyo and Sabel as creatures who are charismatic and beautiful, highlighting the difficulty of knowing, as one townsperson puts it, who among them is an *aswang* and who is human, who is good and who is evil.

In contrast, Elias is marked out by his "human" desire for love and self-hood, a need that extends beyond his hunger as *aswang*. Elias discovers his purpose and identity not by learning from Tasyo and Sabel but because of his love for a human woman who is sold like an object, held captive, and repeatedly abused. They meet when Salome manages to free herself and lies in wait for Damaso, who is then attacked by the three *aswang*. She reveals herself to Elias when he is left to finish off the priest. Wielding a rosary wrapped around the cross-shaped letter opener that she used to break her chains, Salome proceeds to mutilate her rapist's face. "Deliver me from evil," she repeats, adapting the final line of "The Lord's Prayer" to her own struggles against her oppressors.[9]

Salome recruits Elias as an avenger of sins committed against her, calling him not only her "angel of death," but also God's answer to her prayers, brought to Earth to destroy the true demons and monsters disguised as holy folk. Through such conflations of angel and *aswang*, the monstrousness of all the characters is repeatedly questioned both visually and textually in Malonzo's series. When Salome targets Padre Salvi, he overpowers her and prepares to violate her, calling her a "demoñita" (female demon) and himself a soldier of God. Elias overturns such religious epithets, when he arrives to save Salome from Salvi, saying as much to himself as to the priest, "How can a detestable creature such as I be an angel?" Staring at the priest's Western features, thin lips, and sharp nose, he asks, "How can a beautiful creature such as you be a demon?" before he violently wrests Salvi's jaw from his face.

Essential to the US definition of a superhero, according to Stan Lee, is the use of their power "to accomplish good deeds" (qtd. in Rosenberg and Coogan 115). Yet the definition of goodness is interrogated by *Tabi Po* which, in doing so, harks back to the historical and mythological sources of superheroes mapped out by Gavaler, figures whose "great privilege" came "with questionable morality" (9). Thus, in terms of typology, Malonzo's text highlights juxtapositions rather than disparities: good along with evil, the normal alongside the supernatural, nineteenth-century Philippine folk beliefs—dubbed "pagan" by the Westerners—simulated in Catholic doctrine, and the monstrous as indistinguishable from the heroic.

THE LIMINAL IDENTITY

The second reconfigured feature is Reynold's "*The secret identity*" which states that "the extraordinary nature of the hero will be contrasted with the mundane nature of his alter ego" (16). Flores's "The private and the public" convention reveals a lack of distinction between the two and thus pays attention to public perceptions of Filipino superheroes. In Malonzo's narrative, the heroic forms and "alter egos" of *Tabi Po*'s characters are not separate. Moreover, public perception—indeed, perception in general—is represented as unreliable, as Elias is illustrated both as a raging monster when Salome first meets him and, through her eyes, as Saint Michael the Archangel, protector and leader of the army of God against the forces of evil.[10]

Elias and Salome are not costumed heroes and, instead exhibit their most powerful and honest selves when they are naked. What is significant is that in both their "benign" and monstrous forms, Elias and Salome remain outsiders, marginal and liminal characters. The monster, especially the shape-shifting one, like the *aswang*, is a creature in between states, on the threshold of human and beast. Malonzo's Elias is unsure of his identity and belongs neither with his kind nor with the humans around him. His appearance and identity also shift, depending on who views him: his victims see him as monstrous while Salome sees him as heroic. Interestingly it is his liminal, monstrous status that grants him agency in the sociopolitical narrative; his actions, motivated by love for Salome, lead to the death of those who subjugated many Filipinos.

Salome, as a woman in nineteenth-century Philippines, has even less agency and power than her male counterpart. At first, she appears in *Tabi Po* to be much like *Noli*'s iconic female characters—the wealthy Maria Clara and the destitute Sisa—quiescent victims who die in misery. Malonzo grants her more power, writing Salome as a working-class hero with a revenge quest that parallels her search for identity. "Who am I?" she asks repeatedly and asserts at one point that she is no object; she has feelings and a name. She demands justice, not just for herself, but also for others like her: marginal, objectified, persecuted. When Quiroga, the man who sold her to Damaso, tells her that she belongs to the lowest rung of society, Salome stabs his hand, and demands, "Who are you to tell me the limits of my place?" Yet after she has killed all her oppressors, Salome feels empty. To Elias's horror, she says, "Here comes the monster," and then murders the wife and young daughter of the *Alperez* who were witnesses to his slaughter. Later, when she presents herself to the townsfolk to save a falsely accused man, she declares, "I am the *aswang*."

Salome's actions lead Elias to examine both her identity and his, and he realizes that, as beings who have learned to accept themselves as they are, they should remain together. He returns to Salome's cottage to tell her this, saying, "I'm not human. I'm not a monster. Neither am I an angel. I am me, and you are you." But he finds Salome on the brink of death, her body torn open by Tasyo. She addresses him as her angel one last time and asks him to consume her so that they will be one (and whole) forever. Their liminality and outsider status make Elias and Salome extraordinary, and this discovery allows the members of the revolution to recognize that it is such a status, in relation to institutions of power during the Spanish Colonial Period, that drives them. Gavaler's notion that oppression is "the original cosmic gamma ray bomb or spider-bite mutation that births the superhero" (52) manifests in how Salome's persecution and both characters' liminality are what make them forces to contend with.

LIGHT AND DARKNESS

This subsection combines two of Reynold's features, "Justice" and "Superpowers and politics," with Flores's "Politics." Reynolds states, "The hero's devotion to justice overrides even his devotion to the law," and, "Although ultimately above the law, superheroes can be capable of considerable patriotism and moral loyalty to the state, though not necessarily to the letter of its laws" (Reynolds

16). Flores's examination of Filipino superheroes sees a respect for government authorities and the law perhaps attributable to "a call for unity that is common in contemporary Philippine politics" ("The Concept" 29) and the idea that "superheroes are symbols of a childlike hope in a better society" ("The Concept" 36). The law, in the case of both Rizal's and Malonzo's texts, is a colonial one, and their protagonists, along with the Filipino revolutionaries, are driven by a desire for freedom and selfhood that overrides any devotion to this. *Tabi Po* returns to some of the earliest revolutionary heroes' disrespect for authority, whose "antinoble nobility" is described by Gavaler as "one of the superheroes' founding paradoxes" (53), by weighing justice and patriotism against the authority of colonialism.

Tabi Po's weighing of patriotism and colonial authority—as well as of good and evil, light and darkness—involves a questioning of this binary, as already discussed vis-à-vis Elias and Salome, and which can also be seen when Filipinos and colonial characters, or humans and *aswang* are set side by side. The ordinary Filipinos of San Diego embrace the very myths and monsters that rule over them; they seek an *aswang* to blame for the deaths in the town and turn on an admirer of Salome, who happens to have ties with the Filipino rebels on the outskirts of town. The townsfolk capture and beat him and prepare to offer his blood as sacrifice to appease an Old Testament God, shouting a prayer-ending "Amen!" as they light a fire to burn him at the stake. These villagers can be viewed as transforming into monsters themselves: although human, they are drawn with horrific and violent expressions not unlike those of Tasyo and the *aswang* Sabel. In the events that follow, the rebels join the crowd to defend Isagani, and Salome takes his place on the stake. She is then whisked away by Elias, causing the bloodthirsty villagers to suspect and turn on the rebels for taking away their victim. The *aswang* Sabel watches, remarking, "Look at them. They are no different from us."

Elias also observes these blurred lines when he questions the reasons for the slaughter. The *aswang* are like animals; they kill out of necessity, eat to survive. However, they are like humans as well, who take lives even when they do not need to and find ways to justify their actions. The rebels talk of the necessity of spilling blood so that they may achieve freedom. Salome embraces the darkness when she kills for her own reasons. The epiphany Elias reaches, however, is that in everyone, even in the woman he loves, "there is light and darkness. Nothing is pure—everything is mixed. There is no evil. There is no good." He concludes, "Yet there is evil *and* good. Everyone has both light and darkness." In the end, when he confronts Tasyo, he tells him that although Tasyo sees himself as a God, he is a monster, and only when he embraces this identity will he truly be whole.

MYTHOLOGY AND HISTORY AS MAGIC

In describing the final features, "*Science as magic*," Reynolds says that superhero stories "are mythical and use science and magic indiscriminately to create a sense of wonder" (16). *Tabi Po* appropriates mythology, religion, and history to evoke a postmodern disorientation, rather than wonder, aimed at a pointed interrogation of colonialism and heroism. The myths that propagate colonialism are taken apart and dissected in the series. First, and most obviously, the myth of the *aswang*, which is transformed from native belief, to colonial tool, to actual monster, to avenging angel. Tasyo and Sabel, in various panels, are represented as superpowered beings, as Western religious figures Jesus and Mary and Adam and Eve, and as Malakas and Maganda, the first man and woman in a Philippine creation myth. They are neither harmed by folk talismans like garlic, nor by setting foot in a church, thus calling into question the validity of both pagan and Catholic modes of belief. At the same time, their existence is possible because of these belief systems; as one villager puts it, "If God exists, then so does the devil, so yes, there is such a thing as an *aswang*."

The comic book's examination of mythology and the superhero myth in the Philippines extends to the destabilizing of the myth of José Rizal as reformist. At the end of issue two, readers find in an epilogue three brief diary entries signed with the name Simon (recalling Rizal's Simoun). These diary entries are curated by a fictional researcher who calls them the notes of a madman. Issue three introduces him as a young man who defeats Sabel with a talismanic necklace that renders her powerless. Elias, after consuming Tasyo, meets Simon, who travels with an invisible *tikbalang*, a half-horse, half-man creature from Philippine mythology, that dwells in Simon's body. Hinting at what is to come in the next *Tabi Po* volume, Malonzo brings together the two radical figures of *Noli* and *Fili* as potential allies. As a superhero comic book crossover, this promises to be a reimagining of Andres Bonifacio and José Rizal no longer pitted against each other but aligned as revolutionary national (super)heroes.

"TABI PO!"

In conclusion, the chapter offers a final look at the graphic novel's title *Tabi Po!* Filipinos, especially young children in rural areas, are taught to use this phrase as a respectful request to avoid offending spirits believed to dwell in trees and mounds of soil. But who says "tabi po" in Malonzo's narrative, and to whom is this request addressed? Considering the treatment of the (super)heroic in the graphic novel, the utterance operates in several ways. First, the townsfolk say this in deference to the *aswang*, whom they have been taught to fear. Second, it is said ironically by the *aswang* Tasyo to the humans he abhors for their weakness and hypocrisy, but whom he secretly desires to be like. Finally, the writer Malonzo uses it to both ask pardon from and pay homage to José Rizal whose characters he appropriates in a way that fleshes out and frees the man from the myths surrounding him.

In a contemporary Philippines that is still arguably subject to American cultural imperialism, and where precolonial lore has been associated with the dangerous and primitive darkness of the past, *Tabi Po*, then, wrestles with both the "American invention" of the superhero (Flores, "Up in the Sky" 15) and the American-associated metanarrative of the triumph of good over evil (Gutierrez 348) that can be read into the US backing of Rizal as reformist hero. *Tabi Po* merges elements of Philippine horror, mythology, religion, history, and sociopolitical critique to reconstruct Philippine (super)heroism as revolutionary and radical, one comprising both monstrous and noble tendencies, and one that comprehends the darkness of night along with the light of dawn.

Notes

1. This chapter's opening quote, "The specters of the past return, seeking justice" (translated by author), refers to the original Filipino text: "*Ang pagbablik ng mga multo ng nakaraan, naghahanap ng hustisya*"; it is found on the back cover of Malonzo's *Tabi Po*, Isyu 3 (2017).

2. Anna Katrina Gutierrez notes that Wonder Woman analog Darna's "strength is signified when she wears her red and gold bikini costume, essentially replacing her conservative Filipina image with a Western form of female power" (348).

3. In English, the title of Carlo Vergara's graphic novel *Ang Kagilas-gilas na Pagsasapalaran ni ZsaZsa Zaturnnah* echoes those of American comics while humorously incorporating its protagonist's flamboyant name: *The Amazing Adventures of ZsaZsa Zaturnnah* (translated by author).

4. Flores refers to Darna as "the generic Filipino hero" in his paper "The Concept of the Superhero in Filipino Films" to "demonstrate how the superhero was assimilated into Filipino popular culture" (26–27). Darna has both Western and Philippine mythological influences, and as the most popular superhero in the Philippines, "like Superman, is almost synonymous" with the word "superhero" (27).

5. *The Marvelous Adventures of the Amazing Dr. Rizal* is listed as a work-in-progress on *Komikero Dot Com*, the official website of Gerry Alanguilan, who died in 2020.

6. In an interview, *Tabi Po* creator Mervin Malonzo explained, "I'm a fan of José Rizal's novels. I used names from his story. I wanted to show the abuses back then—is it any different now?" (qtd. in Palumbarit).

7. Historian John Schumacher references the importance of Rizal's novels in the Philippines' revolt against Spain in his essay "The *Noli Me Tangere* as Catalyst of Revolution" (1991).

8. Several screen and drama adaptations of *Noli* include Rizal's missing chapter and even highlight this. In 1996, University of the Philippines' theater group Dulaang UP produced "Elias at Salome," a musical retelling of *Noli* but centering on the titular characters.

9. Salome's line "Deliver me from evil" in *Tabi Po* is translated by the author from the original Filipino/Tagalog text, as are the rest of the quotes in English in this chapter.

10. In the Philippines, the image of Saint Michael the Archangel is typically associated with the label of a cheap local brand of gin, Ginebra San Miguel. Malonzo's conflation of this religious image with both Elias and, in one scene, the rapist Padre Damaso, complicates the notion of nobility and degeneracy.

Works Cited

Acibo, Libert, and Estela Galicano-Adanza. *José P. Rizal: His Life, Works, and Role in the Philippine Revolution*. Quezon City: Rex Bookstore, 1995.

Alanguilan, Gerry. "About." *Komikero Dot Com*. Blogger, 2017, http://komikerodotcom.blogspot.com/p/about.html.

Aquino, Benigno III. "Speech of His Excellency Benigno S. Aquino III, President of the Philippines, On the Celebration of the 150th Anniversary of José Rizal's Birth" (English translation). *Official Gazette*, Republic of the Philippines, 19 June 2011, https://www.officialgazette.gov.ph/2011/06/19/president-aquino%E2%80%99s-speech-on-the-150th-birth-anniversary-of-José-rizal-june-19-2011-english-translation.

Chua, Michael. "Did the Americans Make Rizal a Hero?" *Manila Times*. The Manila Times, 20 July 2019, www.manilatimes.net/2019/07/20/opinion/columnists/did-the-americans-make-rizal-a-hero/586664/.

Coates, Austin. *Rizal—Filipino Nationalist & Patriot*. Manila: Solidaridad Publishing House, 1992.

Constantino, Renato. "Veneration without Understanding: Does Rizal Deserve to Be Our National Hero?" *Journal of Contemporary Asia*, vol. 1, 1971, pp. 3–18.

Flores, Emil M. "Comics Crash: Filipino Komiks and the Quest for Cultural Legitimacy." *Journal of English Studies and Comparative Literature*, vol. 7, no. 1, 2004, pp. 46–58. www.journals.upd.edu.ph/index.php/jescl/article/view/2530. Accessed 15 Nov. 2019.

Flores, Emil M. "The Concept of the Superhero in Filipino Films." *Plaridel: A Philippine Journal of Communication, Media, and Society*, vol. 2, no. 3, 2005, pp. 23–38. http://www.plaridel journal.org/article/the-concept-of-the-superhero-in-filipino-films/. Accessed 18 Nov. 2019.

Flores, Emil M. "Up in the Sky, Feet on the Ground: Cultural Identity in Filipino Superhero Komiks." *Negotiating Culture through Comics*. Ed. Maciej Sulmicki. Oxford: Inter-Disciplinary Press, 2014, pp. 3–18.

Gavaler, Chris. *On the Origin of Superheroes: From the Big Bang to Action Comics No. 1*. University of Iowa Press, 2015.

Gutierrez, Anna Katrina. "American Superheroes, Manga Cuteness and the Filipino Child: The Emergence of Glocal Philippine Comics and Picturebooks." *Journal of Graphic Novels and Comics*, vol. 5, no. 3, 2014. 5:3, 344–60, DOI: 10.1080/21504857.2014.905486.

Haliya Publishing. "About Us—Haliya Publishing." 2018–2020, haliyapublishing.com/about.ga.

Malonzo, Mervin. *Tabi Po*. Isyu 1. Pasay City, Visprint, Inc. 2014.

Malonzo, Mervin. *Tabi Po*. Isyu 2. Pasay City, Visprint, Inc. 2014.

Malonzo, Mervin. *Tabi Po*. Isyu 3. Manila, Haliya Publishing, 2017.

Ocampo, Ambeth. *Rizal without the Overcoat (Expanded Edition)*. Mandaluyong City: Anvil Publishing, 2003.

Palumbarit, Oliver M. "Homegrown Monsters Wreak Havoc in 'Tabi Po' Adaptation." *Philippine Daily Inquirer*, 25 Oct. 2017, https://entertainment.inquirer.net/247624/homegrown-monsters-wreak-havoc-tabi-po-adaptation#ixzz64w9pX6Fc. Accessed 7 Nov. 2019.

Philippines. Republic Act No. 1425 (Rizal Law): An Act to Include in the Curricula of All Public and Private Schools, Colleges and Universities Courses on the Life, Works and Writings of José Rizal, Particularly His Novels Noli Me Tangere and El Filibusterismo, Authorizing the Printing and Distribution Thereof, and for Other Purposes. Quezon City, Philippines: Congress of the Philippines, 1956.

Reposar, Eleanor Sarah. "Carlo Vergara's ZsaZsa Zaturnnah and the Tradition of Subversion in Philippine Komiks." *Philippine Studies: Have We Gone beyond St. Louis?* Ed. Priscelina Patajo-Legasto. Quezon City: University of the Philippines Press, 2008, pp. 427–43.

Reyes, Soledad. "The Philippine 'Komiks': Text as Containment." *Southeast Asian Journal of Social Science,* vol. 25, no. 1, 1997, pp. 79–91.

Reynolds, Richard. *Superheroes: A Modern Mythology.* University Press of Mississippi, 1992.

Rizal, José. *El Filibusterismo (Subversion).* 1891. Translated by Leon Ma. Guerrero. Longman: 1965.

Rizal, José. *Noli Me Tangere (Touch Me Not).* 1887. Dover Thrift edition, translated by Leon Ma. Guerrero. Dover Publications Inc., 2019.

Rizal, José. *The Social Cancer: A Complete English Edition of Noli me Tangere.* 1887. Translated by Charles Derbyshire. The Floating Press, 2009.

Rosenberg, Robin S., and Peter Coogan. *What Is a Superhero?* Oxford University Press, 2013.

San Juan, Epifanio Jr. "Sisa's Vengeance: Rizal and the Mother of All Insurgencies." *Kritika Kultura,* vol. 17, 2011, pp. 23-56. www.kritikakultura.ateneo.net.

Schumacher, John. The *Noli me Tangere* as Catalyst of Revolution. *The "Noli me tangere" a Century After: An Interdisciplinary perspective.* Edited by Soledad Reyes. Quezon City: Phoenix Publishing House, Inc. and Ateneo de Manila University, 1987, pp. 97–107.

Chapter 13

IS THERE A COLOMBIAN NATIONAL SUPERHERO?

How Colombian Superheroes Help Define Ethnicity and Race in a Multicultural Society

ENRIQUE URIBE-JONGBLOED and HERNAN DAVID ESPINOSA-MEDINA

Identifying the Colombian comic book superhero is not an easy task. The lack of a true comic book industry in the country makes it challenging to track down its heroes. Nevertheless, looking into the forgotten pages of Colombian comics, we can find hints of past heroes and long-lost adventures. This chapter traces the evolving depictions and definitions of Colombian national identity across three superhero comics: *Makú, Tukano,* and *Zambo Dendé*.

Drawing on the work of key scholars and theoretically engaged artists (Rabanal; Rincón; Suárez; Ossa; Aguilar-Rodríguez and Uribe-Jongbloed), this chapter begins with an introduction to the comics scene in Colombia. This background provides the context for the chapter's reflection on ethnicity and race in a multicultural Colombia. Following Andrew J. Kunka's analysis of the role of visual representation in the construction of Black identities (275), the chapter then reviews how comic book representation defines racial and cultural identities in Colombian superhero comics. These concepts are helpful to distinguish how members of a group come to understand and see their identity versus how outsiders see them. Placing these concepts in the Colombian context, the chapter shows how the definitions of group identity are not clear cut. The implication of these scattered definitions demonstrates that the ideas of "us" and "them" are in constant negotiation, fluidly constructing multiple conceptions of group membership and the different definitions of national cultural identity.

Using these ideas as an analytical lens, the chapter provides a textual analysis of three locally produced Colombian superhero comics. The chapter also undertakes an ideological analysis of the texts (Rifas 224–25) to investigate who Colombian national (super)heroes are, or should be, and what these definitions say about Colombian national identity. Out of the three (super)heroes, the first two, Makú and Tukano, were created, drawn, and developed by Jorge Peña. The single-issue comic *Makú*, with its namesake hero, was published in 1967, while Tukano appeared at various points throughout the 1980s. In these two comics, the main characters are white heroes raised within Indigenous cultures. The third comic, *Zambo Dendé*, which was created by Nicolás Rodríguez and drawn by various artists since its inception in 2010, represents a hero of mixed heritage, the son of an African slave and an Indigenous mother, who becomes a *cimarron* (freer of slaves). This chapter explores how Peña and Rodríguez define their characters' identities and how these characters exemplify the national and historical ideologies that often shape the depictions of race and ethnicity in Colombian comics and broader culture. Finally, in its review of how Colombian representations of different groups of people might relate to those seen in US comics, the chapter engages with Michael A. Sheyahshe's work on the representation of Native Americans in comics.

Ultimately, this chapter cannot offer definitive answers to the questions regarding cultural ascription and national identity in Colombian comics. Instead, this analysis seeks to enrich the discussion around representation in Colombian superhero comics by exploring how these depictions relate to national identity, the implications of this construction, and the lessons learned from tracing the paths that some heroes have already walked.

AN OVERVIEW OF COMICS IN COLOMBIA

After the heyday of Colombian readership of foreign comics between the 1960s and 1980s (Pareja, *El Nuevo Lenguaje Del Cómic*), the 1990s saw most of the Colombian comics scene disappear (Uribe-Jongbloed and Aguilar-Rodríguez). Despite a broad readership, comics made by Colombian artists and published nationally were few and far between. However, in the late 1990s, Colombia experienced an increase in the production and recognition of different types of comics (Rabanal, "Panorama de La Historieta En Colombia," sec. "A modo de conclusión"; Suárez and Uribe-Jongbloed 56–58). In the 2010s, there was a general growth in the number of publications, including autobiographical graphic novels and comic adaptations of notable books (Ossa 247–48). During this period, highlights included the critically acclaimed comic memoir *Virus Tropical* by Power Paola (adapted into an animated film in 2017); the international manga award won by *Two Aldos* in 2018; and the increase in comic-related events such as conventions (Merino, sec. Introduction; Ossa 247–48).

Despite this greater interest, print comics have not regained the popularity they enjoyed in Colombia between the late 1960s and early 1980s (Pareja, *El Nuevo Lenguaje Del Comic*; Pareja, "El Nuevo Contenido Temático Del Cómic";

Ossa 241). Back then, comics were ubiquitous, and American and Mexican small-size booklets were bought at magazine kiosks and exchanged in informal fan clubs in the main cities (Uribe-Jongbloed and Aguilar-Rodríguez). Comics collector Felipe Ossa noted in 2019:

> [I]t can be said that the development of comics in Colombia is just beginning. [. . .] Until the early 1970s there was no restriction [for imports] and comics were plentiful, mainly from Mexico, the US and Argentina. Through them, we, the fans, were nurtured and reading them helped motivate local artists to begin their own comics. [. . .] But national production was incipient and had no support from newspapers or the publishing industry (241).[1]

The 1980s saw an increase in the tax for comic imports and a general criticism of their impact on children (Pareja, "El Nuevo Contenido Temático Del Cómic"). The rising import costs and moral panic precipitated comics' slow disappearance from book stands and kiosks (Uribe-Jongbloed and Aguilar-Rodríguez). Moreover, two factors prompted the near-extinction of comics by the mid-1990s. First, comics sales and social recognition declined following the 1993 Book Law (Law number 98 of December 22, 1993). This law described comics as lacking cultural value (akin to pornography) and prevented them from enjoying the same tax exemptions of other culturally valued printed publications. Secondly, between 1992 and 1995, two magazines that printed various short comic strips and page-long featurettes, *ACME* and *T.N.T.*, ceased publication amidst financial failure (Suárez and Uribe-Jongbloed 55–56).

Nevertheless, the hope for a better future based on university-educated comic book artists of the late 1990s (Rabanal, "Panorama de La Historieta En Colombia," sec. "1980 en adelante") took hold by the 2010s (Ossa 247–48). The work of those artists was able to flourish partly due to lower printing costs, more informal production and distribution systems, and, by 2013, the addition of comics into the tax-exempted printed works of the Book Law (Suárez and Uribe-Jongbloed). Additionally, in the 2010s, the participation of comic sellers and publishers in national book fairs, such as Bogotá's International Book Fair, and the rise of large-scale entertainment events, such as Medellín's Comicon and Bogotá's SOFA festival, provided new spaces for comics to find a readership. These events increased the visibility of underground and self-published comics creators who used these events to reach the shelves of more traditional bookstores and hobby shops (Uribe-Jongbloed and Aguilar-Rodríguez).

Given this discontinuous nature, a history of Colombian superheroes and comics must account for the peak readership of the 1960s through to the 1980s and the rebirth of local comics in the 2010s. Colombian superheroes and the national identity they depict cannot be uncoupled from how the nation has defined and imagined itself in those periods. The case studies presented in this chapter have thus been selected based on how they reflect formative periods in Colombian comics. *Makú* was one of the first efforts to create an entirely Colombian comic magazine back in the late 1960s, *Tukano* was emblematic of the Sunday Funnies era of the 1980s, while *Zambo Dendé* has been described as representative of comics as IP in the creative economy of the 2010s (Espinosa-Medina and Uribe-Jongbloed 115–18).

A CHANGING NATION ACCEPTS ITS MULTIETHNIC HISTORY

1991 is seen as a pivotal year in Colombian history. The nation experienced a crucial political change by the end of the 1980s, developing a new constitution that redefined the state. This redefinition implied a different way to conceive the imagined community that made up the national boundaries. The demand for a new constitution came after the peace process with the M-19 revolutionary guerrilla organization and received massive popular support in a national presidential election in 1990. The country then elected a constitutional assembly, and a new constitution was written. The 1991 constitution changed the previous constitution's monocultural perspective that had survived since its inception in 1886. The constitution now conceptualized Colombia as a "pluriethnic and multi-cultural nation," dismantling the one-country, one-nation, one-language definition of the State (Uribe-Jongbloed and Salawu 185). The aim was to allow for excluded minorities—Indigenous peoples, Blacks, Afro-Caribbeans, or Afro-Colombians—to gain constitutional recognition in the national territory. The 1991 constitution also brought about the opening of the Colombian market to the world, reducing tariffs and other protectionist measures, and demanding the creation of a Ministry of Culture, set up in 1994. This Ministry would eventually enact cultural policies from the 2010s onward to support the development of national cultural products, including comics and graphic novels, through various grants (Uribe-Jongbloed and Aguilar-Rodríguez). These grants are partially responsible for the recent increase in Colombian comics and graphic novel production.

Superheroes and other Colombian comic book characters reflect the industrial and political changes that the country went through between the 1960s and the 2010s. During the late 1960s' heyday of comics distribution and sales, Colombian artists tried to create the first set of locally developed comics with national heroes under the brand of *Súper Historietas*, published in 1968 (Rincón, sec. "Cronología 1960"). There were only five individual comics published under the *Súper Historietas* title, among them *Makú* by Jorge Peña and *El Dago* by

Carlos Garzón (Rincón, sec. "Cronología"; Ossa 242). These characters can be considered the first two Colombian superheroes following Scott McCloud's (114) definition of the superhero genre, which identifies exceptional power as a key convention.[2] In the 1970s, Carlos Garzón created *Calarcá*, a historical heroic figure of an Indigenous leader who would appear in single-page stories in the weekend edition of the national newspaper *El Tiempo*. Years later, from 1981 to 1988, Jorge Peña's Tukano would appear almost uninterrupted in *Los Monos*, the Sunday Funnies magazine of the national newspaper *El Espectador*. These latter publications made Tukano the longest-running national comic book character.[3] After this, the next time a clearly identifiable Colombian superhero character appeared in printed form was *Zambo Dendé* in 2010. *Zambo Dendé* was published as booklets included with a local free-distribution newspaper in 2013 and, after that run, the story was all collected as a graphic novel compilation. The comic was followed by a short animated series and even a live-action trailer, which sparked a newly revised storyline of the main character published in 2019. Meanwhile, in 2018, superheroes finally became a prominent part of the Colombian comic book scene with the graphic novel *Espectaculares Héroes Colombianos* and the comic books series *Heroes Latinos*. These publications suggest that the time of the Colombian superheroes has finally arrived.

ISSUES OF RACE AND ETHNICITY IN COLOMBIAN (SUPER)HEROES

The expanded publication of Colombian superhero comics in the late 2010s has raised the question of how Colombian national superheroes can be characterized. Exploring the national superheroes subgenre, Jason Dittmer touches upon how "nationalist superheroes have been used in the past as a way of 'localising' the comic book as a commodity and trying to subvert nationalistic pride to sell American-style comic books in countries with their own publishing tradition" (6). This observation points to how comic creators in particular cultural contexts can approach the creation of culturally proximate superhero narratives as an exercise in cultural transduction.[4] Cultural Transduction is a framework that serves to describe how "certain cultural products . . . [have] been modified or altered to become available, appealing or relevant in other cultural contexts" (Uribe-Jongbloed and Espinosa-Medina, 616). This strategy can help comic creators reach audiences that, though interested in the American-style superhero narratives, might be attracted to characters that touch upon local issues and represent some of their cultural values. Nevertheless, this representation is complicated and goes beyond portraying stereotypical attributes of a particular ethnicity or visual elements of a country (Nama 257–63). For the Colombian case, it would mean that there was a need to portray a national hero that could at once seem similar enough to the typical American and Mexican comic book heroes of the time while also going beyond the simple transformation of adding a Colombian flag, name, or traditional dress.

Dittmer (2–3) also points out how superhero narratives can coconstruct the values and identities they supposedly represent. Applying Dittmer's observation to Colombian comics, the evolution of the hero rooted in indigenous identity can be understood as an attempt by the comic creators to structure, not just portray, a cultural identity for the nation.

NATIONAL IDENTITY AND THE COLOMBIAN SUPERHEROES

As mentioned earlier, the definition of what it means to be Colombian has changed, at least according to the constitution. As a culturally and ethnically diverse country, trying to pin down a single representation of Colombia's culture and its people is an on-going problem that artists and authors have addressed in various media. In superhero comic books, there is a thematic thread that connects multiple heroes that have tried to fill the void of a Colombian national superhero. This thread is the trope of the hero rooted in indigenous identity which Dittmer identifies. To better understand this trope's evolution, this chapter examines it under the lens of race and ethnicity as defined by Andrew J. Kunka (275). Following this perspective, race is understood as a cultural identity which is assigned to a group of people by someone outside the group. In contrast, ethnicity represents the cultural identity that members of a group ascribe to themselves. These two competing definitions of identity are found in this chapter's three case studies.

First, let us examine how national identity is represented in each of the case studies' narratives. In the comic *Makú*, which was published in 1967, the protagonist is a muscular white man dressed in indigenous garments. As a character, Makú conforms to some of the core elements of the superhero genre defined by Peter Coogan (30).[5] Makú wears a mask to conceal his identity, and his name is the autonym of the tribe that adopted him as a child, which speaks to his secret identity. Also, Peña depicts the character as an exceptional fighter and, in his origin story, it is mentioned that the hero is a messianic figure destined to save the Makú people, which evidences both his special powers and altruistic mission. Nevertheless, it is interesting to see how Peña presents the aesthetic and narrative elements representing the Indigenous people and their context through the white man's gaze. In this narrative, non-Indigenous characters define the Indigenous people's cultural identity as a race.

Moreover, the tension between ethnicity and race is also present on the meta-level of the comic. Peña, as a Colombian author, uses the pre-colonial and

Figure 13.1. Kimu and Makú fighting two white villains in *Super Historietas* (1968).

colonial past of the nation as the main narrative for his hero, using the image of the Indigenous peoples as a representative of national identity. Nevertheless, Jorge Peña was born and raised in Bogotá, Colombia's capital, and he is a white author. Regardless of his intentions, he is offering a definition of Indigenous people from the perspective of someone who is not part of the group; he is defining them from the outside. His depiction of the Indigenous people is in line with that of similar comics of the time, having the Indigenous characters speak broken Spanish, whereas our main hero speaks in clear Spanish. It also

Figure 13. 2. Tukano Jungle Adventurer Cover from Los Monos (No 12, December 6, 1981)

presents those Indigenous people as requiring the presence of a white savior, supporting a colonial view of the national identity, where the white race is superior to the Indigenous one.

These tensions are also present in the comic book superhero Tukano, developed by Peña thirteen years after Makú in 1981. Tukano is also a white man who operates in the jungle with extraordinary fighting abilities. However, there is a crucial narrative change from Makú to Tukano. Peña does not present the latter as a messianic figure destined to save his tribe. Instead, in this second comic, it is the Indigenous people and the jungle who save Tukano. The story is set in the present day. Tukano was a homeless child struggling to survive on the streets of Bogotá. The future superhero sneaks onto a plane that takes him as a stowaway to the jungle in the Vaupés region (part of the great Amazon rainforest) where the Tukano tribe, from which he derives his name, adopt him.

A key characteristic that distinguishes Tukano from Makú is how the hero's story tries to address Indigenous culture more directly by treating Tukano as a member of the community dealing with the problems and traditions of his tribe. Interestingly, the villains in *Tukano* are Indigenous people from the same tribe or neighboring tribes and mythical creatures drawn from their folklore and traditions, including the Jaguar Man (figure 13.2). In a sense, at least in the narrative, there is a turn from defining the Indigenous people's identity from an outsider's perspective to that of someone who is becoming part of the group and learning how they define their ethnicity.

Both Makú and Tukano are examples of what Michael A. Sheyahshe describes as the "*Mohican Syndrome*, in which a white man becomes Indian, manifest[ing] itself through non-Native participation in Indigenous way of life" (13).[6] Looking at the depictions of Native Americans in US comics, Makú is akin to Magazine Enterprises' *White Indian* and Tukano to DC's *Vertigo Visions: Tomahawk*. Where the former "celebrates the white protagonist's 'greatness,'" the latter is considered more nuanced because "while the fact remains that the central, and thereby entire story, revolves around a white protagonist, at least we now are given details about the Indigenous culture that empowers [him]" (Sheyahshe 27). Similar to the referenced Western comics, both Makú and Tukano had Indigenous sidekicks to whom they exhibit a paternalistic attitude where in "the white man . . . is seen as protector of the helpless red man and must fight those who would do him harm" (39). In the comic books, Makú is depicted rescuing his Indigenous sidekick Kimu (figure 13.1). Meanwhile, Tukano often saves or helps Peye, a white priest turned Indigenous wise man, reminiscent of Sancho Panza.

These culturally specific elements help establish the stories' settings and are part of the creator's "world-building" (Wolf). Peña expresses his interpretation of the Colombian ethnicity through his construction of Tukano's narrative world. In contrast to his earlier comic book hero Makú, the author develops more elements relating to the individuals in the tribe and their interpretation of their world. Perhaps due to the longer run of Tukano, or because of the political debates the country was experiencing at the time regarding Indigenous peoples, the representation of the white hero in an Indigenous setting becomes more complex. Still, the representation keeps the white hero narrative at its core.

Nicolás Rodríguez further develops this world-building approach in his comic book *Zambo Dendé*, which was first published in 2010. Set in Latin America during colonial times, *Zambo Dendé* contributes to the fuller representation of a Colombian ethnicity by addressing elements of the Indigenous cultures as well as many other historical elements and cultural groups that are part of the Colombian nation.

In *Zambo Dendé*, Rodríguez creates a character who is not part of a particular tribe or group of people but a son of *mestizaje*.[7] The name of the character comes from the colonial Hispanic and Portuguese socioeconomical caste order. Under this system, people from different genealogies occupied different positions in the colony's political and social structures (Martínez). In this case, the category of zambo referred to someone born of Black and Indigenous parents, representing the lowest social level. In this story, the main character is born of a Black father and an Indigenous mother. He gets his powers from mystical forces that are also a mixture of Latin-American and African folklore. According to

Figure 13.3. Zambo Dendé and Katherine O´Brien Hernández as portrayed in Zambo Dendé's 2019 iteration—image provided by Nicolás Rodríguez, 7gLab, art by Javier de la Pava, colors by Carlos Moreno Diaz.

Oscar Perdomo Gamboa, the character Zambo Dendé, like Batman, conforms to the vigilante archetype:

> a being that takes justice in their own hands without any respect for the current authorities, working outside the law, but fighting for an ideal that slides between vengeance and righteousness. This dark and ominous aspect, more defined in the fear inspired by the vigilante than in the uprightness that the hero exudes, is present in Rodríguez's work (64).[8]

Initially, the comic depicted Zambo Dendé as a freer of slaves. However, with time, he has evolved so that he is now a protector of the oppressed. The comic's 2019 iteration follows a contemporary girl, Katherine O´Brien Hernández, who is guided by the spirit and memories of the original hero (figure 13.3). Furthermore, the narrative core of *Zambo Dendé* has shifted from the single plotline focused on the hero to explore the world that surrounds him, populated by an array of characters that represent, in many ways, the multiple peoples and identities that make part of the Colombian and Latin American ethnicity.

Zambo Dendé is part of a proliferation of local superheroes, with several other examples appearing during this resurgence in Colombian comic book production. In the 2018 comic *Espectaculares Héroes Colombianos* (GoUp Comics), the leading Colombian superhero, Protector, is a white, brown-haired male. Protector seems to fit Dittmer's conception of a nationalist hero—comparable to Captain America or Captain Canuck—since he sports the colors of the Colombian flag in his suit. In a change from earlier traditions, Protector is only one among many heroes in that graphic novel. Two other superheroes, both women, exhibit Indigenous heritage, Iraya and Karin. However, these two characters are magical, exemplifying the stereotype that all Indigenous people are mystical and magical—instant shamans (Sheyahshe 55). *Espectaculares Héroes Colombianos* also includes a superhero from the Colombian North, Kid, who is an African Colombian boxer from Barranquilla. Like Zambo Dendé, Kid acknowledges the African heritage shared by many Colombians ignored in earlier comics.

Despite Colombia's multicultural make-up, the country's superhero comics still privilege white superheroes. Yes, *Héroes* adds Iraya, Karin, and Kid, to the pantheon. However, including three characters in *Espectaculares Héroes Colombianos*, who portray some general cultural traits, seems insufficient to represent the diverse spectrum of Indigenous and African Colombian people of Colombia. Similarly, in another recent entry to the genre, Mikealdi Comics' *Héroes Latinos* 3, the unnamed Colombian superhero is also white. Thus, the impact of recent characters like Zambo Dendé on the development of the Colombian superhero is still uncertain.

The examples in this section reveal the struggle to portray and construct a national identity in a diverse culture such as Colombia. There is still a white narrative prevalent in the comics, be it through the Mohican Syndrome or relegating Indigenous or mixed-race characters to magical or mystical beings. This white-washing and racial stereotyping complicates attempts to connect Colombian multi-ethnic heritage to a "national" superhero.

IS THERE A SPACE FOR A COLOMBIAN NATIONAL HERO?

As mentioned above, the comic book scene in Colombia relied heavily on foreign imports, and that reliance can also be seen as a potential explanation for the lack of superheroes with a strong national identity. From the 1960s to the 1980s, Colombian comic book creators struggled to match the superheroes

Figure 13.4. Cover of "Fantomas en Colombia" issue of *Fantomas*, vol. 5, no. 102, December 1972.

produced by the larger Mexican comics market, such as *Kalimán, the Incredible Man*, and *Aguila Solitaria*.

This struggle is highlighted in the difference between the efforts to localize some of the adventures of foreign heroes in Colombia, and the attempts to place Colombian-created heroes within their own context. For instance, in 1972, the masked Mexican hero Fantomas's adventures took him to Colombia in search of emerald smugglers (see figure 13.4). Depictions of Colombia in the comic include two panels of Bogotá City Centre, two panels for the towns of Sogamoso and Támara, pages of a generic hacienda (where some characters dance a renowned Colombian cumbia of the Caribbean north of the country), and, finally, an encounter with Guahibo Indigenous people in a thick jungle. The story pays attention to Colombian geography, customs, and landscape, including specific dialect used in the region. The inclusion of these details is an exercise in cultural transduction. The creators were trying to localize their product, to make it more relatable to a foreign audience. In this case, since Fantomas had a large readership in Colombia, this was an interesting concession to their audience.

Meanwhile, similar strategies of cultural transduction failed to help audiences connect with the locally created heroes of *Super Historietas*, Makú, and El Dago. The creators drew heavily from the stories and style of international publications. However, the audience did not seem to connect with these characters, even though they inhabited their cities and jungles. The fact that they shared parts of their audience's history or cultural background did not seem to matter either. Despite the effort, the characters and situations were not as nuanced as Fantomas, both in the quality of the work and in the depth of the story and the local depictions, and the readership did not provide the support required for these stories to take hold.

The success of Tukano as part of *Los Monos* never turned it into a standalone comic. Its spot in *Los Monos*, which started as several pages per issue from November 1981 (*Los Monos* 10) to February 1982 (*Los Monos* 23), withered into one-page sections that were commissioned per week upon its return in April 1983 (*Los Monos* 82), sometimes making the stories lose coherence from one to the next. In fact, the last *Tukano* page was published on November 27, 1988, in *Los Monos* 374, leaving his last story unfinished. Despite its improved quality, both in the drawings and in the depth of the story and characters, Tukano remained limited to the Sunday Funnies.

Zambo Dendé offers a different perspective on the evolution of Colombian superheroes. It is interesting, in this case, to see how Zambo's creator, Nicolás Rodríguez, has adapted different development strategies from foreign production companies to project the image of quality linked to foreign products and use this perception to bolster the value and success of his own product (Espinosa-Medina and Uribe-Jongbloed 115–18). To be more specific, Rodríguez has negotiated the development of different products around Zambo Dendé as intellectual property (IP) This includes deals with various global media conglomerates, such as Disney and Sony, to develop Zambo as a transmedia property that goes beyond the classic publishing and distribution models of past Colombian comics. While some of the developments came to fruition, like the animated short available at the Zambo Dendé website since 2020, it remains to be seen if it develops into a full animated series. Similarly, an international cast was used to develop the property's live-action teaser trailer that included action stars like Chilean and American martial artists Marko Zaror and Michelle Lee, respectively.

Rodríguez has talked proudly about Zambo's association with international production companies, which he considers an accomplishment and an important step towards building a successful brand and intellectual property. Rodríguez has also faced criticism by local creators and comic book critics who believed that this global approach might compromise the character's identity in favor of a more international image of the Latin American superhero (Espinosa-Medina and Uribe-Jongbloed 115–18).

This strategy of delocalizing the product fits into the cultural transduction framework, as it is a way in which creators can try to reduce the disinterest experienced by products when they reach other markets. It could be considered as the opposite strategy of the one presented by *Fantomas* above, which rested on adding local content for the target market that would at once work as exotic (for the native Mexican market) and as local (for the Colombian one).

Whereas Zambo Dendé was originally positioned as a Colombian superhero and its story anchored in renown Colombian sites, it has obscured this setting as time has gone by. Zambo Dendé draws on the city of Cartagena de Indias' features to suggest its setting and localize the story, without explicitly naming its location. This creative choice is part of Nicolás Rodríguez's development of the property. In more recent iterations, the creator has steered away from specific mentions of times and places towards displaying Colombia as a generic version of a fictional Latin America (Espinosa-Medina and Uribe-Jongbloed 118). As has been explored before,

> [This choice] entailed two considerations: first, the need to be careful and avoid offensive national stereotypes, and second, they had to use a universal code that made the product accessible to a larger audience. In other words, they were trying to universalise the content, to make it more transparent, by consciously reducing cultural lacunae. In Zambo Dendé's world you will find that Spain, England and Portugal are not mentioned as antagonists—instead, the story talks about the "invaders." No particular century is cited—instead, the story is set back in ancient times of humanity. The Americas are not stated as the location—instead, the story unfolds in "The New World." (Espinosa-Medina and Uribe-Jongbloed 118)

Zambo Dendé tries to remain unique, setting itself apart from Western superheroes by bringing the Afro-Indigenous and Latino roots of the character into play. However, this wider canvas also frees the character from a narrow Colombian national perspective to embrace a more ample Latin American symbolic value. It even extends the comic to reach the Latino connection to the US. In the 2019 iteration of *Zambo Dendé*, the mixed-heritage orphan protagonist, Katherine O'Brien Hernández, lives in California. The story links her with the Indigenous mythology that connects the Americas as one single narrative world, but this time based in the US. Zambo Dendé is no longer a Colombian hero, but rather a more universal one that inspires Katherine in her own path. Although the story now connects Indigenous, Black and modern-day hybrid identities of the Americas, it also dislodges Zambo Dendé from any claim as a Colombian national superhero.

CONCLUSION

The chapter looked at how race and ethnicity were portrayed in Colombian comics to highlight the complex issues of portraying Colombian people's multicultural identity. From the white savior depicted in *Makú* and *Tukano*—representative of the State's monocultural idea before the 1991 constitution—to the multiethnic hero Zambo Dendé and other recent comics, attempts at creating a national superhero repeatedly illustrate how the Colombian national struggle with identity has had many phases and continues to evolve.

Recent comic books such as *Espectaculares Héroes Colombianos* with its multiethnic cast of superheroes might try to bridge the gap between the hegemonic white male identity and the Colombian diversity it seeks to portray, yet it falls short by embracing certain racial stereotypes. As Dittmer has pointed out for these new types of heroes more broadly, "the attempt to negotiate multiculturalism in this context has thus far reproduced some of the gendered/racialised understandings of the nation that the storylines were intended to overcome" (62). That is the case in Colombian comics, where the stereotypes of Black, Afro and Indigenous Colombians as magical or somehow connected to the supernatural remains a common trope. However, at least in the move away from the white savior narrative, Colombian comics seem to be trying to challenge the hegemonic colonial narrative. There may also be cause for some optimism in a new iteration of *Zambo Dendé*, which connects a modern-day mixed heritage girl living in the US with the Afro-Indigenous vigilante of the unnamed Latin American mythos. In this way, the comic is able to explore different approaches to engage with and depict a complex national identity. Interestingly, it is a superhero that aims to increase its international appeal by detaching itself from the specificity of Colombia that seems to address the ethnicity of the people it represents in a layered and sophisticated manner.

Despite their shortcomings, the various attempts to produce a Colombian superhero mirrored the historical difficulties of trying to portray a cohesive national identity that would reflect and represent the multicultural reality of Colombia. This case study underscores the need to expand our understanding of superheroes beyond the United States. As Frederick Luis Aldama charts in his foreword to this collection, the superhero has now become a global "daydream." How Colombian comics have struggled to articulate ethnicity and national identity provides an object lesson in why the simple cultural transduction of US archetypes is insufficient in producing national superheroes that reflect their cultural context. As superheroes increasingly become a social mechanism by which we navigate and negotiate identity, it is hoped that this chapter can provide insights for future research that probes how superheroes define ethnicity and race in a multicultural world.

Notes

1. Translation of the original Spanish by the authors.

2. McCloud (114) includes two aesthetic characteristics in his definition of superhero comics that are also seen in these texts: musclebound anatomy and exaggerated depth of field. Also, present are two narrative elements that McCloud considers: the character is defined by his power and the stakes are ever-escalating.

3. Although comic strip characters have run for longer—Copetín by Jorge Franco, for instance—Tukano was a multi-page color-printed narrative, closer to comic book characters than to comic strips.

4. Cultural proximity is understood as the measurement of shared cultural elements, such as history, language, and values, between the cultural market in which a product is created and the markets it is attempting to reach. In this sense products that reflect a high level of shared elements are seen as culturally proximate to a particular readership (Uribe-Jongbloed and Espinosa-Medina, "Clearer Picture").

5. Coogan defines the superhero as a "A heroic character with a selfless, pro-social mission; with superpowers—extra ordinary abilities, advanced technology, or highly developed physical, mental, or mystical skills; who has a superhero identity embodied in a codename and iconic costume, which typically express his biography, character, powers, or origin (transformation from ordinary person to superhero); and who is generically distinct, that is, can be distinguished from characters of related genres (fantasy, science fiction, detective, etc.) by a preponderance of generic conventions. Often superheroes have dual identities, the ordinary one of which is usually a closely guarded secret" (30).

6. Sheyahshe explains that the concept of the Mohican Syndrome arises from the *Leatherstocking Tales* of James Fenimore Cooper, published between 1823 and 1841. He adds that the idea of the non-Native character transforming into an Indigenous person became a literary standard, concluding that, "as far as comic books are concerned, little has changed in literature since Cooper's time" (13).

7. "Mestizaje" is the common term used in Latin America to refer to the offspring of people classified under different races and is used as a description of Latin Americans as descendants of European, African, and Native American lineage (García Canclini x–xi).

8. Translated from its original Spanish by the authors.

Works Cited

Coogan, Peter. *Superhero: The Secret Origin of a Genre*. MonkeyBrain Books, 2006.

Dittmer, Jason. "Introducing Nationalist Superheroes." *Captain America & the Nationalist Superhero*, Temple University Press, 2013, pp. 1–23.

Espinosa-Medina, Hernán David, and Enrique Uribe-Jongbloed. "Latin American Contraflow in Global Entertainment Media: Kingdom Rush Series and Zambo Dende as de-Localised Media Products." *Media International Australia*, vol. 163, no. 1, 2017, pp. 107–21, doi:10.1177/1329878X16686204.

García Canclini, Néstor. *Culturas Híbridas: Estrategias Para Entrar y Salir de La Modernidad*. Grijalbo, 2000.

Harris, Michael D. *Colored Pictures: Race & Visual Representation*. University of North Carolina Press, 2003.

Kunka, Andrew J. "Comics, Race, and Ethnicity." *The Routledge Companion to Comics*, edited by Frank Bramlett et al., Routledge, 2016, pp. 275–84.

Martínez, María Elena. *Genealogical Fictions: Limpieza de Sangre, Religion, and Gender in Colonial Mexico*. Stanford University Press, 2008.

McCloud, Scott. *Reinventing Comics*. Perennial Editions, 2000.

Merino, Ana. "Comics in Latin America." *The Routledge Companion to Comics*, edited by Frank Bramlett et al., Routledge, 2017, pp. 70–78.

Nama, Adilifu. "Color Them Black." *The Superhero Reader*, edited by Charles Hatfield et al., University Press of Mississippi, 2014, pp. 252–67, doi:10.14325/mississippi/9781617038068.003.0021.

Ossa, Felipe. *Cómic. La Aventura Infinita*. Planeta, 2019.

Pareja, Reynaldo. "El Nuevo Contenido Temático Del Cómic." *Chasqui*, vol. 16, 1985, pp. 24–27.

Pareja, Reynaldo. *El Nuevo Lenguaje Del Comic*. Ediciones Tercer Mundo, 1982.

Perdomo Gamboa, Óscar. "Cimarronaje En El Cómic." *Nexus*, no. 18, 2015, pp. 46–69, doi:10.25100/nc.v0i18.

Rabanal, Daniel. "Panorama de La Historieta En Colombia." *Revista Latinoamericana de Estudios Sobre La Historieta*, vol. 1, no. 1, 2001, http://rlesh.mogno.com/01/01_rabanal.html.

Rabanal, Daniel. "Panorama de La Historieta En Colombia." *Revista Latinoamericana de Estudios Sobre La Historieta*, vol. 1, no. 1, 2001, pp. 15–30.

Rifas, Leonard. "Ideology. The Construction of Race and History in Tintin in the Congo." *Critical Approaches to Comics*, edited by Matthew J. Smith and Randy Duncan, 2012, pp. 221–34.

Rincón, Bernardo. "Museo Virtual de La Historieta Colombiana." *Museo Virtual de La Historieta*, 2014.

Sheyahshe, Michael A. *Native Americans in Comic Books*. McFarland & Company, 2008.

Suárez, Fernando, and Enrique Uribe-Jongbloed. "Making Comics as Artisans: Comic Book Production in Colombia." *Cultures of Comics Work*, edited by Casey Brienza and Paddy Johnston, Palgrave Macmillan, 2016, pp. 51–64, doi:10.1057/978-1-137-55090-3_4.

Uribe-Jongbloed, Enrique, and Abiodun Salawu. "Minority Languages, Cultural Policy and Minority Language Media." *The Routledge Handbook of Global Cultural Policy*, edited by Victoria Durrer et al., Routledge, 2017.

Uribe-Jongbloed, Enrique, and D. Aguilar-Rodríguez. "The Comics Scene in Colombian Cities." *Comics beyond the Page in Latin America*, edited by James Scorer, U.C.L. Press.

Uribe-Jongbloed, Enrique, and Hernán David Espinosa-Medina. "A Clearer Picture: Towards a New Framework for the Study of Cultural Transduction in Audiovisual Market Trades."

OBSERVATORIO (OBS*), vol. 8, no. 1, 2014, pp. 23–48, http://obs.obercom.pt/index.php/obs/article/view/707/642.

Uribe-Jongbloed, Enrique, and Hernán David Espinosa-Medina. "An Introduction to Cultural Transduction." *Palabra Clave*, vol. 20, no. 3, 2017, pp. 615–21, https://doi.org/10.5294/pacla.2017.20.3.1.

Wolf, Mark J. P. *Building Imaginary Worlds: The Theory and History of Subcreation*. Routledge, 2012.

Chapter 14

WHERE DOES *BLACK PANTHER'S* MUSIC COME FROM?

Authorship, "the Other," and the Musical Representation of Africa in Hollywood

DAN GOLDING

Black Panther (Ryan Coogler, 2018), as a major entry in the Marvel Cinematic Universe (MCU), and a film that features a largely Black cast and engages with themes of history, identity, and the African diaspora, has been widely discussed and critiqued. Sheena C. Howard (who also contributes to this volume) argues in her edited collection *Why Wakanda Matters* that "viewers, particularly African American audiences, had a profound cultural connection to the film and an enormous emotional response" (Howard, xxiii). However, Swedish composer Ludwig Göransson's score for the film represents a complex case study for how we understand not just superhero music, but musical self-representation in Hollywood. Indeed, Göransson is one of the few white creatives involved with *Black Panther* in a major role, and his score both amplifies and, in some ways, stands at odds with both praise and criticism for the film. Where is the *Black Panther* musical sound from, and whose is it?

Black Panther offers opportunity to move away from the superhero paradigm of the "otherwise binary nation-state being identifiable in a single human body" (Dittmer 25) or at least to move from the broad association of the superhero with American or the western nation state towards an association with the African continent, pan-African movements, or a fictionalized nation state ostensibly free from colonial history. Questions of on-screen representation and creative direction for superhero films are also illuminated by listening closely to one of the genre's most defining traits: its music. Superhero conventions usually see the genre's music located within a kind of patriotic, Aaron Copland, New Deal-era musical Americana (Golding 141). Does the contemporary superhero score, in the guise of something like *Black Panther*, represent an opportunity for genuine self-representation and a break from harmful stereotypes, or does it instead represent a covert retreat into standard Hollywood tropes about race, "the Other," and difference? In short, who can compose T'Challa's music?

This chapter will engage with such questions in order to explore not just contemporary debates around representation and the superhero genre, but also long-standing discussions about the power of film music to reify and exoticize the cinematic "Other" and to tell stories from outside the United States and the Anglosphere. The ability (or inability), as Edward Said famously put it, for the Orient, or in this case the cinematic "Other," to represent themselves is key to understanding broader debates about *Black Panther*, and indeed its music (283). Despite *Black Panther*'s many achievements in terms of representation and grappling with the complex legacy of colonialism in the context of Hollywood (Bucciferro; Thomas; White), a debate remains regarding the film's relationship with Africa and the African diaspora. The critical response to the film was nuanced and disparate across the African continent and the diaspora. As Jelani Cobb wrote in *The New Yorker*, *Black Panther* "exists in an invented nation in Africa, a continent that has been grappling with invented versions of itself ever since white men first declared it the 'dark continent' and set about plundering its people and its resources" (Cobb). Kenyan journalist Larry Madowo alternatively critiques the film's American perspective, contending that *Black Panther* remains "an approximation of African culture, an outsider's version of what African culture might be like" (cited in Madowo and Attiah). For Godfried A. Asante and Gloria Nziba Pindi, *Black Panther* is both "a welcome shift from the dominant white Western gaze" and a film that "deserves a critical reading as an ongoing and imperfect project of emancipation from the dominant gaze" (Asante and Pindi).

The film's music is credited to a white man: Ludwig Göransson, a Swedish composer who trained and works in the United States, and a long-time collaborator of *Black Panther* director Ryan Coogler. Somewhat unusually for a film composer, Göransson also has a career as a producer and writer for the mainstream music industry, particularly with musician (and actor) Childish Gambino/Donald Glover, who he met on the set of TV series *Community* (NBC, 2009–14). *Black Panther* also notably features an accompanying album of songs heard in the film, curated by American rapper Kendrick Lamar and featuring a mix of American and South African artists. However, as only a small selection of the songs from this curated album are heard in the film, this chapter will largely focus on the film's original music (the film score), credited to Göransson.

There are three main musical elements to the *Black Panther* score. First, the film contains elements that could broadly be thought of as "traditional" Hollywood superhero music. This is orchestral in sound, heavy on brass fanfares and strings, with occasional choir and percussion to suit the contemporary predilection for the "epic" blockbuster style. In some ways this is in keeping with, and an evolution of Göransson's work on previous blockbusters like *Creed* (2015), which builds on composer Bill Conti's music for the original Rocky film franchise that that film develops and subverts (Albarrán Torres and Golding).

Second, *Black Panther* contains elements of hip hop in its music, largely to represent the US-based antagonist Erik "Killmonger" Stevens (Michael B. Jordan). In particular, Göransson uses the sound of a Roland TR-808 drum machine, characteristic of contemporary hip hop, to drive the Killmonger theme with a trap-style beat, complete with typically complex hi-hat patterns and boomy, deep kick drums. Here, Göransson was on familiar ground from his work with Childish Gambino—their 2018 hit, "This Is America," for example, uses an at-times similar sound.

Finally, *Black Panther* contains what might be thought of as "African," or, perhaps, pan-African musical elements. Largely, these elements are derived from Senegal and Senegalese musicians, as Göransson traveled to Senegal and South Africa for a period of four weeks while preparing the film's music. Göransson toured with Senegalese musician Baaba Maal and spent time at the International Library of African Music in Grahamstown, South Africa. This time spent within these two nations was used in the promotion of the film to emphasize the music's authentic "African-ness." Recordings of African musicians (in particular the voice of Maal, who sings over the film's introduction) were directly used in the score as a part of what was ultimately credited as Göransson's music. Further prominent inclusions include a Senegalese talking drum ensemble, key to the sound of the film, and a Fula flute. I will go into further detail about the use of these instruments and the musicians who performed them for *Black Panther* later in this chapter.

All three of these musical elements interact and often derive ideas from each other. Their combination, unusual for any context, let alone cinema, let alone superhero cinema, is what gives *Black Panther* its unfamiliar musical identity. *Black Panther*'s main T'Challa theme, for example, is played on both talking drum and orchestral brass, and is at times accompanied by a different, but complimentary rhythm on the Roland TR-808 drum machine. This leaves the *Black Panther* score as possibly unique in Hollywood film music history in the way it hybridizes styles and traditions—as well as a unique case study in Hollywood's musical history of representing Africa and the Other. *Black Panther*'s score also makes it the first MCU film to make such a clear geographic musical consideration. Previous entries in the franchise with scenes set in Africa, Wakanda, or featuring Wakandans, such as *Avengers: Age of Ultron*, (score by Brian Tyler, 2015) and *Captain America: Civil War* (score by Henry Jackman, 2016) make no noticeable musical gestures to any "African" soundscape. This is not true of the films and TV shows that follow *Black Panther*, however, and echoes of the film's music, specifically its Senegalese elements, can be heard in the film *Avengers: Infinity War* (score by Alan Silvestri, 2018), as well as the streaming service show *The Falcon and the Winter Soldier* (score by Henry Jackman, 2021). *Black Panther*'s hybridized music has, in the context of the MCU, become a musical leitmotif for the franchise.

BEYOND THE SOUND OF "THE OTHER"

It is not controversial to assert that the history of Hollywood film music, and more broadly, film music from the Anglosphere, has been dominated by white men. The major figures in any standard study of the history of the Hollywood sound will include both white American men (Alfred Newman, Bernard Herrmann, John Williams, Danny Elfman) and white European émigrés (Miklos Rosza, Max Steiner, Erich Korngold, Franz Waxman, Hans Zimmer), but few women, few people of color, few African Americans, and certainly very few African émigrés working in Hollywood. "Female screen composers sit at the intersection of two industries—music and film—that have both been recognized as being male-dominated," argues Catherine Strong. The same could be said of practically any minority in film composition.

The monoculture of film composing may explain, in part and alongside other systemic factors, the lack of compositional representation for characters and environments broadly constituting the "Other" for Hollywood. Indeed, Hollywood film composers, particularly in the Golden Age, excelled when it came to musical stereotypes. When the French appear in *Casablanca* (Curtiz, 1941), for example, composer Max Steiner gives us a rendition of "La Marseillaise." The same goes for Steiner's array of southern folk tunes like "Beautiful Dreamer," "Louisiana Belle," and "Old Folks at Home," that he incorporated into his score for *Gone with the Wind* (Fleming, 1939). This same logic also gives us an array of "Asian" musical sounds for films set in Hollywood's imagined "Far East" (*55 Days at Peking*, 1963, score by Dimitri Tiomkin). At its most clichéd, this stereotyping resulted in variations on the infamous "oriental riff" (usually in cartoons, such as Disney's Silly Symphony short *The China Plate*, 1931, score by Frank Churchill); a burst of sitar for Indian characters (*The Party*, 1968, score by Henry Mancini); and lush strings in a double harmonic scale for middle eastern deserts (*Lawrence of Arabia*, 1963, score by Maurice Jarre). These are musical templates of the broadest strokes: of course, the exnominated (Barthes 146) white Christian heroes usually get no such treatment that aligns their musical identity with their race or geography, and instead have access to the widest possible traditions of music for villainy, heroism, emotion, success, and failure. While the Other in Hollywood had music that is similarly othered—"exotica," or "ethnic" music as it is sometimes known—white characters simply had *music*.

Many of these musical clichés are there to match on-screen stereotypes. Henry Mancini's sitar accompanies Peter Sellars's brownface and deplorable "Indian" accent in *The Party*, for example. Yet as Claudia Gorbman notes, Hollywood film music historically also lagged behind progressive developments in on-screen representation, too. To take Gorbman's example, as Hollywood entered the 1950s and 1960s, interiority, complexity, and agency were slowly afforded to Native American characters in Westerns such as *Broken Arrow* (1950, score by Hugo Friedhofer) and *The Searchers* (1956, score by Max Steiner). However, the music in these films still fell back on the old clichés for Native Americans, of "savage" drum patterns (four beats in a row, emphasis on the first) and simple melodies on brass, either without harmonization or in "primitive" parallel fourths. Dimitri Tiomkin even expressed concern in the 1950s that if less stereotypical music was used in such films, audiences may not understand who was on screen at all (Gorbman, 106). That this stereotyped sound was largely an invention of film composers themselves (something Tiomkin himself admitted (Buhler, 194)) seemingly made little difference. The music was "driven by the desire to 'cement' musically the meanings onscreen, and thus became highly codified, calling on a style of music that antedated the musical modes of the day" (Gorbman, 106). The more that stereotyped music was used, the harder it became for these composers to break away from it.

Musical representations of "Africa" in Hollywood unsurprisingly follow a similar pattern of simplicity, reification, and homogenization. Africa, as an uncritically totalized continent, has a long musical history in Hollywood. However, even today musical clichés of Otherness persist. Although totally unimaginable in other contexts (such as representations of Native Americans, or Asian cultures, where anything resembling the racist clichés of the past would today be rightly and immediately seized upon by critics), Hollywood's film music for Africa still shares a strong lineage with the clichés of yesterday.

A very brief survey of the musical sound of Africa in Hollywood and the cinema of the Anglosphere, for example, reveals some stark continuities. Films like *Zulu* (1964, score by John Barry) and *Hatari!* (1962, score by Henry Mancini) are largely reliant on a general and nonspecific sense of "African" drumming to populate the place-specific elements of their scores. Barry's 1966 Oscar-winning film score for *Born Free*, a film about white naturalists raising a lion in captivity in Kenya, also employs miscellaneous drums, as well as woodwinds and xylophone to suggest a sense of geographic location. In 1996, Jerry Goldsmith's music for *The Ghost and the Darkness*, a film about British colonial railroad engineers in turn-of-the-century Kenya, features more nonspecific drumming, as well as "ethnic" flute melodies and voices.

There are some exceptions to this imagined sense of musical Africa. For the television mini-series *Roots* (1977), Quincy Jones made efforts to create a musical score that included "traditional African and African Diaspora instruments such as *shekere* (rattle), *mbira* (thumb piano), log drums, *gakoqui* (bell), and other instruments from West Africa (Yoruba) and Afro-Cuban traditions," (Henry 8) also making Jones one of the few African American composers to write music for an American production set in Africa or involving the slave-era colonial diaspora. This is despite the presence of numerous African and African American film composers in Hollywood history. As another prominent example, Lebohang Morake (credited as "Lebo M") worked with Hans Zimmer in the 1990s to help write and arrange music for South African choirs for *The Power of One* (1992) and *The Lion King* (1994). Both films have African settings, and in the 1990s most of Morake's collaborations involved both well-known Hollywood composers and African settings, such as *Congo* (score composed by Jerry Goldsmith, 1995), or *Outbreak* (score composed by James Newton Howard, 1995).

The most relevant prior example of a composer pushing back against the dominant, imagined musical sound of Africa is also a direct predecessor to Göransson's *Black Panther* score. This is the Black Entertainment Television (BET) produced, Marvel Knights Animation television series, *Black Panther*, from 2010. This series stands in marked contrast to most other attempts at musical representation of Africa and likely deserves its own serious study. The show's composer, Stephen James Taylor, already had experience working within more authentic African musical sounds (his previous credits include *Namibia: The Struggle for Liberation*, 2007) and created a Wakandan language for the series' opening musical theme based on Xhosa (Taylor).

However, actually hiring diasporic African American (let alone African) musicians to move beyond generalizing stereotypes of African music is still the exception for blockbusters and superhero films, rather than the rule. When James Bond visits Madagascar at the beginning of *Casino Royale* (2005, score by David Arnold), when Jason Bourne visits Tangiers, in Morocco, in *The Bourne Ultimatum* (2007, score by John Powell), and when Wolverine visits Lagos in *X-Men Origins: Wolverine* (2009, score by Harry Gregson-Williams), the audience hears "African" drums in each instance to underscore the geographic flavor of the moment. This mode of film scoring promotes a musical tourist-like gaze, largely unchanged since the era of *Zulu* and *Hatari!*, including elements of a reified "African" soundscape composed and usually performed by white musicians and with little of the specifics of these musical traditions. As already established, while Hollywood music has made such stereotypical ethnoscapes its logic when it comes to depicting the Other, its music for Africa is particularly pronounced in this fashion because it homogenizes an entire continent with disparate musical styles and traditions into a single reliable trope: anonymous drumming. There is frequently little consideration given to the type of drum used, and it is not particularly unusual to hear two of the most popular cinematic drums, the taiko drum (from Japan) or conga (from Cuba) used to represent a sense of "Africanness." As already noted, the MCU films prior to *Black Panther* make no attempt at any sense of "African-ness" in their music, and accordingly avoid this issue altogether.

Both the popular and the folk musical traditions of Nigeria and Ethiopia are as different as that of France and Russia, yet in Hollywood they (along with most other African nations and traditions) are often combined in a unitary, reductive "African" ethnographic soundscape. It is also a "folk" or "traditional" African sound that is employed in these film scores. We do not usually hear Fela Kuti-style Afrobeat for Nigeria, Mulatu Astatke-style jazz for Ethiopia, or Amadou et Miriam-style Afro-blues for Mali, let alone any sort of contemporary pop or hip-hop sound. Hollywood's musical Africa is one that is stuck in an imagined—possibly colonial—past, where the sounds of today, markers of postcolonial culture, and a musical agency free of condescending gestures to primitivism do not intrude. As musicologist Kathryn Kalinak writes: "From Indian music in the classic Hollywood western to African polyrhythms in films set in colonial Africa, non-Western rhythms connote savagery . . . even something as simple as rhythm can powerfully (and largely subconsciously) position the spectator according to the logic of white ethnocentrism" (Kalinak 326). To put it simply: when Hollywood goes to Africa, it is frequently time for a composer to delve once again into the long and storied catalogue of drums, xylophones, and "primitive" singing. How else would we know where we are?

LAYERED MUSICAL IDENTITIES

The music of *Black Panther* represents a complex layering of musical cultures, eras, and composers that marks a departure from Hollywood and superhero standards. It uses a developed and largely specific musical framework, as well as the performances—and compositions—of African musicians to musically describe the fictional nation of Wakanda and the key characters of the Black Panther superhero universe. Though allowing some space for African creatives to musically represent a fictional African culture, this strategy is also not without its own problems and complexities.

Ludwig Göransson spent four weeks in Africa—first in Senegal and then in South Africa at the International Library of African Music—researching local music in an attempt to create what he and director Ryan Coogler saw as an "authentic" soundtrack (Carmichael). In particular, after contacting

Senegalese music industry veteran Baaba Maal, Göransson spent the majority of his time in Africa on tour with Maal and his band. In the process, Göransson was introduced by Maal to Senegalese music, musicians, and even used Maal's recording studio for material that would later be incorporated into *Black Panther*'s score. "That was the beginning of the *Black Panther* score," acknowledges Göransson (Genius).

The results of this work with Senegalese musicians can be clearly heard in *Black Panther* itself. Göransson imbued his score with instruments unusual for a Hollywood score like kora (a West African instrument with plucked strings like a harp or guitar), kalimba (a type of thumb piano), and balafon (a West African instrument similar to a xylophone). However, it is his collaborations with Maal and other Senegalese musicians that give *Black Panther* its musical complexity, resonance, and any sort of authentic appeal to a musical "Africanness." Göransson keenly documented his travels in Senegal on social media, and several of these performances and moments of collaboration can still be heard and seen in their original form on Göransson's Instagram account. From these, I want to highlight four important instances of collaboration throughout the score and discuss them in some detail.

The first key collaboration is with Maal himself. Given the extensive time Göransson spent on tour with Maal and the curatorial role that Maal played in guiding Göransson through Senegalese and West African music and musicians, Maal's influence over *Black Panther*'s score is difficult to overstate. It is also difficult to fully capture; much of Maal's work for *Black Panther* was as a kind of "cultural intermediary" (Bourdieu 318), introducing Göransson to the right musicians and providing information and resources. Yet one direct trace of Maal is left in *Black Panther* itself: his voice. Maal can be heard singing early in the film when T'Challa, Okoye, and Nakia return to Wakanda (in the track "Wakanda" at 0:05). This was inspired by Maal's performances on tour in Senegal, where he would usually begin with solo singing. According to Göransson, director Coogler briefed Maal on *Black Panther*'s story over video chat, and a few minutes later Maal recorded the vocals heard in the film. The lyrics, in Fulani, are "about an elephant that died, an elephant being a synonym for a king" (Grobar). The resulting cue, titled "Wakanda," is cocredited to Göransson and Maal in the film's credits. It is the only cue from the film to be cocredited.

Second, the musical theme for antagonist Erik "Killmonger" Stevens was created in collaboration with fula flute player Amadou Ba. One of the musicians introduced to Göransson by Maal and recorded in his studio, Ba was given a similar brief to respond to as Maal, as well as details about the character of Killmonger (Hirway). Ba then improvised a performance, using both fula flute and his voice, both of which are in the *Black Panther* score and serve as the basis for Göransson's "Killmonger" theme (Ba is not credited in the film; an

Figure 14.1. Musical transcription of Black Panther's talking drum inspired T'Challa theme.

example of his performance can be heard in the track "Killmonger" at 0:28). Continuing Göransson's predilection for geographic specificity as leitmotif, the "Killmonger" music is almost always augmented by the most clearly hip-hop-inspired elements of the score, intended to evoke the African-diasporic identity of the Oakland-raised Killmonger.

The third important instance of collaboration in the *Black Panther* score is the sound for the elite Wakandan female bodyguards, the Dora Milaje. This is one of the most unusual and prominent musical sounds on a recent Hollywood soundtrack. The sound of the Dora Milaje is created through a rhythmic "yipping" made by the women of the Voquality Choir. Voquality is a session choir (that is, a group contracted for recording rather than performance) based in London, otherwise generally known for gospel and religious music (Voquality). Used as leitmotif for the Dora Milaje, and sometimes for just their most prominent member, Okoye (Danai Gurira), the Milaje motif cuts through usual assumptions about unobtrusive Hollywood film music and is an extremely active element in the *Black Panther* sound mix. This is music that is meant to be noticed. One remarkable instance of this motif is the Korea-set casino fight midway through the film (in the track "Casino Brawl" at 2:36). The camera cranes upwards towards the second level of the casino, where, having removed her wig, Okoye is fighting several of the arms dealer Ulysses Klaue's goons. She is dressed in a bright red dress, and the "yipping" choir seems to match the high key situation: this is not a sound that is meant to dwell in the background. Having defeated her opponents, Okoye jumps down to the ground level of the casino, her red dress billowing behind her, the camera following in a single movement. This is one of the boldest audiovisual moments in all of *Black Panther*.

Finally, and perhaps most pervasively throughout the score, is the use of talking drum. This is an instrument characteristic of music and culture in Senegal and West Africa more broadly, and its presence in *Black Panther* stands in contrast to Hollywood's more usual implementation of generic, and even stereotyped drumming to suggest "Africa." Because of its semipitched nature (players compress and release the drum's skin through strings while performing to adjust pitch) the talking drum is named literally, as it is also used as a means of communication. Words and names can be spelled using the drum's pitch and rhythm. For *Black Panther*, Göransson asked Senegalese talking drum players in Maal's studio to perform the protagonist's name, "T'Challa." This rhythm performed by these talking drum musicians (Massamba Diop and Magatte Shaw in particular are named as "drum soloists" in *Black Panther*'s end credits) subsequently formed the basis of Göransson's orchestral theme for the character (in the track "United Nations / End Titles" at 1:07; see also figure 14.1). The talking drum rhythm was echoed by Göransson on his Roland TR-808 kick drum, as well as taken up by layers of orchestral brass and, in the end credits at least, a choir literally chanting T'Challa's name.

WAKANDAN COLLABORATIONS

What can we make of Göransson's collaborations, so important to the creation of the *Black Panther* sound? "In an era where white artists and producers, from Ariana Grande to Diplo, are frequently called out as cultural appropriators, Göransson is a true collaborator," writes NPR's Rodney Carmichael in relation to Göransson's work both on *Black Panther* and with recording artists like Childish Gambino. It is difficult to entirely disagree. We need only to turn to the briefest survey of "African" music in Hollywood to imagine how *Black Panther*'s score may have played out in the hands of a white composer more content with stereotypes and clichés. Instead, Göransson saw travel to Africa and engagement with individual African musicians as an essential part of the composition process and has hardly hidden the influence of his Senegalese collaborators (indeed, he has on multiple occasions highlighted their individual work on social media).

Yet it was still Göransson alone who got up on stage to receive the film's Oscar for Best Original Score (something perhaps made more complicated by the Academy's strict rules on musical collaboration). It is Göransson who receives the lion's share of public acknowledgement for the music's potency and its break with Marvel's otherwise staid musical output. It is still Göransson who is subsequently engaged for Hollywood's biggest projects and not his collaborators (for Göransson, after *Black Panther* came *The Mandalorian* and Christopher Nolan's *Tenet*).

Even the way that Göransson's success with *Black Panther* was reported by the press reinforces the impression that the influences for the score stemmed wholly from "traditional" African music. Indeed, the presence of a genuine star like Baaba Maal in *Black Panther*'s score is worth exploring in a bit of detail. Despite some of the more breathless reporting on *Black Panther*'s music portraying Maal as some kind of hidden Senegalese cult or folk figure uncovered by Göransson. For example, the *Hollywood Reporter* noted that Göransson "spent months researching African tribal music," when in fact the majority of this time was spent on-tour with Maal [Burton]. In fact, Maal is a music industry veteran both locally in Senegal and on the global stage. After studying music at both an undergraduate and postgraduate level in Dakar and then Paris, Maal has been recording and performing since the late 1980s. Although aware of and influenced by Fulani tradition, Maal is no strict traditionalist and is better described as an international recording artist who works in a fusion of pop, reggae, rock, and blues. He is also an in-demand collaborator. Maal's career highlights include work not just in Senegal and throughout Africa, but at innumerable international music festivals, with the BBC (recording "God Only Knows" alongside One Direction, Elton John, Lorde, and Kylie Minogue, among others), and collaborations with the likes of Brian Eno, Taj Mahal, The Roots, and Mumford and Sons. Nor was Maal in any sense new to Hollywood when it came to *Black Panther*. Maal had already collaborated with Hans Zimmer on the soundtrack to *Black Hawk Down* in 2001 (something Zimmer himself keenly pointed out in the *Hollywood Reporter* composer's roundtable discussion in 2018), and Alberto Iglesias on *Exodus: Gods and Kings* (2014). Maal has also appeared on both *Later . . . with Jools Holland* and *The Tonight Show with Jimmy Fallon*.

Maal is a figure of contemporary Africa, someone who incorporates tradition into a rich union of international musical genres for audiences in Senegal, in West Africa, across broader Africa, and around the world. "The way it comes across in the film is that the culture is ancient, but also it talks to the future as well," notes Maal himself of the final *Black Panther* score (Perry). In contrast, much of the film industry media coverage of his involvement in the score positions him—and the music of Africa generally—as not agents of a contemporary society but as gateways to ancient, possibly primitive cultural history.

Black Panther's music contains layered temporalities, traditions, geographies, diasporas, and composers. The question that began this chapter of who can compose T'Challa's music remains complicated: though Ludwig Göransson's name is listed as the film's composer, it is more complex and nuanced than that. Baaba

Maal quite clearly had significant influence over the score, as did other Senegalese musicians Maal introduced Göransson to, like Amadou Ba and Massamba Diop. Even then, questions of diaspora and musical specificity remain: Wakanda is a fictional nation, yet its nondiegetic film music is largely Senegalese, a country with a very real and specific colonial, cultural, and musical history.

It is worth noting as well that such genre and geographic blending is a musical strategy open to white film composers, but rarely offered to others. As Stephen James Taylor, composer for the animated *Black Panther* television series, argued in 2007, "White composers do it all the time . . . listen to any score by Danny Elfman, John Powell or James Newton Howard and you hear everything from hip hop loops to elaborate 19th century orchestral gestures. (But) for some reason black composers don't seem to be given (m)any of those opportunities" (Brown). Indeed, despite the clever and deliberate inclusion of other voices and traditions across the entirety of the *Black Panther* score, Göransson's creative centrality and the orchestral Hollywood sound as the "default" for the superhero cinematic genre still means that the inclusion of Baba Maal and others in the soundtrack can be positioned (especially by marketing and press) as a somewhat exotic "flavoring" that marks *Black Panther* out from the usual superhero soundtrack. "Göransson's mission, therefore," wrote Charles Burchell for *SoundFly*, "was to consider all of these elements and find suitable, and exciting, ways to combine traditional African musical styles, timbres, and rhythms, with the modern high-fidelity production and orchestral arrangements you'd expect from an action-packed blockbuster" (Burchell).

The perceived hierarchy between what we might see as, on the one hand, "Hollywood-European-orchestral" and on the other "African-Senegalese-traditional" is quite clear. Imagining what press coverage for the film might have looked like had an African composer with no orchestral background—such as Baaba Maal—been tasked with creating the soundtrack by traveling to the United States to "consult" with traditional orchestral composers is revealing. Instead, it is the inverse scenario, and one that, despite good intentions and collaborations, nonetheless reaffirms that the "home" musical sound for the superhero is one based in a white European orchestral tradition.

Larry Madowo's contention that *Black Panther* remains "an approximation of African culture, an outsider's version of what African culture might be like," is particularly complex to think through when it comes to the film's score (cited in Madowo and Attiah). For Göransson's part, it is undeniably true: he is an admitted outsider to African culture, and no one could credibly argue that his four weeks spent on the continent does anything to substantially change that. However, his collaborators on the score—Baaba Maal in particular—are far from outsiders to African culture. Indeed, in contrast to many of the film's other cast and crew members, who are of the African diaspora, Maal is African, was born in Senegal, and has spent a life building a career and making music across the continent.

Who represents themselves, and who represents others when it comes to the music of *Black Panther*? The *Black Panther* score is undoubtedly both a product of the diaspora and also not; it is potentially appropriative in its use of Senegalese sounds and musicians; problematic in its authorship and promotion; and also, still likely significantly better in terms of self-representation than it could have been if assigned to a less collaborative white composer. In many ways it does little to move the sound of the cinematic superhero beyond the Copland Americana tradition heard in everything from *Superman* to all three live-action *Spider-Man* cinematic incarnations. Indeed, *Black Panther* itself still continues this tradition with Göransson's brassy orchestral style. Yet the lack of attentiveness to geographic or cultural specificity in previous MCU films, and the subsequent leitmotif-like inclusion of talking drums to represent Wakanda in the franchise following *Black Panther*, illustrates the score's complicated impact. Through its combination of Senegalese elements, the score does challenge—in whatever compromised, problematic way—what it sounds like to be a superhero at the cinema, and where such film music can come from.

Works Cited

Albarrán Torres, César, and Dan Golding. "Creed: Legacy Franchising, Race and Masculinity in Cntemporary Boxing Films." *Continuum*, vol. 33, no. 3, 2019, pp. 310–23.

Asante, Godfried A., and Gloria Nziba Pindi. "(Re)imagining African Futures: Wakanda and the Politics of Transnational Blackness." *Review of Communication*, vol. 20, no. 3, 2020, pp. 220–28.

Barthes, Roland. *Mythologies*. Vintage Classics, 1993.

Bourdieu, Pierre. *Distinction: A Social Critique of the Judgement of Taste*. Harvard, 1984.

Brown, Samm. "Ebony and Ivory: The Door Only Swings One Way." *Film Music Magazine*, 9 February 2007, http://www.filmmusicmag.com/?p=527. Accessed 10 December 2020.

Bucciferro, Claudia. "Representations of Gender and Race in Ryan Coogler's Film *Black Panther*: Disrupting Hollywood Tropes." *Critical Studies in Media Communication*, vol. 38, no. 2, 2021, pp. 169–82.

Buhler, James. *Theories of the Soundtrack*. Oxford, 2019.

Burchell, Charles. "Straight Outta Wakanda: How the "Black Panther" Score Fixed Marvel's Music Problem." *Soundfly*, 2 March 2018, https://flypaper.soundfly.com/write/straight-outta-wakanda-how-the-black-panther-score-fixed-marvels-music-problem/. Accessed 10 December 2020.

Burton, Bryan. "'Black Panther' Composer Scored a 4-Hour Cut of the Movie." *Hollywood Reporter*, 23 February 2018, https://www.hollywoodreporter.com/heat-vision/black-panther-composer-ludwig-goransson-scored-4-hour-cut-1087475. Accessed 10 December 2020.

Carmichael, Rodney. "How Ludwig Göransson Helped Orchestrate America's Conversation on Race In 2018." *NPR*, 23 February 2018, https://www.npr.org/2019/02/23/697124438/how-ludwig-g-ransson-helped-orchestrate-americas-conversation-on-race-in-2018. Accessed 10 December 2020.

Cobb, Jelani. "'Black Panther' and the Invention of 'Africa.'" *New Yorker*, 18 February 2018, https://www.newyorker.com/news/daily-comment/black-panther-and-the-invention-of-africa. Accessed 10 December 2020.

"Composers Hans Zimmer, Terence Blanchard, and Ludwig Göransson." *YouTube*, uploaded by Hollywood Reporter, 28 November 2018, https://www.youtube.com/watch?v=Lp9H-0EKCvs.

Dittmer, Jason. *Captain America and the Nationalist Superhero: Metaphors, Narratives, and Geopolitics*, Temple, 2012.

Golding, Dan. "The Sound of the Cinematic Superhero," *The Superhero Symbol: Media, Culture, and Politics*, edited by Liam Burke, Ian Gordon, and Angela Ndalianis, Rutgers, 2019, 135–48.

Gorbman, Claudia. "Drums along the LA River: Scoring the Indian," *Cinema and the Sound of Music*, edited by Philip Brophy, AFTRS, 2000, 97–116.

Grobar, Matt. "'Black Panther' Composer Ludwig Göransson on Grammy Wins & His Surreal Journey through Senegal." *Deadline*, 12 February 2019, https://deadline.com/2019/02/black-panther-ludwig-goransson-ryan-coogler-oscars-grammys-interview-1202555562/. Accessed 10 December 2020.

Henry, Clarence Bernard. *Quincy Jones: A Research and Information Guide*. Routledge, 2014.

Hirway, Hrishikesh. "Episode 131: Black Panther." *Song Exploder*, 14 March 2018, https://songexploder.net/black-panther.

Howard, Sheena C. *Why Wakanda Matters: What* Black Panther *Reveals about Psychology, Identity, and Communication*. BenBella Books, 2021.

Kalinak, Kathryn. "Disciplining Josephine Baker: Gender, Race, and the Limits of Disciplinarity," *Music and Cinema*, edited by James Buhler, Caryl Flinn, and David Neumeyer, Wesleyan, 2000, 316–38.

Madowo, Larry, and Karen Attiah. "'Black Panther': Why the Relationship between Africans and Black Americans Is So Messed Up." *Washington Post*, 17 February 2018, https://www.washingtonpost.com/news/global-opinions/wp/2018/02/16/black-panther-why-the-relationship-between-africans-and-african-americans-is-so-messed-up/. Accessed 10 December 2020.

"The Making Of 'Wakanda' with Ludwig Göransson." *YouTube*, uploaded by Genius, 11 February 2019, https://www.youtube.com/watch?v=fcO5klPyfX4.

Perry, Kevin. "Senegalese Singer Baaba Maal on Being the Sound of Black Panther's Wakanda." *NME*, 21 March 2018, https://www.nme.com/blogs/nme-blogs/baaba-maal-soundtracking-black-panthers-wakanda-2270695. Accessed 10 December 2020.

Said, Edward W. *Orientalism*. Penguin, 1995.

Strong, Catherine. "Why Are There So Few Women Screen Composers?" *The Conversation*, 1 August 2017, https://theconversation.com/why-are-there-so-few-women-screen-composers-81689. Accessed 10 December 2020.

Taylor, Stephen James. "Scored Scenes," *Stephen James Taylor*, no date, https://www.stephenjamestaylor.com/sjt/video_clips.html.

Thomas, Dominique. "Killmonger and the Wretched of the Earth," *Why Wakanda Matters: What* Black Panther *Reveals About Psychology, Identity, and Communication*, edited by Sheena C. Howard, BenBella Books, 2021, 59–70.

Voquality. "About Us," *Voquality*, no date, https://kenburton.wixsite.com/voquality/about-us-.

White. "I Dream a World: *Black Panther* and the Re-Making of Blackness," *New Political Science*, vol. 40, no. 2, 2018, pp. 421–27.

THE PHANTOM IN ABORIGINAL AUSTRALIA

Educational Comics, National Identity, and Indigeneity

AARON HUMPHREY

Superheroes have often been used as symbols for civic virtues. Groups from across the political spectrum, from indigenous activists and community health organizations to government agencies, have taken superheroes beyond their roles as crimefighters to demonstrate the heroism of participatory democracy and promoting public health. As Henry Jenkins has argued, "Superheroes are now a vital element in our collective civic imaginations" (25). However, the roles of these heroes in community service campaigns can vary widely, constructing differing versions of heroism, conflicting civic virtues, and even widely divergent versions of the characters themselves. Accordingly, studying the ways that different groups have employed superheroes in community service campaigns can illuminate the multifaceted meanings of superheroes and heroism in the civic imagination.

This chapter examines community service campaigns conducted for Aboriginal Australians between 1986 and 1996 that repurposed The Phantom, a hero created by Lee Falk for United States newspaper comic strips in 1936. Comics scholar Kevin Patrick has discussed how Australian adaptations of The Phantom reflect different interpretations of colonialism alongside "the needs and aspirations of Indigenous people" ("The Wisdom of the Phantom" 120). This chapter will chronicle the evolution of The Phantom as a spokescharacter for Aboriginal Australians. The chapter will outline how Aboriginal health organizations came to establish The Phantom as a vehicle for indigenous community service messages by ironically recasting Falk's character as a member of the Indigenous community.[1] While the earliest Aboriginal uses of The Phantom subverted the copyright of King Features Syndicate (which owns the character), later publications licensed the character, and brought it closer in line to the comic strip version. As King Features and larger Australian government organizations became involved in deploying The Phantom for community service campaigns, the character became a voice of conventional authority, and the authenticity and humor of the earlier community-led projects was lost.

A useful lens to understand the history of these uses of The Phantom is John Fiske's concept of "excorporation" and "incorporation." For media scholar Fiske, popular culture comprises the uses and meanings that people make out of mass-produced cultural products, such as comic strips and comic books. Writing before the Internet had rewired the structures of popular culture and fan communities, a time contemporaneous with the publications examined in this chapter, Fiske argued that since many subordinated subcultures lacked the resources and means of production to create mass culture, they instead refashioned the products of mass culture into expressions of meaning that could be quite different from what their producers initially intended. He designates "excorporation" as this "process by which the subordinate make their own culture out of the resources and commodities provided by the dominant system" (15). Its opposite force is "incorporation," where the manufacturers of mass culture seek to "adopt" these alternate or oppositional permutations of popular culture "into the dominant system and thus attempt to rob them of any oppositional meanings" (18). Fiske thus sees popular culture as an unsettled struggle over the meanings of mass culture, with subordinate subcultures repurposing media symbols to suit their needs, and the dominant producers seeking to tame those subversions to maintain the status quo.

It is important to note that not all adaptations or variations of a popular culture text are excorporations. For example, the version of The Phantom that became popular in Australia was changed in some ways from the US original. However, this should be better understood as a cross-cultural, transnational adaptation, where the meaning of the character is slightly modified to suit a local context, rather than subverted. Indeed, although Falk created The Phantom for King Features Syndicate to be published in American newspapers, the character has seen greater success beyond America. As Patrick documents in his monograph *The Phantom Unmasked*, The Phantom has "unrivalled status as an adopted national hero" in Sweden, India, and Australia (3). Patrick has argued that "more than just another instance of American cultural imperialism," The Phantom's popularity beyond the strip's country of origin "demonstrates the process whereby one culture can take a product of another and refashion it in often surprising and contradictory ways" ("Phans" Not "Fans" 151). When King Features licenses international incarnations of The Phantom, it not only builds the value of its own intellectual properties, but also potentially creates a common cultural good that links the countries where the comic is distributed. This has the potential to bring readers into mutual "civic imaginings" of authority, community, and control.

While King Features generally looks to control international variations of the character at a national level by granting country-specific licenses to publishers in Australia, Sweden, and others, The Phantom has also been appropriated in more specific, subnational, and hyper-local ways. For example, the comics examined in this chapter present versions of The Phantom that are specifically linked to particular communities in remote, Outback Australia—a Phantom from Broome, Western Australia who parties at local music gigs; a Phantom from Katherine in the Northern Territory who meets with elders under a gum tree, far away from the urban publishers that have typically printed The Phantom's exploits, such as Sydney-based Frew Publications.

The comics examined in this chapter were created for Aboriginal communities and feature an (often unofficial) excorporation of The Phantom as a civic symbol in an indigenous context. This is intriguing because the character is typically presented as a European man who lives amongst, and is revered by, Indigenous people. The Phantom can be understood as a superheroic version of Tarzan (Knowles), but his lineage traces back farther. Both Tarzan and The Phantom have been interpreted as fantastical extrapolations of white captivity memoirs like Mary Rowlandson's *The Narrative of the Captivity and Restoration of Mary Rowlandson*, published in 1682 (Hübinette and Arvanitakis 695–96), and as iterations of the Orientalist convention exemplified in Defoe's *Robinson Crusoe* (1719) of "a European who creates a fiefdom for himself on a distant, non-European island" (Friese 10). In their contribution to this collection, Uribe-Jongbloed and Espinosa-Medina identify how a similar white savior trope, the "Mohican Syndrome," influenced the development of Columbian superheroes.

In some ways, the nonspecific, Orientalist tropes of "Othering" in Falk's Phantom makes the character very easy to translocate. The Phantom's home base is a skull-shaped cave in a jungle called "The Deep Woods," located in a fictional third world country that Falk first dubbed Bengal, then Bengali, and later Bengalla. Located originally near Java, then in India, then eastern Africa, the location of the Deep Woods and the nationality of its indigenous Bandar people were fluid for the American Falk, who was concerned only with setting his hero's adventures in a mythical, mystical, Oriental wilderness.

The creators of the Australian comics examined in this chapter used the mutability of The Phantom, and of his milieu, to cast The Phantom as member of the Indigenous Australian community, at times coded unambiguously as Black and Aboriginal. These comics see him take on roles far beyond what is usually expected of costumed heroes: a mediator in custody battles, a lover converted to the virtues of safe sex, and an election candidate in a remote shire council. The earlier comics excorporate, parody, and subvert the colonialist and Orientalist tropes of Falk's Phantom, while the later comics, authorized by both King Features and the Australian Government, mostly serve to reinforce those tropes. This allows us to see how The Phantom becomes a site for negotiating visions of the civic imagination, as the character is first used in subversive ways before ultimately being incorporated back into a more conventional role, and made to serve the status quo.

THE PHANTOM IN AUSTRALIA

To understand the Aboriginal variations of The Phantom, it is important to briefly discuss the national Australian context of the character. The prominence of the American-created Phantom in remote Aboriginal Australian communities may seem unusual, but, as Russell Marks notes, "The Phantom *is* Australia's favourite comic hero" where he out-sells heroes like Batman and Spider-Man, "by as much as ten-to-one" ("The Legend and the Phantom").

The first Australian version of *The Phantom* debuted in the September 1, 1936, issue of *The Australian Woman's Mirror*, roughly six months after the feature began in American newspapers. The weekly woman's magazine printed a page of four daily American *Phantom* strips each week, preceded by a short synopsis of the previous episodes. This synopsis set the Australian context for *The Phantom*, by initially presenting the female lead Diana Palmer as the protagonist of the story. Beginning with the second instalment, the *Woman's Mirror* synopsis also served to localize the strip, describing the location of a besieged ocean liner as "off the coast of Sydney." By the third strip, Diana herself was described as a "Sydney girl." Diana would shortly go on to become The Phantom's love interest, and Falk had the characters get married in a 1977 storyline.

Patrick argues that "*The Phantom*'s longstanding tenure in the *Woman's Mirror*—where it remained until the magazine's closure in 1961—cemented the character's status as a widely recognised fixture in Australian popular culture for years to come," and explains why *The Phantom* "retains a strong following amongst Australian women" ("Phans" Not "Fans" 136). It also served to create a readership of the character among the children, husbands, and relatives of the women who bought the *Woman's Mirror*. As journalist Troy Bramston recalls, "My grandfather and father read The Phantom when they were kids. His appeal transcends generations" ("Art Shows").

In 1948, more than a decade after The Phantom entered the pages of the *Woman's Mirror*, Sydney-based Frew Publications began publishing a comic book for the Australian market that featured reprints of *The Phantom*. Sales of the comic were strong. By 1950, Frew's version of *The Phantom* had reached a circulation of 90,000 copies a month (Snowden, 1973, p.6, quoted in Patrick 2012). Frew celebrated its seventieth anniversary of continually publishing *The Phantom* in 2018 with regular issues of their comics still available in newsagents across Australia, from the city to the Outback. No other comic book in Australia comes close to matching its storied publication history.

As the Aboriginal lawyer and land rights advocate Noel Pearson has recalled:

> When I was a kid, the old and the young read comic books, cowboy stories and magazines. These reading materials would make their way around the village, read by all of the interested members of one household and then passed on to the next. *The Phantom* was, of course, premium. (51)

This availability in the farthest corners of Australia may also partly account for *The Phantom*'s enduring popularity amongst remote Aboriginal communities.

POSTCOLONIAL CRITIQUE

Considering Australia's shameful legacy of subjugating and annihilating its Indigenous people and cultures, it is unsettling but perhaps not surprising that its most popular superhero is essentially, as Mark A. Peterson writes, "a Colonialist fantasy about Black tribal peoples who live in peace thanks to the guidance of a line of wise and powerful white men" (107).

Marks comments on the absurdity of the strip's racial politics: "Despite living in the 'deep woods' for more than four hundred years and twenty-one generations, the Phantom has nearly always married a white woman" ("The Legend and the Phantom"). Even though Kai Friese notes that in Falk's stories of The Phantom's ancestors, the hero does occasionally marry non-Europeans, "[s]o our twenty-first Phantom is not quite white as a ghost," the character remains a man who essentially wears a bodysuit of dark skin when out on adventures that can be removed to reveal a blond European underneath (13). Whatever family lineage Falk or other writers give him is beside the point. The Phantom is a character whose duality allows him to alternatively "pass" as either Western or Indigenous. The appeal of this fantasy to non-Indigenous readers is obvious. Marks muses, "[m]any non-Indigenous Australians would like to imagine their contact with the 'tribes' of this land in Phantom terms [...] deputy sheriffs keeping the peace among tiny Pacific nations and modernising the local tribespeople?" ("The Legend and the Phantom").

Few scholars have considered the way Indigenous readers regard The Phantom, but the wealth and variety of educational comics produced for Aboriginal Australian communities that feature different versions of The Phantom make it clear that the character has resonance for many Aboriginal readers. Some of the appeal of the character seems to be the way that "Falk's imaginary geography recapitulates the disorientations of colonial discovery and loss," and while these discoveries and losses are starkly different for indigenous communities, The Phantom still provides an opportunity for readers to explore these facets (Friese 11). The excorporations of The Phantom discussed below should be understood in this context: not just as a pop culture messenger for civic and public health messages, but as a vehicle for exploring indigenous identities and agency in the frontiers of postcolonial trauma.

"WHY WANDA SAID NO IN BROOME"

The first example of The Phantom being re-created as an educational tool is a three-page comic published by the Kimberly Aboriginal Medical Services Council in 1986 and reprinted in a 1989 issue of the *National AIDS Bulletin* (O'Riordan). This comic is a key publication for understanding both The Phantom in Australia, and the history of health communication in Indigenous Australian communities, but it has not been reprinted since the 1980s and currently remains unacknowledged in the many online fan communities that catalogue the character's appearances.

The comic resembles a fanzine and repurposes photocopied drawings from the comic strip overlaid with new dialogue (figure 15.1). It tells a winkingly risqué story about The Phantom's attempts to romance Wanda, a girl from Broome who refuses to sleep with him unless he uses condoms. The opening narration tells us "Phantom is peeved . . . after a month in Sydney and Perth fighting crime, he can think of only think of one way to really relax. But the lovely Wanda was not born yesterday. Being a Broome girl, she knows what the score is. She's not coming across!" The comic is entirely unauthorized by King Features Syndicate.

This version of The Phantom is rowdier than his canonical counterpart. He is shown downing a pint of beer in the story's first panel and lamenting to Wanda that her refusal of unprotected sex is driving him to drink. While the King Features version of The Phantom is chastely devoted to Diana, the Broome Phantom and Wanda have an implied past together. He implores her for "just one more time? Just for old time's sake?," but she is wary: "How do I know you didn't moonj around while you were in Sydney fighting crime?" The use here of "moonj," a Nyoongar word for "something a little stronger than a kiss!" ("Moonj"), and other indigenous colloquialisms marks this incarnation of The Phantom as distinctly Aboriginal. Like the officially authorized serialization of The Phantom in *Woman's Mirror*, this excorporated version of the strip has been localized. While The Phantom himself is depicted as well traveled, Wanda is portrayed as a local "Broome girl" in the same way that *Women's Mirror* positioned Diana Palmer as a "Sydney girl." In addition to these references to

The Phantom's travels to Australian capital cities, the comic includes hyperlocal callouts. The Phantom first tries to romance Wanda at Gantheaume Point, a popular cliffside rendezvous spot ten minutes outside of Broome. He meets her again at the Broome Civic Centre for a concert by Scrap Metal, the legendary Broome band who released their debut record in 1987, some months after the comic was published.

Wanda tells the Phantom "I think you're deadly . . . but I don't want to be dead. Get condoms!," to which he replies "Can't be! I've never worn a frenchy in my life." The word "deadly" means "awesome" in Aboriginal vernacular, while "frenchy" is a slang word for condom. The comic plays up the camp aspect of the normally virtuous hero being shown as sexually frustrated. He is insecure about needing condoms and worried that Wanda's insistence on them means she thinks he is gay, reflecting a common myth at the time that AIDS was a "gay disease." Wanda finally persuades him by simultaneously breaking the fourth wall and reassuring him of his masculinity, by saying "If Superman can use condoms, so can you." This brings more of The Phantom's insecurities to light, as he broodingly muses "How does she know Superman uses frenchys?" Reluctantly, The Phantom relents to Wanda's request.

The Phantom goes off to study up on AIDS and meets Wanda at the Scrap Metal gig prepared. When she asks him, "Did you get wise and get condoms?" he replies "28 of them my love." Wanda tells him "that should do for tonight." Just how the couple uses those twenty-eight condoms is left to the reader's imagination, but a caption box reassures the reader, "After a night of passion, Phantom is still a he-man—condoms didn't change that!" The comic ends on a panel of Wanda proclaiming, "You're solid Phantom . . . better than before. It's a good thing I've got some spares in my bag."

This punchline serves to highlight that Wanda herself is just as resourceful as The Phantom. Similar to Diana Palmer in the *Women's Mirror*, she can be read as a protagonist in this comic, as she works to manage a romantic partner as unusual as The Phantom. For female readers of this comic, she could serve as a role model in her steadfast insistence on safe sex. Ultimately, Wanda stays resolute throughout the comic and is successful in convincing The Phantom to change.

If The Phantom is the other protagonist in this comic, his arc follows the archetypical "hero's journey" common in adventure comics: he is faced with a challenge that he initially refuses, until he undergoes a search for wisdom, overcomes his fears, and finally emerges triumphant. Even though the comic features no scenes of conventional action or adventure, its narrative adheres to a story structure that would be familiar to readers of Phantom comics.

However, even as the comic excorporates art and story structures from the King Features strips, the hyperlocal setting, the modern, regional slang, and

Figure 15.1. "Why Wanda Said No in Broome," page 1. Published by the Kimberly Aboriginal Medical Services Council in 1986.

the previously unknown character of Wanda draw upon Aboriginal cultural resources in equal measure. The hero is repurposed and subverted into an expression that is unique to Broome and beyond the norms and conventions for the character that had been established in American newspapers fifty years prior. Despite everything it repurposes from King Features, this comic by the Kimberly Aboriginal Medical Services Council essentially creates a new character, The Broome Phantom, an excorporation of King Features' Phantom. While parodic, the character drew upon the earlier American and Australian iterations of *The Phantom* for a novel purpose: to improve the public health conditions for Indigenous people.

CONDOMAN

In public health terms, there is no record of how the Broome Phantom comic was distributed or received in 1986, but many of its tactics were repurposed by public service agencies over the next several years. A similarly tongue-in-cheek excoporation of The Phantom as an agent for public health was used in the more widespread Condoman campaign developed in 1987 by Aboriginal Health Workers of Australia. Like the Broome Phantom, the Condoman campaign combined imagery derived from The Phantom with local references and slang and had the same aim of promoting condom use in Aboriginal communities. The focus of this campaign was a poster that features an excorporated version of The Phantom wearing a variation of his usual purple costume that is red, yellow, and black, the colors of the Aboriginal flag (figure 15.2). He poses heroically beneath a cloudless sky, a bright blue ocean behind him, and holds a small package of condoms in his right hand. A yellow title emblazoned across the top of the poster in the unmistakable style of the Frew Phantom logo christens this character "CONDOMAN." Next to this title, a smaller word, "SAYS," and directly below his catch phrase appears in a word balloon straight from the masked figure's mouth: "DON'T BE SHAME BE GAME." A comic-strip style caption box at the bottom of the poster proclaims: "USE FRENCHIES!"

From the font used in the poster's title, to the style Condoman is drawn in, to the costume he wears, the poster designers clearly intended their audience to draw connections between Condoman and The Phantom. Besides the characters' names and costume colors, there are small differences in their costumes (Condoman sports a letter C logo and lacks a domino mask). The most significant difference, though, is that Condoman is Black.

Considering Condoman was designed by and for Indigenous Australians, the decision to make him Black seems entirely appropriate. In terms of copyright, it also serves to distinguish the character from King Features' incarnation of The Phantom. Crucially, this race-bending draws attention to the racial identity of the character, and serves as a critique of The Phantom's canonical "Whiteness." The absurd duality of his skin-tight, full-body costume also does double duty in terms of promoting safe sex, as it renders The Phantom almost impossibly fully clothed and yet essentially naked.

The Condoman poster became a minor classic of health communication, "internationally-recognized" as an example of "culturally-appropriate health promotion" (Ward et al.,). The copyright-infringing Wanda comic has become essentially forgotten, while the Condoman posters were frequently reprinted (Hill; Laird et al.; Ward; Ware). The character was revived and updated in 2009 with a modified, less obviously Phantom-inspired costume, as well as a female partner named Lubelicious (Mooney and Sariago). While successful in their

Figure 15.2. Condoman poster, published by the Aboriginal Health Workers of Australia in 1987.

own right, the modern Condoman campaign materials lack the subversive playfulness of the original poster, which not only invite its audience to rethink their previous conceptions of safe sex, but also heroism and authority. Like the Broome Phantom, Condoman presents safe sex as virile and masculine, and power as not white, but Black.

AUSTRALIAN ELECTORAL COMMISSION COMICS

While these safe sex campaigns adapted The Phantom and demonstrated the power of repurposing the character for Indigenous communities, they did so unofficially. The Broome Phantom quite possibly passed under the radar of King Features, but Condoman had international visibility and would not have escaped notice. So, when the Australian Electoral Commission (AEC) decided to make use of The Phantom for another campaign targeting Aboriginal communities, they got King Features involved. The AEC officially licensed The Phantom from King Features for two comic books intended to educate remote indigenous communities about the process of voting: *The Phantom Enrols and Votes* (1988) and *Vote 1 Phantom* (1990). While this official licensing arrangement represents a step towards the subversive aspects of the Broome Phantom and Condoman being incorporated into the official, dominant version of The Phantom, the AEC comics seem to have been inspired by the aesthetics and aims of those earlier unauthorized iterations.

Although this version of The Phantom is not shown to be explicitly Aboriginal, he is depicted as a member of an Indigenous community. In *The Phantom Enrols and Votes*, the hero comes across a group of Aboriginal women who are discussing the fact that Aunt Jess, a local elder, is running for Parliament. The Phantom has been away and was unaware of this development, as he explains, "You miss out on a lot of news at home when you're fighting crime." A woman called Dot tells him, "I hope you're enrolled to vote Phantom." Like the Broome Phantom, this version of The Phantom is also shown to be both a community member and a traveler who is out of touch.

As a group, the women and children take The Phantom to see the Community Electoral Person, a young man who is sitting under a gum tree with a folder of election documents. Eventually The Phantom receives a letter at the Skull Cave that he can vote in the next election. When the election comes around, his name and address are verified on the electoral roll as "Phantom, Skull Cave via Katherine." Katherine is a regional town in Australia's Northern Territory and a historically important meeting place for local tribes. This address, in addition to his neighborly interactions with the Aboriginal characters, codes The Phantom as a member of the Indigenous community.

There is a sense of catharsis in seeing how some of the colonialist tropes of King Features' version of The Phantom are excorporated and upended in this comic. In contrast to the colonial fantasy of the King Features comic strip, where a masked, White hero presides as a benevolent dictator over a remote, indigenous community, *The Phantom Enrols and Votes* is a post-colonial fantasy. In this civic (re)imagining, The Phantom is cast as a bumbling relic of Western colonization who can only participate in democracy because he listens to the patient advice of Aboriginal women. Of course, this is still a fantasy, and it should be acknowledged that the voices of Aboriginal Australians, who comprise a geographically dispersed population, are systematically drowned out of the Australian democratic system by White and urban voters. Nonetheless, the Katherine Phantom is optimistic at the end of the comic, encouraging readers that "[v]oting in elections means we can all have a say in what happens!"

Figure 15.3. *The Phantom Enrols and Votes*, page 3. Published by the Australian Electoral Commission in 1988.

The fantasy element of Aboriginal representation in Australian parliament is made more apparent in the second instalment of the adventures of the Katherine Phantom, published in 1990. While the eight-page *The Phantom Enrols and Votes* had a perfunctory, procedural plot designed primarily to familiarize readers with the mechanisms of voting, the sixteen-page sequel *Vote 1 Phantom* recast that comic as the first in a series of adventures into parliamentary democracy. This second comic more closely incorporates the

Figure 15.4. *Vote 1 Phantom*, page 8. Published by the Australian Electoral Commission in 1990.

previously subversive, ironic version of The Phantom back to his conventional role established by King Features of fighting villains and acting as an authority for indigenous people. Faced with "fellas who don't even live here" destroying the local land, the local Aboriginal community appeal to The Phantom to run for election. After a moment of hesitation, he agrees. Soon he is presenting a stump speech on horseback: "Are you tired of outsiders ripping you off? Then do something about it! Vote for me and I'll do my best to put it right." Dot asks him, "Why should we believe you?" and The Phantom replies "You have trusted me before, you can trust me again!" Although this is incongruous with The Phantom's lunkheaded portrayal in *Enrols and Votes*, we are given no specific reasons for why the other characters in this community see him as a leader. From this point on, The Phantom himself does not appear again until the end of the comic, as the narrative focus shifts to the community in the run up to the election. On election day, there are long lines at the polls, and someone handing out "how to vote" cards for the incumbent, a candidate called Joe Pug. Eventually, the results are in and The Phantom is declared the winner, as "the new member of Skull Cave Shire Council."

We then see The Phantom attending his first council meeting. A white councilman in a tie adjusts his glasses and muses, "Business as usual gentlemen, heh heh heh," but The Phantom replies "No—I don't think so. . . . those days are over & it's time for a change." Seeing the Phantom take on a position of authority moves the character closer to his traditional role, but this also moves the comic from the realm of pedagogy to one of fantasy—readers are encouraged not to learn with The Phantom, but to watch him ascend to a place of power, as he so ably does in the traditional comics.

The last pages of the comic are devoted to the Indigenous community members reflecting on the good that The Phantom is doing for their shire and on the power of democracy: "We can choose our *own* leaders who get things done our way." However, as the leader these characters have chosen is an actual phantom both textually (his character is a cipher with no defining traits beyond campaign rhetoric) and metatextually (he is an imported American comic strip hero from a fantasy world), this conclusion is rather unconvincing.

THE WISDOM OF THE PHANTOM

Ten years after the Kimberley Aboriginal Medical Services Council created the Broome Phantom as a unique subversion of King Features' hero, the Family Court of Australia officially licensed the character for a public service campaign that incorporated this idea of using The Phantom as a champion for civic virtue for indigenous audiences, aligning the character even closer to the conventional version. The result was a 1996 comic book called *The Wisdom of the Phantom*, which was designed to provide "counselling information for Aboriginal and Torres Strait Islander communities." While superficially polished, it lacked the Aboriginal cultural perspective that had made the earliest campaigns spark. The comic begins once again with The Phantom returning "home" after adventuring. Although his home community is depicted as Aboriginal Australian, this incarnation of The Phantom shares many similarities with the canonical Falk Phantom, and includes supporting characters such as his wife Diana and their children, Heloise and Kit. On page two, The Phantom sits with Diana on their sofa next to a fireplace, with his wolf Devil at their feet like a domestic dog, as she takes his arm and explains that while he was away, "Our friends Pug and Ruby have had big family trouble."

This sofa-sitting Family Court Phantom is a far cry from the carousing Broome Phantom. Diana explains that Pug and Ruby have broken up and are fighting over custody of their children—Pug wishes for them to stay with him "in the community," while Ruby wants to take them to live with her family in Bengali. The use of Bengali here is unusual, and not just because Falk changed the country's name to Bangalla in the 1970s. In the other comics examined in this article, Broome and Katherine seem to replace Bengali/Bangala as The Phantom's indigenous homeland. However, in the Family Court comic, The Phantom is said to live in "the community," while Bengali is depicted as both geographically distinct and culturally distant from the community, somewhere that Pug fears his children will not be able to learn "the ways of our people and understand our traditions and culture."

The Phantom recommends to Pug and Ruby that they meet with councilors from the Family Court of Australia. Ruby expresses skepticism about seeing the court and asks, "But do they understand the ways of our people and our traditions?" The Phantom replies in a full-page illustration where he is juxtaposed against an intricately rendered tableau of scenes of Aboriginal culture, "They will respect our ways and traditions." As in *Vote 1 Phantom*, the comic positions The Phantom as a trusted figure within indigenous communities, although the use of slang and references to specific locations that had marked the earlier incarnations is gone, replaced with a generic collage of "indigenousness" that looks like it belongs on a souvenir tea towel.

The Family Court Phantom's sole role in the story is to advertise the Family Court of Australia to Pug and Ruby. The Family Court members then recommend that Pug and Ruby share custody of their children, and that Ruby be allowed to take them to Bengali if she agrees to bring them back to Pug and the community. Pug exclaims "But how can I TRUST HER to do this? What if she does not return?!!" a rational outburst in the context of generations of Aboriginal children being forcibly removed from their families and communities and made wards of the state, a policy that only officially ended in 1967.

In the comic, this problem is solved because one of the Family Court councilors is revealed to be Ruby's sister, who vouches that Ruby will keep her word, which satisfies Pug. The episode ends with a scene of Pug's children returning to him after visiting Bengali. The last page of the comic features a final panel of The Phantom's sidekick Guran in front of a portrait of an Aboriginal child next to a fluttering Aboriginal flag. In the stories of Falk's Phantom, Guran is the medicine man of the Bandar pygmy tribe and one of The Phantom's best friends. Here, he

Figure 15.5. *The Wisdom of the Phantom*, page 16. Published by the Family Court of Australia in 1996.

speaks directly to the audience about the Family Court: "They are good people who respect our ways. They can help us if we have family troubles."

The fact that the character of Guran embodies a variety of racist, Orientalist tropes makes this final benediction almost shockingly tone-deaf, as if the creators of the comic found it suitable to equate their intended Indigenous readers with members of a fictional "tribe" of pygmies. While earlier uses of The Phantom in educational comics for indigenous readers subverted or satirized the colonialist fantasies of the original comics, each successive publication became less subversive and more beholden to the tropes of the King Features version Phantom, to the point where the racist power relationships are essentially replicated in *The Wisdom of the Phantom*. This is perhaps the end goal of incorporation—the character is returned to a more conventional and recognizable form, while the subversive, culturally specific meanings that had animated the earlier excorporation of the character by Aboriginal community groups are stripped away.

CONCLUSION

The earliest comic discussed in this chapter was an unauthorized parody published by an Aboriginal activist group that was a rather radical interpretation of The Phantom. Later examples, which were published by branches of the Australian government and licensed from King Features, increasingly depicted iterations of The Phantom that were incorporated to be closer to the official version of the character. As Jenkins notes, "Superhero comics provide alternative conceptions of the social good and different models for how to make change" (35), and a close analysis of these comics makes it possible to trace different models for how superheroes can be repurposed for different kinds of civic imaginations. The ways that The Phantom was excorporated and changed by the Aboriginal Australian communities that created the Broome Phantom, Condoman, and the earlier Kathrine Phantom suggests that those communities saw heroism quite differently than how it is conventionally depicted in The Phantom comics.

Although "Why Wanda said No in Broome," Condoman, and *Enrols and Votes* depict versions of The Phantom who is an accepted member of the Indigenous community, they also parody the official Falk and Frew Phantoms in a wry way, letting their audience in on the joke of the absurdity of the traditional version of the character and the colonialist values he represents. In these comics, The Phantom himself is either shown as Indigenous or as someone who learns from women in the Indigenous community. In *Vote 1 Phantom* and *The Wisdom of the Phantom*, the milieu of indigeneity is incorporated on a surface level into stories that hew much closer to The Phantom of Falk, Frew, and King Features. In these stories, The Phantom is an authoritative figure who spends more time doling out advice rather than listening to the Indigenous community he is nominally part of. In particular, in *The Wisdom of the Phantom* he is shown in his more conventional role of being a White protector. While this returns the character to his "canonical" role and is presented in a way that more closely matches the visual style of the official Phantom Comics, the civic reimagining of the character as community member is lost. Heroism in these latter comics is depicted as coming from an outside figure, a savior like The Phantom who can run for office or recommend government agencies to attend. By contrast, the power of the earlier excorporations of The Phantom is in showing heroism and responsibility as characteristics that originate and are shared within the community.

Note

1. In this chapter, the term "Indigenous" refers to First Nations peoples in general, while "Indigenous Australians" refers to both Aboriginal and Torres Strait Islander people, and "Aboriginal" refers to Australian Aboriginal people in particular.

Works Cited

Bramston, Troy. "Art Shows Pay Tribute to Comic Book Hero the Phantom." *Weekend Australian*, 15 August 2017. http://www.theaustralian.com.au/arts/visual-arts/art-shows-pay-tribute-to-comic-book-hero-the-phantom/news-story/756dd736fffd6d5dd4f1a797721d84ce19.

Fiske, John. *Understanding Popular Culture*. Unwin Hyman, 1989.

Friese, Kai. "White Skin, Black Mask." *Transition*, no. 80, 1999, pp. 4–17.

Hill, Peter S. "Reading the Phantom in Condoman: Semiotics in Health Promotion." *Health Promotion Journal of Australia: Official Journal of Australian Association of Health Promotion Professionals*, vol. 6, no. 1, 1996, p. 32.

Hübinette, Tobias, and James Arvanitakis. "Transracial Adoption, White Cosmopolitanism and the Fantasy of the Global Family." *Third Text*, vol. 26, no. 6, 2012, pp. 691–703.

Jenkins, Henry. "What Else Can You Do with Them?: Superheroes and the Civic Imagination." *The Superhero Symbol: Media, Culture, and Politics*, edited by Liam Burke, Ian Gordon, and Angela Ndalianis. Rutgers, 2019, pp. 25–46.

Knowles, Christopher. *Our Gods Wear Spandex: The Secret History of Comic Book Heroes*. Weiser Books, 2007.

Laird, S., et al., "Fifteen Years of Health Promotion in Kimberley Aboriginal Community-Controlled Health Services." *Health Promotion Journal of Australia: Official Journal of Australian Association of Health Promotion Professionals*, vol. 8, no. 1, 1998, p. 46.

Marks, Russell. "The Legend and the Phantom." *Overland*, 2013. https://overland.org.au/2013/06/the-legend-and-the-phantom/31 August 2017.

Mooney, Brett and Phillip Sariago. "2spirits: Providing a Multi-Generational, Culturally Competent Approach to Health Promotion for Aboriginal and Torres Strait Islander Communities." *HIV Australia*, vol. 13, no. 3, 2015, p. 34.

"Moonj." *Australian Word Map*, vol. 2019, Macquarie Dictionary. https://www.macquariedictionary.com.au/resources/aus/word/map/search/word/moonj/Perth%20Region/.

O'Riordan, Maurice. "Everyone's Business: Love, Magic and the Art of Resistance." *National AIDS Bulletin*, vol. 12, no. 3, 1998, http://reconciliation.tripod.com/nab_everyone.htm.

Patrick, Kevin. "Phans" Not "Fans": The Phantom and Australian Comic-Book Fandom." *Participations: Journal of Audience & Reception Studies*, vol. 9, no. 2, 2012, pp. 133–58.

Patrick, Kevin. *The Phantom Unmasked: America's First Superhero*. University of Iowa Press, 2017.

Patrick, Kevin. "The Wisdom of the Phantom: The Secret Life of Australia's Indigenous Superhero." *Graphic Indigeneity: Comics in the Americas and Australasia*, edited by Frederick Luis Aldama. University Press of Mississippi, 2020, pp. 100–124.

Pearson, Noel. *Radical Hope: Education and Equality in Australia*. ReadHowYouWant.com, 2011.

Peterson, Mark Allen. "Response to John Postill." *Social Anthropology*, vol. 17, no. 3, 2009, pp. 337–40.

Ward, James. "The Road Travelled and the Road Ahead: Anwernekenhe 6 Keynote Address." *HIV Australia*, vol. 13, no. 3, 2015, p. 14.

Ward, James et al., "So Far, So Good: Maintenance of Prevention Is Required to Stem Hiv Incidence in Aboriginal and Torres Strait Islander Communities in Australia." *AIDS Education and Prevention*, vol. 26, no. 3, 2014, pp. 267–79.

Ware, Cheryl. "Living by the Code of the Condom." *HIV Survivors in Sydney*, Springer, 2019, pp. 87–110.

"Why Wanda Said No in Broome." *National AIDS Bulletin*, vol. 3, no. 3, 1989.

ABOUT THE CONTRIBUTORS

MITCHELL ADAMS is lecturer and director of the Bachelor of Laws at Swinburne Law School. His specialization lies at the intersection of law and technology, as an expert in intellectual property law, entertainment law, and legal innovation. Mitchell is an intellectual property lawyer, being a registered Trademarks Attorney and admitted to practice as an Australian Legal Practitioner in the Supreme Court of Victoria. His current research is focused on empirical legal methods to investigate the registration systems for intellectual property rights in Australia and internationally. Other areas of research include those in the field of entertainment law and the legal protection afforded to fictional characters. He holds a Bachelor of Laws (Honors) and Bachelor of Science (Chemistry) from Monash University and completed his PhD in Law at Swinburne University of Technology.

FREDERICK LUIS ALDAMA, aka Professor Latinx, is the Jacob & Frances Sanger Mossiker Chair in the Humanities at UT Austin. He is author/editor of over fifty books including the Eisner winning *Latinx Superheroes in Mainstream Comics* (University of Arizona Press, 2017), *Multicultural Comics: From Zap to Blue Beetle* (University of Texas Press, 2020), and the University Press of Mississippi volumes *Graphic Indigeneity: Comics in the Americas and Australasia* (2020), and *Jeff Smith: Conversations* (2019).

JASON BAINBRIDGE is executive dean of the Faculty of Arts and Design at the University of Canberra and author of over fifty publications. He has published widely on comics, toys and merchandising, media representation, and popular representations of law and is currently working on a book around supervillains.

DJOYMI BAKER is lecturer in cinema studies at RMIT University, Australia, and formerly worked in the television industry. She has published work on children's television history, television stardom, and intergenerational television fandom. Djoymi is chief investigator on the project Australian Children's Television

Cultures, funded by the Australian Children's Television Foundation. Her other research interests include film and television genres, myth in popular culture, and the ethics of the nonhuman on screen. Djoymi is author of *To Boldly Go: Marketing the Myth of Star Trek* (2018) and coauthor of *The Encyclopedia of Epic Films* (2014).

LIAM BURKE is the discipline leader in cinema and screen studies at Swinburne University of Technology, Australia. Liam has published widely on comic books and adaptation. His books include *The Comic Book Film Adaptation: Exploring Modern Hollywood's Leading Genre*, *Superhero Movies*, and the edited collections *Fan Phenomena Batman* and *The Superhero Symbol*. Liam was chief investigator of the Australian Research Council–funded project *Superheroes & Me*, which has produced *Cleverman: The Exhibition*, the VR experience *Superheroes: Realities Collide*, and the award-winning documentary film *Superheroes & Me*.

OCTAVIA CADE is a New Zealand writer. She has a master's in biology and a PhD in science communication. Her academic work on science in speculative fiction has appeared in *Horror Studies*, *MOSF Journal of Science Fiction*, *Supernatural Studies*, *Interdisciplinary Studies*, in anthologies from Routledge and McFarland, and more. She has had over sixty short stories published in various markets, including *Clarkesworld*, *Fantasy & Science Fiction*, and *Asimov's*. She has won four Sir Julius Vogel Awards for speculative writing, is a Bram Stoker nominee, and was the 2020 writer in residence at Massey University.

HERNAN DAVID ESPINOSA-MEDINA is a PhD candidate at the School of Media and Communication at RMIT University, UX Designer, and lecturer. As a researcher at La Sabana University (Bogotá, Colombia), much of his work focused on exploring the nature of creative audiovisual products in the current media environment. Currently, in his doctoral research, he is exploring how user experience designers can use machine learning to create products that positively impact the lives of their users.

DAN GOLDING is associate professor in Media and Communications at Swinburne University and host of "Screen Sounds" on ABC Classic. He is an award-winning writer with over two hundred publications (*ABC Arts*, *Crikey*, *Buzzfeed*, *Meanjin*, *Kotaku*), a video essayist with more than one million views on YouTube, and in 2018 was the cohost of *What Is Music* for ABC + iView and Triple J. He cowrote *Game Changers* (Affirm Press, 2016) and made the soundtrack to *Untitled Goose Game* (2019). His latest book is *Star Wars after Lucas* (University of Minnesota Press, 2019).

IAN GORDON taught history and media studies at the National University of Singapore for many years. His books include *Comic Strips and Consumer Culture* (Smithsonian Institution Press, 1998), *Kid Comic Strips: A Genre Across Four Countries* (Palgrave, 2016), *Superman: The Persistence of an American Icon* (Rutgers University Press, 2017), and several edited collections including University Press of Mississippi volumes *Film and Comic Books* (2007), *The Comics of Charles Schulz: The Good Grief of Modern Life* (2017), *Ben Katchor: Conversations* (2018), and *The Superhero Symbol: Media, Culture, and Politics* (Rutgers University Press, 2019).

SHEENA C. HOWARD, a professor of communication at Rider University, is an award-winning author, filmmaker, and scholar with a PhD in Intercultural and Rhetorical Communication from Howard University. In 2014 Sheena became the first Black woman to win an Eisner Award for her first book, *Black Comics: Politics of Race and Representation* (2013). The Eisner Awards are considered the "Oscars of Comics," the highest award you can win in the comics industry. She is also author of several critically acclaimed books and comics books. In 2014, Sheena *published Black Queer Identity Matrix* and *Critical Articulations of Race, Gender and Sexual Orientation*. Sheena is the author-editor of the award-winning book, *Encyclopedia of Black Comics* (2017) and the cowriter of the critically acclaimed comic book, *Superb*, about a teenage superhero with Down Syndrome.

AARON HUMPHREY is lecturer in Media and Digital Humanities at the University of Adelaide. His academic writing has been published in the *International Journal of Comic Art*, *The International Journal of Cultural Studies*, *a/b: Auto/Biography Studies*, *Media International Australia*, and *The Comics Grid*. He is also a cartoonist and has published academic comics in *Persona Studies*, *Composition Studies*, and *Digital Humanities Quarterly*. He is a member of the J. M. Coetzee Centre for Creative Practice.

NAJA LATER is an academic tutor at Swinburne University of Technology. They study sociopolitical allegories in pop culture, with a focus on superhero, science fiction, and horror genres. They have recently published papers in the *Quarterly Review of Film and Video* and *Participations: Journal of Audience & Reception Studies*, and chapters with Rutgers University Press, University of Mississippi Press, and Syracuse University Press. They are a cofounder of the All Star Women's Comic Book Club.

CORMAC McGARRY completed his PhD at the Huston School of Film & Digital Media, University of Galway. His research examined the post-medium specificity of comic books in the digital age. He has developed modules in critical and cultural studies on the Animation program at the Institute of Art, Design, and Technology, Dún Laoghaire.

ANGELA NDALIANIS is adjunct professor at Swinburne University of Technology. Her research focuses on entertainment media and the horror, science fiction, and superhero genres. Her publications include *Neo-Baroque Aesthetics and Contemporary Entertainment* (2004), *Science Fiction Experiences* (2010), and *The Horror Sensorium: Media and the Senses* (2012), and the anthologies *The Contemporary Comic Book Superhero* (2009) and *Super/Heroes: from Hercules to Superman* (2007).

JULIAN NOVITZ is senior lecturer in writing at the Swinburne University of Technology. He is author of two novels and a collection of short stories, and his fiction and criticism have been published in a wide range of journals, magazines, and anthologies.

ALEXANDRA OSTROWSKI SCHILLING graduated with her BA in Film and Media Studies from Smith College, and received academic honors on her thesis work, "*Superheroes Aren't Born—They're Built*"—*An Exploration of the Interactions between Technology and Humanity in the Marvel Cinematic Universe*. She has an enduring passion for the modern superhero film, and for the Marvel Cinematic Universe in particular. She has also explored disability studies, film sound studies, and the topics of post- and transhumanism, often using these as lenses through which to examine the Marvel Cinematic Universe. Alex has had her work selected for presentation at conferences in the United States, Canada, and Australia. She currently works in Boston at Harvard University's Edmond and Lily Safra Center for Ethics.

MARIA LORENA M. SANTOS has published and delivered talks based on her research on adaptation and appropriation, intertextuality, and fandom and popular culture. Her PhD work at the National University of Singapore was on the cultural phenomenon of global fan communities surrounding the works of—and inspired by—Jane Austen. She is currently working on a book project on Jane Austen in the Philippines based on a paper delivered at the 2021 Jane Austen in the Pan Pacific conference and recently contributed a book chapter to *Robinson Crusoe in Asia*, edited by Steve Clark and Yukari Yoshihara. She is associate professor of the Department of English and Comparative Literature at the University of the Philippines.

JACK TEIWES received a PhD from the University of Melbourne for his thesis "Crisis of Infinite Intertexts! Continuity as Adaptation in the Superman Multimedia Franchise." Publications include "A Man of Steel (by any other name)" in *ImageTEXT*, "The New 'Man of Steel' is a Quiche-Eating Wimp!" in Joseph Darowski's *The Ages of Superman: Essays on the Man of Steel in Changing Times*, and "The Man of Steel vs. Reactionary Meta-Reboots!" in *Refractory*. Jack has presented at San Diego's Comic Art Conference (2009), PopCAANZ Conference (2010), Superhero Identities Symposium (2016), Superheroes Beyond Conference (2018), and is a longstanding theatre critic for AustralianStage.com.

ENRIQUE URIBE-JONGBLOED is professor and researcher of the Recasens Communication Research Group at the School of Social Communication and Journalism, Universidad Externado de Colombia. Uribe-Jongbloed has done research on a variety of media, including comics. His interest lies at the crossroads of culture, identity and media. He is the main researcher on the *Contemporary Comics and Sequential Image Studies* research project at Universidad Externado de Colombia. He has published the book chapters "Making Comics as Artisans: Comic Book Production in Colombia" with Fernando Suarez in the collection edited by C. Brienza and P. Johnston, *Cultures of Comics Work* (Palgrave-MacMillan, 2016) and "The Comics Scene in Colombian Cities" with Daniel Aguilar in the collection edited by J. Scorer, *Comics Beyond the Page in Latin America* (UCL Press, 2020).

INDEX

Aboriginal Australians, 15, 240, 250
Action Comics, 95, 123, 132, 180
Action for Children's Television, 99, 106
Adams, Mitchell, 13, 96, 122–23, 126, 132, 135
adaptation, 15, 77, 95, 99, 101, 103, 105, 119, 151, 158, 198, 241
Africa, 14–15, 76–77, 84, 87–90, 90n1, 209, 216, 218, 223n7, 226–37, 242
African Americans, 69, 75–76, 78, 81–82, 84, 87, 89, 90n1, 146, 226, 231; viewers, 11; young adult audiences, 75, 78–80, 82–83, 85–86, 88–89
Afrofuturists, 19
Agents of S.H.I.E.L.D. (2013–20 TV series), 147
All-New, All-Different (ANAD), 22–29, 31–33, 34n1
Ally Sloper, 95
Aldama, Frederick Luis, 20, 175, 223
Almost Infamous (2016), 62, 64
altruism, 163
Ancient One, The, 46
animation, 7, 12, 95–107, 117, 139, 141, 146, 209, 212, 220, 231, 237, 256
Apple, 135
Aquaman, 12, 20, 98–107, 128, 176
Arad, Avi, 117–18
arc reactor (Iron Man), 43–44, 47
archetype, 3–7, 9–11, 13–15, 34, 125, 175, 189, 199
aswang, 192, 198–205
AT&T's Warner Media. *See* Warner
Australia, x, 14–15, 50, 151, 174–90, 190n1, 190n5, 240–57, 257n1
Avengers, the, 22, 44, 47, 118

Avengers, The (2012), 176
Avengers: Age of Ultron (2015), 228
Avengers Assemble (2013–19 animated TV series), 118
Avengers: Endgame (2019), 47, 116
Avengers: Infinity War (2018), 47, 116, 229

Bale, Christian, 138
Banner, Bruce, 32, 53, 55
"Bat-embargo," 97, 141–42
Batman, 13, 106, 114, 127, 132, 138–39, 153, 155, 162, 168, 178, 187, 217, 243
Batman, The (2004–8 animated TV series), 141
Bazin, André, 5–9
Beaty, Bart, 7, 15n1
Bendis, Brian Michael, 32, 118
Bickle, Travis, 163–64
bildungsroman, 11, 62–63, 65, 68–73
biodiversity, 52
Black blockbuster, 76
Black community, 75–76, 78, 83–84, 88–89
Black history, 75, 79
Black Panther, 34n1, 75–77, 85–86, 186
Black Panther (2018), 11, 14–15, 19–20, 75–77, 79–83, 88, 226–29, 231–38
Black Panther: Wakanda Forever (2022), 8, 146
Black-led superhero blockbuster, 11, 75
Brightburn (2019), 64, 168n6
Bruns Publications, 125
Bukatman, Scott, 7, 58–59
Burke, Liam, 14, 20, 97, 101, 107, 139, 147, 151, 158, 168n2, 174

Cage, Luke, 19
Campbell, Joseph, 162, 173
Captain America, 10, 22–23, 27, 29, 32, 37, 40, 42, 116, 118, 120, 173–74, 184, 218
Captain America: Civil War (2016), 47, 228
Captain America: The First Avenger (2011), 40
Captain Marvel, 22, 25, 27, 29, 35n2, 35n4, 147
Captain Marvel (comic book), 29, 35n4
Captain Marvel (Shazam), 124–25, 131, 193. *See also* Shazam
Captain Marvel (2019), 19, 20, 22
Children's Television Workshop (CTW), 99–100
Cho, Amadeus, x, 20
Chronicle (2012), 64
Cleverman, x, xiii, 14, 177, 179, 186–90, 190nn1–2
Coates, Ta-Nehisi, 32, 76
Cocca, Carolyn, 8, 19, 20
cognitively atypical protagonists, 153. *See also* neurodivergence
coherent continuousness, 138
Colombia, 14, 175, 208–33
colonialism, 77, 197, 203–4, 227, 240
comic book stores, 20, 29, 30
comic books, x, 3–4, 6–14, 19–20, 24–26, 29–30, 35n4, 63–65, 69, 75–76, 95, 97, 98–107, 112–15, 119, 122–26, 128–32, 135–36, 138–39, 143, 147–48, 148n1, 148n3, 148n6, 151–52, 155, 157–58, 162, 165, 167, 169n13, 173–74, 176–78, 180–81, 185–86, 188–89, 190n1, 192–93, 196, 198–99, 204, 208, 210–13, 215–16, 218, 221–22, 223n3, 223n6, 241, 243–44, 250, 253
comic club, 30
comic strips, 95, 98, 122, 126, 210, 223n3, 240–41
Comics Code Authority, 98
comix, 19
ComiXology, ix, 30
Condoman, 248–50, 256
Coogler, Ryan, 77, 226–27, 232–33
Cooper, Ben, 112–14
copyright, 96, 122–26, 129–33, 133n4, 133n6, 152, 240, 248; legal basis for protecting superheroes, 123–26. *See also* intellectual property (IP); trademark
costume, 4–6, 8–9, 20, 69–70, 113–14, 116, 125, 128, 130, 152–59, 163–64, 166, 169n11, 173–74, 176, 179, 182, 185, 193–94, 199, 201, 205n2, 223n5, 242, 248
critique of superhero, 7, 20, 62, 64–65, 164, 166, 174, 205, 244, 248
Crocodile Dundee, 177, 181, 182, 190
cultural cringe, 177, 184–87, 189
Cumberbatch, Benedict, 54, 47
Cyborg, 115, 188

damsel-in-distress, 163, 169n12. *See also* woman's agency
Danvers, Carol, 22, 25, 35n2, 35n4
Dark Knight Returns, The (1986 comic book), 64
Dark Knight trilogy (2005–12), 141, 173, 176
Darkseid, 115
DC Comics, 28, 35n4, 76, 96, 112–17, 120, 122–23, 125–32, 141–42, 148n3, 148n7, 176–78, 185–86, 189
DeConnick, Kelly Sue, 29
deconstruction of superheroes, 64–65, 194
Defendor (2009), 13, 151, 156–57, 163, 164–65
Detective Comics, 138, 177–78
diaspora, 15, 84, 90, 226–27, 231, 236–38
disability, 9–10, 26, 37–48, 48n1
Disney, 25, 76, 100–101, 112, 114, 124, 135–36, 140, 146, 148n1, 176, 188, 220
Dittmer, Jason, 174–75, 212–13, 218, 222, 226
diversity, 25, 167
Do It Yourself (DIY) Superhero, 13, 96, 152–53, 155–58, 160–68, 169nn15–16
Doctor Strange, 10, 37, 45–47
Doctor Strange (2016), 45
Doctor Strange in the Multiverse of Madness (2022), 146
Downey, Robert, Jr., 10, 43
Dyer, Richard, 137–38, 140, 142

Eco, Umberto, 4–5, 63, 182
ecological superhero, 51. *See also* sustainable superheroes
El Filibusterismo, 196–97

empowerment, 33; and Blackness, 82, 85–86, 88–89
ethnicity, 14, 80, 81, 83–84, 89–90, 208–9, 212–13, 215–16, 218, 222–23
Evans, Chris, 40

Falk, Lee, 15, 179, 240
fandom, 20, 34, 155, 158, 164, 167
fans, 14, 20, 26, 28–31, 33, 35nn4–5, 53, 77, 96, 102, 111, 116, 141, 147, 152, 155, 164–66, 168, 177, 180, 184–86, 190n1, 196, 205n6, 210, 241, 243, 245
Fantastic Four, 4, 19, 66
Fantastic Four (1967–68 animated TV series), 101, 111, 116, 118
Fawaz, Ramzi, 6, 9, 24, 173, 182
Fawcett, 125–26, 131
Federal Communications Commission (FCC), 99, 106
Filipino culture, x, 14, 192–204, 205n1, 205n4, 205n9
Filipino Heroes League, The, 193–94
Filmation, 102–3, 105, 128, 131
Flash, the, 141
Flash, The (2014–23 TV series), 141
Flores, Emil, 192–94, 199, 202–3, 205, 205n4
Floronic Man, The, 51, 57, 59
Fortress of Solitude, The (2003 novel), 11, 62–65, 69, 72–73
Foster, Jane, 22, 33
franchises, x, 12–13, 55, 57, 112, 116–17, 132, 135–36, 140, 143–46, 228–29, 238. *See also* transmedia
Frankenstein, 58
Fritz, Ben, 135, 139, 143

Gabriel, David, 23, 29
Gavaler, Chris, 62, 64, 66, 69, 173, 197, 201, 203
gay, 24, 32, 193, 246. *See also* LGBTQ+ community
Gay, Roxane, 32
geek, 29, 151, 158, 163–67
gender, xi, 3, 8, 10, 19–20, 26, 81, 83, 89; identities, 22, 28, 89
generational taste, 12, 98, 101–7
Genette, Gérard, 112, 142

Geraghty, Christine, 147
Geraghty, Lincoln, 147
Godzilla, 11, 54–57, 59
Godzilla (1954), 56
Goodman, Martin, 96
Göransson, Ludwig, 226–28, 231–38
Gordon, Ian, 4, 95, 127, 131–32, 139
Gosling, Ryan, 138
Gould, Jack, 99, 107
Grace, Sina, 29, 32
Grantray-Lawrence Animation, 101, 103
gratifications theory, 11, 75, 80, 82, 88
Gravity's Rainbow, 62–64
Gray, Jonathan, 112, 119, 137, 142
Grey, Jean, 19
Griff the Invisible (2010), 151, 157, 159, 162, 164, 169n11, 169n13
Gwenpool, 31

Hanks, Tom, 140
Hanna-Barbera Productions, 101, 103, 106
Harmonized Tariff Schedule, 111
Hasbro, 118–20
Helfand, Michael Todd, 123–24, 127–28, 130–31
Hero (2007), 62
heroism, 3, 37, 42, 45, 64, 68, 70, 73, 152, 192, 197–98, 204–5, 229, 240, 249, 256–57
Hiroshima, 56
Holland, Alec, 51
Hudlin, Reginald, 77
Hulk, the, x, 20, 22–23, 27, 32, 53, 55, 116, 128–29, 139
hypermasculine identities, 42, 62, 163–64, 167
hypotexts, 139–40, 145–48

Iceman, 29, 32, 116
Ideal Toy Company, 113
identity, xi, 3, 8, 11, 14, 39, 51, 55–56, 62–65, 67, 69–70, 72–73, 78–79, 89, 132, 135, 139, 152, 153, 155–56, 163, 165, 177, 179–80, 182–84, 186, 189, 193, 199–203, 208–9, 211, 213–15, 218, 221–23, 223n4, 226, 228–29, 234, 240–48
independent comics, 31, 194

Indigenous Australians, 14, 179, 186–89, 240–57
Indigenous communities, 14, 65, 177, 179, 186–89, 209, 211–22, 223n6, 240, 242, 244–45, 247–56, 257n1
Inseparable (2011), 151, 157, 159, 164, 168n8, 169nn9–10, 169n12
intellectual property (IP), 12–13, 28, 95–96, 117, 122–24, 128–33, 135–37, 140–42, 148n1, 148n3, 152, 211, 220–21. *See also* copyright; trademark
intergenerational trauma, 85, 89
intertextuality, 136–41, 144, 148n6, 152, 160–66, 192
Invincible Iron Man, The. *See* Iron Man
Iron Man, 10, 22–23, 25, 27, 32, 37–38, 43–44, 47, 50, 116, 118
Iron Man trilogy (2008–13), 43–44, 118
Ironheart, x, 27, 29, 136, 146

Jenkins, Henry, 12, 113, 240, 256
Johnson, Derek, 143
Joker (2019), 154–55, 168n3, 169n15
Joker, The, 127
Jones, Chuck, 100, 102
Jones, Jessica, 181
Jones, Quincy, 231
Jungle Action, 76

Keaton, Michael, 138
Kenner, 113–15, 120
Khan, Kamala, 22, 25, 27, 34, 35n2, 136
Kick-Ass (2010), 13, 64, 151, 156–58, 163–64, 166, 168nn2–8, 169n14
Kidman, Shawna, 95–96
Killmonger, 83–84, 87–89, 228, 233–34
Kingdom Come, 64
Kinney, Laura, 20, 22
Kirby, Jack, 76, 114–15

Lane, Cort, 146
Lane, Lois, 155, 157, 160, 162, 169n12
Latinx, x, xiii, 20, 136, 175
Lawrence, Bob, 101–3
Lee, Stan, 4–5, 96, 117, 201
lesbian, 24. *See also* LGBTQ+ community

Levitz, Paul, 141
LGBTQ+ community, 20
Los Monos, 212, 215, 220
Lu, Chen, 53

Maal, Baaba, 228, 233, 235–37
Mad Max, 177, 182–83
magic, 46, 204
Makú, 208–16, 220, 222
Malonzo, Mervin, 14, 192–98, 200–205, 205n1, 205n6, 206n10
manga, 28–30, 209
Manifold (*Avengers* character), 179
manifold embodiment, 141–42, 145, 147
marginalized readers, 26, 30
Marston, William Moulton, 19
Mattel, 96, 115–16, 120
Marvel Cinematic Universe (MCU), 10, 14, 37, 40, 42–48, 97, 112, 116, 118–20, 135–36, 139, 143–46, 148n1, 151, 166, 168n2, 226, 228–29, 232, 238
Marvel Comics, 3, 10, 29, 69, 76, 103, 112, 117–18, 129, 186
Marvel Rising, 13, 136, 140, 143–47
Marvel Super Heroes (1966 animated TV series), 12, 98, 101, 103–6, 116
Marvels, The (2023), 146
McCloud, Scott, 212, 223n2
McDonald, Paul, 136–37, 139
Mego Corporation, 112–14, 120
Melbourne, Australia, 50, 176–77, 184, 186, 188, 190n1
men, 3, 6, 9–10, 20, 27, 41–43, 45, 80, 85, 125, 152, 163–65, 167, 168n3, 200, 227, 229, 244
Metcalf, Stephen, 135, 139, 143
Mexico, 210
Meyer, Christina, 95
Mickey Mouse, 100
Midnight's Children, 62–69, 72–73
Miller, Ezra, 141
Miller, Frank, 64
misogynists, 33, 167. *See also* toxic masculinity
Miss America (Marvel character), 136, 146
Mittell, Jason, 101–2, 136–38, 143–46
monopoly value, 13, 140–42, 147, 148n4

monsters, 54, 56, 58–59, 64, 192, 198, 200–204
Monstress, 31
monstrous, the, 11, 14, 51–56, 58–59, 192, 198, 200–203, 205
Moon Girl, 31
Moore, Alan, 51, 56, 62, 64, 194
Moore, Ellen, 11, 50, 56
Morales, Miles, x, 3–5, 8, 19, 22, 25–27, 35n2, 35n4
morality, 37, 40, 44, 58, 202
Morrison, Grant, 6–7, 180, 182, 185
Ms. Marvel, x, 19–20, 22, 25, 27–32, 34, 35n2, 136, 146
multiplicity of Blackness, 82–83, 88
Murray, Chris, 174–75
Murray, Mitch, 7–8
music, 14–15, 70–71, 123, 143, 160, 187, 205n8, 226–38, 242
mutant superheroes, 11, 54–59, 66, 132
myth, 4–7, 9, 14, 62–64, 73, 79, 100, 173–75, 177, 181–84, 187, 189, 192–94, 199–205, 205n4, 215, 222, 242, 246

Nagasaki, 56
national identity, 4, 177, 180, 182, 184, 186, 189, 208–9, 211, 213–14, 218, 223, 240–57
nationalism, 14, 77, 180–81, 192, 197
Ndalianis, Angela, xiii, 4, 20
nemesis, 111, 157, 162, 169n13
neurodivergence, 151, 155, 162, 165, 167. *See also* cognitively atypical protagonists
New York, 30, 69, 77, 99–100, 128, 174, 179, 186
Noli me Tangere, 196–97, 205n7

Okoye, 81, 85–86, 88, 233–34
Old Man Logan, 64
origin stories, 10, 37–38, 40, 45, 63–64, 72–73, 193–94
originating instance, 138, 140
Other, The, 15, 70, 226–38
Outback, the, 177–78, 180–82, 184, 186, 242, 244

Pangborn, Jonathan, 45–46
Paper Girls, 31

paratext, 12, 112–15, 119, 137, 142, 160
Parker, Peter, 26–27, 35n4, 69
Patrick, Kevin, 179–80, 184, 186, 240–41, 243
Peña, Jorge, 209, 211–16
Perelman, Ron, 117
Perlmutter, David, 99, 102–4, 107, 108n3
Perlmutter, Isaac "Ike," 117
Phantom, The, 15, 179–80, 240–57
Philippines, 14, 175, 192–206
Plastic Man, 115, 128, 193
postcolonial culture, 14–15, 65–66, 193, 232, 244–45
postmodern disorientation, 204
posttraumatic stress disorder (PTSD), 44
presold, 135–36. *See also* franchises; transmedia
Priest, Christopher, 76–77
Prophecy (1979), 55, 57–58
proto-superhero characters, 69
psychological turmoil, 167

Quinn, Harley, 19, 177

race, 3, 10, 14, 22, 26, 75, 80–81, 83, 89–90, 208–9, 212–13, 215, 218, 222–23, 223n7, 227, 229, 248
racebending, 26
racial identities, 26
racism, 81, 89
Radioactive Man, 54
Rambeau, Monica, 25
Rawhide Kid, 23–24
Real Life Superhero (RLSH), 152
Red Skull, 42
reflexive economies of scope, 142–43
religion, 204–5
representation, 8–10, 12, 15, 19–20, 22–26, 28–30, 32–33, 37, 40, 43, 45–48, 78–79, 81–88, 164, 166, 208–9, 212–13, 216, 226–27, 229–31, 238, 251
Reynolds, Richard, 182, 199, 202, 204
Rhodes, James Rupert "Rhodey," 25, 47
Rizal, José, 192, 194–200, 203–5, 205nn5–8
Robbins, Trina, 19
Rogers, Steve, 26–27, 32, 37, 40–42, 45

Sabin, Roger, 95
Saga, 31
Saga of the Swamp Thing (1984–87), 51
Scheimer, Lou, 102
science, 153, 182, 199, 204, 223n5
science fiction, 185, 189
secret identity, 69, 72, 153, 165, 182, 199, 201
Secret Wars (comic book miniseries), 96, 115–16, 120
Senegal, 175, 228–29, 232–33, 235–38
Shang-Chi and the Legend of the Ten Rings (2021), 19–20, 176
Shazam, 69, 131
She-Hulk, 19, 27, 116
Shooter, Jim, 116
Silk, 32, 34n1
Singer, Bryan, 139
Smallville (2001–11 TV series), 148
Soon I Will Be Invincible (2007), 62, 64
Special (2006), 13, 151, 156–57, 159, 162
Spider-Man, 3–4, 19, 25, 27, 29, 35n2, 35n4, 38, 111, 116–18, 238, 243
Spider-Man (1967–70 animated TV series), 103, 106
Spider-Man: The Animated Series (1994–98), 139
Spider-Man: No Way Home (2021), 176
Staiger, Janet, 140–42
star personas, 136–37, 140
star systems, 13, 136–37. *See also* superhero stars
Stark, Tony, 26, 32, 37, 43–45, 47, 50
stereotype, xi, 19, 78–81, 83, 88–89, 162, 164–66, 174, 179, 181, 186, 190, 218, 221–22, 227, 229–31, 235
Storm, Sue, 19
streaming, x, 8, 135–36, 142, 229
subgenre, 13, 64, 151–53, 155–56, 158, 160–61, 163, 166–67, 212
Sub-Mariner, 98–99, 101, 104, 107
Suicide Squad, 177, 189
Super (2010), 151, 157–59, 163–64, 168n6
Super Friends (1973–85 animated TV series), 115
Super Powers Collection, 114–15
Supercrip, 37, 39–40, 43, 46

Superfolks, 62–64
superhero as ecological monstrous, 51
superhero stars, 13, 138–45, 148n6. *See also* star systems
superhero trademark, 112–14
superhuman, the, 42, 44, 53–54, 153, 155, 199
Superman, xi, 6, 10, 13, 63, 95–96, 99, 105, 114–15, 122–27, 130–32, 133n4, 133n6, 139, 179–83, 186, 192, 194, 197, 199, 205n4, 238, 246
Superman/Aquaman Hour of Adventure (1967–68 animated TV series), 12, 98, 102–3, 105–6
Superpowers, 62
superpowers, 37, 46, 66, 68, 72, 153, 155–56, 179, 184, 199, 202, 223n5
sustainable superheroes, 50. *See also* ecological superhero
Swamp Thing, 11, 51–59
Sydney, Australia, 176, 180, 187, 242–43, 245

Tabi Po, 14, 192–206
Taxi Driver (1976), 163–64, 168n17, 169n15
T'Challa, 78, 83–85, 88, 228, 234
Teen Titans, xi, 20
Thor, 10, 22–23, 27, 30–33, 116, 118, 176–77
Thor Girl, 27
Thor: Love and Thunder (2022), 176
threshold value, 140–48
Time-Warner. *See* Warner
toxic masculinity, 84, 89, 152, 163, 167. *See also* misogynists
Toy Biz, 111–12, 117–18, 120
toyesis, 12, 118–19; toyetic, 113, 119
trademark, 112–14, 122–23, 126–33; legal basis for protecting superheroes, 126–29. *See also* copyright; intellectual property (IP)
Transformers, 118–19
transmedia, 8–9, 12–14, 95, 97, 99, 112, 118–19, 123, 131–32, 135–38, 140–41, 143–45, 147–48, 148n2, 167, 220; centrifugal, 136, 144–46; centripetal, 136, 144–45, 147; coextensive, 143–48. *See also* franchises
tropes, 10, 13–14, 38, 40, 62, 152–53, 155, 160–63, 165–66, 168n3, 190, 193, 227, 242–43, 250, 255–56

Tukano, 208–9, 211–12, 215–16, 220, 222, 223n3
Turner, Victor, 51
TV Guide, 98–101

übermensch-like, 32
Unbeatable Squirrel Girl, The, 31
United States of America, 7, 9–10, 14, 15n1, 75, 96, 111, 113, 123–25, 127–32, 173–75, 177, 180, 223, 227, 237, 240
Urbont, Jack, 102

video games, 7, 142, 185
vigilantes, 153–55, 160, 163, 173, 192, 217, 222
vigilantism, 152, 156–57, 159–60, 162, 166
villain, 25, 42, 46, 51, 55, 115, 155, 163, 169n13, 177, 186
violence, xi, 12, 72, 99, 101, 103, 106–7, 107n1, 162–63, 165, 167

Waid, Mark, 22
Wakanda, 8, 76–79, 85, 146, 175, 226, 228, 232–33, 237–38
War on Terror, 173
Warner, 96, 100–102, 112, 124, 126, 131, 148n3
Warner, Kristen J., 25–26, 31–32
Warner Bros. *See* Warner
Watchmen (1986–87), 19, 62, 64, 185, 194

Wertham, Frederic, 98–100, 103
Western, the (genre), 5–7, 9, 182, 230
Williams, Riri, x, 8, 22, 27, 136, 146–47
Wilson, G. Willow, 29, 32, 34
Wilson, Rainn, 158, 163
Wilson, Sam, 22, 27
Wolverine, 20, 22–23, 177, 181, 188, 231
woman's agency, 8, 19, 22, 29, 31–32, 81, 136, 163, 169n16. *See also* damsel-in-distress
women, 19, 20, 22, 24–25, 28–32, 34, 34n1, 80, 82, 85–86, 88, 146, 159, 165, 169, 218, 229, 234, 243, 250, 256
Wonder Woman, 19–20, 114, 130, 139, 148n7, 183, 186, 193, 205n2
Wonder Woman (2017), 82
Wonderman, 124–25
Woo, Benjamin, 164, 166
World's Greatest Superheroes (WGSH), 113–14, 120

xerography, 101, 105
X-Men, 19–20, 66, 111–12, 117–18, 132, 139, 178, 181, 186–87, 231
X-Men Origins: Wolverine (2009), 231

Yellow Kid, 95

Zambo Dendé, 208–9, 211–12, 216–18, 220–22

www.ingramcontent.com/pod-product-compliance
Lightning Source LLC
Chambersburg PA
CBHW021836220426
43663CB00005B/266